To Oscar and Marika Rodríguez Razzeto

For their appreciation of the archaeology of Northern Peru, and their generous support of scholars and institutions devoted to its study.

A Oscar y Marika Rodríguez Razzeto

Por su aprecio de la arqueología del Norte del Perú y por su generoso apoyo a los investigadores y a las instituciones dedicadas a su estudio.

THE PACATNAMU PAPERS
Volume 2

The Moche Occupation

Edited by
Christopher B. Donnan
Guillermo A. Cock

Fowler Museum of Cultural History
University of California, Los Angeles

This publication was supported by funding from
The Ahmanson Foundation
The Times-Mirror Foundation
Manus, the Support Group of the UCLA Fowler Museum of Cultural History

International Standard Book Number 0-930741-56-0 (Hardcover)
0-930741-57-9 (Softcover)

Library of Congress Catalog Card Number: 86-061112

UCLA Fowler Museum of Cultural History
405 Hilgard Avenue
Los Angeles, California 90095-1549

Printed and bound in Hong Kong by Golden Cup Printing Co., Ltd.

Table of Contents

Acknowledgments

The Pacatnamu Project was made possible by the generous support of various institutions and individuals, and it is a pleasure to have this opportunity to acknowledge their assistance. Primary funding for the project was provided by the National Geographic Society and the National Endowment for the Humanities. This was generously augmented by support from the Ahmanson Foundation and the Ethnic Arts Council of Los Angeles.

Of critical importance at the inception of the Pacatnamu Project, and continuously through its completion, was the support, both financial and spiritual, of ten very special people: Wendy and Ross Cabeen, Lloyd Cotzen, Geraldine Ford, Joan and Jack Hoch, Debbie and Jay Last, and Ann and Bill Lucas.

The Pacatnamu Project involved a formal convenio between the Instituto Nacional de Cultura in Lima and the Fowler Museum of Cultural History at the University of California, Los Angeles. We are very grateful to Lili de Cueto Fernandini and José Antonio del Busto, former Directors of the Instituto Nacional de Cultura, Hugo Ludeña, then Director of The Center for Conservation of Archaeological Monuments in Peru, and Elwin Svenson on behalf of the University of California, for their support in making the convenio possible.

The office of the Instituto Nacional de Cultura in Trujillo was very helpful in supervising the field excavation and providing facilities for the permanent storage of the Pacatnamu collections. We are particularly grateful for the assistance of Cristóbal Campana, Ricardo Morales, Ana María Hoyle, Daisy Barreto, and Carlos Deza.

The project benefited in many ways by the hospitality and friendship of the people in the town of Guadalupe. In particular, we are grateful for the assistance that was provided by Oscar Lostaunau and his brother Luis Lostaunau.

Ramiro Matos, Amalia Castelli, Franklin Pease, and María Rostworowski provided valuable advice and assistance to the project. The same is true of Werner Haeberle, Betty Meggers, Franklin Murphy, and Gene Sterud, each of whom took a personal interest in the research. David Scott assisted with the identification of inorganic materials.

Preparation of this publication has been assisted by Daniel R. Brauer, Alana Cordy-Collins, Kerry Cox, and Debbie Last. Support for the preparation of the line drawings was made possible by a grant from the Research Committee of the Academic Senate at UCLA.

Donna and Don McClelland are due special recognition for their help with this publication. They patiently edited multiple versions of each of the individual papers, and Don McClelland was instrumental in refining the publication design. This volume has been greatly enhanced by the skill, talent, and devotion that they brought to nearly all stages of its production.

Christopher B. Donnan
Guillermo A. Cock

Introduction

Christopher B. Donnan

Pacatnamu is a uniquely important archaeological site, located at the mouth of the Jequetepeque Valley on the North Coast of Peru (Figs. 1, 2). Ringed by precipitous cliffs on two sides and guarded by high city walls on the third, it is one of ancient Peru's most spectacular archaeological sites (Fig. 3). The core of the sprawling architectural complex, which has an area of approximately one square kilometer, is dominated by more than fifty truncated pyramids that once supported elaborate summit structures and sanctuaries. Flanking these mud brick pyramids are attendant complexes of spacious courts, corridors, and elite quarters (see Site Map, pages 18-19). Cemeteries are scattered inside and outside the city's perimeter walls.

Because of the arid climate and Pacatnamu's location high above the irrigated valley floor, archaeological preservation is extraordinary. Many walls stand nearly to their original height, painted facades survive, and elaborate tombs preserve their original contents—cane coffins, gourds, ceramic vessels, jewelry, and exquisitely woven fabrics which comprise the largest collection of ornate textiles ever discovered in northern Peru. Thus, Pacatnamu offers "laboratory conditions" for a study of the art, architecture, and population of a major religious center, shaped by the dynamics of local development and foreign conquest.

Previous Research

Although Pacatnamu was mentioned by various explorers (e.g., Hutchinson 1873; Middendorf 1894), it was not studied in detail until 1925, when Alfred Kroeber made a sketch map of several pyramids in the central portion of the site and recorded some observations about the architecture (1930:88-89). Subsequently, the site was mentioned sporadically in the archaeological literature (Garcia Rosell 1942:123-124; Schaedel 1951:235; Ishida et al. 1960:435; Kosok 1965: 123). The first archaeological excavation was conducted in 1937-39 by Heinrich Ubbelohde-Doering. He continued his excavations there in 1952-53 and again 1962-63. Ubbelohde-Doering's work resulted in the excavation of two of the pyramid complexes. He uncovered numerous burials containing remarkable textiles, basketry, cordage, leather, and plant remains. The human remains were exceedingly well preserved—some of the bodies were mummified and in some cases tattoos were still visible (Ubbelohde-Doering 1959, 1967; Keatinge 1978; Hecker and Hecker 1985).

Wolfgang and Giesela Hecker accompanied Ubbelohde-Doering on his 1962-1963 expedition to Pacatnamu. They produced excellent maps of the site and of some of the major architectural features (Hecker

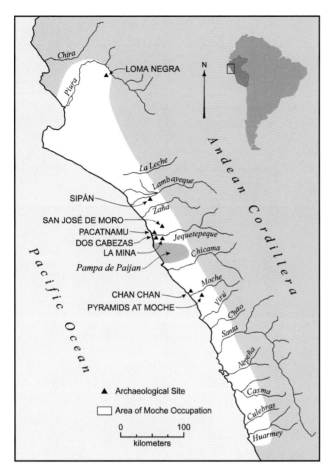

Figure 1. Map of the North Coast of Peru.

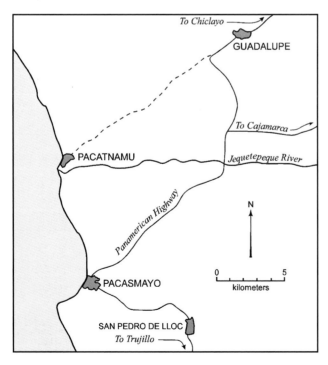

Figure 2. Map of the lower part of the Jequetepeque Valley.

and Hecker 1977, 1982, 1985, 1990, 1991).[1] Richard Keatinge conducted a surface survey of Pacatnamu in 1974 and subsequently published several brief reports on his findings (Keatinge et al. 1975; Keatinge 1977, 1982).

The Pacatnamu Project

In February 1983, the Instituto Nacional de Cultura in Lima formally approved a request by the Fowler Museum of Cultural History at the University of California, Los Angeles for a five-year excavation permit at Pacatnamu. This was to be a multidisciplinary research effort, combining archaeological excavation with physical anthropology, botany, zoology, textile analysis, ethnography, and ethnohistory.

During the five field seasons, which took place between June and September of 1983 through 1987, Pacatnamu was systematically surveyed, portions of it were surface collected, and excavations of many architectural features were completed. In the process, many burials were excavated. These five seasons of fieldwork were very successful, producing abundant artifacts with associations that provide valuable insights into the nature of the people who inhabited this spectacular site.

Considerable effort was focused on developing a chronology of the ancient occupation at Pacatnamu. This began with a seriation of the ceramics and was supported by a seriation of the mud bricks used to construct the architecture (McClelland 1986). The chronology based on ceramic and brick seriation was augmented by controlled stratigraphic excavations, as well as a seriation of textiles and of burial types. Radiocarbon determinations supported the chronology, and permitted the assignment of absolute dates to the periods of occupation.

When *The Pacatnamu Papers, Volume 1* was published in 1986, we proposed a preliminary chronology of the site's occupation based on the information we had a that time. In doing so, we stressed that "the chronology is subject to change and refinement as more evidence is uncovered" (Donnan 1986a:22). Since that time, we completed our final two field seasons at Pacatnamu, which produced a great deal of new evidence. Moreover, excavations elsewhere on the north cost of Peru provided new information that has refined our understanding of Pacatnamu's chronology.

There are two important differences between what we knew about Pacatnamu when we published *The Pacatnamu Papers, Volume 1* in 1986 and what we know now. First, in 1986 we stated that "It appears that Pacatnamu was unoccupied before the end of Moche IV or

---

1. The Heckers assigned numbers and letters to most of the architectural features at Pacatnamu. In almost all instances we have followed their designations.

Figure 3. Air photo of Pacatnamu. Courtesy of Servicio Aerofotográfico Nacional, Lima.

the beginning of Moche V (ca. A.D. 600)" (*ibid.*). Since 1986, we excavated considerably more Moche material at Pacatnamu, and the Heckers published a detailed account of the burials that had been excavated by Ubbelohde-Doering between 1939 and 1963 (Ubbelohde-Doering 1983). Moreover, the Moche material from Pacatnamu could be examined in light of important Moche material that has been excavated since 1986 at Sipán (Alva 1988, 1990, 1994; Alva and Donnan 1993), La Mina (Narvaez 1993), San José de Moro (Donnan and Castillo 1992, 1993; Castillo and Donnan 1993, 1994), and Dos Cabezas (Donnan ms.). These excavations have provided critical information about the sequence of Moche ceramics in the lower Jequetepeque Valley. We now realize that the Moche occupation of Pacatnamu may have begun with early Moche (Moche I) and that its most intensive period was probably middle Moche (Moche II-III). A late Moche (Moche IV-V) occupation is present at the site, but appears to have been smaller than the middle Moche occupation.

Second, in 1986 we suggested that the site had essentially two periods of occupation—an early period when Moche ceramics were in use and a later period characterized by the use of Chimu ceramics. We now realize that the later period ceramics, and hence the later period occupation, is more accurately referred to as Lambayeque. It has recently become clear that the cultural history of the north coast of Peru is best understood in terms of two distinct geographic spheres: a northern sphere and a southern sphere, separated by the Pampa de Paiján (Fig. 1). This division is clearly present in the Moche period, with the valleys in the northern sphere sharing a style of Moche ceramics that is distinct from that shared by the valleys in the southern sphere (Donnan 1990, Castillo and Donnan 1995). Following the Moche occupation of the north coast, the distinction between the northern and southern ceramic styles not only continued, but became even more pronounced. South of the Pampa de Paiján, the Chimu style predominated, but north of the Pampa de Paiján, the style was sufficiently distinctive that most researchers are now using the term Lambayeque (Donnan 1993, Cordy-Collins 1996). Thus, throughout this volume, the term Lambayeque will be used for what we referred to as Chimu in *The Pacatnamu Papers, Volume 1.*

The articles included in the first volume of *The Pacatnamu Papers* dealt with various aspects of the Lambayeque occupation. This volume focuses on the Moche occupation, which was considerably less extensive than the Lambayeque occupation, and was restricted to the central portion of the site (Fig. 4). Some ceremonial architecture was constructed during the Moche occupation, including an incipient stage of both Huaca 1 and Huaca 31—probably the two most

important ceremonial structures at Pacatnamu during the Moche occupation.

In the area between Huaca 1 and Huaca 31 there are remnants of Moche architecture which was damaged by later construction. Some walls were made of rounded cobbles set in mud mortar, but most were of mud brick. The walls created rectangular rooms and patio areas that appear to have been well planned and constructed. Outside the areas around Huacas 1 and 31, most of the Moche architecture consisted of simple wattle and daub (quincha) buildings that apparently were domestic structures for the common people.

There were numerous Moche cemeteries, nearly all of which have been extensively looted by grave robbers. Some are in the central portion of the site, but most are scattered north of the occupied area. Nearly all are small, isolated clusters of burials that appear to have contained between 15 and 70 individuals, including both males and females, as well as individuals of all ages (see Verano, this volume).

Nearly all of the Moche burials appear to be of common people—they have neither the quantity nor quality of associated objects that characterize elite burials. The individuals were generally buried in simple pits or in shallow boot-shaped chambers. Only one cemetery, located in the area north of Huaca 31, contained some high-status Moche burials (Ubbelohde-Doering 1967; Hecker and Hecker 1985).

We located one unlooted Moche cemetery near the central portion of the site (H45 CM1). It was extensively excavated (see Donnan and McClelland, this volume), and appears to have been typical of the majority of Moche cemeteries at the site.

The motivation for the Moche occupation of Pacatnamu is uncertain. There is no evidence that the site was fortified at that time; thus, its natural defensive potential was probably not a factor. There may, however, have been environmental factors that made the location desirable. Recent excavations at the site of Dos Cabezas, located on the valley floor beneath Pacatnamu, indicate that it was an important center prior to the beginning of the Moche era and had a major Moche I occupation. Then it began to be inundated with windblown sand. Floors and walls were built over thick layers of sand, and eventually the inhabitants were forced to abandon the site. This abandonment occurred at the time that Pacatnamu was first inhabited, suggesting that the inhabitants moved up onto the high cliffs, above the valley floor, to create a new settlement that would be free of accumulating sand. In moving to Pacatnamu, the people would have maintained proximity to their agricultural fields, as well as to the intertidal and maritime resources on which they had depended.

The Moche occupation at Pacatnamu continued until approximately A.D. 900. Just before it ended, new

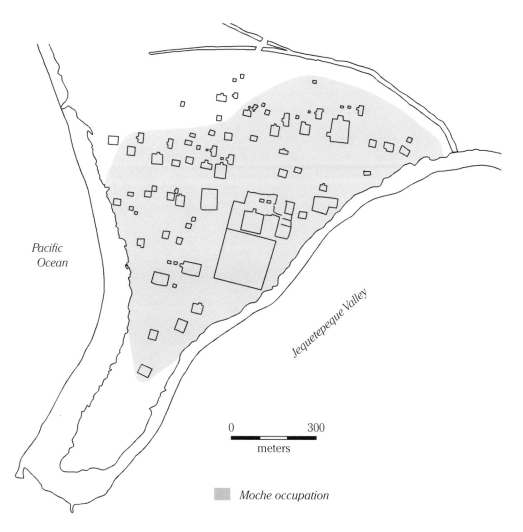

Figure 4. Area of the Moche occupation at Pacatnamu.

forms were added to the ceramic assemblage. Most notable are jars with necks that depict an adult male with long tresses and a small mustache at the corners of his upper lip. Ubbelohde-Doering referred to this form as the "King of Assyria" (1967:24).[2] Also associated with the terminal part of the Moche occupation are cooking and storage ollas with distinctive rim profiles (Fig. 5).

At the end of the Moche occupation, some ceramics also reflect Huari influence (see Cordy-Collins, this volume), but this influence is not evident in the Moche textiles. Nor is it reflected in burial practices: Huari burials are seated and tightly flexed, while Moche burials at Pacatnamu are consistently extended and lying on their backs.

At approximately A.D. 1050, there was a major break in the sequence between the Moche and the Lambayeque occupations. This hiatus appears to cor-respond to a period of major flooding—presumably a severe Niño which would have created a crisis for the local population. As a result, Pacatnamu was either abandoned or retained only a small residual popula-tion.

There was a second major florescence at Pacatna-mu beginning approximately A.D. 1100-1150, with an altogether new inventory of ceramics, textiles, bricks, and architectural forms. The vast majority of the archi-tecture visible today was constructed during the follow-ing two centuries.

This second florescence, which we refer to as the Lambayeque occupation, was at least partially motivated by the need for defense. Major walls were built across the northern and southern margins of the site to com-plement the high cliffs on the east and west, enabling easy control of access to the central part of Pacatnamu. The unfinished portions of major walls along the north-ern side suggest that the site was being expanded in that direction shortly before the Lambayeque occupation ended (Donnan 1986b).

---

2. Jars of this type were also found by Disselhoff in Moro (1958:185) and by Hecker and Hecker at Pacatnamu (1977:30, Table 1, Photos 15 A, B).

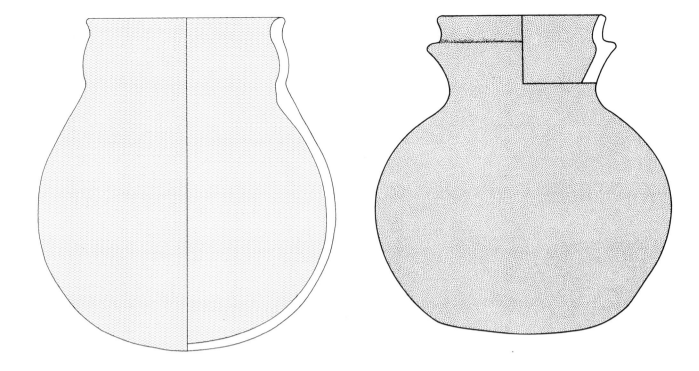

Figure 5. Rim profiles from terminal Moche cooking and storage ollas.

It is not yet known what ended the Lambayeque occupation, tentatively dated at around A.D. 1370. However, it is tempting to speculate that it may, in part, have been related to the conquest of the lower Jequetepeque Valley by the Chimu, who had their capital at Chan Chan, approximately 150 kilometers to the south (Fig. 1).

After A.D. 1370, a small population may have continued to live at Pacatnamu, but by the time the Inca conquered the North Coast (ca. A.D. 1470), the site was largely in ruins—most of the earlier architecture was heavily eroded, and windblown sand was banked against the leeward side of the walls and pyramids. A few Inca period offerings suggest that Pacatnamu continued to maintain some ceremonial significance, but it clearly had been eclipsed as a major center.

Offerings continued to be made at Pacatnamu during the early part of the Colonial Period, and some small cemeteries from that time have been identified. It is unlikely, however, that the site continued to be occupied. No Colonial Period architecture or refuse have been found, and no Colonial Period document has been discovered that mentions a settlement at that location.

Changing Perspective on the Function of Pacatnamu

Pacatnamu has often been viewed as a ceremonial complex and pilgrimage center, analogous to the site of Pachacamac on the Central Coast. Ubbelohde-Doering (1959, 1960, 1967) first suggested this interpretation, and Keatinge (1977, 1978, 1982) has been its most recent proponent.

Our excavation, as well as those by other archaeologists, cast doubt on the pilgrimage center hypothesis. No ceramics or artifactual material have been found that clearly indicate that anyone other than members of the local valley population is buried at Pacatnamu. Furthermore, the vast majority of ceramic sherds found in test pits within the architectural complexes are fragments of simple utilitarian vessels—not the elite ritual ware we would expect to find at a major ceremonial center.

Nevertheless, Pacatnamu clearly constitutes one of the largest concentrations of ceremonial architecture on the North Coast of Peru. During its second period of florescence Pacatnamu undoubtedly served as a focus of ceremonial activity and political power for the population of the lower Jequetepeque Valley.

RESUMEN:
Introducción

Pacatnamú es un importante sitio arqueológico. Ubicado en la desembocadura del río Jequetepeque (Figs. 1 y 2), está rodeado de barrancos por dos lados y resguardado por una muralla en el tercero (Fig. 3). El área central mide alrededor de 1 km2 y tiene más de 50 pirámides truncas. Hay cementerios dentro y fuera de los límites de la ciudad.

Por su ubicación, la preservación de los restos arqueológicos es óptima, por lo que ofrece "condiciones de laboratorio" para el estudio de la arquitectura, arte y la población de un importante centro religioso a través del tiempo.

Investigaciones Anteriores

Aunque fué mencionado por viajeros (p. ej. Hutchinson 1873; Middendorf 1894), no fué estudiado hasta que Kroeber (1925) bosquejó los planos de algunos de sus edificios y escribió sobre su arquitectura (1930:88-89). Las primeras investigaciones fueron conducidas por Heinrich Ubbelohde-Doering en 1937-39, 1952-53 y 1962-63, cuyos resultados han dado origen a numerosas publicaciones (ver Bibliografía).

Wolfgang y Giesela Hecker acompañaron a Ubbelohde-Doering en 1962-63 y han realizado una serie de publicaciones sobre el sitio (ver Bibliografía). Richard Keatinge condujo exploraciones de superficie en 1974, publicando luego una serie de reportes (ver Bibliografía).

El Proyecto Pacatnamú

En Febrero de 1983, el Instituto Nacional de Cultura del Perú aprobó la solicitud del Museo Fowler de Historia Cultural de la Universidad de California, Los Angeles, para conducir investigaciones multidisciplinarias en Pacatnamú, por cinco años. Estas se realizaron entre junio y setiembre de los años 1983 a 1987.

Se invirtió considerable esfuerzo en el desarrollo de una cronología que fuese el resultado de la seriación cerámica, la de adobes (McClelland 1986), estratigrafía, seriación de tejidos, tipología de entierros y fechados Radiocarbónicos. En 1986 propusimos una cronología preliminar, la que ha sido refinada con las excavaciones de 1986 y 1987.

Hay dos importantes diferencias entre el Volumen I (1986) y éste. Primero, en 1986 afirmábamos que la ocupación del sitio empezó al final de Moche IV o el comienzo de la Fase V (ca. 600 DC). Hoy sabemos que ésta habría comenzado durante la Fase Temprana de Moche (Moche I) y que tuvo su etapa más intensiva durante el Moche Medio (Moche II-III); la ocupación Moche Tardía (Moche IV-V) fué mas reducida que la del Moche Medio.

Segundo, en 1986 soteníamos que habían habido basicamente dos periodos de ocupación: Moche y Chimú, basándonos en la evidencia cerámica. Hoy nos damos cuenta que el periodo tardío debe ser llamado "Lambayeque", que define mejor las características de la cerámica tardía en el sitio.

Los artículos incluidos en el Volumen I de los Pacatnamú Papers trataron varios aspectos de la ocupación Lambayeque. Este se centra en la ocupación Moche, que fue menos extensa y se restringió a la parte central del sitio (Fig. 4). Durante ella, se inició la construcción de la Huaca 1 y de la 31, probablemente las estructuras ceremoniales más importantes durante la ocupación Moche. En el área entre ellas, hay restos de arquitectura Moche dañada por las construcciones posteriores. Fuera de las áreas que están entre y alrededor de las Huacas 1 y 31, la arquitectura Moche es de quincha, aparentemente doméstica y para la gente del común.

Hay numerosos cementerios (ver Verano, este volumen) tanto dentro como fuera de la ciudad. La mayoría de ellos parece haber contenido sólo entre 15 y 70 individuos. Casi todas las tumbas parecen pertenecer a gente del común y solo uno, ubicado frente a la Huaca 31 y excavado por Ubbelohde-Doering, parece haber contenido individuos Moche de alto rango.

Ubicamos y excavamos un cementerio Moche que no estava huaqueado (ver Donnan y McClelland, este volumen) y que parece ser típico y representativo de la mayoría de los ubicados en el sitio.

El motivo de los Moche para ocupar Pacatnamú es desconocido. Podría ser que al desocupar Dos Cabezas, los Moche se hayan instalado en este sitio; la desocupación de uno y el inicio de la ocupación del otro parecen coincidir.

La ocupación Moche en Pacatnamú continuó hasta, aproximadamente, el 900 DC. Hacia el final, nuevas formas aparecieron en el inventario cerámico y algunas reflejan influencia Huari (ver Cordy-Collins, este volumen), pero su influencia no aparece en los tejidos o en las prácticas funerarias.

Aproximadamente en el 1050 DC, se produce un abandono total del sitio, o sólo una población muy reducida queda en él, probablemente como consecuencia de un Niño de grandes proporciones. El segundo Florescimiento comienza entre el 1100 y 1150 DC. Un nuevo inventario cerámico, tejidos, adobes y formas arquitectónicas lo caracterizan. La mayoría de las construcciones visibles son de este periodo. A él nos referimos, ahora, como Ocupación Lambayeque y fué cuando el sitio se fortificó. Termina alrededor del 1370 DC y es tentador especular que estuvo relacionado con la conquista Chimú del Valle.

Despues de 1370 DC, una pequeña población continuó en el sitio, pero para el momento de la conquista Inca (ca. 1470 DC), la mayor parte del sitio estaba en ruinas. Algunas ofrendas Inca sugieren que Pacatnamú *continuó siendo un importante centro ceremonial, pero menor que en el periodo precedente.*

Las ofrendas continuaron durante el periodo Colonial y pequeños cementerios de ese periodo han sido identificados.

Cambio de Perspectiva en las Funciones de Pacatnamú

Pacatnamú ha sido frecuentemente visto como un centro ceremonial y de peregrinaje (Ubbelohde-Doering 1959, 1960, 1967; Keatinge 1977, 1978 y 1982). En las excavaciones, no se han recuperado evidencias que sugieran que fué un centro de peregrinaje; sin embargo, es claro que se trata de una de las concentraciones mas vastas de arquitectura ceremonial y que sirvió de centro de actividad religiosa y política para la población del valle bajo del Jequetepeque.

Moche Burials at Pacatnamu

Christopher B. Donnan
Donna McClelland

Eighty-four Moche burials were excavated at Pacatnamu between 1983 and 1987.[1] These are summarized in Table 1, page 38, in which each burial is assigned a number. The burials are described in detail beginning on page 40. Throughout this report, reference to a specific burial will be made by citing the burial number assigned to it (e.g., Burial 23).

Burials 1 through 67 were from a single cemetery (H45 CM1) located in a ravine that cuts across the center of the site (see Site Map, pages 18-19). The cemetery lay along the southern margin of the ravine, in accumulated windblown sand and soft soil that provided a place where shallow burial pits could be dug much more easily than in the hard conglomerate geological base of the Pacatnamu plateau.[2] The cemetery extended over an area 40 meters east-west and between 6.5 and 12.5 meters north-south (Figs. 1, 2). The outline of the area in Figure 1 shows the limit of excavation, within which the entire area was investigated. The cemetery yielded the largest number of Moche burials ever excavated from a single cemetery and included the burials of males and females, as well as individuals of all ages.

In addition to the burials from H45 CM1, three burials (Burials 68, 69, 70) were from an area that may have been reserved for children, for only child burials were found there. It was on the western edge of the site, again in an area where sand and loose soil facilitated the excavation of burial pits (see Site Map).

The remaining 14 burials (Burials 71-84) were found during excavation of seven other parts of the site (see Site Map). They appeared to be isolated individuals, or small clusters of individuals, who were buried outside of any regularly utilized cemetery area. Several were located in refuse, or under the floors of structures.[3] The 84 individuals comprised 28 males, 27 females, 2 adults whose sex could not be determined, and 27 children.

Burial preservation varied greatly. Many were in poor condition—organic materials were decomposed, and little or no evidence of them remained. In these burials we were unable to determine the original grave contents or to reconstruct the treatment of the corpse.

In some instances, however, organic materials such as textiles, basketry, cordage, feathers, and gourd containers were remarkably well preserved, and it was possible to make detailed reconstructions of what the grave

---

1. This is the total number of *individuals* excavated. Some graves contained two or three individuals. There was a total of 79 graves.

2. In most areas of the site there would have been very little soft soil above this conglomerate—especially during the Moche occupation, before extensive refuse and the remains of decomposed architecture began to accumulate.

3. Burials under floors of structures have been previously reported from Huanchaco in the Moche Valley (Donnan and Mackey 1978: 188-207).

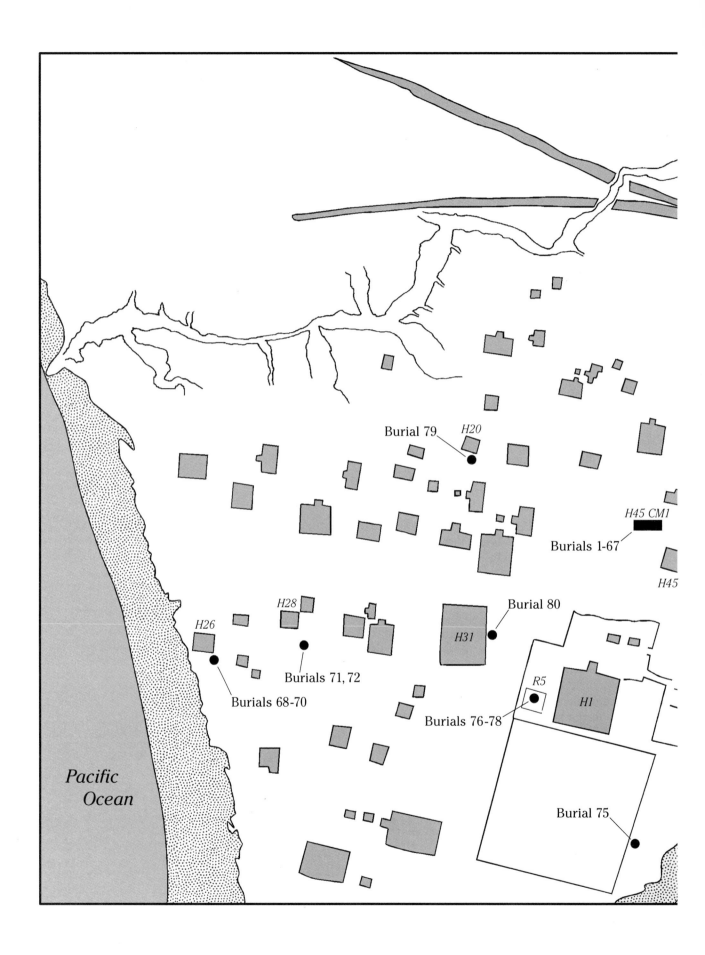

Burial 79 *H20*

H45 CM1
Burials 1-67

H45

Burial 80

H31

H28

H26

Burial 75

R5

H1

Burials 76-78

Burials 71, 72

Burials 68-70

Pacific
Ocean

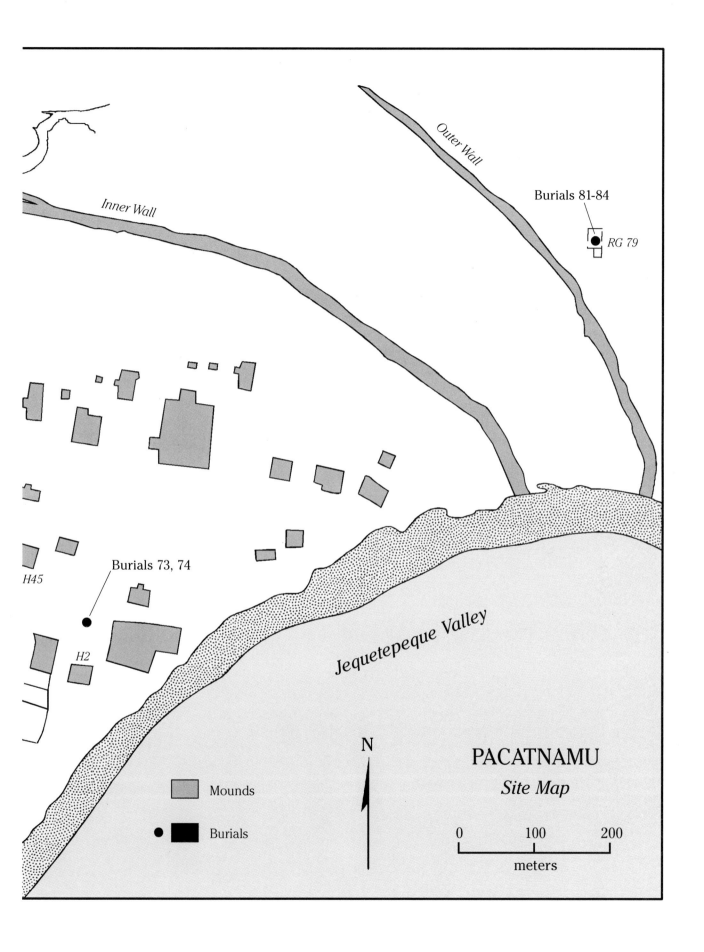

Outer Wall

Inner Wall

Burials 81-84

RG 79

Burials 73, 74

H45

H2

Jequetepeque Valley

Mounds

Burials

N

PACATNAMU

Site Map

0   100   200

meters

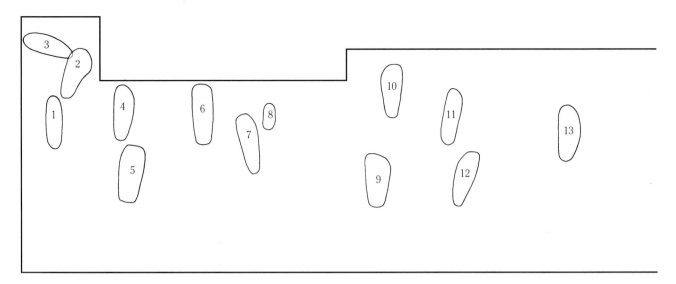

Figure 1. Plan of H45 CM1.

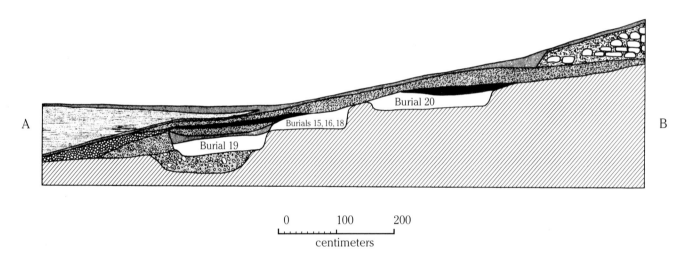

Figure 2. Profile A-B of H45 CM1.

contained and how the corpse was dressed and encased. The well preserved burials suggest that those without good preservation were more complex, contained a greater range of grave contents, and involved more elaborate preparation and encasing of the body than was reflected in the archaeological record.

Preparation of the Body

On the north coast of Peru at the time of European contact, it was said that the death of an individual was followed by a five-day mourning period when the corpse was washed and prepared for burial (Calancha 1977-81: 1247). We do not know if the Moche practiced a similar mourning period, or if they washed the corpse, but on the basis of the few well preserved graves in our sample, we noted several procedures they used to prepare the body for burial.

The woman in Burial 2 had braided hair (Verano, Fig. 4, this volume). In many burials wool yarn was wrapped around the heads, hands, wrists, ankles, feet, or legs.[4] The head was wrapped with multiple windings around the forehead, or with multiple strands of yarn that formed a headband knotted at the center of the forehead (Burial 4). The hands were wrapped individually around the palm and the back of the hand, leaving the thumb free. Wrist wrapping sometimes extended

---

4. Ubbelohde-Doering also reported this practice in Moche burials at Pacatnamu (Ubbelohde-Doering 1983:Abb. 40).

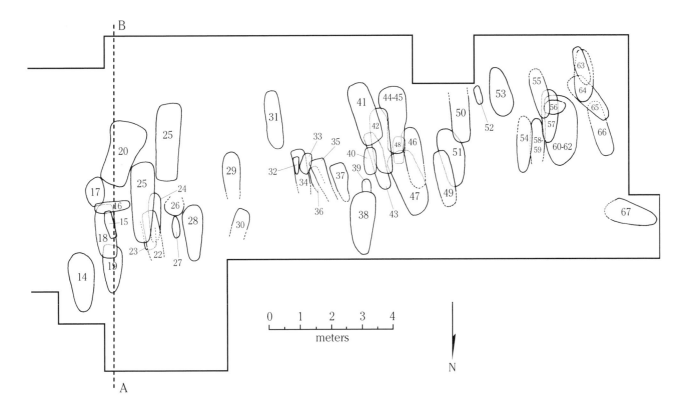

over the palm of the hand. Each foot was wrapped separately, below the arch and over the top of the foot (Fig. 3). One two-year-old child (Burial 17) had yarn wrapped around the left leg at mid-calf.

All bodies were in a fully extended position, on their backs. The ankles sometimes were crossed, but more commonly positioned side by side. The hands usually were placed at the sides or over the pelvic area, although one adult female (Burial 83) was buried with her left hand near her face.[5]

Although we do not know how many individuals were buried wearing articles of clothing, most of the well preserved burials were not dressed. A few, however, were wearing a shirt (Burials 4, 17), a loincloth (Burial 80), or both (Burial 75). Nothing was worn on the feet except the yarn wrapping described above.

Many of the well preserved burials had unspun cotton placed over the eyes or face before the body was wrapped in textiles. Several burials had unspun cotton under the head as though serving as a pillow, or had a thin layer of unspun cotton placed under the entire body. In other burials the head was resting on a stack of textiles, and a few had one or more folded textiles beneath the entire body. Many had textiles placed over the face or wrapped around the head.

Figure 3. Yarn wrapped around a foot of Burial 4.

---

5. One female Moche burial from the Moche Valley also was buried with the left hand near the face (Donnan and Mackey 1978: 160, 161).

Encasing the Body

In our sample of Moche burials from Pacatnamu, five distinct procedures were used to encase the body. These reflect an increasing complexity of funerary practice with an increase in both raw materials and labor invested.

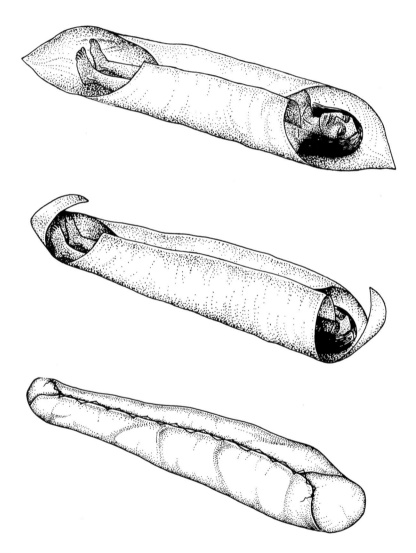

Shroud Wrap

The simplest procedure was to wrap the body in a plain cotton shroud and subsequently to sew the shroud closed along the top of the bundle (Fig. 4). Some bodies were wrapped successively in two or three shrouds. The inner shrouds usually were a finer weave than the outer shrouds and not sewn closed.

Figure 4. Shroud Wrap encasing procedure.

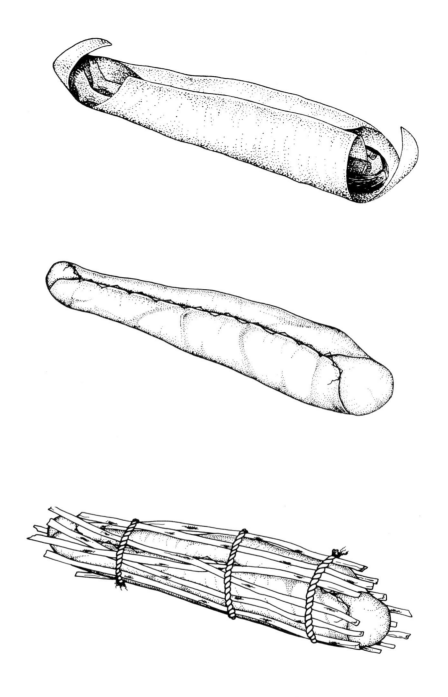

Figure 5. Splint Reinforced encasing procedure.

Splint Reinforced

The body was encased in a Shroud Wrap. Wood or cane splints then were tied to the outside of the bundle, keeping the body rigid (Fig. 5).

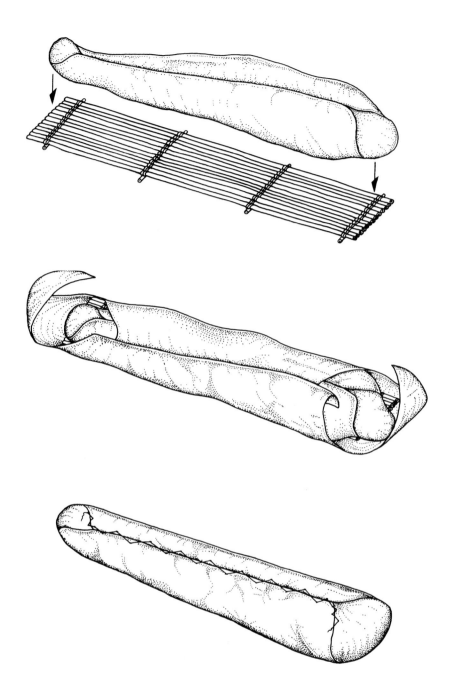

Figure 6. Cane Frame encasing procedure.

Cane Frame

The body was encased in a Shroud Wrap, and the bundle subsequently placed on a rigid cane frame. Generally, the bundle and frame then were wrapped in another large textile that was sewn closed (Fig. 6). In Burials 1 and 24, the bundle was simply placed on a cane frame, but not wrapped in a second textile. In Burials 7 and 17, the body was not wrapped in a shroud before being placed on the cane frame, but the body and cane frame were wrapped together in a shroud.

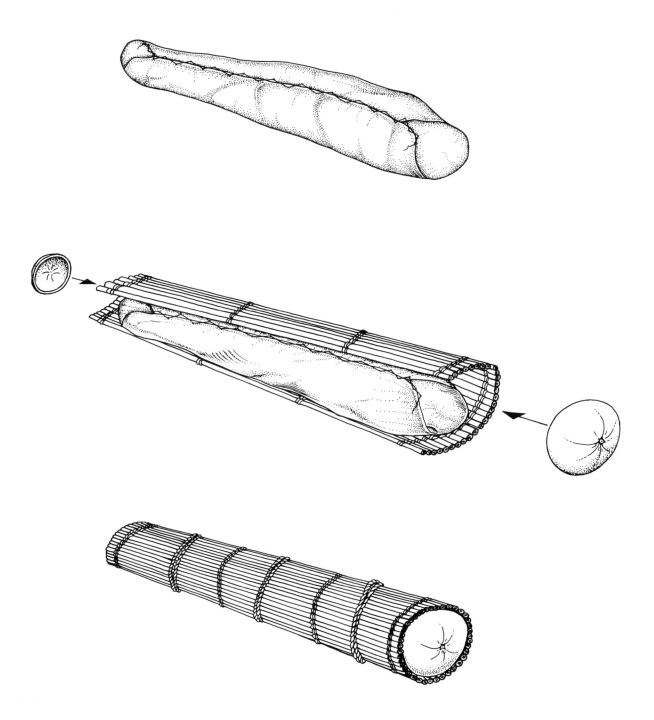

Figure 7. Cane Tube encasing procedure.

Cane Tube

The body was encased in a Shroud Wrap. Then it was wrapped in canes that previously had been twined together (Fig. 7) to form a tube around the bundle, which was tied with ropes. The ends of the tube sometimes were closed with shallow gourd plates. In Burial 17, the cane tube was wrapped around a body that was lying on a Cane Frame.

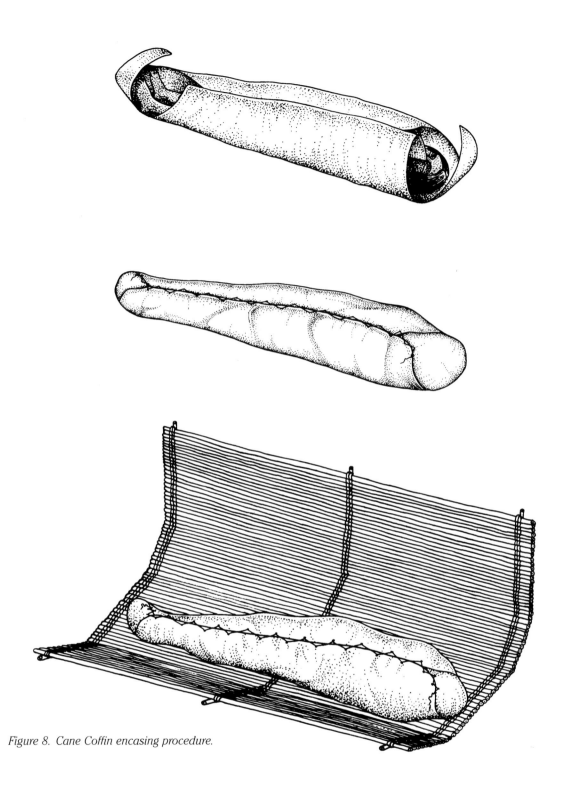

Figure 8. Cane Coffin encasing procedure.

Cane Coffin[6]

The body was encased in a Shroud Wrap. Then it was wrapped with a large cane frame that had been crimped to fold into four sections forming the sides, top, and bottom of a cane coffin (Fig. 8). The two ends of the coffin consisted of separate cane frames which were tied into place as the larger frame was wrapped around the body (Fig. 9). Some cane coffins subsequently were wrapped with rope, creating an elaborate pattern on their exterior surfaces. In Burial 25, the cane coffin

6. For a detailed description of a cane coffin, see Donnan and Barreto, this volume.

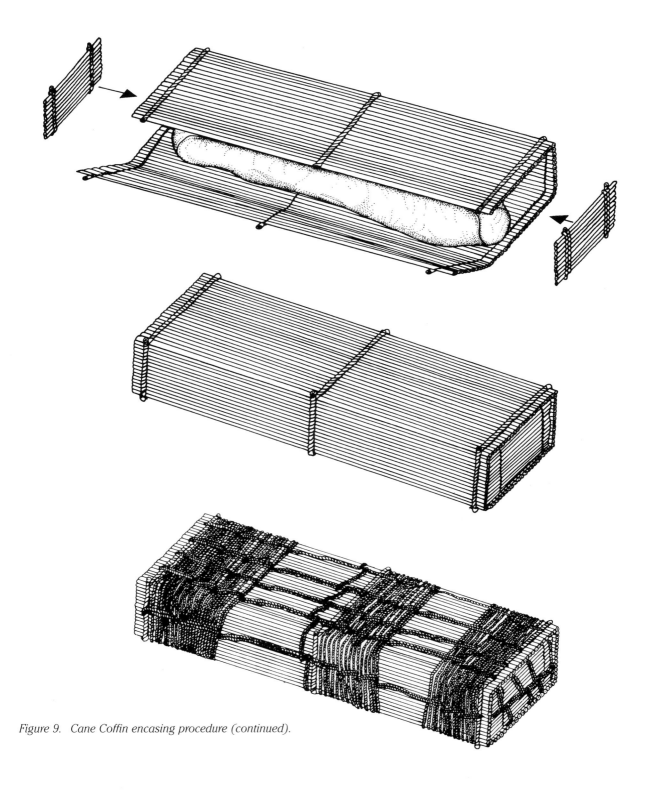

Figure 9. Cane Coffin encasing procedure (continued).

appears to have been wrapped with a textile. In Burial 21, the body inside the coffin was lying on a Cane Frame.

It is possible that some corpses lacked clothing or wrapping when placed in their burial chambers, but there is no good archaeological evidence of this. Nor is there any evidence of a corpse wearing clothing, but not wrapped. Wrapping of the body is so universal that it probably was a standard aspect of Moche funerary practice.

The five procedures for encasing the body probably correlate to economic and social status, as well as age. Infants and young children usually were buried with Shroud Wrap or Splint Reinforced procedures and with few accompanying objects. The Splint Reinforced procedure was only used with infants and young children. When adults were buried with only the Shroud Wrap procedure, they also were accompanied by few, if any, objects, and the objects generally were of poor quality.

Cane Frame, Cane Tube, and Cane Coffin procedures usually were for males and females older than 15 years, and generally were associated with more grave goods than Splint Reinforced or Shroud Wrap burials. Cane Coffin burials were exclusively for adults (male and female) and were accompanied by numerous grave goods, many of which were more elaborate and/or better crafted than those found in simpler burials.

One notable exception to this pattern was Burial 17, a child approximately 2 years of age, who was placed on a cane frame, shroud wrapped, and then enclosed in a tube of twined canes. Not only was this an unusually elaborate treatment for a child, but it was a unique combination of elements with which to encase the corpse.

It should be noted that our burial sample lacks three burial procedures reported from other Moche sites: a variation on the Cane Tube (Strong and Evans 1952: 140-141,150-167; Donnan 1995: 125, Fig. 7); Ceramic Casing (Larco 1945: 37 left; Donnan 1995: 125-130, Fig. 8); and Plank Coffin (Alva 1988; Alva and Donnan 1993; Donnan 1995: 133, Fig. 11).

Funerary Chambers

All 84 burials were found in simple pits that generally were rectangular or oval-shaped with flat or slightly concave floors. Most pits were not much larger than the bundles or coffins placed in them, and were rather shallow—from 40 to 100 centimeters deep.

In Burials 75 and 84, the encased body was supported by three stones or mud bricks rather than lying directly on the chamber floor. Burial 80 had mud bricks on top of the corpse.

Most burial chambers were oriented north-south, and the individuals were placed inside with the head to the south. A few were oriented east-west, with the head to the east (Burials 3, 16, 56, 67). One burial (82) was oriented north-south with the head to the north. No one was buried with the head to the west.

Heinrich Ubbelohde-Doering found Moche graves at Pacatnamu in shaft tombs, each consisting of a vertical shaft with an enlarged chamber at the bottom, making them boot-shaped in profile. Those intended for a single individual were small and rather shallow, while larger ones were for multiple individuals. The largest (EI) had a shaft approximately 2.5 meters deep, providing access to the burial chamber which was approximately 2 meters long and 3 meters wide (Ubbelohde-Doering 1967: 25, 62). An irregular wall made of wood beams and mud bricks sealed the chamber at the bottom of the shaft. Inside the chamber were a stack of nine cane coffins and a large assortment of grave contents.

Although we did not excavate any shaft tombs, there was clear evidence of them in looted Moche cemeteries on the northern margin of the site. These appear to have occurred sporadically, in cemeteries where most individuals were buried in shallow pits. They had small chambers and do not appear to have contained the quantity of grave associations that are found in elite burials. This suggests that shaft tomb burials were by no means restricted to the highest social class. Rather, they could occur in the cemeteries of common people as a more elaborate procedure than burial in a shallow trench.[7]

Although burials in rectangular funerary chambers, with walls lined with rocks or mud bricks, have been reported from other Moche sites (Donnan 1995: 136-142, Figs. 14-17), we found none at Pacatnamu.

Associated Objects

Ceramic vessels were found in most of the graves (Figs. 10-13). Those of adult males and females contained similar quantities of ceramics, but graves of children contained fewer. No grave contained more than six ceramics.

No clear distinction in vessel forms was found by comparing the graves of males and females, or adults and children, nor was there a standard inventory of ceramic forms. The variety of ceramic forms was usually proportional to the number of ceramic objects; apparently a variety of vessel forms in the grave was preferable to multiple examples of a limited number of forms. The only clear exception to this, Burial 38, contained five ceramic vessels, all of which were jars. There is no obvious correlation between the iconography of ceramic vessels in a burial and the role or status of the deceased.

Gourds were found in nearly all Moche burials that had good preservation of organic materials (Fig. 14).

---

7. The association of shaft tombs with burials of commoners is supported by the Moche burials recently excavated at San Jose de Moro (Castillo and Donnan 1994a).

a. Burial 38 2.

b. Burial 34 1.

c. Burial 53 1.

d. Burial 63 1.

Figure 10. Ceramics from Moche burials at Pacatnamu.

a. Burial 5 2.

b. Burial 47 2.

c. Burial 20 2

d. Burial 46 1.

Figure 11. Ceramics from Moche burials at Pacatnamu.

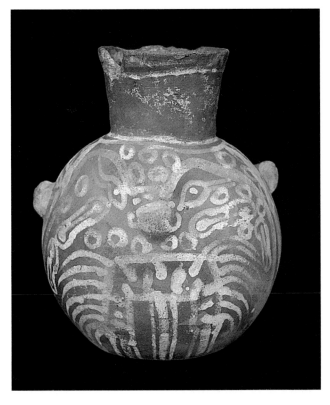

a. Burial 9 1.

b. Burial 34 3.

c. Burial 60 2.

d. Burial 37 1.

Figure 12. Ceramics from Moche burials at Pacatnamu.

a. Burial 20 1.

b. Burial 64 1.

c. Burial 5 1.

d. Burial 34 2.

Figure 13. Ceramics from Moche burials at Pacatnamu.

They were found in more graves and in greater numbers than ceramics. One burial (44) contained 21 gourds, and more than 20 percent of the burials contained at least 6 gourds. The number of gourds in a grave was not related to the number of ceramic vessels. The grave with the greatest number of gourds (Burial 44), for example, contained only two ceramic vessels.

Gourds were found in burials of both sexes and all ages. A few gourds were whole and uncut. Most, however, were in the form of cups, bowls, or plates. One burial (21) contained a gourd in the form of a jar with a gourd stopper, which had a carrying harness of sedge rope (Fig. 15). There were no small, narrow-necked gourds of the type used to contain lime for coca-chewing.

Nearly all gourds were cut horizontally, resulting in a container with an indentation near the center of the bottom. A few, however, were cut vertically, leaving the indentation on the side (Burial 2 G1, Burial 7 G2).

Several were broken and had been mended by lashing with string through holes drilled along the sides of the breaks. One gourd (Burial 25 G1) had remnants of a textile sewn to holes around its rim. Only two gourds had any evidence of decoration. One (Burial 21 G4a) was pyroengraved with two double lines and an unidentified figural motif; the other (Burial 21 G4b) was decorated with a series of perforations filled with unspun cotton.

The gourd bowls and plates often were empty, but sometimes contained plant or animal remains. They often were upside down as lids on gourd bowls, ceramic bottles, or jars. An upside-down gourd bowl or plate sometimes covered the face or other parts of the body in burials of both sexes and all ages.

Plants other than gourds seldom were recovered and only were found in well preserved graves (Gumerman, this volume). They usually were in gourd or ceramic containers. Corncobs also were found wrapped in wool yarn (Burial 53 G2) or cotton string (Burial 2). The most common plant remains were maize (almost always on the cob), edible seaweed, and bottle gourd seeds. Less common were beans, coca, peanuts, squash, *lucuma*, and *espingo*. There was no consistent combination of plants, and only small quantities of plant foods were recovered. Generally there was scarcely enough plant food in a grave to provide a small meal.

In addition to identifiable plant remains found in burials, many gourd and ceramic containers had organic residue or insect pupae, suggesting that they originally contained food.

Burial 21 contained a shallow spoon made of *tutuma* (*Crescentia Cujete*; Towle 1961:88), a gourd-like fruit from the calabash tree, with a thin, woody shell.

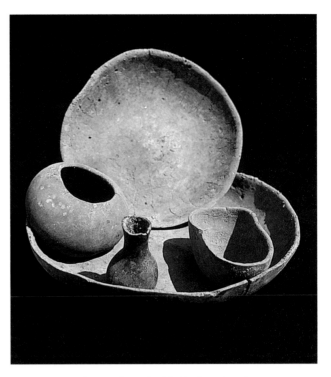

Figure 14. Gourds from the Moche burials at Pacatnamu.

Figure 15. Gourd jar from Burial 21.

Animals, both complete and partial, were found in many Moche graves of men and women, but seldom in graves of children. The most frequently identified animals are llamas—perhaps because their bones are large and tend to be preserved, while smaller skeletal materials may have decomposed. Thirteen graves contained llama bones. Only one (Burials 60-62) contained a complete llama. All others contained only llama parts—most frequently the skull, scapulae, lower legs, feet, and teeth. Burial 80 contained ribs. There is little meat is on these parts of the llama; apparently, they were not placed in graves because of their food value.

A common offering of llama parts consisted of the four lower legs (with toes) and the head stacked alongside the human corpse. In Burial 25 they were wrapped in textiles. Llama remains generally occurred in graves of adults who had elaborate burial treatments (Cane Coffins, Cane Tubes, or Cane Frames) and/or numerous associated objects.

In addition to llama remains, Burial 80 contained guinea pig and fish bones. Burials 9, 21, 73, and 79 contained fish, and Burial 2 contained fish scales.

Metal objects were found in graves of both sexes and all ages. All were copper except for a thin sheet of silver in the mouth of Burial 76.

The weight of copper per burial varied considerably, from less than 2 grams (Burial 12) to more than 247 grams (Burial 61). Most burials, however, contained between 10 and 50 grams. Copper was most often found in the mouth (47 burials), the right hand (27 burials), or the left hand (31 burials). Eighteen burials had copper in the mouth and both hands, whereas six had it in the mouth and only one hand. In only four burials was it found in the hands, but not in the mouth. This suggests that the mouth was the primary location for copper objects, and the hands were secondary. It is noteworthy that of the 25 burials with copper in the mouth and in one or both hands, there were only two cases in which the copper in one of the hands weighed more than the copper in the mouth. However, the weight of the copper in both hands frequently exceeded the weight of the copper in the mouth. There appears to have been no preference for placing copper in either the right or left hand.

Only 13 burials contained copper somewhere other than in the mouth and/or hands. All but one of these also had copper in the mouth, hands, or both. The copper found outside of the mouth and hands consistently weighed less than the copper in the mouth and hands, indicating that it was less important than that in the mouth and hands.

Copper objects in the hands and mouth of the deceased usually were wrapped, either in unspun cotton or in cotton string that had been wound around them many times. A few copper objects appear to have been wrapped in textile fragments.

It is curious that three burials (6, 17, 31) had ceramic sherds rather than copper in their hands. In two cases (17, 31) the sherds were carefully wrapped with unspun cotton.

Most copper in the burials consisted of amorphous chunks; some may have been fragments of ingots (Lechtman, this volume). Also common were thin copper sheets, often folded into multiple laminae. Some recognizable ingots and ingot fragments were recovered. In some instances, such as Burial 61, a single ingot was broken in half, and one half was placed in each hand.

The relatively few copper implements in the graves appeared to be a rather random selection. Burial 47 had a copper bell fabricated from a single sheet of copper. It was bent double, like a pair of tweezers, and was decorated with an owl face in low relief on each half. It originally would have had a loose clapper inside. Part of a spatula blade was found in Burial 11, and two pieces of another spatula were in Burial 47, which also contained a cluster of perforated copper disks and a hook-shaped object that may have been the engaging spur of a spear thrower. A copper fish hook was found inside a gourd in Burial 42. Burials 34 and 76 each contained a copper spindle whorl. The only copper bead was found in Burial 2.

Decorative elements associated with the burials included ear ornaments, necklaces, bracelets, and a feathered headdress ornament.[8] Ear ornaments were found only in the graves of adult females (Burials 2, 53, 73, 76). They were made of wood or bone, and some still had stone inlay (Fig. 16).[9]

Only 12 of the 84 burials contained beads. Five were burials of adult females and seven were of children. The beads were of various types and were made of the following materials:

Spondylus shell
Olivella shell
Black stone
Turquoise
Faustile (similar to turquoise)
Chrysacola
Lapis lazuli
Copper
Gourd
Unidentified shell (white, pink, reddish-white, nacre)

---

8. Nose ornaments were not found in the burials that we excavated at Pacatnamu, but they were found in some of the elaborate Moche graves that Ubbelohde-Doering excavated at this site (Ubbelohde-Doering 1983:85, Abb. 37).

9. Two of the four burials with ear ornaments (Burials 2 and 76) also contained large numbers of beads.

Figure 16. Ear ornaments from Moche
burials at Pacatnamu.

One shell bead (in Burial 68) was carved in the form of a bird and had an inlaid eye of turquoise. All other beads were simple forms, generally disk-shaped or tubular. There appears to have been no rigid symmetry in stringing beads for necklaces or bracelets. Sometimes portions of strands were predominantly one type of bead, and sometimes two or more alternating types. However there was usually no consistent pattern.

Several infants and children were found with "bead strings" tied around their wrists and/or neck. These consisted of 3 to 30 beads, generally of varying sizes, colors, and materials, that were strung in a random sequence. With the exception of the burial shroud, a bead string around the wrist or neck was the artifact most commonly associated with infant and child burials.

A feathered headdress ornament (Fig. 17) was found in Burial 80. It consists of a long, tapered bone pin with feathers attached at its upper end. It is particularly interesting because it correlates closely with feathered headdress ornaments depicted in Moche art (Fig. 18).[10] Large feathered headdress ornaments were excavated in the tomb of the Warrior Priest at Sipán (Alva and Donnan 1993: 106, Figs. 117, 118). They consisted of large copper pins with feathers attached at their upper ends. The Sipán examples may be among the most elaborate feathered headdress ornaments made by the Moche, and probably were meant to be used by individuals of high

10. A similar headdress ornament was excavated by Ubbelohde-Doering at Pacatnamu (Ubbelohde-Doering 1983: Abb. 15).

Figure 17. Feathered headdress ornament
from Burial 80.

Figure 18. Feathered headdress ornament
in Moche art.

status. In contrast, the one from Pacatnamu, which is considerably smaller and made with a bone rather than a copper pin, may have been more characteristic of those used by people of lower status.[11]

Textiles were found in many burials (Donnan and Donnan, this volume). Males tended to have more textiles than females. Most infants and children had fewer textiles than adults, but this may be due to the simpler manner in which these burials were wrapped. A few child burials contained elaborate textiles.

Some burials contained textile garments and accessories, including shirts, loincloths, headcloths, cloaks, and bags (Donnan and Donnan, this volume). A few garments clearly were worn by the deceased, but most appear to have been simply placed adjacent to the body, generally inside the shroud wrapping. Loincloths were found only in adult male graves. Headcloths also appear to have been found only in adult male graves, although the sex of the individual in Burial 25 could not be determined, and a child burial (16) contained a possible headcloth.

Spindle whorls were found only in burials of adult females.[12] Of the 27 adult females in the sample, 20 were buried with spindle whorls. Thirteen of these had one spindle whorl and seven had two spindle whorls. The spindle whorls were either ceramic or stone, except for two made of copper (Burials 34, 76) and one made of a section of corncob (Burial 31). The latter was probably nonfunctional. The ceramic, stone, and copper spindle whorls were small, and weighed between 5.8 and 11 grams. In most cases, the position of the spindle whorl in the grave suggested that it was on a wood spindle lying parallel to the body, generally near the elbow or wrist. The spindles were not in weaving baskets, and no other weaving implements were associated.

Net spacers (malleros) are flat rectangular objects of bone, stone, or wood, which are used in tying fishing nets to insure a consistent mesh size. Today, fishermen in the lower Jequetepeque Valley still tie their nets using net spacers, which they refer to as "*malleros*."

Moche *malleros* vary considerably in size. The critical measurement of a *mallero* is the distance around its narrow dimension (a function of its width and thickness), for this determines the mesh size of the finished net. The mesh size will be equal to twice this distance. The size of the *mallero*, and, thus the size of the mesh, are related to the size of the fish that are to be caught in the net.

Malleros were as exclusive to males' graves as spindle whorls were to females' graves, though not as prevalent. They were found in only three burials (9, 15, 75). Perhaps spinning was practiced by a higher percentage of females than net tying was practiced by males.

Multiple Burials

There were a few graves in which two or three individuals appear to have been buried together. These multiple burials take many forms, and probably resulted from a variety of circumstances. In one grave (Burials 60, 61, 62) an adult male and an adult female were buried together with an infant. In another (Burials 76, 77), a female was buried with a fetus, and in another (Burials 44, 45) a female was buried with a child. In one instance (Burials 58, 59) a male may have been buried with a child.

We must consider the possibility that some individuals in these multiple burials had been dead for a considerable time before being placed in the grave. Early accounts of native Andean people report that bodies of some stillborn infants were kept in households as sacred objects (Arriaga 1968:31). Some infants in the multiple Moche burials may have been kept as sacred objects prior to burial. There is no evidence that sacrificed humans were included in the burials we excavated, but Ubbelohde-Doering reported finding skeletons of individuals at Pacatnamu that he thought had been sacrificed (Ubbelohde-Doering 1983; Hecker and Hecker 1992).

Chronology

Our sample of Moche burials from Pacatnamu is difficult to evaluate in terms of chronological periods. Most burials did not contain ceramics that could be assigned to one of Larco's (1948) phases. The exceptions, Burials 20 and 64, each contained one stirrup spout bottle that would be classified as Phase III (or late Phase II) by Larco's chronology, and thus these two burials can be assigned to that phase.

In attempting to assess the chronology of the other burials in our sample, we compared their ceramics with the ceramics excavated by Ubbelohde-Doering in Moche burials at Pacatnamu. Particularly relevant are Ubbelohde-Doering's burials A IV (1983:44) and E I (1983:52-92), both of which appear to be Phase III by

---

11. A "plume of yellow feathers" and a "large fan of green parrot feathers" were excavated from a Moche burial at Huaca de la Cruz in the Viru Valley (Strong and Evans 1952:154, Plate XXI). Neither is reported to have a headdress pin, but one or both may have been headdress ornaments.

12. One infant burial excavated at the site of San Jose de Moro (Donnan and Castillo, n.d.) and one juvenile burial excavated by Ubbelohde-Doering at Pacatnamu (Ubbelohde-Doering 1983:41) contained spindle whorls. These may have been females, but their sex could not be determined. A spindle whorl has been found in only one grave of a Moche male. It had been placed inside a jar (Donnan and Mackey 1978: 102-115). These are the only examples in more than 325 excavated Moche burials (Donnan 1995) where spindle whorls were not with adult females.

Larco's chronology.[13] Comparison of the ceramics from our Moche burials with those from burials A IV and E I reveals striking overall similarities—many ceramics are nearly identical. This strongly suggests that most, if not all, of the ceramics we excavated are contemporary with Ubbelohde-Doering's A IV and E I ceramics, and pertain to Phase III of the Larco chronology.

The assessment of our ceramics as Phase III is supported by the absence of diagnostic ceramics from Phases I, IV, or V, although each of these ceramic phases was represented in other burials excavated at Pacatnamu by Ubbelohde-Doering.[14]

Moreover, our Moche burials contained no examples of ceramic forms characteristic of terminal Moche occupation at Pacatnamu: special rims and New King jars (Donnan Introduction, this volume). Thus, it seems likely that most, if not all, of our ceramics are Phase III, and that the burials containing these ceramics belong to that phase.

Many burials in the H45 CM1 cemetery were contiguous or superimposed above one another in clusters. The upper burials in the clusters almost always disturbed the lower ones, implying that the people who interred these later burials did so without knowing, or without being concerned about, the locations of previous burials.[15]

The contents of superimposed burials suggest that there was no significant elapsed time between the upper and lower burials in any of the clusters. The only exception to this may be Burial 48, which is at the bottom of one of the deepest clusters (Fig. 1). It contained a face neck jar that is unique in having coffee bean eyes—a feature common to the pre-Moche style of Viru (Gallinazo). This feature, plus its location at the bottom of its cluster, suggest that it may be earlier than most, if not all, of the other burials in the cemetery. It should be noted, however, that the chamber of this face neck jar with coffee bean eyes, in the form of an armless person, is nearly identical to the chamber of a jar in Burial 58, which has Moche-style eyes. Consequently, if Burial 48 is earlier than the others, it may not be much earlier.

Two other burials (35, 37) contained jars with faces rendered primarily with punctation and incision. Jars of this type are generally thought to be pre-Moche Viru (Gallinazo) style. In each instance, however, the jars were in burials with Moche ceramics similar to those from other burials in the cemetery. Recent excavation at the nearby site of Dos Cabezas (Donnan ms.) has demonstrated that ceramic jars with faces rendered primarily with punctation and incision continued well into the Moche period, and often are associated with typical Moche-style ceramics. Therefore, their presence in these two burials is no indication that the burials are necessarily earlier than the other burials in the H45 CM1 cemetery.

Burial 5 may be slightly later than the others in the H45 CM1 cemetery. It contained a press molded blackware jar and a jar with three colors of slip paint.[16] Both are different from other jars in the sample, and neither is similar to any of the ceramics in Ubbelohde-Doering's burials. Unfortunately, since this burial was not part of a cluster of burials, it is not possible to assess its stratigraphic relationship to Moche burials with the more common ceramic forms.

The burials that lacked ceramics are difficult to assign to a phase. These include 23 burials (approximately one-third of the sample) from cemetery H45 CM1, but since these burials were so similar to the others in the cemetery and often were stratigraphically mixed with others that contained Phase III ceramics, it is likely that they too were Phase III. Outside of cemetery H45 CM1, the Moche burials without ceramics cannot be assigned to a phase at this time.

We have three radiocarbon dates for burials from cemetery H45 CM1:

Burial 20	1260 ± 80 B.P.	A.D. 750 (Calibrated)[17]
Burial 25	1480 ± 80 B.P.	A.D. 510 (Calibrated)
Burial 80	1350 ± 80 B.P.	A.D. 600 (Calibrated)

All three dates seem late. If the burials in this cemetery are Phase III, we would have expected the dates to be approximately A.D. 400. The date of A.D. 750 is particularly surprising since similar dates have been reported for Moche material known to be Phase V. On the other hand, radiocarbon dates recently obtained from Phase I material at the nearby site of Dos Cabezas suggest that Phase I did not begin until after A.D. 350 (Donnan ms.). Clearly, before an absolute Moche chronology can be developed we need a careful assessment of all available radiocarbon dates, augmented by additional dates to fill out missing portions of the sequence.

---

13. The stirrup spout bottles from these two burials were exclusively Phase III, and the ceramic vessels from the two burials had many features in common.

14. Most of the burials excavated by Ubbelohde-Doering were either not diagnostic as to phase, or were clearly mixtures of ceramics from several distinct phases.

15. Probably nothing marked the burials to indicate their location. The disturbed burials do not appear to have been systematically searched for associated objects, since the disturbance is generally localized to only a portion of the burial, while the other portions remain undisturbed.

16. The three colors are white, red, and an unusual purple slip. The purple, however, also occurs on two other ceramic vessels from this cemetery (Burial 20 Ceramic 2, Burial 44 Ceramic 1). The first of these is associated with a stirrup spout bottle that would be classified as Phase III (or late Phase II) by Larco's chronology, implying that the unusual purple slip was used well before the late part of the Moche sequence.

17. Calibrated date (rounded to the nearest decade) is the mean of the 95% confidence interval, based on a revised calibration of radiocarbon dates agreed upon at the 1979 "Workshop on Calibrating the Radiocarbon Time Scale" in Tucson, Arizona (Klein et al. 1982).

Table 1. Moche burials at Pacatnamu

Archive Burial Number	Condition	Sex	Age	Burial Type	Ceramics	Gourds	Copper	Textile	Spindle Whorls	Malleros	Yarns	Llama	Beads	Additional
Burial 1	B	M	16-18	CF				2			1			
Burial 2	U	F	35-45	CF	1	10	3	4	1				199	String around corncob, wood ear ornament, and splints
Burial 3	U	M	15-17	I				1						
Burial 4	U	M	30-35	CF	1	4	4	6			4			
Burial 5	U	M	50+	CC	2	19	3	4						Wood staff, string
Burial 6	D	M	35-45	CC	2	3	1	2			1	1		Bast fiber rope
Burial 7	D	M	30-35	CF	1	5	3	4			4			
Burial 8	U	?	8 mo*	SW		1	1	4					3	
Burial 9	U	M	50+	CC	2	19	3	1		2	4	1		Fish bones, wood post
Burial 10	U	F	50+	CF	1	2	3	1	1		1			Mytilus sp. shell
Burial 11	U	F	30-40	CF	1	3	3	3	2		3			Spindle fragments
Burial 12	U	M	25-35	CF		8	1	3			1			
Burial 13	U	F	50+	I	3			2		2		1		
Burial 14	U	M	20-25	CC	3	3	1	2			3			Stone mace head, shell inlays
Burial 15	U	?	6 mo*	SR		2	1	5						
Burial 16	U	?	4-5	SR			2	4						
Burial 17	B	?	2*	CFCT	1	6	2	4			5			1 sherd in unspun cotton
Burial 18	D	F	40-50	CC	2	7	2	2	1		2			
Burial 19	D	F	50+	I	1	5	3		1			1		Foot missing
Burial 20	B	M	25-35	CC	3	8	1	10						Bundle of 11 animal bones, cotton cord and tassels
Burial 21	B	M	35-45	CC	3	16	2	8			4			2 bone objects, 1 spoon, cord
Burial 22	B	F	50+	I		1	1	2						
Burial 23	B	?	ADULT	I		1					4			
Burial 24	D	F	25-35	CF			1	1						
Burial 25	B	?	ADULT	CC		2		8				2		Totora disk
Burial 26	B	?	1-2	SR ?		5		1			1			String
Burial 27	U	?	Fetus	SR		1	1	1			1			
Burial 28	U	F	50+	I	3	2	4		1					
Burial 29	B	F	50+	CT ?	1	6	1	3			1			
Burial 30	B	F	50+	I	2			1	1					
Burial 31	U	F	50+	SW		1		4	1		1			Sherd in unspun cotton in hand, corncob spindle
Burial 32	U	?	0-6 mo	SR			3	2						
Burial 33	U	?	18 mo*	SR	1	9	2	1			2			
Burial 34	B	F	30-40	CC	4		5	1	1		2			
Burial 35	D	M	15-17	I	2	4								
Burial 36	B	?	18 mo*	CT ?	1	1	1	1						
Burial 37	U	?	4-5	I	2	15	4							Pacae pods
Burial 38	D	F	50+	I	5		2		2		1	5		
Burial 39	B	?	1-1.5	I		3	1							
Burial 40	U	?	3.5-4	SR	2	6	3	1			2		5	
Burial 41	D	M	25-30	CT	6	7		2						
Burial 42	U	F	30-40	I	5	19	6		1			1	1	
Burial 43	B	M	25-45	CF ?	1		2	2						
Burial 44	U	F	25-35	CT	2	21	2	2			1	1		1 ceramic sherd
Burial 45	U	?	6 mo*	CT				1			3			
Burial 46	B	M	ADULT	I	1	1		1						
Burial 47	U	M	25-30	I	2			7						Blue pigment, white chalk, canine skull, cordage
Burial 48	B	?	18 mo*	I	1	2	2	1			1			
Burial 49	B	F	50+	I		1	2		1		1			
Burial 50	B	F	ADULT	I										
Burial 51	U	M	25-35	I	2		4			1				Sea mammal bone
Burial 52	B	?	1*	I	1	3								
Burial 53	D	F	50+	CF	2	4	3	2	2		3			Ear ornaments, wood staff, Spondylus labret
Burial 54	D	M	30-40	CF				4						2 wood objects, Mytilus sp. shell
Burial 55	B	M	30-35	I				2						
Burial 56	U	?	6 mo*	SR	2			2						
Burial 57	U	F	35-45	I	1			3			2			
Burial 58	B	M	35-40	I	2									
Burial 59	B	?	2-2.5	I										
Burial 60**	U	M	35-45	I	3	4	4							Bone spatula
Burial 61**	U	F	30-40	I				5	1	2				
Burial 62**	U	?	6 mo*	SR				4					78	
Burial 63	D	?	3-3.5	SR	2	3	1	5			3		118	String, twined mat
Burial 64	B	M	20-35	I	1	3		1			2			
Burial 65	D	F	30-40	I	3	5	3		2					
Burial 66	B	F	30-40	I	2			2			1			
Burial 67	D	M	25-30	I	1	1						1		Skull missing
Burial 68	U	?	9 mo*	SW ?				1			2		55	
Burial 69	U	?	1*	SW				1			2		157	
Burial 70	U	?	1-1.5	SW				1						
Burial 71	U	?	4-5	SW	2	10		1					4	
Burial 72	B	?	1.5-2	CT				4						
Burial 73	D	F	50+	CF		4	2	12	1		1	1	1	1 wood ear ornament, fish bones, spindle
Burial 74	U	M	40-50	I				7			1			
Burial 75	U	M	25-30	CF		1	3	9		1	3			Wood objects
Burial 76	U	F	19-22	SW			2	1	1				161	Bone ear ornaments, silver ornament in mouth
Burial 77	U	?	6 mo	SW				1						
Burial 78	U	?	11-13	CF				1						
Burial 79	U	F	25-35	CF	2	7	3	1	1					Fish, dark sand
Burial 80	U	M	30-40	CC	1	2	1	16			2	2		Guinea pig bones, fish, feather plume
Burial 81	D	?	6 mo*	SW				2						Mat
Burial 82	B	M	20-25	I				1						
Burial 83	D	F	30-35	SW				3						
Burial 84	U	M	20-25	SW				1						
Burials 60-62 ***					4	10						1		Compacted llama dung

* = Approximately
** = Individual burial contents. See also group contents Burials 60-62
*** = Contents associated with all three burials. See also individual contents in Burials 60-62.
CONDITION: U = Undisturbed burial   D = Disturbed burial   B = Badly disturbed burial
BURIAL TYPE: CC = Cane Coffin   CF = Cane Frame   CT = Cane Tube   SW = Shroud Wrap   SR = Splint Reinforced   I = Indeterminate

Conventions

Burial Descriptions

1. Reference to the "left side" or "right side" of the skeleton refers to the skeleton's proper left or right.

2. "Head to the south" indicates that the head is south of the torso and does not refer to the direction the head is facing.

3. Some associated objects were so poorly preserved that they could not be reconstructed or illustrated. If, however, the object could be identified, it was counted and listed in the contents of the burial. For example, the statement "Eight ceramic vessels (1-7)," means that there were eight ceramics, but only seven of the eight could be illustrated.

4. Individual gourds and ceramics are described only when (i) they have contents, (ii) they have dimensions but are not individually illustrated, or (iii) their position or orientation is unclear in the burial drawing. Many of the gourds were so badly decomposed that they could not be recovered from the excavation, but their dimensions could be recorded. The dimensions are given when it was not possible to illustrate the gourd.

5. The textile numbers in in the burial descriptions are the original field numbers (see Donnan and Donnan, Table 1, pages 233-240, this volume). All cotton and wool products, including string, yarn, and unspun cotton were given textile numbers; however, string, yarn, and unspun cotton, as well as textiles that were too fragmentary to be analyzed, are not included in the burial descriptions. Thus, some textiles numbers are missing (e.g., Textile 1 in Burial 73 which was unspun cotton).

6. "Wool" refers to camelid fiber.

7. In listing the associated artifacts, Arabic numerals are used for ceramic vessels, and the following capital letters are used for other items:
   B1, B2 = Bag 1, Bag 2
   Cu1, Cu2 = Copper 1, Copper 2
   G1, G2 = Gourd 1, Gourd 2
   T1, T2 = Textile 1, Textile 2

8. The term "cane" is used frequently in the descriptions. The type of cane rarely could be identified, but it would have been either Carrizo (*Phragmites communis*) or Caña brava (*Gynerium sagittatum*).

Burial Illustrations

1. North arrows indicate magnetic north.

2. The method used to encase the body is illustrated as fully as possible, except when size, form, or construction could not be determined. When the outline of a Cane Frame, Cane Wrapping, or Cane Coffin was determinable, it is indicated with a solid line.

3. A dashed line on a drawing of an associated artifact indicates the probable shape of the original specimen.

4. "Fire-blackened" written adjacent to an illustration indicates that the ceramic object had a carbon deposit on its surface when it was found, suggesting that it had been used over an open fire.

5. All ceramic specimens are color coded to indicate which areas are slip painted, unslipped, or painted with organic black pigment. Also, smudge fired blackware is indicated. The following color coding is used:

   □ White slip
   ▦ Red slip
   ▩ Purple slip
   ■ Organic black
   ░ Paste
   ▤ Blackware

Burial 1

Original Field Number: H45CM1 B53
Sex: Male
Age: 16-18
Burial Type:
  Cane Frame. Constructed with 14 long pieces of cane.
Contents:
  Two textiles.
      Textile 1, a shroud wrapped around the body, but not the cane frame.
      Textile 2, a loincloth at midsection of the body.
  Yarn around the left hand was badly decomposed.
Comments:
  The skeleton was badly disturbed prior to excavation. For further information on the textiles see Donnan and Donnan, this volume.

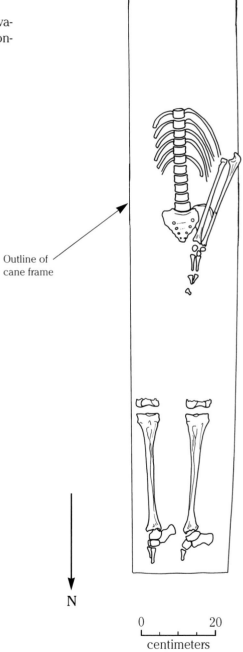

Outline of cane frame

N

0   20

centimeters

Burial 2

Original Field Number: H45CM1 B55
Sex: Female
Age: 35-45
Burial Type:

Cane Frame. Constructed with 16 long pieces of cane at least 150 cm long, 30 cm wide at the head, 22 cm wide at the feet. Three cane cross braces 5 cm, 47 cm, and 93 cm from the head end.

Contents:

One ceramic vessel (1) contained insect pupae.
Ten gourds (G1-G10).

G2 contained insect pupae.

G3 contained 10 bottle gourd seeds (*Lagenaria siceraria*).

G5 contained 0.5 g of seaweed (*Gigartina chamissoi*).

G6, large irregular fragment of a gourd bowl, positioned upside down over G7.

G7, bowl (15 cm diameter x 8 cm high), positioned upright. It contained 43.2 g of seaweed (*Gigartina chamissoi*) and insect pupae.

G8, positioned upright, contained fish scales.

G9, positioned upright, contained 26.7 g of seaweed (*Gigartina chamissoi*) and 4 corncobs (*Zea mays*).

G10, upside down over 1.3 g of seaweed (*Gigartina chamissoi*).

One copper chunk (12.1 g) in the mouth.
One copper chunk (2.3 x 0.9 x 0.7 cm, 4.0 g) in right hand.

One copper chunk (2.3 x 1.3 x 0.7 cm, 6.6 g) in left hand.
Beads around the neck.

1 copper (A).

2 carved white shell (B, C).

18 pink/white *Spondylus* shell (D).

115 black stone (E). In some areas there were up to 12 consecutive black beads, and in other areas black and pink/white beads alternated.

Beads around the right wrist.

11 pink/white *Spondylus* shell (D).

7 black stone (E).

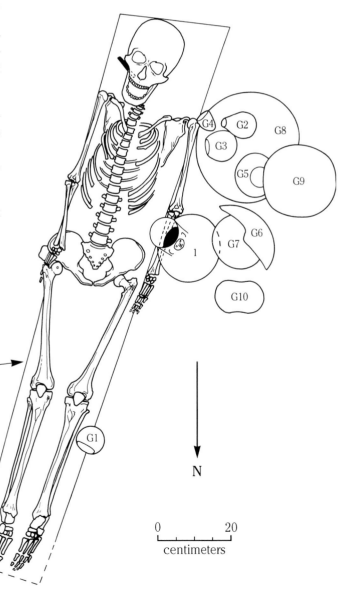

Outline of cane frame

N

0   20
centimeters

Beads around left wrist.

> 12 pink/white *Spondylus* shell (D).
>
> 2 black stone (E).

Mat fragment at left ankle.

Four textiles.

> Textile 1, an outer shroud, wrapped around the entire body and the cane frame; then gathered over center axis of the body, folded up over the head and feet, and sewn up the central axis.
>
> Textile 2, an inner shroud, in the area from the middle of the lower legs to the collarbone.
>
> Textile 3 covered the face and top of the head, and was tied at the back of the head with a single knot.
>
> Textile 4 was massed under the head.

Brown unspun cotton over the eyes.

String, brown cotton, S-Z2, wrapped around a small corncob inside Textile 4 under the head.

Stone spindle whorl (8.8 g) (F).

One wood ear spool (G).

Bound wood splints by the right arm.

Fish scales in G8.

Comments:

> The hair was braided (Verano, Fig. 4, this volume). For further information on the textiles see Donnan and Donnan, this volume.

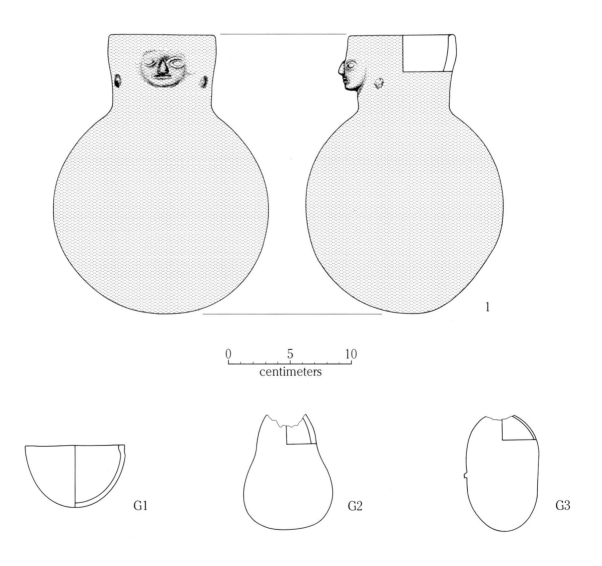

1

centimeters

G1   G2   G3

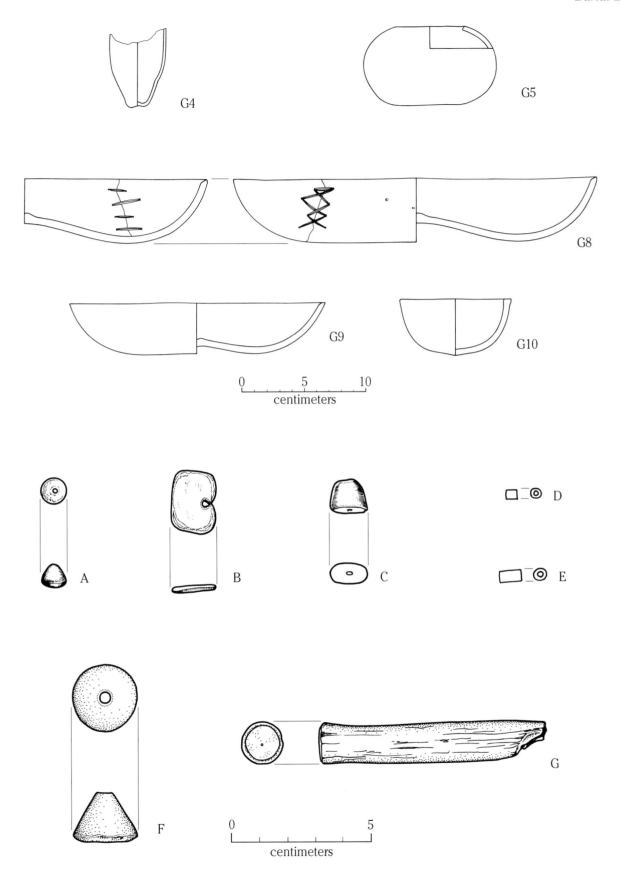

Burial 3

Original Field Number: H45CM1 B62
Sex: Male
Age: 15-17
Burial Type:
   Indeterminate.
Contents:
   One textile.
      Textile 1 in the areas of the feet and pelvis.
Comments:
   The body was positioned east-west with the head to
   the east, instead of the more usual position of north-
   south with the head to the south. This individual
   appears to have been in poor health as a child, and
   to have suffered from an infectious disease at the
   time of death. See Verano, this volume, for skeletal
   analysis. For further information on the textiles see
   Donnan and Donnan, this volume.

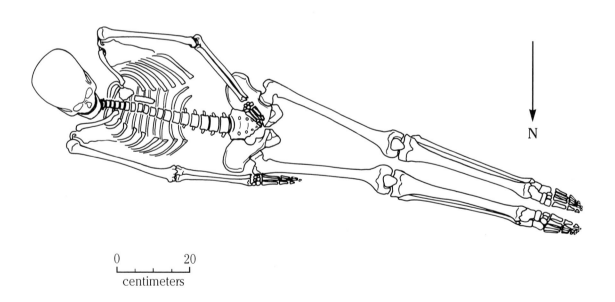

N

0 _____ 20
centimeters

Burial 4

Original Field Number: H45CM1 B46
Sex: Male
Age: 30-35
Burial Type:
  Cane Frame.
Contents:
  One ceramic vessel (1) contained insect pupae.
  Four gourds (G1-G4).
    G1, positioned upright, contained 5 corncobs (*Zea mays*).

G2 contained 6.3 g of seaweed (*Gigartina chamissoi*) and 3 corncobs (*Zea mays*).

G3, plate (27 cm diameter x 3 cm high), positioned upright over G4. It contained several fragments of seaweed (*Gigartina chamissoi*) and organic residue.

G4, positioned upright, below G3.

One copper ingot (2.7 cm diameter x 0.7 cm thick, 14.0 g) in the mouth.

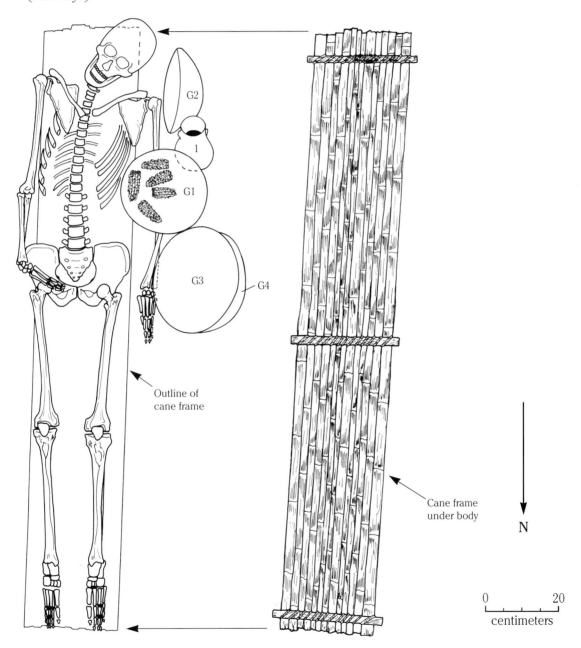

Outline of cane frame

Cane frame under body

N

0   20
centimeters

One copper chunk (1.5 x 1.5 x 0.4 cm, 0.1g) (Cu2) in right hand.

One copper chunk wrapped in yarn (2.6 x 2 x 0.8 cm, 11.3 g) in right hand.

One copper chunk (2.2 x 1.6 x 1.2 cm, 12.2 g) in left hand.

Six textiles.

> Textile 1, an outer shroud, wrapped around the body and the cane frame and folded up over the feet.

> Textile 2, wrapped around the waist.

> Textile 3, a shirt, worn by the individual. The right arm was still inside the remaining sleeve.

> Textile 4, directly on top of the cane frame, extending to within 10 cm of the south end and 5 cm of the north end.

> Textile 5, a head cloth, wrapped around the head over textile 6.

> Textile 6, a headcloth, folded in half diagonally and wrapped around the head, but not covering the face.

Unspun cotton from the feet to midthigh under the shroud.

Unspun cotton on top and possibly below the textile covering the cane frame.

Yarn, yellowish brown wool, Z-S2. At least 50 strands around the right foot.

Yarn, yellowish brown wool, S-Z2. At least 40 strands around the left foot.

Yarn, gold wool, S-Z2. At least 20 strands formed a headband that was knotted in a single knot at the front of the head.

Yarn, gold wool, S-Z2, around the right hand that contained a copper object.

Comments:

> In addition to the cane frame, there was a mass of north-south cane and some rope along the northwest side of the body, and some east-west cane at the south end. This cane and rope apparently were not used to wrap the body. For further information on the textiles see Donnan and Donnan, this volume.

1

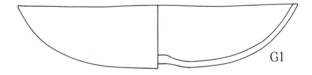

G1

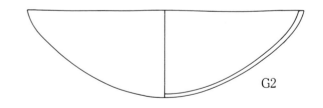

G2

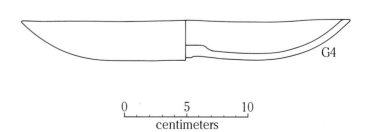

G4

0 5 10
centimeters

Burial 5

Original Field Number: H45CM1 B44
Sex: Male
Age: 50+
Burial Type:
  Cane Coffin.
Contents:
  Two ceramic vessels (1, 2) contained insect pupae.
  Nineteen gourds (G1-G12).
      G1, bowl (16 cm diameter x 5 cm high), contained 6.1 g seaweed (*Gigartina chamissoî*) and 5 corncobs (*Zea mays*).

G2 positioned under G3.
G3, bowl (5.5 cm x 2.5 cm high), positioned upright inside G2, contained 5 bottle gourd (*Lagenaria siceraria*) seeds.
G4, lidded bowl (14 cm diameter x 7 cm high, lid 2.5 cm diameter), contained 2 corncobs (*Zea mays*).
G5, positioned upright, contained 8.6 g of seaweed (*Gigartina chamissoî*).
G6, whole gourd (9 cm diameter x 10 cm high), positioned on its side with the stem to

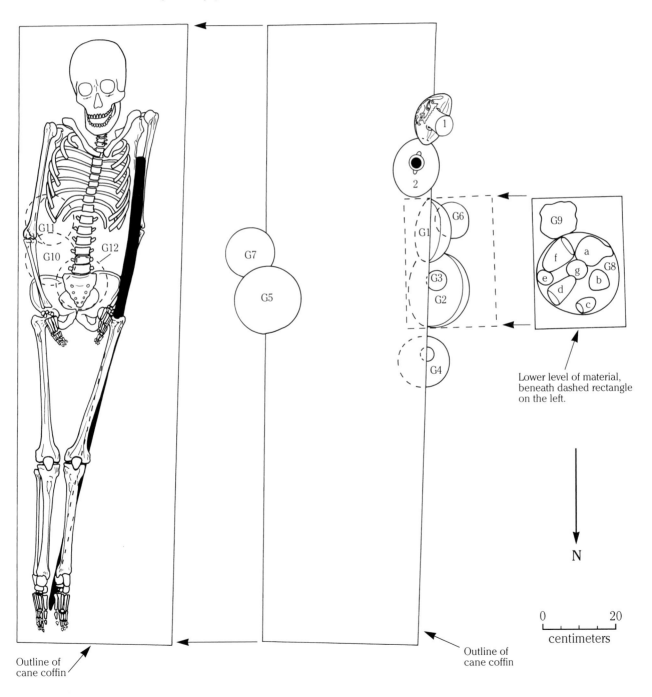

Lower level of material, beneath dashed rectangle on the left.

N

0   20
centimeters

Outline of
cane coffin

Outline of
cane coffin

northwest, contained 11 bottle gourd (*Lagenaria siceraria*) seeds.

G7, bowl (14 cm diameter x 13 cm high), positioned upside down, contained 4 corncobs (*Zea mays*).

G8, positioned upright, contained an additional 7 small gourds (G8a-G8g). G8a, whole gourd (7.5 cm lower diameter x 3.9 cm upper diameter x 11 cm high), contained insect remains. G8b, narrow end of gourd (4.7 cm diameter x 6.6 cm high). G8c, narrow end of gourd (3.5 cm diameter x 5.5 cm high). G8d, narrow end of gourd (5 cm diameter x 9 cm high). G8e, G8f, and G8g were too decomposed to determine their form or size.

G9 was too decomposed to determine its form or size.

G10, positioned upright, contained 3 corncobs (*Zea mays*).

G11, bowl (13 cm diameter), positioned upright, contained 5 corncobs (*Zea mays*).

G12, positioned upright, contained 5.0 g of seaweed (*Gigartina chamissoi*) and insect pupae.

One folded copper sheet (14.2 g) (Cu3) in mouth.

One folded copper chunk (3.6 x 2.4 x 1 cm, 6.9 g) wrapped in unspun cotton in right hand.

One folded copper chunk (3.8 x 2.6 x 1.0 cm, 5.4 g) wrapped in unspun cotton in left hand.

Four textiles.

Textile 1, an outer shroud, wrapped around and over the top of the head.

Textile 2, a head cloth, wrapped around the forehead.

Textile 3, a head cloth, wrapped around the head, closest to it.

Textile 4 near the head.

String, possibly human hair, near the ears.

One pointed wood staff (19 cm diameter x 122 cm long).

Comments:

It was not possible to determine what was in and what was out of the coffin because of extreme decomposition. The condition of the bone around the left eye suggests a serious infection and possible loss of the left eye. See Verano, this volume, for skeletal analysis. For further information on the textiles see Donnan and Donnan, this volume.

1

```
0        5        10
|   |   |   |   |   |
    centimeters
```

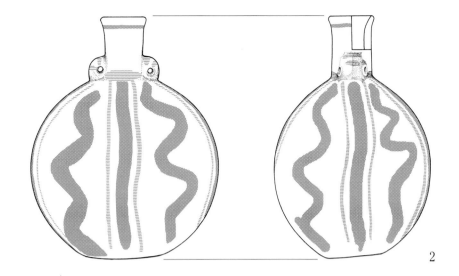

2

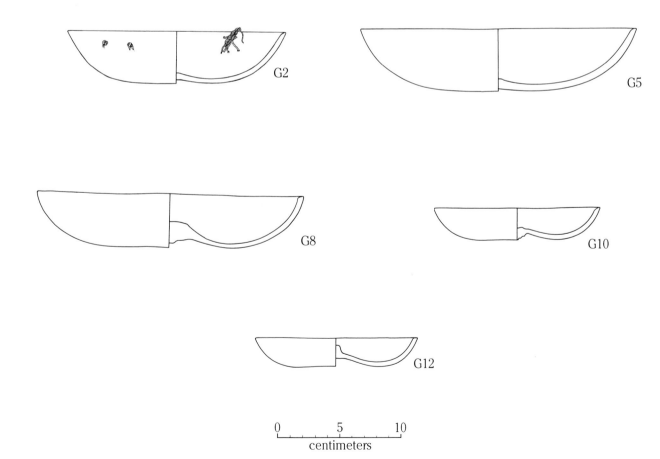

G2

G5

G8

G10

G12

0   5   10
centimeters

Burial 6

Original Field Number: H45CM1 B52
Sex: Male
Age: 35-45
Burial Type:
Cane Coffin.
Contents:
Two ceramic vessels (1, 2) and two sherds, one in each hand.
Three gourds (G1-G3).
G1, bowl (17 cm diameter x 6 cm high), positioned upright. It contained 1.5 g of seaweed (*Gigartina chamissoi*).
G2, bottle shaped (4 cm diameter x 11 cm high).
G3, whole gourd (14 cm diameter), too decomposed to determine its height.
Copper stains on the teeth.
Two textiles.
Textile 1, a shroud, around the feet and lower legs.
Textile 2 associated with the llama bones.
Bast fiber rope around the llama bones.
Yarn, brown wool, S-Z2. At least 15 strands around the left hand.
Llama bones. The four ankles and feet were tied together with a bast fiber rope, and a llama head was placed on top of them. Small amounts of net were present.
Comments:
The end of the coffin near the head had been disturbed prior to excavation. For further information on the textiles see Donnan and Donnan, this volume.

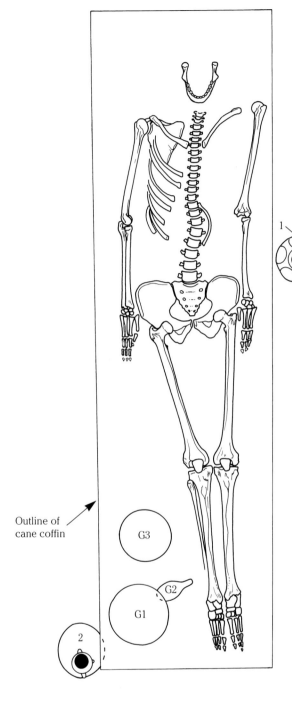

Outline of cane coffin

N

0 _____ 20
centimeters

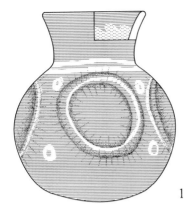

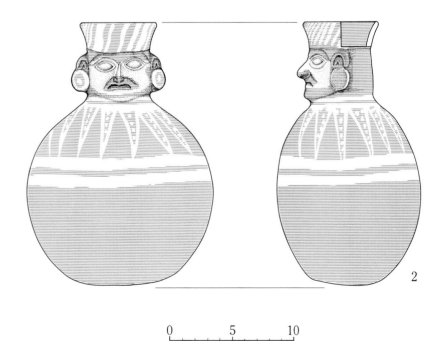

Burial 7

Original Field Number: H45CM1 B48
Sex: Male
Age: 30-35
Burial Type:
  Cane Frame.
Contents:
  One ceramic vessel (1) contained insect pupae.
  Five gourds (G1-G5).
    G1 contained insect pupae.
    G2 contained insect pupae.

G3 contained organic residue and insect pupae.
G4, upright, over G5, contained 3 corncobs (*Zea mays*).
G5, upright, under G4, contained insect pupae and unidentifiable plant material.
Two copper objects (2.3 x 1.4 x 0.7 cm and 2.4 x 1.4 x 0.6 cm, 11.0 g total) in mouth.
One copper chunk (2.3 x 1.8 x 0.3 cm, 3.2 g) in right hand.

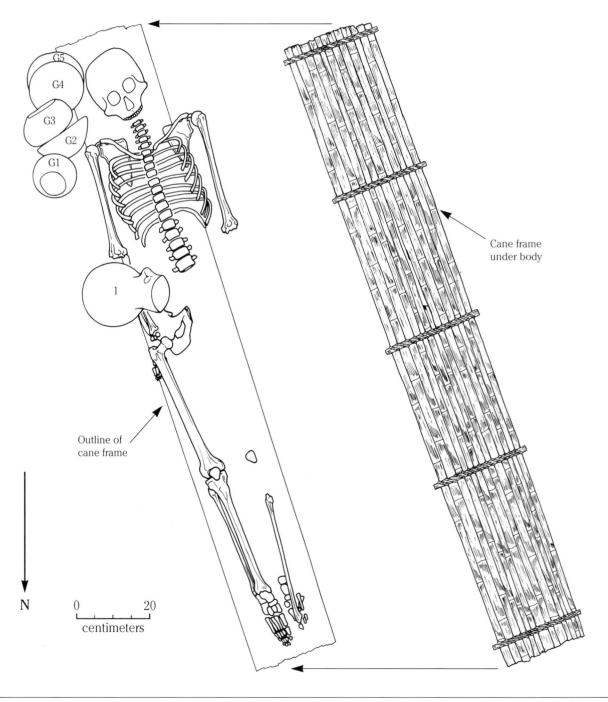

Outline of cane frame

Cane frame under body

N

0   20
centimeters

Four textiles.

Textile 1, a shroud, wrapped around the body and the cane frame. The body and frame were placed diagonally on the shroud, its corners folded up over the head, feet, and torso. The excess was pulled together along the central axis of the body and sewn closed.

Textile 2, a shirt, in the area of chest. The individual may have been wearing it.

Textile 3, in the area of waist.

Textile 4, a head cloth, folded and rolled diagonally before wrapping twice around the head, covering the unspun cotton over the eyes.

Unspun cotton over the eyes.

Yarn, brown wool, S-Z2, wrapped around the fingers of right hand.

Yarn, yellowish brown wool, S-Z2, wrapped around right foot.

Yarn, yellowish brown wool, S-Z2, wrapped around left foot.

Yarn, yellowish brown wool, Z-S2. At least three groups of 30 strands wrapped around the head, on top of the head cloth.

Comments:

The left side of the body was disturbed prior to excavation. Many bones were missing including the jaw. For further information on the textiles see Donnan and Donnan, this volume.

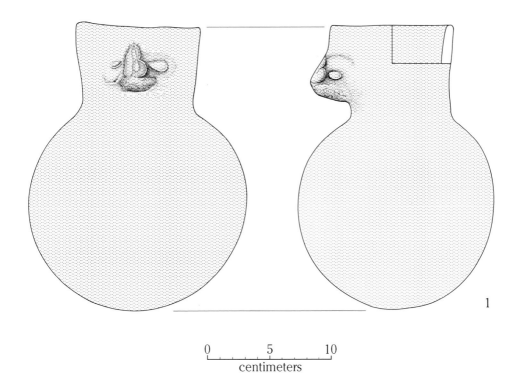

0   5   10
centimeters

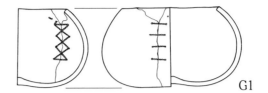

G1

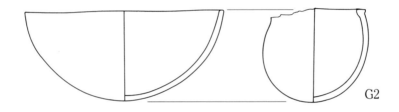

G2

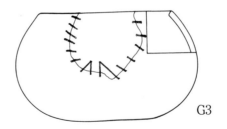

G3

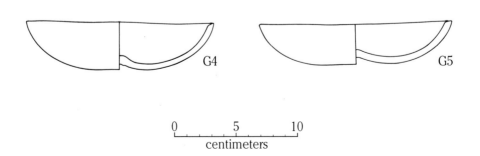

G4   G5

0   5   10
centimeters

Burial 8

Original Field Number: H45CM1 B47
Sex: ?
Age: Approximately 8 months
Burial Type:
  Shroud Wrap.
Contents:
  One gourd (G1), placed upside down over the head.
  One folded copper needle (2.1 cm long x 0.2 cm diameter) in mouth.
  Four textiles.
    Textile 1, an outer shroud, wrapped around the body, completely covering head and feet.
    Textile 2, a middle shroud, folded in half lengthwise then wrapped around the body, completely covering head and feet.
    Textile 3, an inner shroud, wrapped around the body, with the excess gathered in folds at the side and top of body.
    Textile 4, a shirt, wrapped around the head.
  Unspun, light tan cotton on the face and top of the head, and under the shirt.
  Beads strung around the neck.
    3 reddish-white shell, tubular.
Comments:
  For further information on the textiles see Donnan and Donnan, this volume.

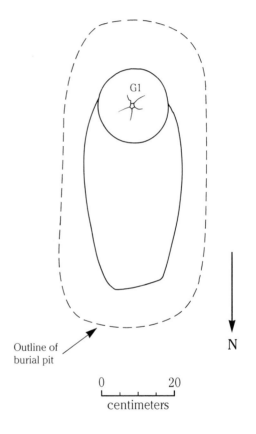

Outline of burial pit

N

0   20
centimeters

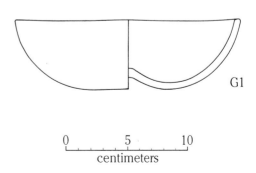

G1

0   5   10
centimeters

Burial 9

Original Field Number: H45CM1 B54
Sex: Male
Age: 50+
Burial Type:
   Cane Coffin.
Contents:
   Two ceramic vessels (1, 2) contained insect pupae.
   Nineteen gourds (G1-G19).
      G2, bowl (25 cm diameter x 3 cm high), positioned upright over G3.
      G3, bowl (24 cm diameter x 3 cm high), positioned upright under G2.

G4, bottle (12 cm high).
G5, lid (10 cm diameter x 2 cm high), upside down over G6.
G6, bowl with incurving rim (16 cm diameter x 6 cm high; rim opening 8 cm), positioned upright under G5 and over G9 and G10. It contained 14 whole peanuts (*Arachis hypogaea*) and 6 fragments of peanut shells.
G7, bowl (8 cm diameter x 4 cm high), positioned upright.
G8 positioned upright.

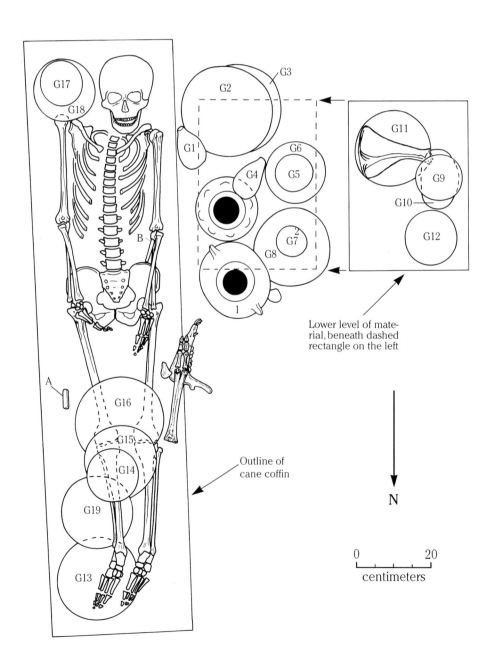

Lower level of material, beneath dashed rectangle on the left

Outline of cane coffin

N

0   20
centimeters

G9, bowl (12 cm diameter x 3 cm high), positioned upright under G5 and G6 and over G10.

G10, bowl (16 cm x 11 cm diameter x 7 cm high), positioned upright under G9.

G11, bowl (20 cm diameter x 3 cm high), positioned upright. It contained animal bones and 29 whole peanuts (*Arachis hypogaea*).

G12, bowl (14 cm diameter x 5 cm high), positioned upright under G7 and G8.

G13 positioned upright, contained 27 whole peanuts (*Arachis hypogaea*) and 3 fragments of peanut shells.

G14, bowl (14 cm diameter x 6 cm high), upside down over G15.

G15, plate (19.5 cm diameter x 3 cm high), positioned upright under G14. It contained 3 corncobs with kernels (*Zea mays*) and fragments of corncobs.

G16, plate (24 cm diameter x 2 cm high), positioned upright.

G17, bowl (11 cm diameter x 3 cm high), positioned upright inside G18. It contained 2 corncobs (*Zea mays*).

G18, bowl (16 cm diameter x 4 cm high), positioned upright.

G19, plate (20 cm diameter x 3 cm high), positioned upright. It contained 49 whole peanuts (*Arachis hypogaea*), 6 fragments of peanut shells, and 1 corncob (*Zea mays*).

One copper chunk (2.7 x 2.7 x 1.2 cm, 23.3 g) in mouth.

One copper chunk (3.4 x 2.0 x 0.9 cm, 16.5 g) in right hand.

One copper chunk (2.9 x 2.2 x 0.9 cm, 17.3 g) in left hand.

One textile.

Textile 1 under the pelvis.

Yarn, yellowish brown wool, S-Z2. At least 6 strands wrapped around right foot.

Yarn, brown wool, S-1. Many fine strands in right hand.

Yarn, brown wool, S-1, plied (?). Many fine strands in left hand.

Yarns (?) wrapped around head.

One stone *mallero* (A).

One bone *mallero* (B).

Llama scapula, beneath G11.

Llama mandible and leg bones outside the coffin on west side of left femur.

Fish bones outside the coffin on west side of left femur.

One short wood post, upright, beside ceramic 1.

Comments:

The two ceramic vessels, gourds G1-G12, the llama scapula beneath G11, fish bones, and the llama mandible and leg bones were outside the coffin. For further information on the textiles see Donnan and Donnan, this volume.

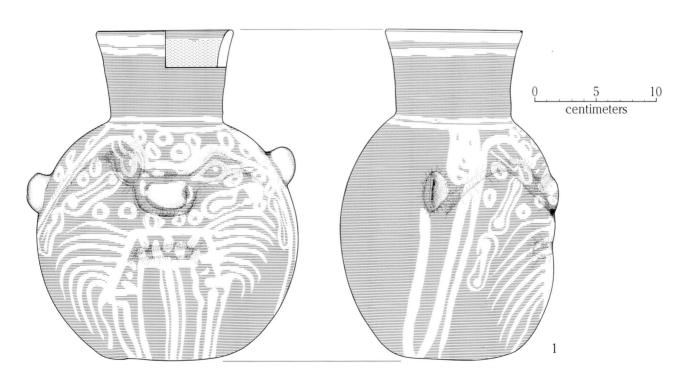

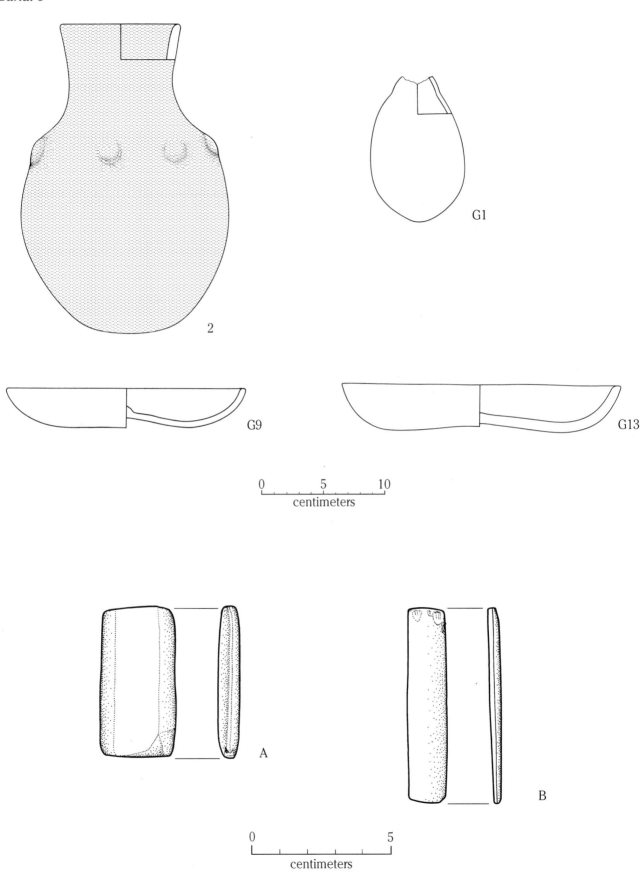

2

G1

G9

G13

0   5   10
centimeters

A

B

0   5
centimeters

Burial 10

Original Field Number: H45CM1 B39
Sex: Female
Age: 50+
Burial Type:

Cane Frame. There were 14 long pieces of cane with one cross brace near the head and another near the hip. The foot end was decomposed, but originally it must have had another cross brace.

Contents:

One ceramic vessel (1).
One ceramic spindle whorl (A).

Two gourds (G1-G2).

G1, incurving bowl (12 cm diameter x 5 cm high; rim opening 7 cm), upside down.

G2, bowl (15 cm diameter x 4.5 cm high), positioned upright (?). It contained 43 squash (*Cucurbita* sp.) seeds and 2 corncobs (*Zea mays*).

One copper chunk (2 x 2 x 0.8 cm, 6.4 g) in the mouth.

One concave copper sheet (bell fragment? 3.4 x 3.1 x 0.5 cm, 4.9 g) in right hand.

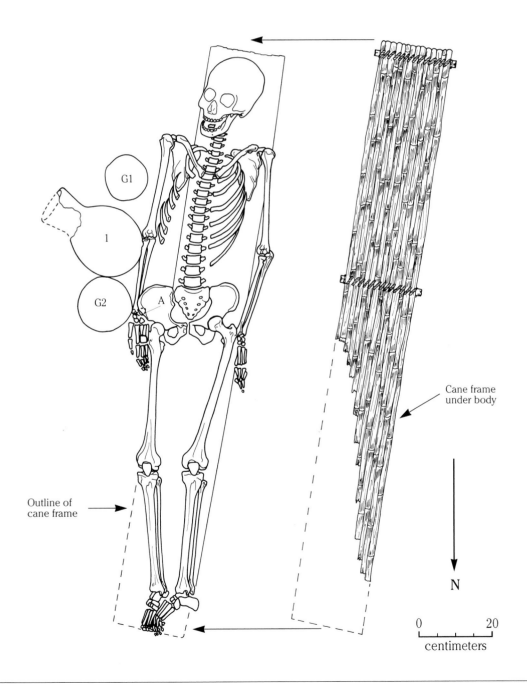

Cane frame
under body

Outline of
cane frame

N

0   20
centimeters

One copper chunk (2.1 x 1.4 x 0.5 cm, 2.6 g) (Cu3) in left hand.
One textile.
  Textile 1 near the back of left arm.
Yarn, yellowish brown wool. At least 10 strands wrapped around the upper part of the head forming a headband.
One-half shell (*Mytilus* sp.) east of right femur.

Comments:
  For further information on the copper see Lechtman, this volume. For further information on the textile see Donnan and Donnan, this volume.

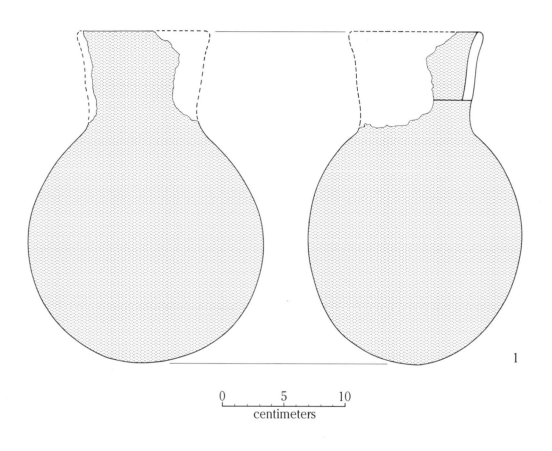

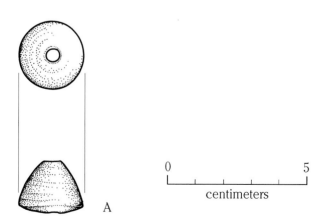

Burial 11

Original Field Number: H45CM1 B36
Sex: Female
Age: 30-40
Burial Type:

Cane Frame. Constructed of eight long canes and at least 3 cane cross braces. Six of the long pieces were half-rounds, 2 were full-rounds, and the cross braces were half-rounds.

Contents:

One ceramic vessel (1).

Two ceramic spindle whorls (8.5 g and 8.2 g) (A, B).

Three gourds (G1-G3).

G1 contained 11.5 g of seaweed (*Gigartina chamissoi*).

G2, inside G3, contained 1 g of seaweed (*Gigartina chamissoi*).

G3 under G2.

One copper fragment (C) (spatula? 4.1 x 1.4 x 0.3 cm, 7.1 g) in mouth.

One copper chunk (1 x 0.65 x 0.5 cm, 3.1 g) in right hand wrapped with unspun cotton.

One copper chunk (2.2 x 1.6 x 1.1 cm, 7.2 g) in left hand.

Three textiles.

Textile 1, an outer shroud, covered the head and torso to the elbow.

Textile 2 under textile 1 next to the head.

Textile 3 in the pelvic area.

Unspun cotton over the eyes under the head cloth.

Yarn, yellowish brown wool, S-Z2. At least 20 strands wrapped around fingers of right hand.

Yarn, yellowish brown wool, S-Z2. At least 20 strands

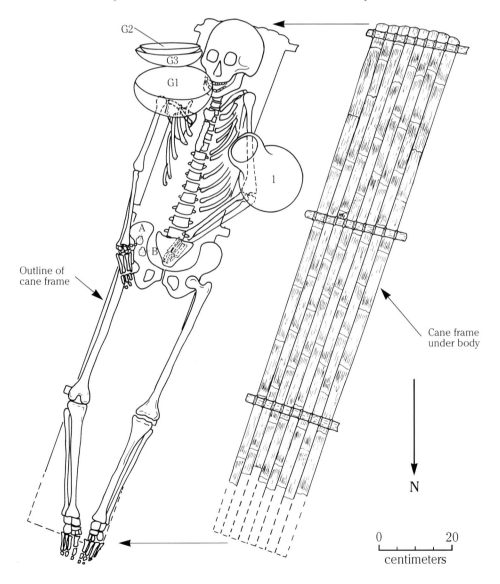

G2
G3
G1
1
A
B
Outline of cane frame
Cane frame under body
N
0   20
centimeters

wrapped around the head on top of the head cloth.

Yarn, wool wrapped around fingers of left hand.

Spindle fragments associated with spindle whorl A.

Comments:

The left hand and lower arm were under the body, below the cane frame. The body and cane frame were wrapped with a textile. There was a dense accumulation of insect pupae south of the head. A layer (3 cm thick) of dung and organic material over upper torso. For further information on the textiles see Donnan and Donnan, this volume.

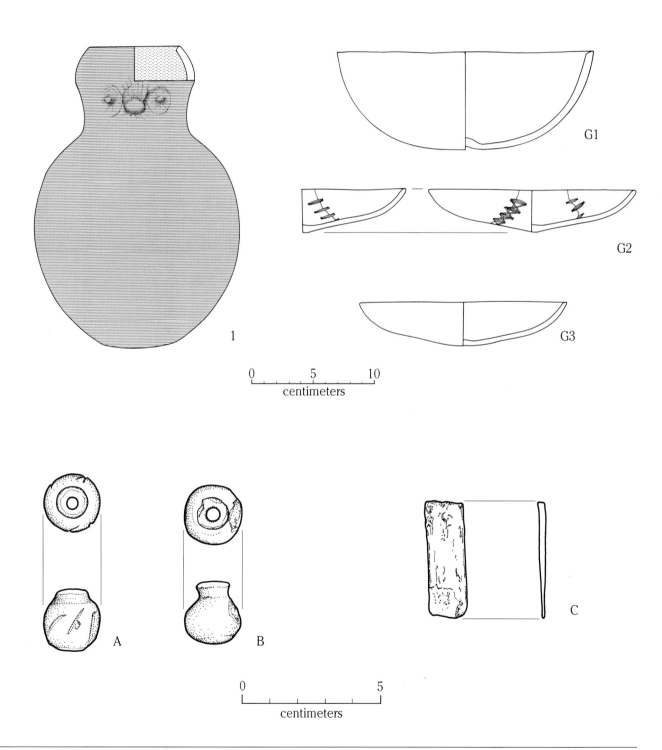

Burial 12

Original Field Number: H45CM1 B37
Sex: Male
Age: 25-35
Burial Type:

Cane Frame. Faint traces of cane beneath the body and parallel to it. One cross brace was visible near north end of frame. No evidence of cane on sides, ends, or top of body.

Contents:

Eight gourds (G1-G8).

G1, bowl (15 cm diameter x 2.5 cm high), positioned upright and tilted northwest. It contained 5.6 g of seaweed (*Gigartina chamissoi*).

G2, bowl (16 cm diameter x 3 cm high), positioned upright and tilted north. It contained 14.4 g seaweed (*Gigartina chamissoi*) and 7 corncobs (*Zea mays*).

G3, bowl (12 cm diameter).

G4, bowl (?), positioned upright and tilted northwest, inside G5. It was badly decomposed.

G5, positioned upright and tilted northwest, under G4. It contained 15.5 g of seaweed (*Gigartina chamissoi*).

G6, bowl (?) (13 cm diameter), positioned upright and tilted west.

G7, bowl (11 cm diameter x 7 cm high), positioned upright under G1, G2, and G6. It contained 24.3 g of seaweed (*Gigartina chamissoi*) and 3 corncobs (*Zea mays*).

G8, fragments inside G5.

One copper chunk (2.0 x 1.3 x 0.3 cm, 1.6 g) in mouth.

Three textiles.

Textile 1 on the face.

Textile 2, a shroud, in the area of the left shin and feet.

Textile 3 in the area of the left shin and feet.

Yarn, brown wool, at least 10 strands on the face.

Comments:

This individual had a benign tumor on the left thumb. See Verano, this volume, for skeletal analysis. For further information on the textiles see Donnan and Donnan, this volume.

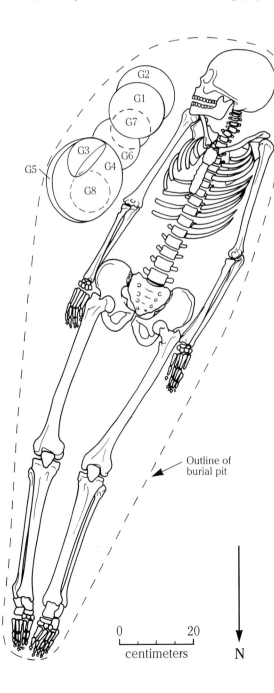

Outline of burial pit

0 — 20
centimeters

N

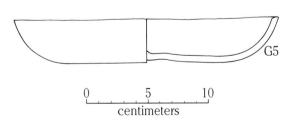

G5

0 — 5 — 10
centimeters

Burial 13

Original Field Number: H45CM1 B38
Sex: Female
Age: 50+
Burial Type:
   Indeterminate.
Contents:
   Three ceramic vessels (1-3).
   One copper chunk (2.2 x 1.6 x 0.8 cm, 8.9 g) in
      mouth.
   One copper chunk (2.4 x 1.3 x 0.8 cm, 5.8 g)
      between knees.
   Two stone spindle whorls (10.1 g and 6.7 g) (A,B) by
      the right elbow under the llama bones.
   Llama bones stacked along the east side of the
      upper torso.

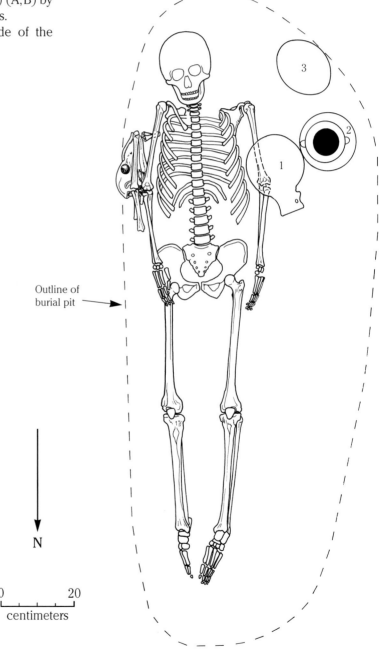

Outline of
burial pit

N

0   20
centimeters

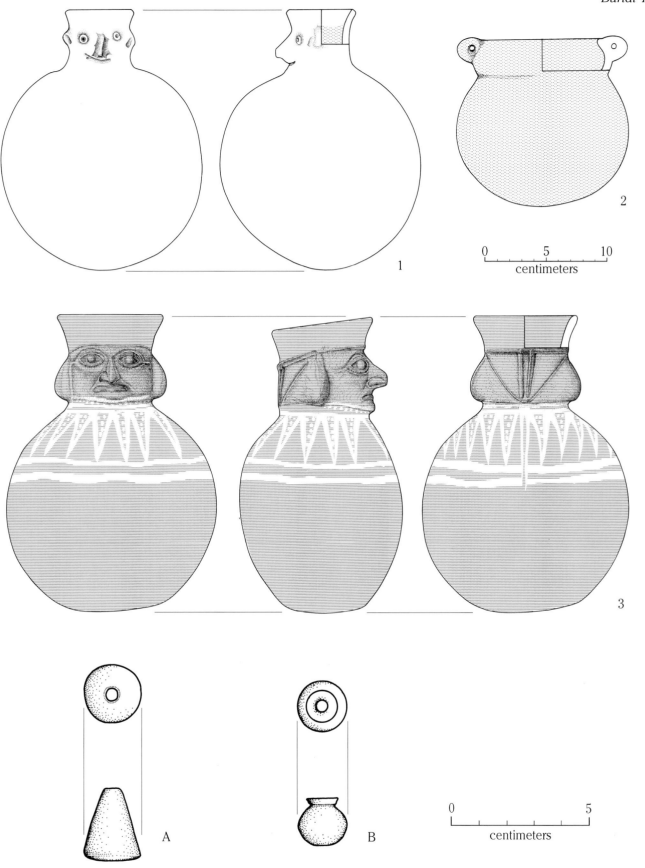

Burial 14

Original Field Number: H45CM1 B43
Sex: Male
Age: 20-25
Burial Type:
    Cane Coffin.
Contents:
    Three ceramic vessels (1-3).
        Ceramic 2 contained insect pupae.
    Three gourds (G1-G3).
        G1, bowl (10.5 cm diameter x 6 cm high), positioned upright.
        G2 contained trace of badly decomposed gourd and leaf fragments.
        G3, bowl (14 cm diameter).
    One copper chunk (4.5 x 3.5 x 1.1 cm, 13.9 g) in the mouth.
    Stone mace head (240.4 g) (A).
    Nacre (?) shell inlays, with adhesive adhering to their backs, near lower right ribs.
    Two textiles.
        Textile 1 in the area of the head.
        Textile 2 near the arms.
    Yarn, S-Z2, brown wool. At least 40 strands wrapped around right ankle.
    Yarn, S-Z2, dark brown wool near left leg.
    Yarn, S-Z2, clump of yellowish brown wool around arm bones.
Comments:
    Because of extensive decomposition, it is unclear which objects were placed inside or outside the coffin. The individual showed multiple bone fractures that appear to have occurred at or around the time of death. Most apparent was the broken right femur. Additional fractures include various ribs and vertebrae, the right humerus and scapula, and the left tibia and fibula. The pattern of fractures suggests that this individual may have fallen from a significant height. None of the fractures shows evidence of healing. See Verano, this volume, for skeletal analysis. For further information on the textiles see Donnan and Donnan, this volume.

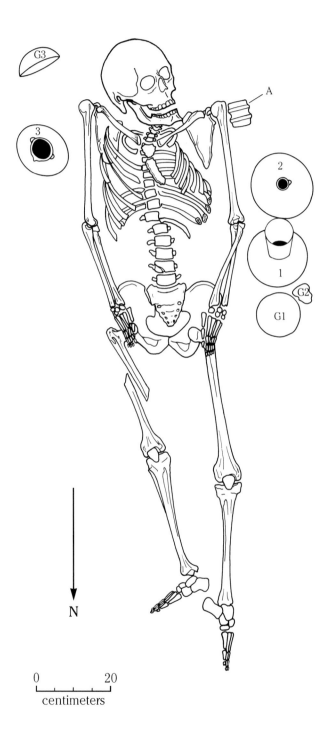

N

0   20
centimeters

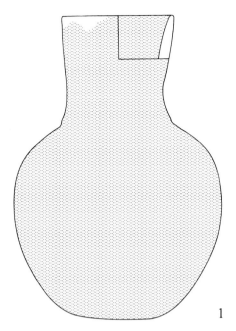

1

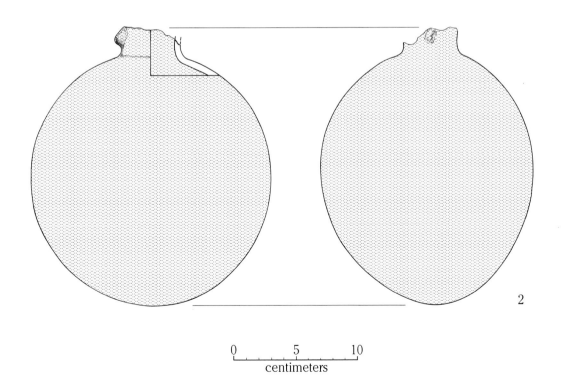

2

0   5   10
centimeters

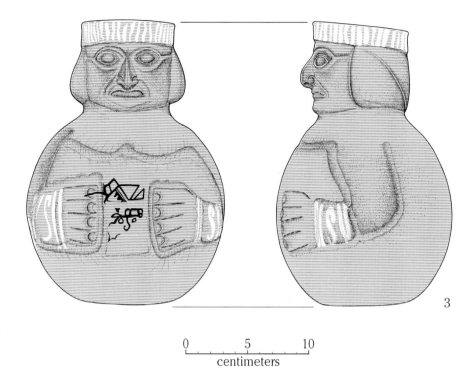

0   5   10

centimeters

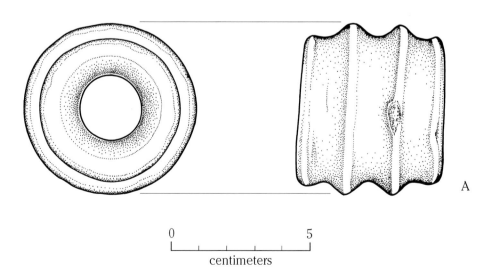

0   5

centimeters

Burial 15

Original Field Number: H45CM1 B16
Sex: ?
Age: Approximately 6 months
Burial Type:
    Splint Reinforced.
Contents:
    Two gourds (G1-G2).
        G1, bowl (10 cm diameter x 4 cm high), positioned upright, contained legumes (?).
        G2, positioned upright, contained two textiles.
    Copper object (1.9 x 1.5 x 0.7 cm, 4.2 g) in mouth.

Five textiles.
    Textile 1, an inner shroud wrapped around body with at least two layers under body.
    Textile 2, an outer shroud wrapped around body.
    Textile 3 between the inner and outer shrouds.
    Textile 4 associated with G2.
    Textile 5 associated with G2.
Comments:
    It was not possible to determine whether the gourds were inside or outside the shrouds. For further information on the textiles see Donnan and Donnan, this volume.

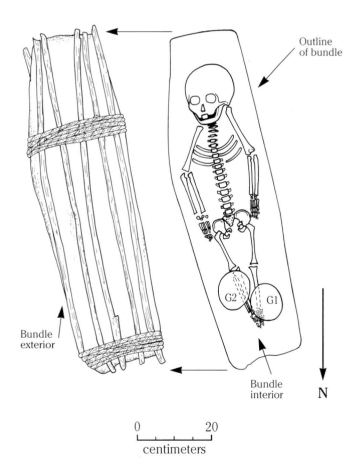

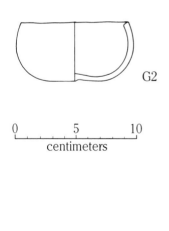

Burial 16

Original Field Number: H45CM1 B14
Sex: ?
Age: 4-5
Burial Type:
    Splint Reinforced.
Contents:
    One copper chunk (1.7 x 1.4 x 0.6 cm, 3.79 g) in right hand.
    One copper chunk (1.8 x 1.6 x 1.1 cm, 1.4 g) in left hand.
    Four textiles.
        Textile 1, an outer shroud. The body was placed diagonally on the shroud, but the shroud was not sewn closed. The corner on the left side of the body was drawn through a hole in the corner that was drawn over from the body on the right side.
        Textile 2, an inner shroud. The body was placed on it diagonally and then it was wrapped around the torso, but not the arms.

Textile 3, cordage, used to tie the splints onto the burial bundle.
Textile 4, a head cloth (?), wrapped over the head (next to the hair) and over the face, prior to the torso being wrapped with Textile 2.
    Abundant unspun cotton between the inner and outer shrouds beneath the entire body and along both sides. Only a few traces of unspun cotton on top of the body.
Comments:
    The body was positioned east-west, with the head to the east, instead of the more usual north-south position, with the head to the south. There were insect pupae around the area of the feet. For further information on the textiles see Donnan and Donnan, this volume.

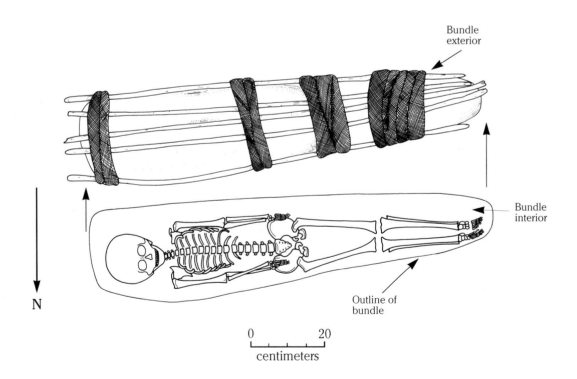

Bundle exterior

Bundle interior

Outline of bundle

N

0   20
centimeters

Burial 17

Original Field Number: H45CM1 B15

Sex: ?

Age: Approximately 2

Burial Type:

Cane Frame and Cane Tube. A thick layer of unspun cotton was put on top of the cane frame, and the body was placed on top of the unspun cotton. The body and cane frame were placed on top of the shroud, parallel to its side selvages. The shroud then was folded up over the feet and lower legs, gathered along the top of the body, sewn closed, and subsequently wrapped in a cane tube.

Contents:

One ceramic vessel (1).

Ceramic 1 was fire blackened and contained organic residue.

One ceramic sherd, wrapped in unspun cotton, in the left hand.

Six gourds (G1-G6).

G1 upside down over ceramic 1.

G2, bowl (12.5 cm diameter x 3 cm high), upside down over G3.

G3, bowl (15 cm diameter x 5 cm high), positioned upright under G2. It contained several fragments of corncobs (*Zea mays*).

G4, bowl (14 cm diameter x 5 cm high), positioned upright. It contained 4 corncobs (*Zea mays*).

G5 positioned upright. It contained 10 corncobs (*Zea mays*).

G6 formed the foot end of the coffin inside the cane wrapping.

Two copper objects (2.8 x 2.5 x 1.1 cm and 2.5 x 1.7 x 1.2 cm, 16.6 g total) in mouth.

Four textiles.

Textile 1, a shroud, wrapped around the body and cane frame.

Textile 2, cordage, used to twine the tube canes together.

Textile 3, a shirt, worn by the individual.

Textile 4 wrapped around the copper, over the unspun cotton, in left hand.

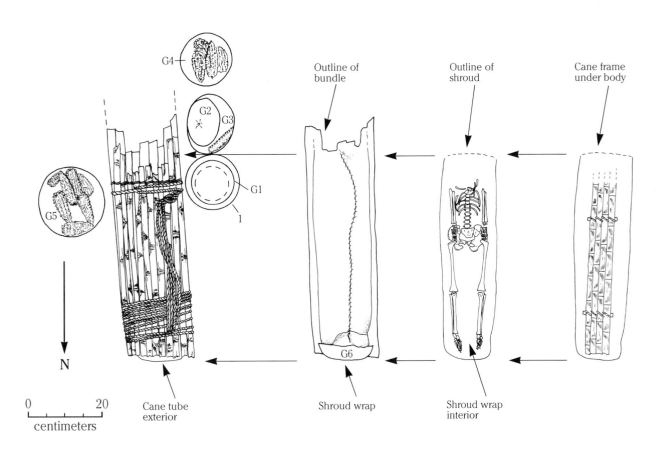

Yarn, yellowish brown wool, S-Z2, approximately 8
    strands around right foot.
Yarn, yellowish brown wool, S-Z2, several strands
    around left foot.
Yarn, yellowish brown wool, S-Z2, about 6 strands
    around left leg at midcalf.
Yarn, yellowish brown wool, S-Z2, around right hand.
Yarn, yellowish brown wool, S-Z2, around left hand.
Unspun cotton under the body on the cane frame.
Comments:
    The upper part of the burial was badly disturbed.
    For further information on the textiles see Donnan
    and Donnan, this volume.

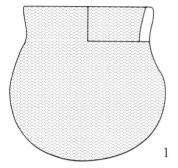

1

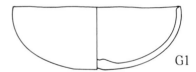

G1

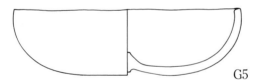

G5

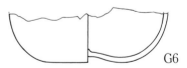

G6

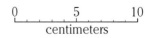

0   5   10
centimeters

Burial 18

Original Field Number: H45CM1 B20
Sex: Female
Age: 40-50
Burial Type:

Cane Coffin. There were at least 5 vertical cane braces, and at least 3 groupings of rope wrapping the coffin.

Contents:

Two ceramic vessels (1, 2).

Ceramic 1 contained seeds, insect pupae, and organic residue.

Ceramic 2, positioned upright, contained insect pupae.

One ceramic spindle whorl (A) near the right hand.

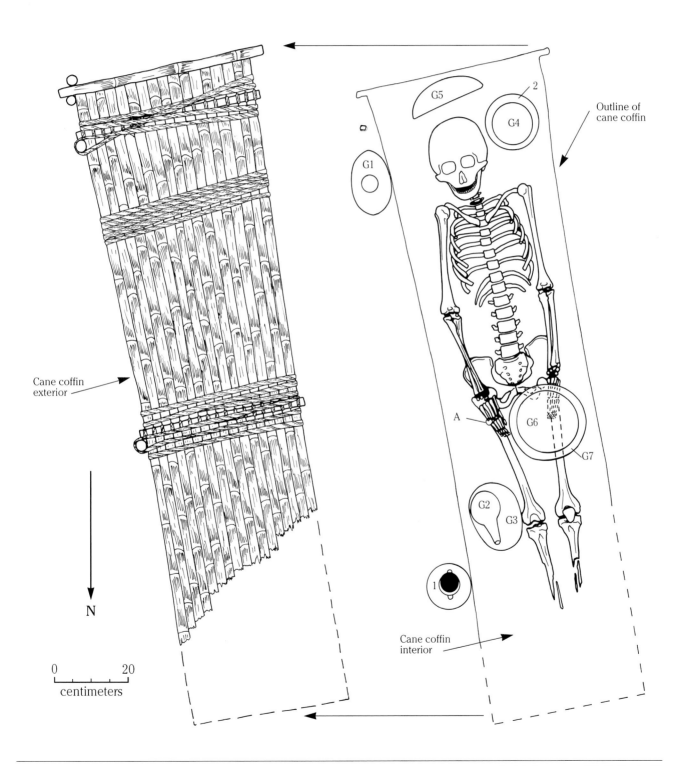

Outline of cane coffin

Cane coffin exterior

Cane coffin interior

N

0   20
centimeters

Seven gourds (G1-G7).

G1, jar, composite gourd. The jar neck was sewn onto the chamber.

G2, bottle (7 cm diameter x 15 cm high).

G3, bowl (13 cm x 19 cm diameter x 7.5 cm high), positioned upright.

G4, bowl (11.5 cm diameter x 4 cm high), upside down, over Ceramic 2, with Textile 2 attached.

G5, bowl (22 cm diameter x 6 cm high).

G6, bowl (16 cm diameter), upside down in G7.

G7, bowl (21 cm diameter), positioned upright.

One copper chunk (3.4 g) outside the coffin near G1.

One copper ingot fragment (2.4 x 2.3 x 0.9 cm, 19.2 g) in mouth.

Two textiles.

Textile 1, a shroud, covering at least the head and torso.

Textile 2 attached to G4.

Yarn, wool, around the right hand.

Yarn, brown wool, S-Z2. At least 15 strands around the left hand.

Comments:

The north end of the burial was disturbed prior to excavation. Ceramic 1, G1, and a chunk of copper were found outside the coffin. All other associated objects were found inside the coffin. For further information on the textiles see Donnan and Donnan, this volume.

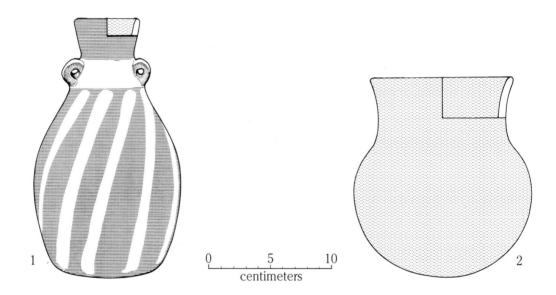

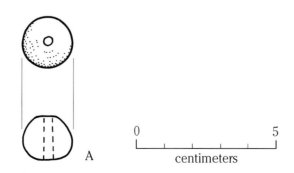

Burial 19

Original Field Number: H45CM1 B45
Sex: Female
Age: 50+
Burial Type:
   Indeterminate.
Contents:
   One ceramic vessel (1).
   Five gourds (G1-G5).
      G1, bowl (13 cm diameter x 5 cm high).
      G2, bowl (13 cm diameter x 5 cm high).
      G3, bowl (11 cm diameter x 6 cm high), positioned upright.
      G4, bowl (12 cm diameter x 5 cm high), positioned upright, under G5.

G5, bowl (12 cm diameter x 5 cm high), positioned upright, inside G4.
One copper chunk (3.9 x 1.5 x 1.3 cm, 6.4 g) in mouth.
One copper fragment and one thin copper sheet (0.7 g) in left hand.
One stone spindle whorl (6.89 g) (A).
Llama bones near the left arm.
Comments:
   Most bones of the left foot were missing. It was not possible to determine whether this was because of disturbance, or if part of the foot was missing at the time of burial.

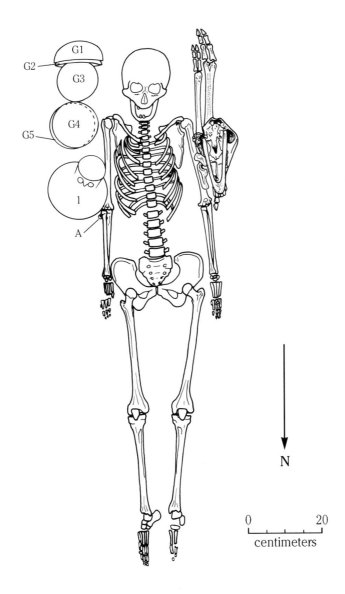

N

0   20
centimeters

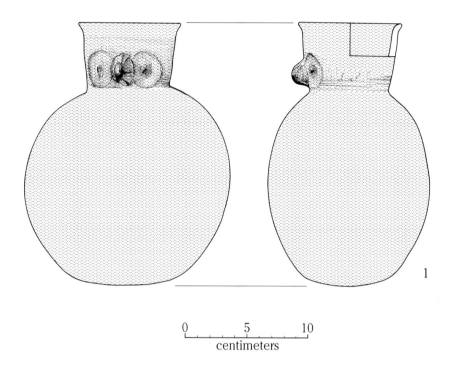

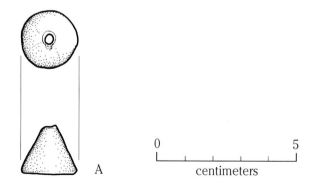

Burial 20

Original Field Number: H45CM1 B11
Sex: Male
Age: 25-35
Burial Type:
    Cane Coffin.

Contents:
    Three ceramic vessels (1-3).
        Ceramic 1 had a ball of unspun cotton in the
            spout and contained organic residue.
        Ceramic 2 contained unidentifiable seeds,
            insect pupae and organic residue.
        Ceramic 3 contained vegetal material.

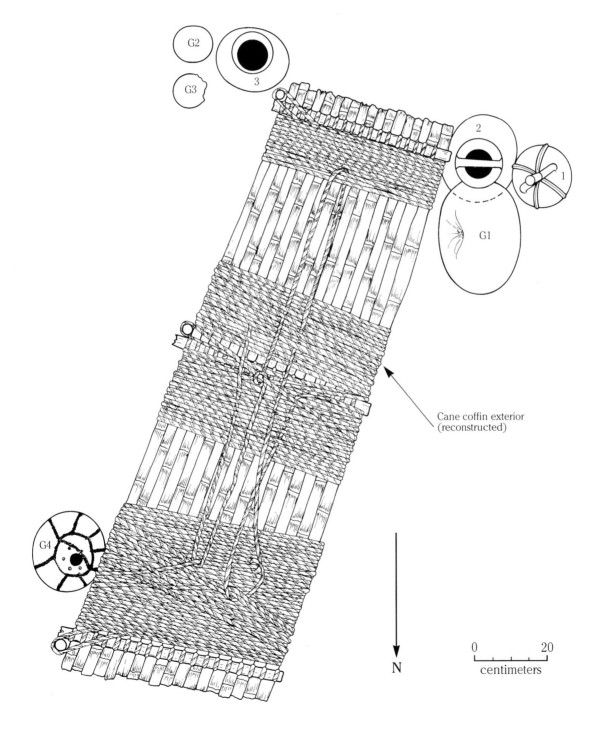

Cane coffin exterior
(reconstructed)

N

0   20
centimeters

Eight gourds (G1-G8).

G1, positioned upside down.

G2, cup (10 cm diameter x 10 cm high), positioned upright.

G3 probably a small cup similar to G2. Completely broken.

G4 with a woven grass harness and gourd disk stopper. It contained a ball of fine net (Textile 10).

G5 upside down over G6.

G6 positioned upright under G5. It contained seven corncobs with some kernels still remaining on the cobs (*Zea mays*).

G7, bowl (17 cm diameter x 4 cm high), upside down over G8.

G8 positioned upright under G7. It contained nine corncobs with some kernels still remaining on the cobs (*Zea mays*) and Textile 11.

One copper object (2.8 x 1.8 x 0.7 cm, 11.6 g), possibly in the area of left hand.

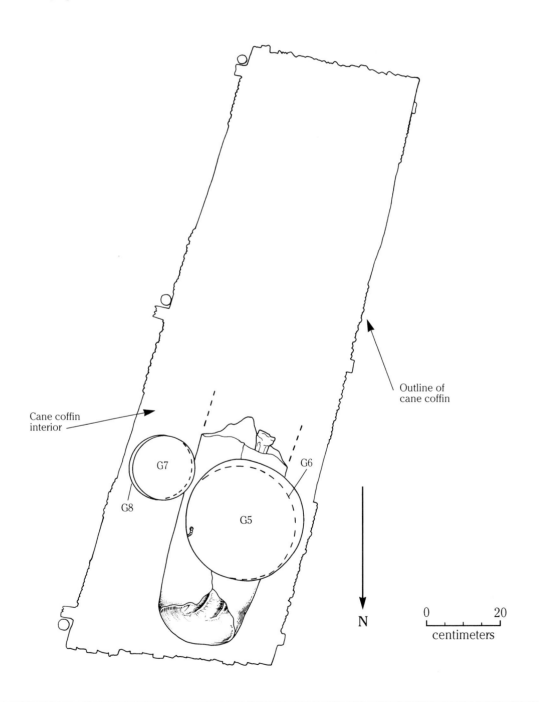

Ten textiles.

> Textile 1, an outer shroud. The body was placed parallel to the side selvages, and the shroud then was folded up over the feet and sewn closed along the central axis of the body.

> Textile 2, an inner shroud, wrapped around the body, but was not sewn closed.

> Textile 3 near feet.

> Textile 4 near feet.

> Textile 5 near feet.

> Textile 7 near midsection of body.

> Textile 8 near knees, but not in the coffin. (Donnan and Donnan, this volume, Fig. 11).

> Textile 9 near knees, but not in the coffin.

> Textile 10 in G4.

> Textile 11 inside G8.

Cotton cord, braided, 3 groups of 6 ply yarn.

Three cotton cord tassels made from heavy cotton braiding. Each braid was secured by a cotton string, which was painted black with a resin-like material after it was wound around the finished braid. Found near the waist.

Eleven small animal bones tied with string at one end, in the area of the pelvis. Three illustrated (A).

Comments:

> The burial was badly disturbed prior to excavation, particularly at its center and south end. The bones above the knees were broken and scattered. G5-G8 were inside the cane coffin. For further information on the textiles see Donnan and Donnan, this volume. For further information on the cane coffin see Donnan and Barreto, this volume. A cotton textile fragment produced a radiocarbon date of 1260 ± 80 B.P. (A.D. 750), Beta-14744.

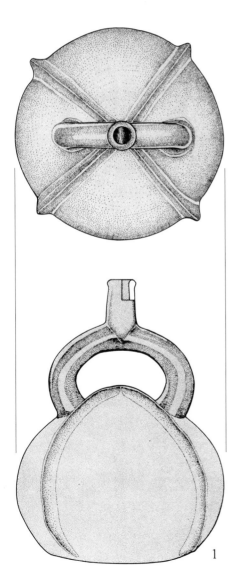

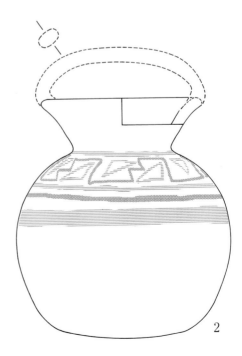

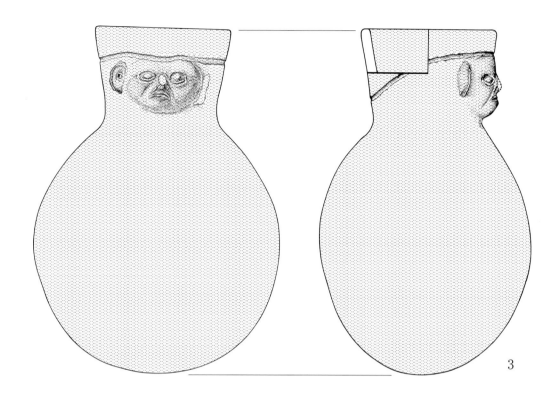

3

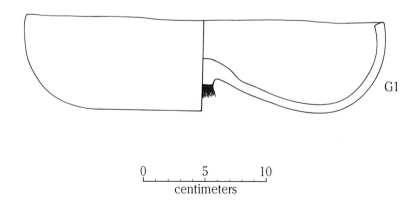

G1

0   5   10
centimeters

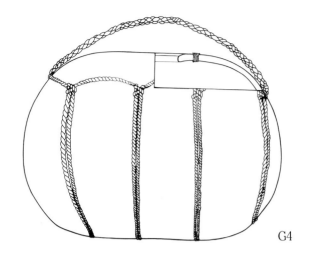

G4

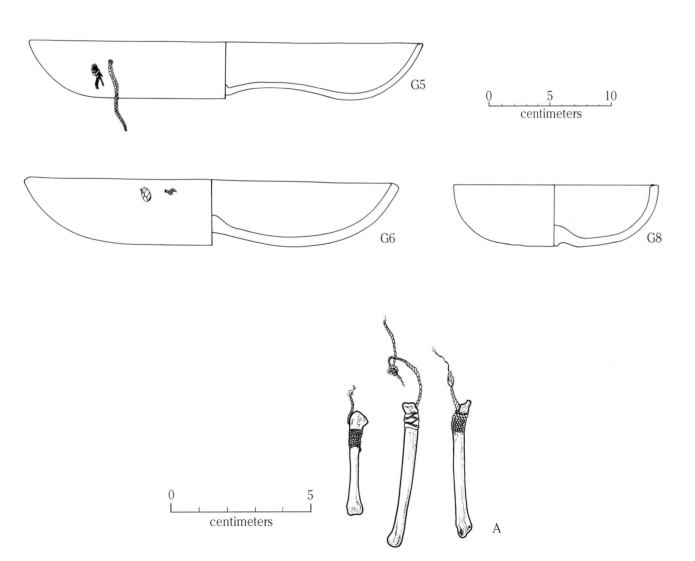

G5

G6

G8

0   5   10
centimeters

0   5
centimeters

A

Burial 21

Original Field Number: H45CM1 B3
Sex: Male
Age: 35-45
Burial Type:

    Cane Coffin. The body was placed inside the coffin on a narrow, short cane frame constructed of four split stalks of cane, twined together with net.

Contents:

    Three ceramic vessels (1-3).

        Ceramic 1 contained insect pupae.

        Ceramic 2 had a bast stopper.

        Ceramic 3 had a gourd lid (G10) upside down over the mouth of the jar that was filled with unspun cotton. A grass rope was tied around the neck of the jar.

    Sixteen gourds (G1-G15).

        G1, bowl (19.5 cm diameter x 6.5 cm high), lying on its side.

        G2 upside down over G5-G9.

        G3 had a grass rope harness and a gourd stopper.

        G4a, bowl (28 cm diameter x 5 cm high), inside G4b. Decorated with 2 double lines around the base and an amorphous figural motif.

        G4b under G4a. Mended with cotton string and decorated with plugs of unspun cotton drawn through perforations.

        G5-G9 were in a cluster beneath G2. All had unspun cotton stoppers, and all contained insect pupae. G5, tall incurving cup (5.5 cm rim diameter x 8.5 cm high), positioned on its side with mouth to west, contained 26 bottle gourd (*Lagenaria siceraria*) seeds. G6 contained 19 bottle gourd (*L. siceraria*) seeds. G9 contained 1 bottle gourd (*L. siceraria*) seed.

        G10, bowl (15 cm diameter), upside down over Ceramic 3.

        G11 had an unspun cotton stopper and contained insect pupae.

        G12, bowl (27 cm diameter x 7 cm high), warped and lying on its side.

        G13, bowl (22 cm diameter x 6 cm high), upside down over G14.

        G14 contained 3 large fish vertebrae, a number of animal teeth (dog?), one piece of worked bone (A), a spiral shell (*Turritellidae*) with the tip missing, an agate chip, a worn halved univalve, a shell (nacre?) fragment, a bone spatula (B), a gourd disk, tiny stone chips (an agate and several red/purple chips), a piece of wood charcoal, a chunk of copper (3.0g) (C), and 5 clam shells. One shell

contained an agate chip and another contained an agate chip and a piece of copper (12.5 cm x 1 cm). G14 also contained more

than 97 bottle gourd (*Lagenaria siceraria*) seeds, four beans (*Phaseolus vulgaris*), insect pupae, yarn fragments, and badly disintegrated textiles (Textiles 1b, 1c).

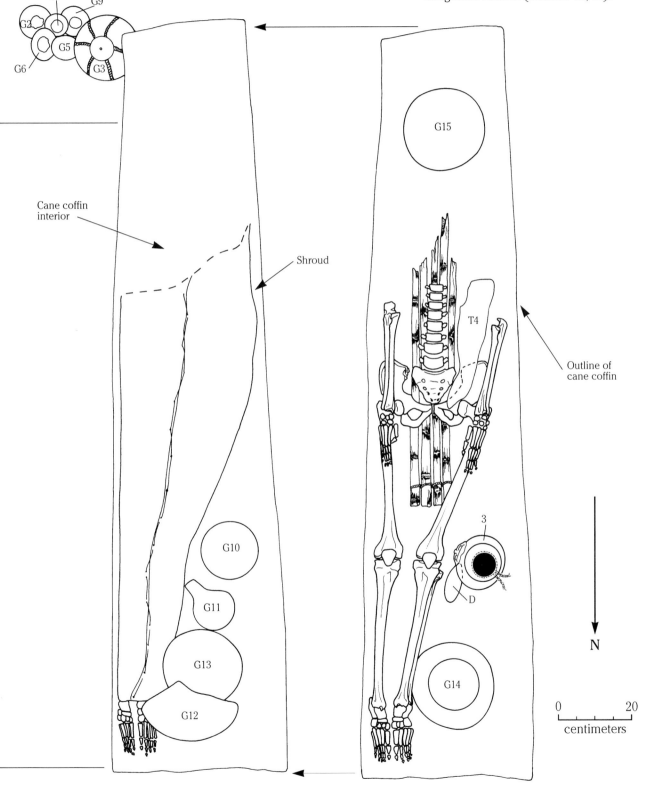

G15, bowl (22 cm diameter x 5 cm high), positioned upright.

One spoon made of *Tutuma* (D).

One copper chunk (ingot fragment? 31.3g) (E) in the area where the head would have been if the body had been complete.

One copper chunk in G14 (C).

Eight textiles.

Textile 1b inside G14.

Textile 1c inside G14.

Textile 2, an outer shroud, wrapped around the body and the cane frame. It extended only to the ankles, leaving the feet exposed.

Textile 3, an inner shroud, wrapped around the body, but not sewn closed.

Textile 4 wadded up and placed on top of the pelvis near the left side.

Textile 5, a loincloth, appears to have been brought up between the legs with the ties wrapped around the waist from front to back and back to front, and subsequently tied.

Textile 6, cordage, used to twine the cane frame together.

Textile 7 in the area where the head would have been if the body had been complete.

Fine grass rope near the south end of the coffin, with one end inside the coffin.

Yarn, two strands of yellowish brown and one strand of brown, Z-2S, was intermingled with a net fragment, and wrapped around the contents of G14.

Yarn, yellowish brown wool, S-Z2, around the wrist and palm of the right hand.

Yarn, brown wool, S-Z2, around the wrist and palm of the left hand.

Yarn, yellowish brown wool, S-Z2, around the lower right leg, just above the ankle.

Yarn, yellowish brown wool, S-Z2, around the lower left leg just above the ankle.

Cord, tan cotton, on top of the coffin.

Unspun cotton above and below the cane frame.

Two bone objects (A, B) in G14.

Fish vertebrae inside G14.

Comments:

The southern portion of the burial was badly disturbed and the upper part was destroyed. Gourds G4a and G4b were on top of the casket near the center of the south end. Their precise position is indeterminate. For further information on the textiles see Donnan and Donnan, this volume.

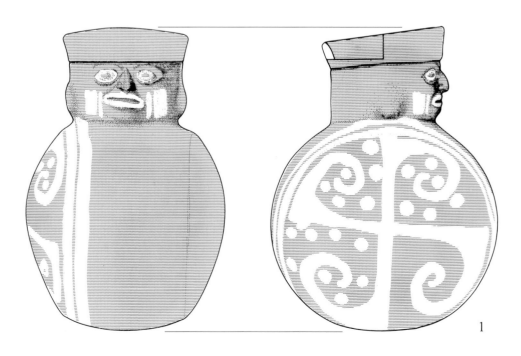

1

0   5   10

centimeters

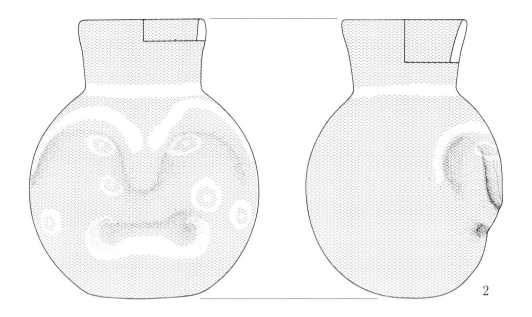

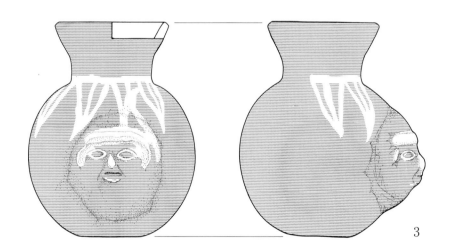

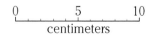

0   5   10
centimeters

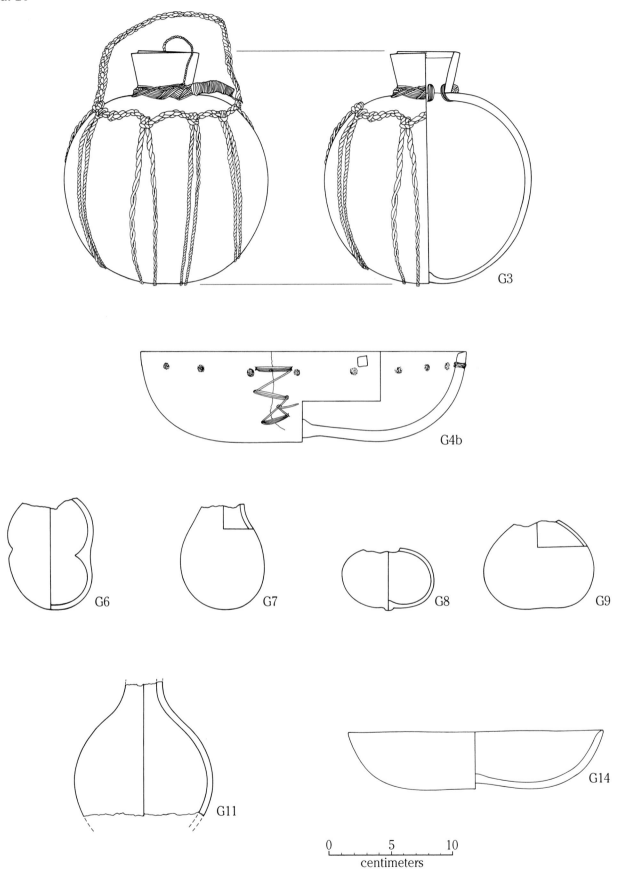

G3

G4b

G6 G7 G8 G9

G11 G14

0 5 10
centimeters

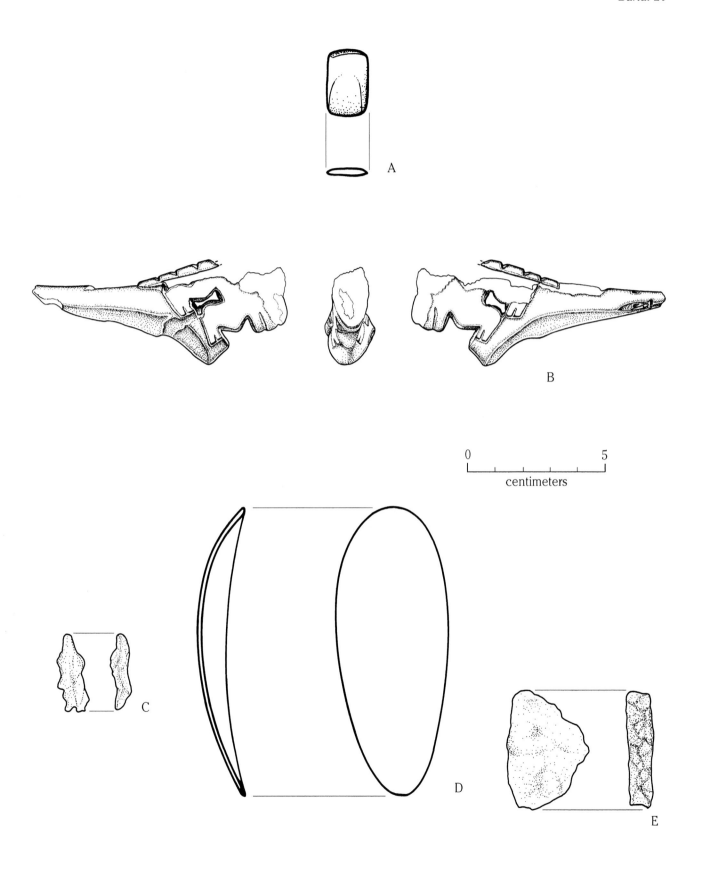

Burial 22

Original Field Number: H45CM1 B4
Sex: Female
Age: 50+
Burial Type:

Indeterminate. There were traces of cane around the body and parallel to it. There was no clear evidence that the canes were tied together.

Contents:

One gourd (G1).

G1, plate (25 cm diameter x 2.5 cm high), upside down over the top of skull.

One copper chunk (10.9 g) in mouth.

Two textiles.

Textile 1 around the head.

Textile 2, a shroud, extended from the shoulders to the lower part of the body.

Comments:

The north end of the burial was badly disturbed. The burial goods were inside the canes that were around the body. For further information on the textiles see Donnan and Donnan, this volume.

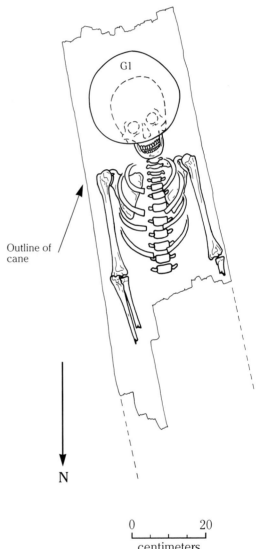

Burial 23

Original Field Number: H45CM1 B33
Sex: ?
Age: Adult
Burial Type:
  Indeterminate. Faint traces of cane under the legs.
Contents:
  Small gourd fragments in the area of the feet.
  Yarn, yellowish brown wool (S-Z2), approximately 16 strands, tied in knot around right foot.
  Yarn, yellowish brown wool (S-Z2), ten strands, around right ankle.
  Yarn, yellowish brown wool (S-Z2), approximately 12 strands, around left foot.
  Yarn, yellowish brown wool (S-Z2), approximately 12 strands, around left ankle.
Comments:
  The burial was badly disturbed prior to excavation, the upper body was completely missing.

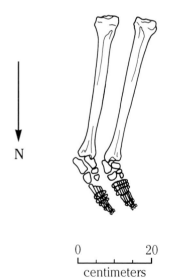

N

0   20
centimeters

Burial 24

Original Field Number: H45CM1 B49
Sex: Female
Age: 25-35
Burial Type:

Cane Frame. The head extended 4.5 cm beyond the south end of the frame. The frame was approximately 23 cm wide at the south end. There was no evidence of cross braces or textile under the frame.

Contents:

Copper fragments (0.9 g) in mouth.

One textile.

Textile 1, a shroud, wrapped the body, but not the cane frame.

Comments:

The burial was disturbed prior to excavation. This individual apparently had a congenital or developmental malformation in the left radius. See Verano, this volume, for skeletal analysis. For further information on the textiles see Donnan and Donnan, this volume.

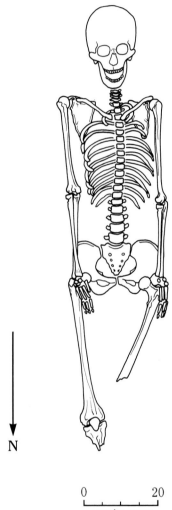

N

centimeters

Burial 25

Original Field Number: H45CM1 B7
Sex: ?
Age: Adult ?
Burial Type:

Cane Coffin. All that remained was the bottom of the coffin and portions of the ropes that formed the elaborate wrappings.

Contents:

Two gourds (G1, G2).

G1, incurving bowl (16 cm diameter x 9 cm high), positioned upright inside the coffin. Textile fragments adhering to the rim, originally sewn to the rim holes.

G2, bowl (19 cm diameter x 4.5 cm high), positioned upright.

Eight textiles.

Textile 1, a shirt, folded and placed beneath the body, on top of Textile 2.

Textile 2 folded and placed on top of the canes forming the bottom of the coffin. It did not completely cover the length of the canes. It was under Textile 1.

Textile 3 adhering to rim of G1.

Textile 4, a head cloth, inside the coffin near its south end. It may have been around the individual's head.

Textile 5 wrapped around Llama 1.

Textile 6 wrapped around exterior of coffin and tied to it with rope.

Textile 7 wrapped around Llama 2.

Textile 8, associated with Textile 7, wrapped around Llama 2.

One circular disk of *totora* (11.5 cm diameter x 1 cm thick) was near the southwest corner of the grave pit.

Four corncobs with kernels (*Zea mays*), inside the coffin near the southwest corner of the grave pit.

Two llamas, L1 and L2, wrapped in textiles (T5 and T7).

Comments:

The burial was badly disturbed prior to excavation. The skeleton was missing except for one adult finger bone. The size of the coffin suggests the individual was an adult. For further information on the textiles see Donnan and Donnan, this volume. A cotton textile fragment from this burial produced a radiocarbon date of 1480 ± 80 B.P. (A.D. 510), Beta-14743.

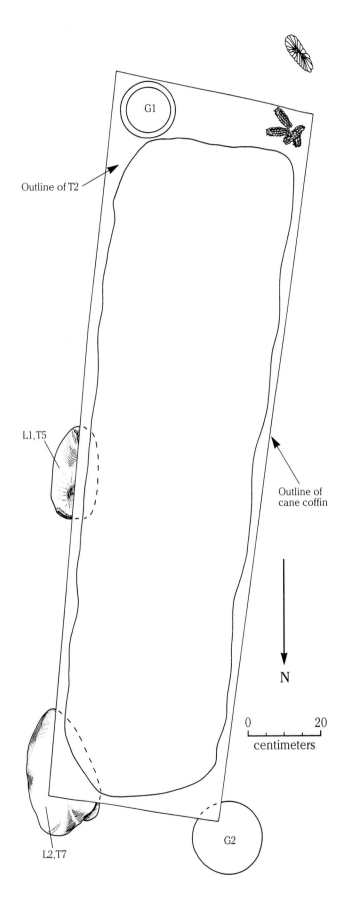

Outline of T2

L1, T5

Outline of cane coffin

N

0   20
centimeters

G1

G2

L2, T7

Burial 26

Original Field Number: H45CM1 B32
Sex: ?
Age: 1-2
Burial Type:

Splint Reinforced (?). Some canes were tied around the outside of the bundle with two bast ropes.

Contents:

Five gourds (G1-G5).

G1, whole gourd (12 cm diameter x 11 cm high).

G2 positioned upside down.

G3, bowl (15 cm diameter x 5.5 cm high), positioned upright.

G4, bowl (19 cm diameter x 4 cm high), positioned upright, tilted south. It was under G5, and contained 29 beans (*Phaseolus vulgaris*).

G5 positioned upside down inside G4. It was pierced with 2 holes threaded with string.

One textile.

Textile 1, a shroud, wrapped around the body.

Unspun cotton around the feet.

Yarn, yellowish brown wool, S-Z2, wrapped around one foot (left or right could not be determined).

String in G5.

Two bast ropes wrapped around the bundle.

Comments:

The burial was badly disturbed prior to excavation. Only foot bones and a portion of one of the leg bones remained. For further information on the textile see Donnan and Donnan, this volume.

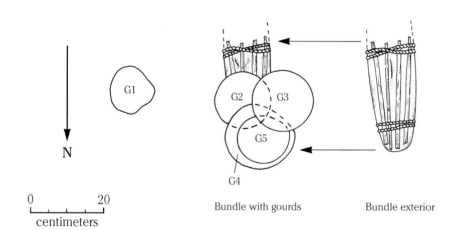

N

0 ____ 20
centimeters

Bundle with gourds   Bundle exterior

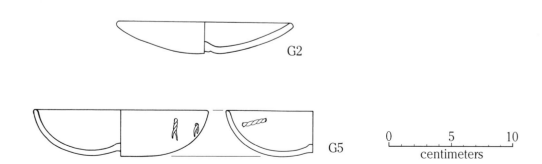

G2

G5   0 ____ 5 ____ 10
centimeters

Burial 27

Original Field Number: H45CM1 B19
Sex: ?
Age: Fetus
Burial Type:

Splint Reinforced. The body was wrapped in a textile. Wood splints were tied around the bundle with bast rope. The body was extended north-south with the head to the south, lying on its right side and facing east. No precise drawing of the body position was possible.

Contents:

One whole gourd (*Lagenaria siceraria*) with 41 seeds, positioned on its side with the stem to the south, outside of the coffin.

One copper object (1.8 x 0.8 x 0.3 cm) in the right hand with a string.

One textile.

Textile 1, a shroud, wrapped around the entire body. The ends were brought up together over the center of the torso and twisted together clockwise creating a "stem" of textile over the navel.

Yarn, yellowish brown wool (S-Z2), approximately 14 strands around the right hand.

Burial 28

Original Field Number: H45CM1 B2
Sex: Female
Age: 50+
Burial Type:

Indeterminate. There were traces of cane running the length of the body, on the top and both sides.

Contents:

Three ceramic vessels (1-3).

Ceramic 1 had cordage around the neck and contained 2 cotton (*Gossypium barbadense*) seeds.

Ceramic 3, unfired broken *ofrenda* (5 cm diameter x 5 cm high), was upside down.

One ceramic spindle whorl (6.8 g) (A).

Two gourds (G1, G2). They were probably outside the canes that surrounded the body.

G1, bowl (8.5 cm diameter x 6 cm high), positioned upright. It contained 3 bottle gourd (*Lagenaria siceraria*) seeds.

G2, bowl (10 cm diameter x 8.5 cm high), positioned upright. It contained 5 bottle gourd (*Lagenaria siceraria*) seeds.

Multiple copper chunks (ingot fragments? 8.4 g) (Cu1) in mouth.

Copper sheeting (2.5 x 2.3 x 0.6 cm, 1.9 g) folded to 5 thicknesses in the right hand.

Copper sheeting (0.5 g) (B) in the left hand.

Rectangular copper sheet (1.8 x 1.5 x 0.2 cm, 0.3 g), pierced and bent double, over right side of pelvis with fiber adhering to outer surface.

Comments:

For further information on the copper see Lechtman, this volume.

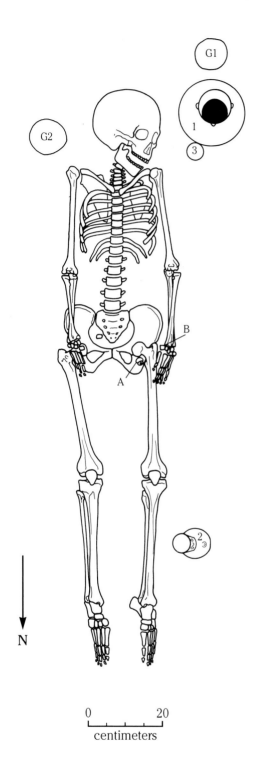

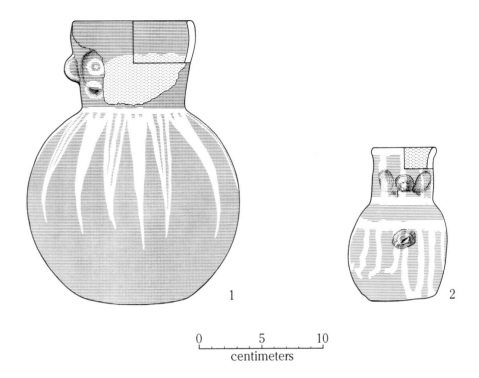

1

2

0   5   10
centimeters

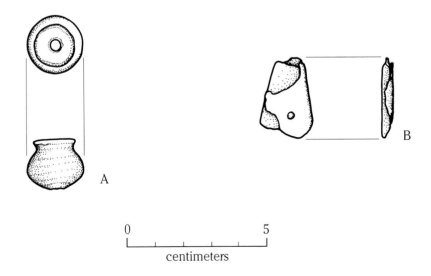

A

B

0   5
centimeters

Burial 29

Original Field Number: H45CM1 B13
Sex: Female
Age: 50+
Burial Type:
> Cane Tube (?). The canes that remained showed no evidence of having been tied together.

Contents:
> One ceramic vessel (1).
>> Ceramic 1 contained rodent (?) bones, insect pupae, and corn kernels (*Zea mays*).
>
> Six gourds (G1-G6).
>> G1 with cotton string remnants in the perforations, upside down over G2.
>> G2 positioned upright under G1. It contained corn kernels (*Zea mays*) and insect pupae.
>> G3 positioned upside down over G4.
>> G4 positioned upright under G3. It contained 14 small corncobs (*Zea mays*).
>> G5, plate (25 cm diameter x 6 cm high), positioned upside down over the top of the head.
>> G6 positioned upside down under G5.
>
> Copper (ingot fragment? 40.2 g) (A) in left hand.
> Three textiles.
>> Textile 1, an outer shroud, wrapped around the body.
>> Textile 2, a middle shroud, wrapped around the body.
>> Textile 3, an inner shroud, wrapped around the body.
>
> Yarn, S-Z2, brown wool around left wrist.

Comments:
> The burial was badly disturbed prior to excavation. The textiles appear to have been wrapped around and over the top of the head, extending north along the body to the disturbed area, presumably covering most, if not all the rest of the body. The three textiles may have been shrouds. G5 and G6 were beneath the canes that were above the body and may have been inside one or more of the three textiles. For further information on the textiles see Donnan and Donnan, this volume.

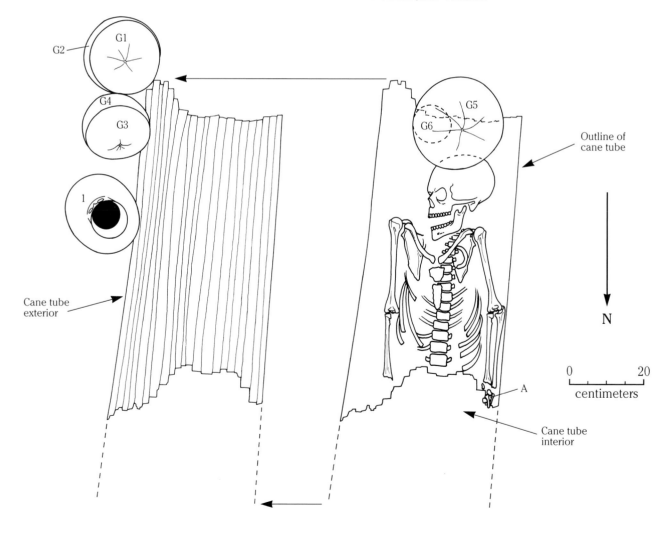

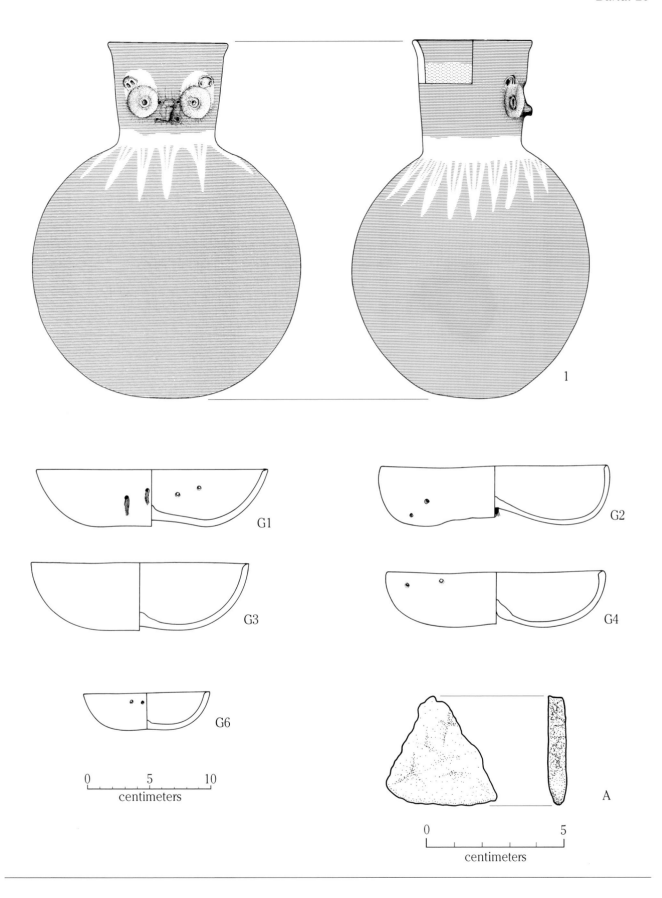

Burial 30

Original Field Number: H45CM1 B1
Sex: Female
Age: 50+
Burial Type:
  Indeterminate. There were faint impressions of cane beneath the body and parallel to it.
Contents:
  Two ceramic vessels (1, 2).
  One ceramic spindle whorl (8.9 g) (A).
  One copper chunk (2.75 x 1.5 cm, 10.3 g) in mouth.
Comments:
  The burial was badly disturbed prior to excavation. Although the ceramic vessels were next to the body, they may actually have been associated with Burial 29, which was immediately south of the disturbed area.

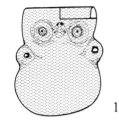

1

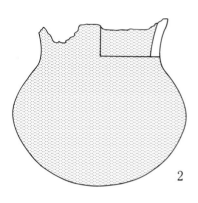

2

centimeters

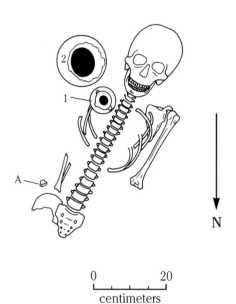

N

0   20
centimeters

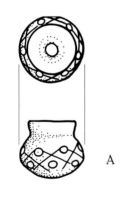

A

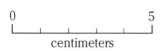

centimeters

Burial 31

Original Field Number: H45CM1 B10
Sex: Female
Age: 50+
Burial Type:

Shroud Wrap. There were a few remnants of canes above the shroud that originally may have extended the full length of the body. A few appear to have been twined together with rope, but no cross braces were visible. There were no canes beneath the body.

Contents:

One small ceramic sherd (6.3 g), wrapped in unspun cotton, in the right hand.

One gourd (G1).

G1 with cotton string in the perforations. The

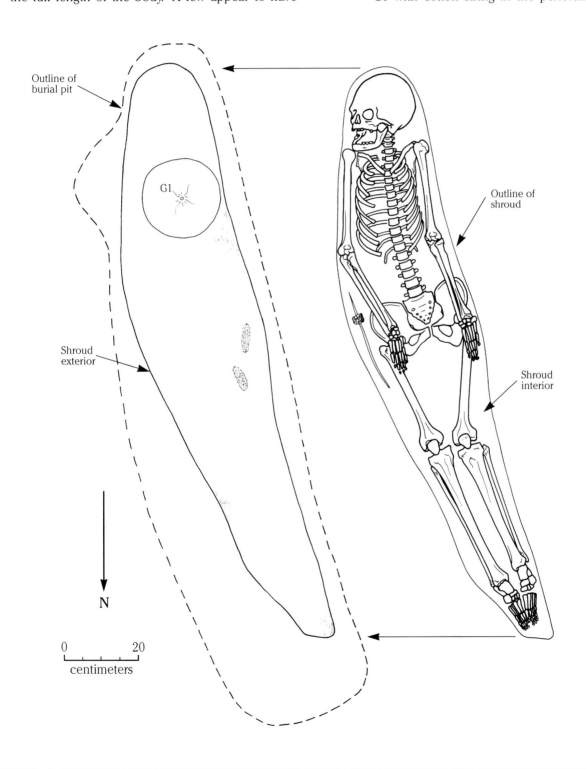

gourd was placed upside down over chest on top of outer shroud.

Four textiles.

Textile 1, an outer shroud. The body was placed diagonally on the textile, the corners were folded up over the head and feet and then over the sides. The bundle was sewn closed, starting at the top of the head and continuing down the central axis of the body, with thick tan cotton string, S-Z11. Stitches were every 10-12 cm.

Textile 2 tied the inner shroud around the body. It encircled the body slightly above the waist, and was secured in front with a simple twisting rather than with a tied knot (see illustration below).

Textile 3, an inner shroud, wrapped over the shoulders and down along lower part of the body, but did not wrap the elbows or lower arms.

Textile 4 wrapped over the face from the brow ridges to the chin. The corners then were gathered on the sides and pulled back around the head and tied together behind the right ear with a simple overhand knot.

Unspun cotton over the face.

Yarn, brown wool, S-Z2, around the palm of the right hand.

Spindle, with a corncob beneath the burial bundle.

Two corncobs (*Zea mays*) on top of the outer shroud.

Comments:

The burial pit was identifiable on all sides of the body. After wrapping and sewing the body in the outer shroud, the bundle was placed on the floor of the burial pit on top of the spindle with a corncob whorl. G1 and the two corncobs were placed on top of the burial bundle and the canes were placed on top of them. For further information on the textiles see Donnan and Donnan, this volume.

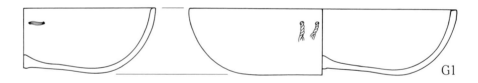

G1

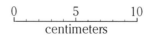

0   5   10
centimeters

T2

Burial 32

Original Field Number: H45CM1 B17
Sex: ?
Age: 0-6 months
Burial Type:

Splint Reinforced. The body was wrapped in a textile from head to foot and then the bundle was made rigid by binding narrow wood splints along its length.

Contents:

One thin copper chunk (0.5 g) in mouth.

Thin copper folded sheets (1.1 x 0.9 x 0.3 cm, 0.7 g) in right hand.

Thin copper folded sheets (1.3 x 1.2 x 0.5 cm, 0.5 g) in left hand.

Two textiles.

Textile 1, a shirt, wrapped the entire body.

Head cloth (?), tan cotton gauze wrapped around the head.

Unspun cotton over the face and perhaps around the entire head under the gauze.

Comments:

For further information on the textiles see Donnan and Donnan, this volume.

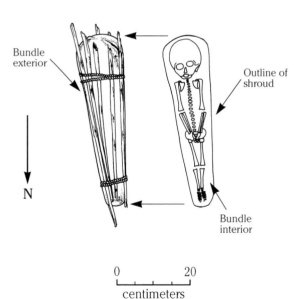

Bundle exterior

Outline of shroud

Bundle interior

N

0   20
centimeters

Burial 33

Original Field Number: H45CM1 B18
Sex: ?
Age: Approximately 18 months
Burial Type:

Splint Reinforced. The body was wrapped in a textile. Lengths of cane were tied around the bundle with cotton string.

Contents:

One ceramic vessel (1) contained 3 small corncobs (*Zea mays*).

Nine gourds (G1-G9).

G1 contained organic residue.

G2, bowl (7.5 cm diameter x 2.5 cm high), positioned upright, contained gourd (*Lagenaria siceraria*) seeds.

G3, ladle (?) (8.5 cm diameter x 12 cm long). This may have been a bowl lying on its side that was compressed so that one edge of the rim was pinched to appear like the handle of a ladle. It was badly decomposed.

G4, bowl (9 cm diameter x 4 cm high), contained insect pupae.

G5, fragmentary bowl (20 cm diameter x 6 cm high), upside down over G6.

G6, bowl (11 cm diameter x 2.5 cm high). It contained fragments of corncobs (*Zea mays*), and unidentifiable leaf fragments.

G7, bowl (13 cm diameter).

G8, positioned on side with the stem to the southeast.

G9, bottle (11 cm diameter x 8.5 cm high), spout broken and missing, contained seeds.

Narrow copper strip (3.2 x 1 x 0.6 cm, 3.8 g) in mouth, folded in half.

Copper strip (2.4 x 0.5 x 0.3 cm, 1.1 g) broken off from the strip in the mouth. It was in the left hand wrapped with yellowish brown yarn.

One textile.

Textile 1, a shroud, wrapped around the body.

Yarn, yellowish brown wool (S-Z2), approximately 20 strands wrapped around left hand.

Yarn, wool wrapped around right hand.

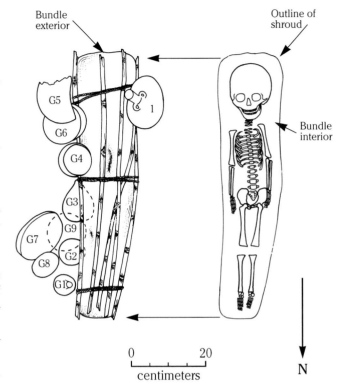

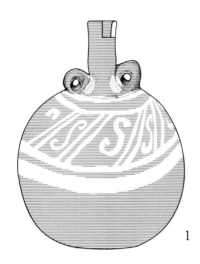

1

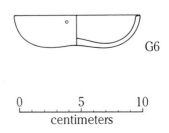

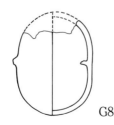

Burial 34

Original Field Number: H45CM1 B24
Sex: Female
Age: 30-40
Burial Type:
  Cane Coffin.
Contents:
  Four ceramic vessels (1-4).
    Ceramic 1 and Ceramic 2 contained insect pupae.
  Two copper objects in mouth: one chunk (ingot fragment? 2.5 cm diameter x 0.6 cm thick, 11.0 g) and one ingot (3 x 1.4 x 0.7 cm, 9.7 g).
  One copper chunk (ingot fragment? 2.6 x 2.2 x 0.6 cm, 13.2 g) (Cu 1) in right hand.
  One copper chunk (ingot fragment? 2.2 x 2.7 x 0.7 cm, 12.4 g) wrapped in unspun cotton in left hand.
  One copper spindle whorl (11.0 g) (A).

One textile.
  Textile 1 along right side of the body.
  Yarn, brown wool. Approximately 12 strands around right wrist, extending to the palm of the hand.
  Yarn, yellowish brown wool. Approximately 20 strands around the left hand.
Comments:
  The burial was disturbed prior to excavation, and the north end was missing. For further information on the textile see Donnan and Donnan, this volume. For further information on the copper see Lechtman, this volume.

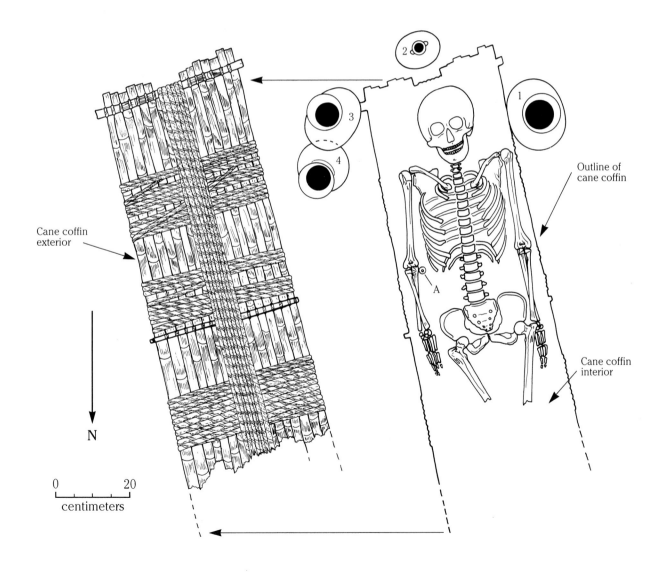

Cane coffin exterior

Outline of cane coffin

Cane coffin interior

N

0   20
centimeters

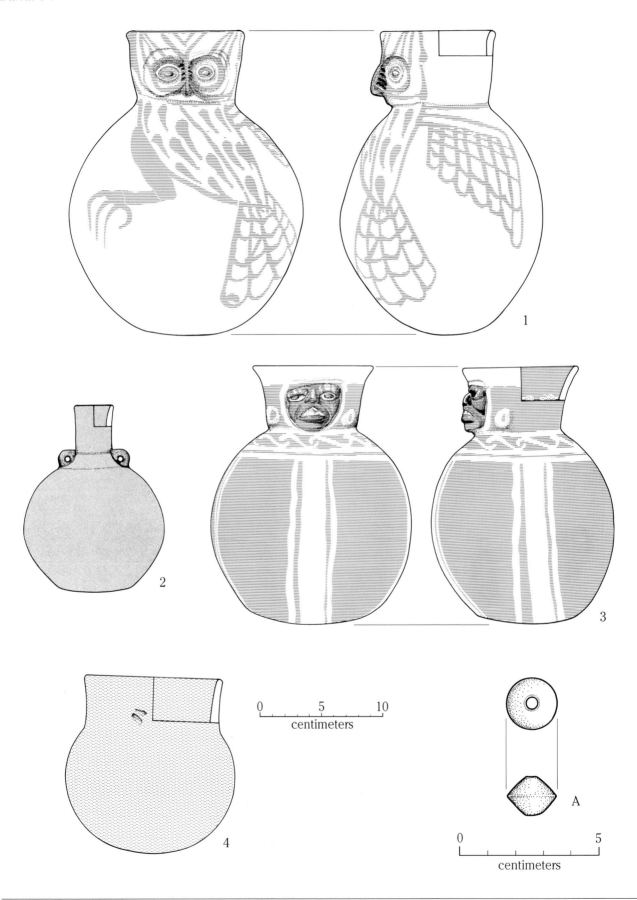

Burial 35

Original Field Number: H45CM1 B22
Sex: Male
Age: 15-17
Burial Type:

Indeterminate. Decomposed, canes were visible on both sides and below the body.

Contents:

Two ceramic vessels (1, 2).

Four gourds (G1-G4).

G1, bowl (18 cm diameter x 3.5 cm high), upside down over G2.

G2, bowl (18 cm diameter x 2.5 cm high), positioned upright under G1.

G3, bowl (19 cm diameter x 2.5 cm high), positioned upright under G2.

G4, bowl (13 cm diameter x 2.5 cm high), positioned upright.

Comments:

All associated objects were found outside the canes. The north end of the burial was disturbed prior to excavation.

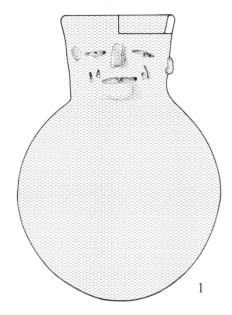

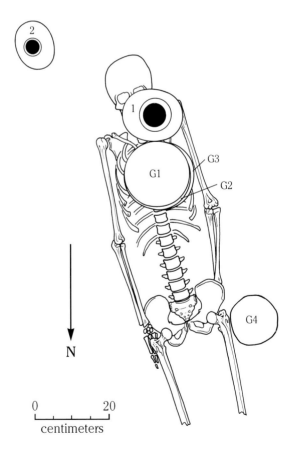

N

0   20
centimeters

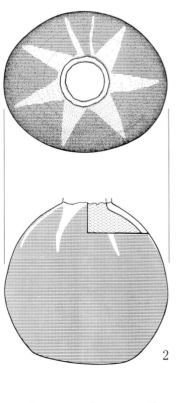

0   5   10
centimeters

Burial 36

Original Field Number: H45CM1 B21
Sex: ?
Age: Approximately 18 months
Burial Type:
  Cane Tube (?). Faint remnants of cane remained along both sides and on top of body.
Contents:
  One gourd (G1).
    G1, bowl (19 cm diameter x 5 cm high). Possibly placed over the south end of coffin.
  One copper chunk (4.2 g) in mouth.
  One textile.
    Textile 1 over face and shoulders.
Comments:
  The burial had been badly disturbed prior to excavation, with only the head and shoulders still intact. For further information on the textile see Donnan and Donnan, this volume.

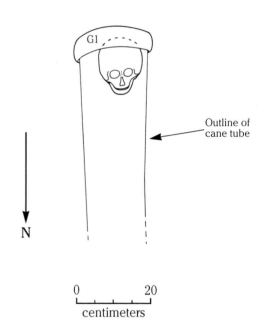

Outline of cane tube

N

0   20
centimeters

Burial 37

Original Field Number: H45CM1 B23
Sex: ?
Age: 4-5
Burial Type:

Indeterminate. Badly decomposed canes were visible around the body and parallel to it.

Contents:

Two ceramic vessels (1,2).

Ceramic 1 contained 2 gourd (*Lagenaria siceraria*) and 2 cotton (*Gossypium barbadense*) seeds, and insect pupae.

Fifteen gourds (G1-G15).

G1, bowl (12 cm diameter x 5 cm high), positioned upright.

G2, bowl, positioned upright contained insect pupae.

G3, bowl (8 cm diameter x 6 cm high),

positioned upright contained 2 gourd (*Lagenaria siceraria*) seeds.

G4, bowl (9.5 cm diameter x 7.5 cm high), positioned upright.

G5, bowl (6 cm diameter x 4.5 cm high), positioned upright.

G6, bowl (8 cm diameter x 6.5 cm high), positioned upright contained insect pupae.

G7, bowl (4 cm diameter x 2.5 cm high), positioned upright contained 3 gourd (*Lagenaria siceraria*) seeds.

G8, bowl (6 cm diameter x 4 cm high), positioned upright.

G9, bowl (?), positioned upright.

G10, bowl (5 cm diameter x 6 cm high), positioned upright.

G11, bowl (16 cm diameter x 5.5 cm high),

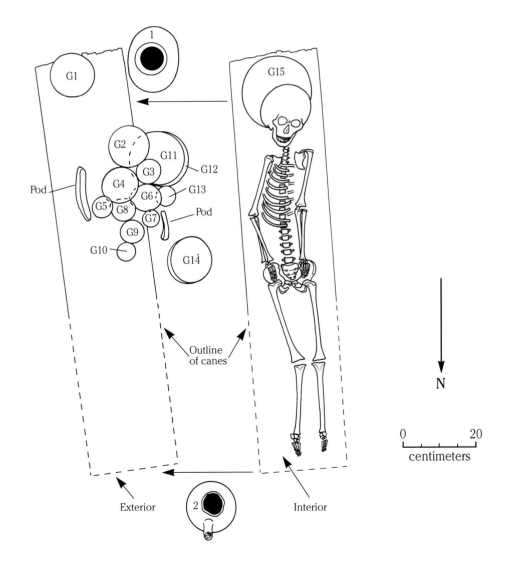

upside down over G12.

G12, bowl, positioned upright under G11.

G13, badly decomposed bowl, positioned upright.

G14, bowl.

G15, bowl (19 cm diameter x 5 cm high), positioned upright and tilted north.

Two thin folded copper sheets (3.1 x 2.4 x 1.1 cm, 1.8 g and 2.9 x 1.9 x 1.2 cm, 0.4 g) in mouth. They were wrapped in a badly decomposed cotton textile. All that remained were faint textile impressions.

One large copper sheet (5.5 x 3.9 x 1.4 cm, 9.4 g), doubled over with textile adhering to it, in right hand. Textile impressions appeared similar to this.

One sheet of copper (3.2 x 3.2 x 1.5 cm, 5.0 g) doubled over in the hand.

Pacae, (Inga Feuillei) pods along the west side and upper east side of coffin.

Comments:

All ceramics and all gourds, except G15, were outside the canes surrounding the body.

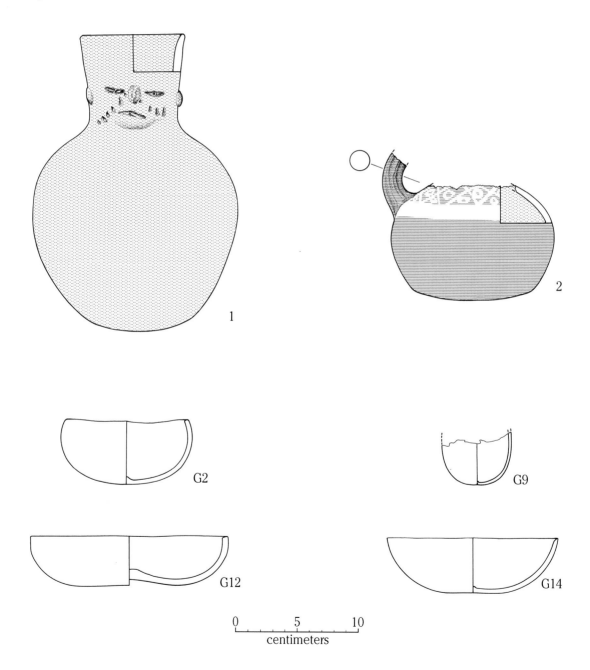

Burial 38

Original Field Number: H45CM1 B34
Sex: Female
Age: 50+

Burial Type:
    Indeterminate. Cane impressions under the body.

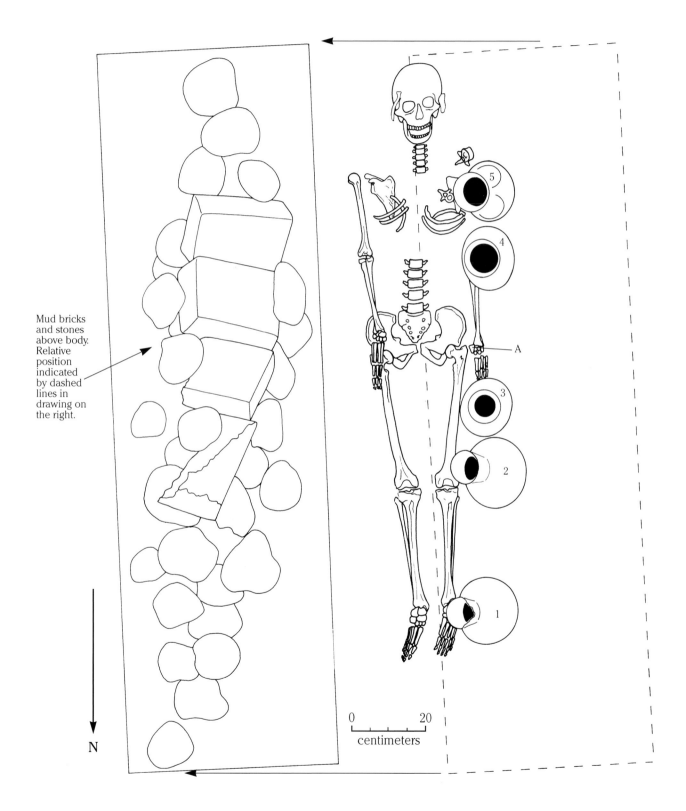

Mud bricks
and stones
above body.
Relative
position
indicated
by dashed
lines in
drawing on
the right.

N

0   20
centimeters

Contents:

Five ceramic vessels (1-5).

One copper chunk (ingot fragment? 4.1 x 2.5 x 1.2 cm, 23.0 g) in the right hand.

One copper chunk (1/8 ingot fragment 4.1 x 1.3 x 0.7 cm, 14.1 g) (Cu 2) in the left hand.

Beads in the area of the neck.

5 short tubular: 1 light pink (fragmented), 2 white, and 2 black.

Two stone spindle whorls.

One (8.4 g) (A).

One near the head, not illustrated.

Llama vertebrae near the left shoulder.

Comments:

Four mud-bricks (approximately 29 cm x 22 cm x 12 cm) and stones (10-20 cm in diameter) were irregularly positioned above of the burial. There was no evidence of mortar. The body was disturbed in the center of the chest prior to excavation. Although many of the bones in this area were displaced, nearly all were present. For further information on the copper see Lechtman, this volume.

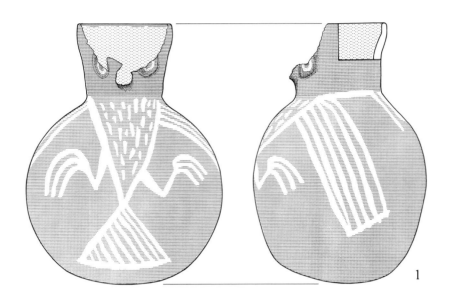

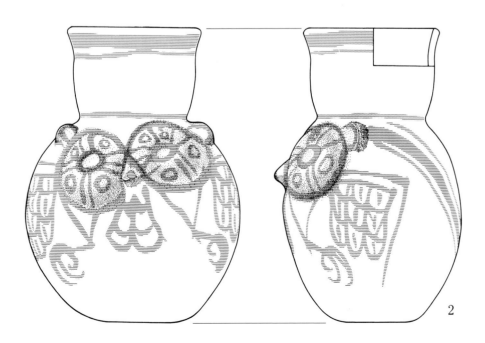

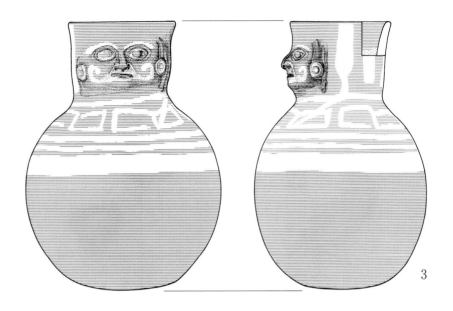

3

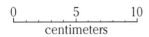

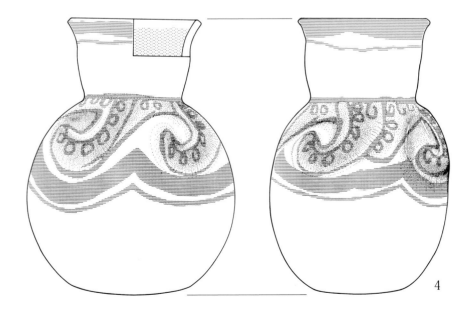

4

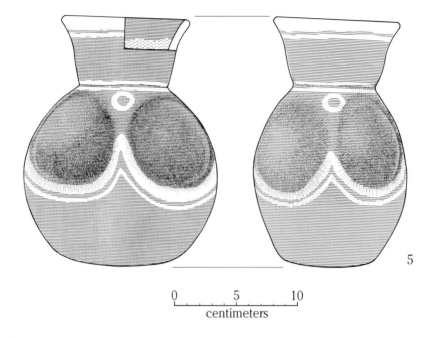

5

0   5   10
centimeters

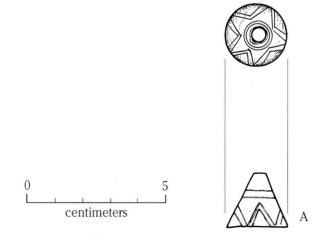

A

0   5
centimeters

Burial 39

Original Field Number: H45CM1 B5
Sex: ?
Age: 1-1.5
Burial Type:
   Indeterminate.
Contents:
   Three gourds (G1-G3).
      G1 upside down over the head.
      G2 (11 cm diameter x 7 cm high), positioned
         upright.
      G3 positioned upright.
   One copper object (3.8 g) (A) in the mouth.
Comments:
   The burial was disturbed prior to excavation. The
   dimensions of G1 and G3 could not be determined.

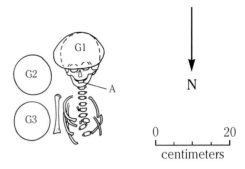

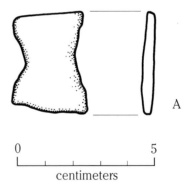

Burial 40

Original Field Number: H45CM1 B6
Sex: ?
Age: 3.5-4
Burial Type:

Splint Reinforced (?). There were very faint traces of wood that may have been splints tied around the burial bundle to make it rigid. The wood and the burial wrappings were almost completely decomposed.

Contents:

Two ceramics. One vessel (1) and one figurine (2). Ceramic 1 was fire blackened.

Six gourds (G1-G6).

G1, bowl (14 cm diameter x 2.5 cm high), upside down over G5.

G2, bowl (12 cm diameter x 4 cm high), positioned upright.

G3, lid (?) (8.5 cm diameter x 0.5 cm high).

G4, bowl with incurving rim (13.5 cm diameter x 5 cm high), upside down over Ceramic 1.

G5, plate (11 cm diameter x 2.5 cm high), upside down under G1.

G6, fragmentary plate, above the head.

Four carved red stone pendants (A-D). Two were on top of the ceramic figurine, one was on the west side, and one was on the east side.

One copper object (13.5 g) in the mouth, fiber on surface.

One copper object (11.6 g) in the right hand appears to have been wrapped with string.

One copper object (3.9 x 3.4 x 0.9 cm, 33.4 g) (Cu 2) in the left hand, textile and yarn adhering.

One shell (*Olivella*) bead (E), with the apex cut off.

One textile.

Textile 1 wrapped around the copper in the left hand.

Yarn, brown wool, S-Z2, around the left hand.

Yarn, yellowish brown wool, S-Z2, around the right hand.

Comments:

For further information on the textiles see Donnan and Donnan, this volume. For further information on the copper see Lechtman, this volume.

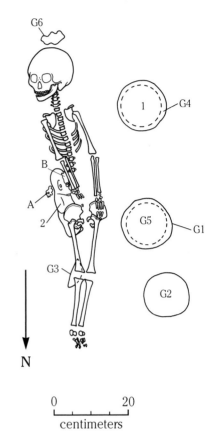

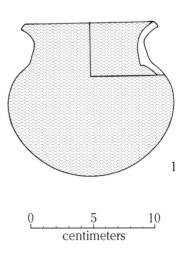

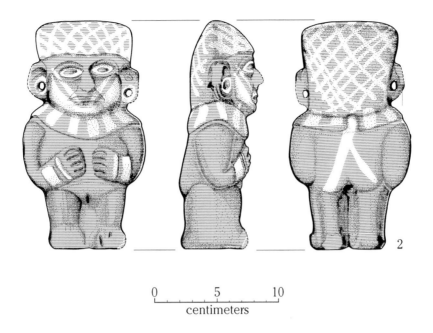

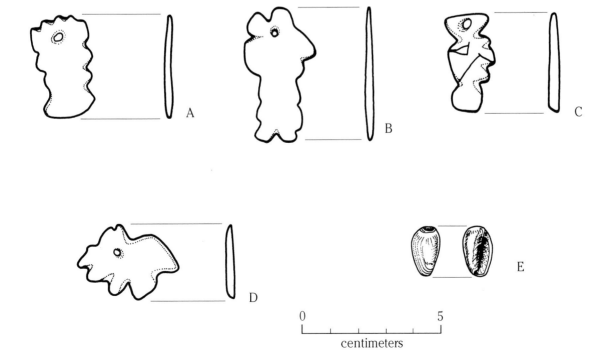

Burial 41

Original Field Number: H45CM1 B8
Sex: Male
Age: 25-30
Burial Type:
    Cane Tube.

Contents:
    Six ceramic vessels (1-6).
        Ceramics 1 and 3 contained organic residue
        and insect pupae.

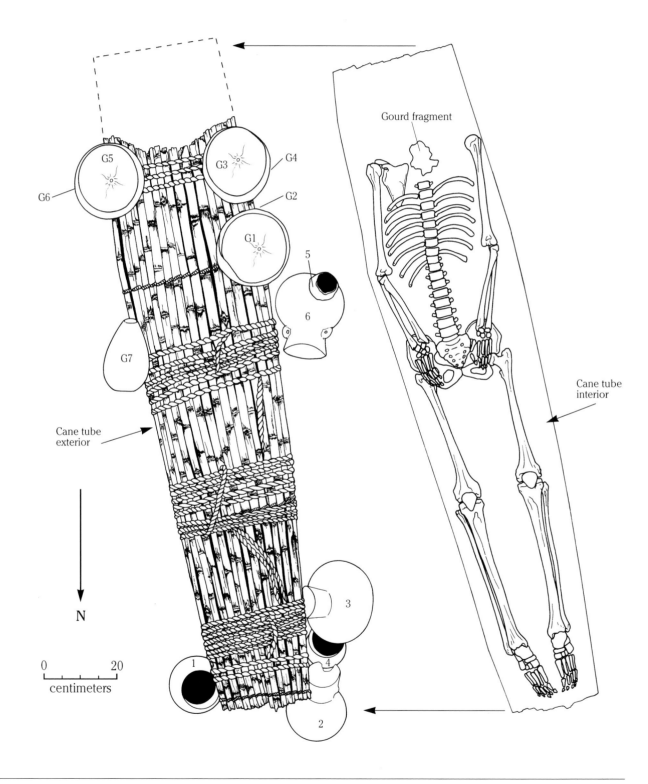

Ceramics 2 and 4 contained insect pupae.

Ceramic 6 contained insect pupae and unidentifiable seeds.

Seven gourds (G1-G7).

G1 upside down over G2.

G2 positioned upright under G1, contained
corncobs (*Zea mays*).

G3 upside down over G4.

G4 positioned upright under G3, contained

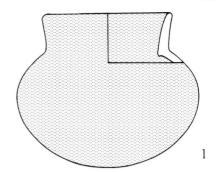

1

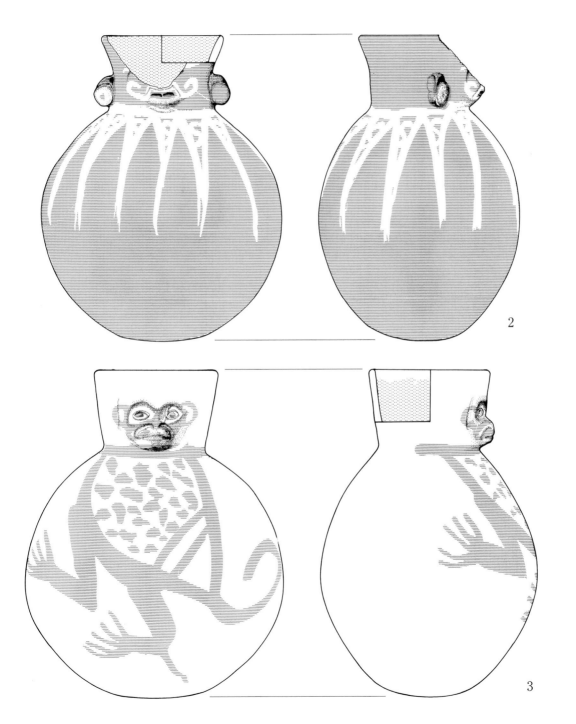

2

3

corncobs (*Zea mays*). It had 3 perforations with string laced through one of them.

G5 upside down over G6.

G6 positioned upright under G5, contained corncobs (*Zea mays*).

G7 contained seeds, insect pupae and organic residue.

Two textiles.

Textile 1, a loincloth, wrapped around the body.

Textile 2, a shroud, wrapped around the body from the top of head to at least the ankles.

Comments:

The south end of the burial was disturbed prior to excavation. The end of the coffin was missing and the skull was badly broken with some portions missing. For further information on the textiles see Donnan and Donnan, this volume.

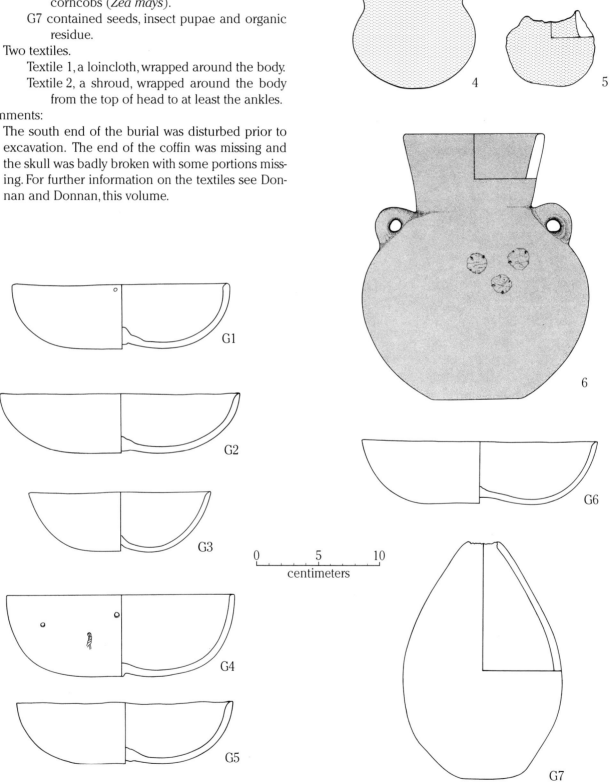

Burial 42

Original Field Number: H45CM1 B9
Sex: Female
Age: 30-40
Burial Type:

Indeterminate. There were a few lengths of cane above the body and parallel to it. They did not appear to have been tied together. Beneath the body and parallel to it were poorly preserved canes. They were tied to at least one cross brace located near the knees. There were traces of cane and groups of ropes along the west side of the body. Remnants of a mat were found over the west side of the body, outside the canes.

Contents:

Five ceramic vessels (1-5).

Ceramic 1 contained insect pupae and corn kernels (*Zea mays*).

Ceramic 4 was fire blackened and contained unidentifiable seeds.

Ceramic 5 was fire blackened and contained organic residue.

Nineteen gourds (G1-G19).

G1-G3 were stacked. G1, bowl (14 cm diameter x 2 cm high), positioned upright inside G2, contained llama teeth and skull fragments. G2 positioned upright inside G3, contained seeds (*Lagenaria siceraria* and *Phaseolus vulgaris*). G3, bowl (17.5 cm diameter x 7 cm high), positioned upright under G2.

G4, bowl (13 cm diameter x 7 cm high).

G5, bowl with incurving rim (13 cm diameter x 4 cm high), upside down.

G6, shallow plate (19.5 cm diameter), upside down over G7, G8, and G9.

G7, bowl (21.5 cm diameter x 6 cm high), upside down over G8.

G8 upside down under G7.

G9, plate (24 cm diameter x 3 cm high), positioned upright.

G10, nearly flat disk (18 cm diameter).

G11, bowl (15 cm diameter x 2.5 cm high), upside down over G12.

G12, bowl (13.5 cm diameter x 3.5 cm high), upside down under G11, over a shell ornament (C).

G13, bowl (14.5 cm diameter x 7 cm high), was so badly decomposed it was impossible to determine whether it was upright or upside down. It contained three copper objects.

G14, bowl (20 cm diameter x 9 cm high), on side and upside down, tilted northwest.

G15 under the palm of the right hand, upside down.

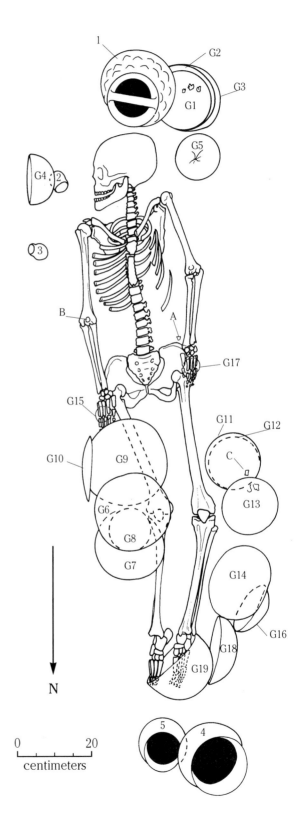

G16, bowl (14 cm diameter x 3.5 cm high), with flaring rim.

G17, bowl, badly decomposed, but almost certainly similar to G15, under the palm of the left hand.

G18, bowl (19 cm diameter x 7.5 cm high).

G19, bowl (20 cm diameter x 15 cm high), contained insect pupae.

One copper chunk (3 x 3.5 cm, 58.5 g) in mouth.

One-fourth copper ingot (3 x 3.5 cm, 35.7 g) under fingers of right hand.

One-half copper ingot (5 cm diameter, 36.2 g) under palm of the hand.

One copper fishhook (1 x 4 cm, 1.6 g) in G13.

One copper chunk (2.1 g) in G13.

One copper fragment (needle? 3 x 4.5 mm, 0.1 g) in G13.

One conical stone spindle (7.0 g) (A).

One lobed stone spindle whorl (7.6 g) (B) with a piece of the wood spindle parallel to the body.

One shell (*Spondylus*) ornament (C) inside G12, with nacre (?) circle at its center. Some adhesive adhering to the back.

Llama teeth and skull fragments in G1.

Comments:

For further information on the textiles see Donnan and Donnan, this volume.

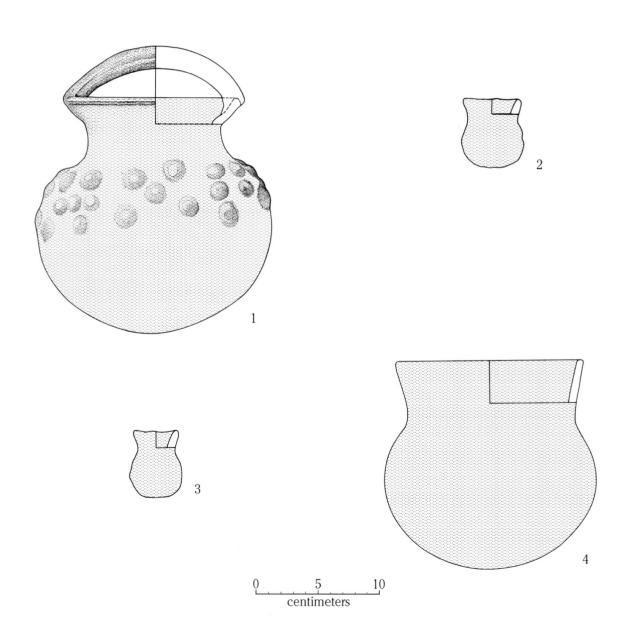

0   5   10

centimeters

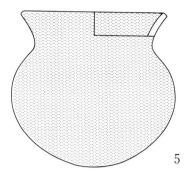

5

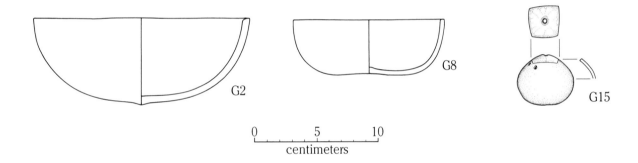

G2

G8

G15

0   5   10

centimeters

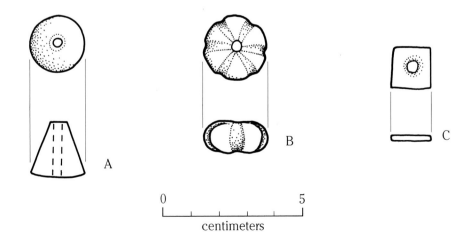

A

B

C

0   5

centimeters

Burial 43

Original Field Number: H45CM1 B12
Sex: Male
Age: 25-45
Burial Type:
Cane Frame (?). There were faint traces of cane under the body and parallel to it.
Contents:
One ceramic vessel (1).
Ceramic 1 contained one *espingo* (*Nectandra* sp.) seed.

One copper chunk (1.8 x 1.2 x 0.7 cm, 2.5 g) with textile fragment adhering in the area of the skull.
One copper object (ingot fragment? 6.0 g) in mouth.
Two textiles.
Textile 1 in the area of the ribs on west side of body.
Textile 2 in the area of the ribs on west side of body under Textile 1.
Comments:
The burial had been disturbed above the pelvis, almost certainly as the result of the excavation of the grave pit for Burial 42 which was placed on top of it. For further information on the textiles see Donnan and Donnan, this volume.

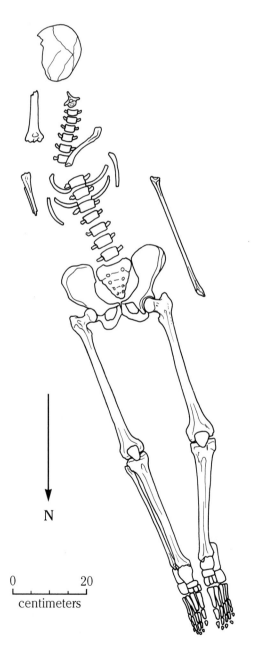

N

0   20
centimeters

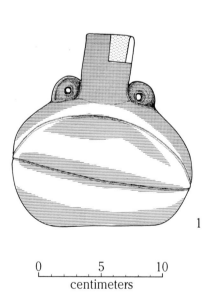

1

0   5   10
centimeters

Burial 44

Original Field Number: H45CM1 B25a
Sex: Female
Age: 25-35
Burial Type:

Cane Tube (?). Badly decomposed canes were found on both sides of the body as well as above and below it. There was no clear evidence that the canes were twined together.

Contents:

Two ceramic vessels and one ceramic sherd (1-3).

Ceramic 1 contained insect pupae and an unspun cotton stopper.

Ceramic 3 is part of an olla rim.

Nineteen gourds (G1-G19).

G1 upside down over G2. A string attaches the rim of G1 to rim of G2.

G2 positioned upright under G1, and attached to rim of G1 with a string. It contained seeds, 8 corncobs (*Zea mays*), and llama teeth.

G3 positioned upright, inside G4.

G4 positioned upright, under G3 and inside G5.

G5, badly decomposed bowl with a diameter greater than 15 cm, under G3 and G4.

G6 upside down over G7.

G7 positioned upright under G6.

G8, bowl (11 cm diameter x 7 cm high x 3 cm opening), positioned upright. It contained 31 bottle gourd (*Lagenaria siceraria*) seeds and insect pupae.

G9 upside down over G10 and G11. It evidenced mending along one side.

G10, bowl (11 cm diameter x 4 cm high), positioned upright under G9 and over G17. It contained corn cob (*Z. mays*) fragments, 1 gourd (*Lagenaria siceraria*) seed and numerous poorly preserved seeds.

G11, bowl (11 cm diameter x 7 cm high), positioned upright under G9.

G12, G13, G14, and G15 were 10 cm above the canes that were on top of the body with Ceramic 3. G12, bowl (16 cm diameter x 6 cm high), upside down over Ceramic 3. G14, a completely warped mass (9 cm diameter x 6 cm high), was possibly a container since it had an unspun cotton stopper. G15 had an unspun cotton stopper and contained 104 bottle gourd (*Lagenaria siceraria*) seeds.

G16, bowl (16 cm diameter x 3 cm high), upside down over the top of the skull. It was the only gourd inside the cane surrounding the body.

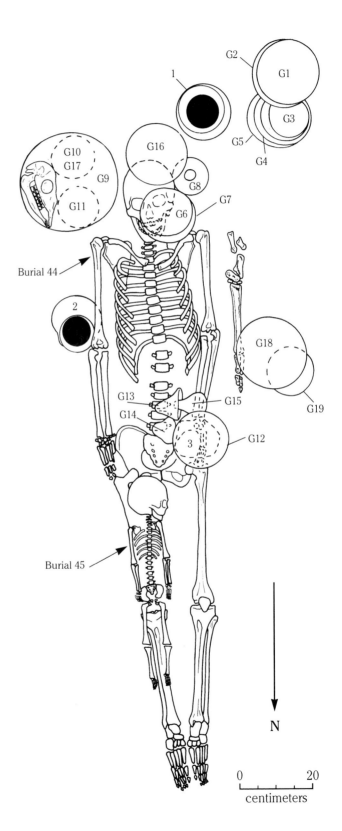

G17, badly decomposed bowl (?), was filled with numerous decomposed seeds under G10.

G18, bowl (19 cm diameter), above G19.

G19, bowl (12 cm diameter), beneath G18.

Copper (2.4 x 1.5 x 0.7 cm, 12.6 g) in mouth.

Copper chunk (1.4 x 1.4 0.9 cm, 5.4 g) in the hand.

Two textiles.

Textile 1 was placed over the unspun cotton on face.

Textile 2 was placed over the face on top of Textile 1.

Unspun brown cotton on face.

Yarn, yellowish brown wool, S-Z2. Approximately 15 strands around left wrist.

Llama bones, probably the skull with brown fur, under G9.

Llama leg bones on left side of coffin.

Matting from the left side of body.

Comments:

This is a double burial of an adult female and an infant. See Burial 45. For further information on the textiles see Donnan and Donnan, this volume.

1

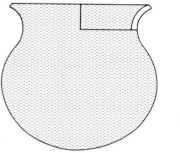

2

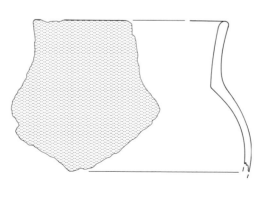

3

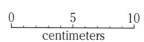

0   5   10

centimeters

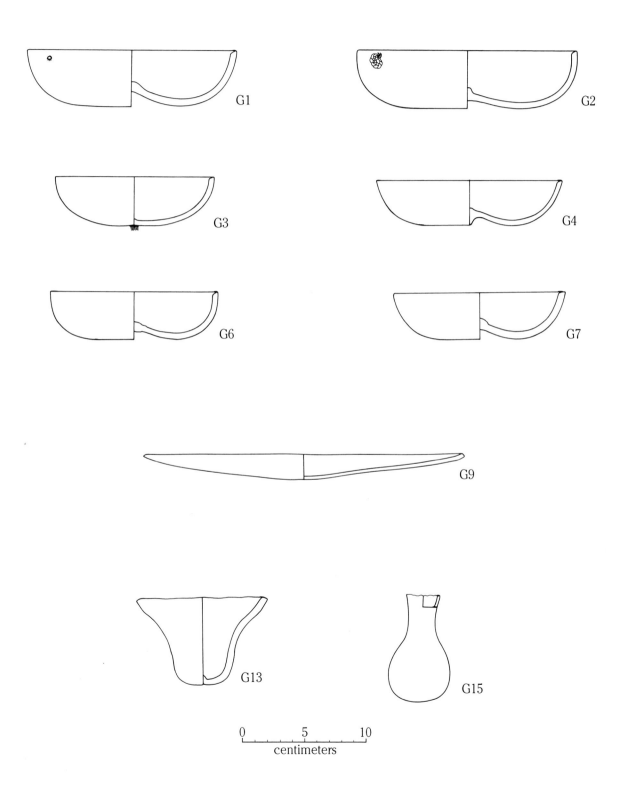

G1

G2

G3

G4

G6

G7

G9

G13

G15

0   5   10
centimeters

Burial 45

Original Field Number: H45CM1 B25b
Sex: ?
Age: Approximately 6 months
Burial Type:
> Cane Tube (?). The body was placed over the right leg of Burial 44.

Contents:
> One textile.
>> Textile 1, a shroud (?), on the skull.
>
> Yarn, yellowish brown wool, S-Z2. Approximately 20 strands around the left wrist.
>
> Yarn, yellowish brown wool, S-Z2. Several strands around the right ankle.
>
> Yarn, yellowish brown wool, S-Z2. Approximately 9 strands around the head, over mouth.

Comments:
> This is a double burial of an adult female and an infant. See Burial 44. Insect pupae were associated with the body.

Burial 46

Original Field Number: H45CM1 B28
Sex: Male
Age: Adult
Burial Type:
  Indeterminate. Cane fragments along each side of the body and under it.
Contents:
  One ceramic vessel (1) contained organic residue.
  One gourd (G1).
      G1, badly decomposed bowl (15 cm diameter x 5.5 cm high), positioned upright contained 10 bottle gourd (*Lagenaria siceraria*) seeds.
  One textile.
      Textile 1 was folded along the west side of left shoulder.
Comments:
  Because the burial was badly disturbed prior to excavation, it is not certain that the contents were originally associated with the burial. For further information on the textiles see Donnan and Donnan, this volume.

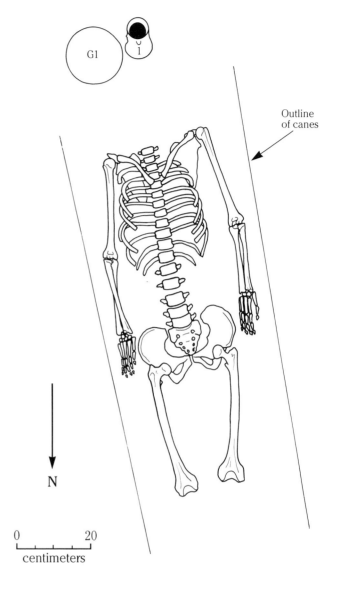

Outline
of canes

N

0   20
centimeters

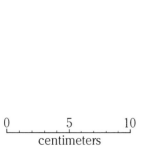

0   5   10
centimeters

1

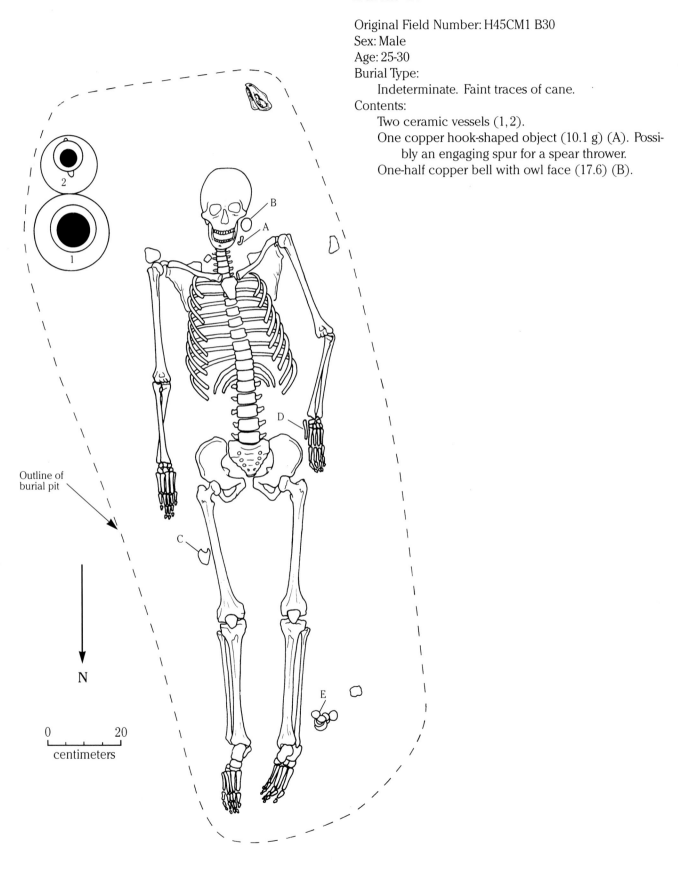

Burial 47

Original Field Number: H45CM1 B30
Sex: Male
Age: 25-30
Burial Type:
    Indeterminate. Faint traces of cane.
Contents:
    Two ceramic vessels (1, 2).
    One copper hook-shaped object (10.1 g) (A). Possi-
        bly an engaging spur for a spear thrower.
    One-half copper bell with owl face (17.6) (B).

Outline of
burial pit

N

0   20
centimeters

One-half copper bell with owl face (10.8 g) (C).

One bent copper spatula missing the tip (10.2 g) (D).

Mass of perforated copper disks (14.0 g, largest single disc, 2.3 g). They were apparently strung together at the time of burial (E).

Tip of copper spatula (?), possibly broken from copper object D, near the left upper arm (12.0 g).

One copper chunk by east side of neck.

Impression of a band of cordage around the head (headband?).

Chunk of blue pigment near left leg and copper disks.

Chunk of white chalk near upper part of right shoulder.

Canine skull south of the head.

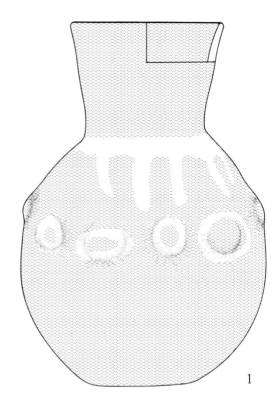

1

2

centimeters

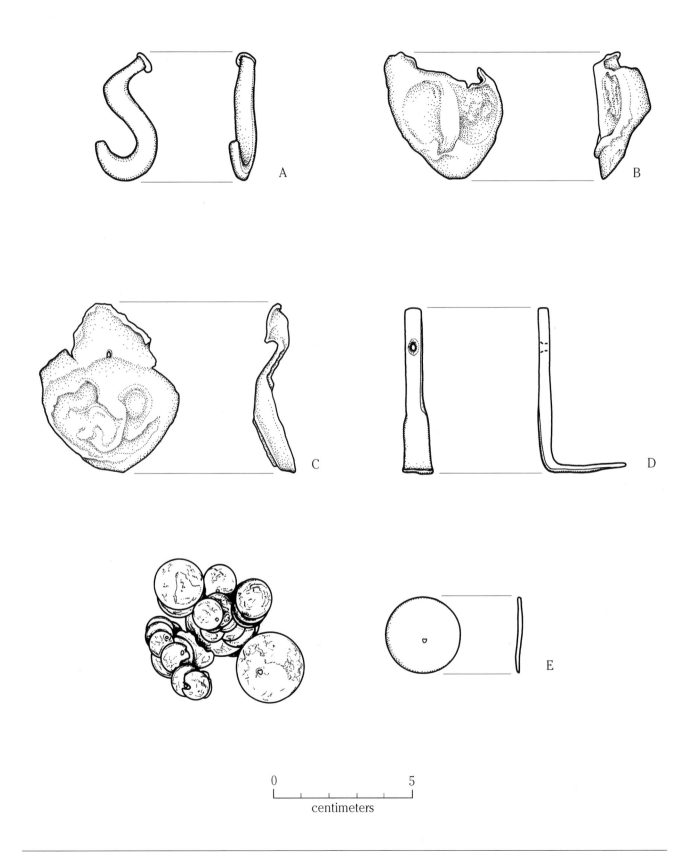

Burial 48

Original Field Number: H45CM1 B29
Sex: ?
Age: Approximately 18 months
Burial Type:

Indeterminate. Cane impressions under the body and parallel to it. No evidence of the canes being tied together.

Contents:

One ceramic vessel (1) contained insect pupae.
Impressions of two gourds (G1, G2).

G1, bowl (10.5 cm diameter x 5 cm high), positioned upright.

G2, bowl (dimensions indeterminate), upside down over the skull.

One copper ingot (1.8 x 1.7 x 0.65 cm, 7.1 g) (A) in mouth.

One copper chunk (2.4 x 1.4 x 0.6 cm, 6.1 g) near right shoulder.

One textile.

Textile 1, a shroud, in the area of the face, apparently wrapped over the top of the head and around most, if not all, of the body.

Llama bone on right side of the skull.

Comments:

The body was disturbed from the middle of the body to the feet, probably when the grave pit for Burial 47 was dug.

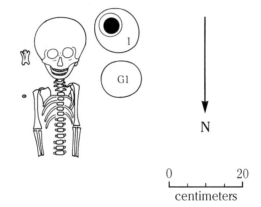

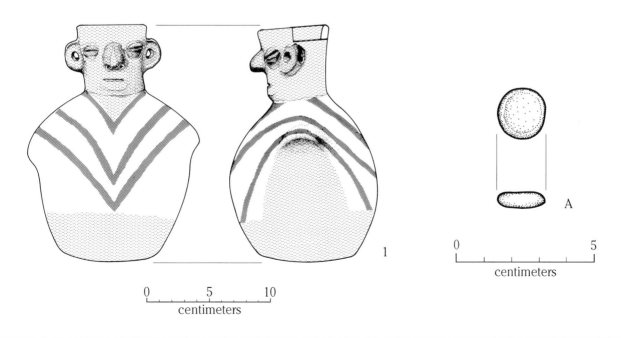

Burial 49

Original Field Number: H45CM1 B26

Sex: Female

Age: 50+

Burial Type:

Indeterminate. Only fragments of cane remained.

Contents:

One ceramic spindle whorl (5.8 g) (A).

One gourd (G1), bowl (16 cm diameter x 6 cm high), upside down over upper part of skull.

Copper chunk (2.8 x 2.7 x 1 cm, 15.3g) in mouth.

Copper chunk (ingot fragment? 2.8 x 2.2 x 1.2 cm, 14.8 g) near right knee.

Yarn, yellowish brown wool. At least 15 strands looped around another group of 15 strands. They were wrapped around the right wrist.

Comments:

Because the burial was badly disturbed prior to excavation, the original position of the contents is not certain.

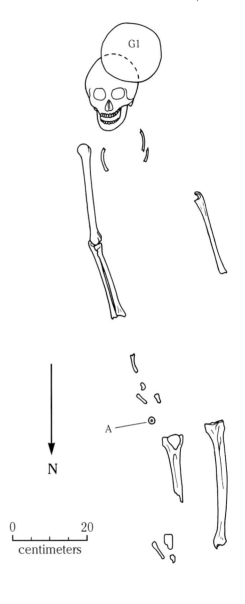

N

0   20
centimeters

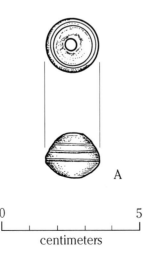

A

0   5
centimeters

Burial 50

Original Field Number: H45CM1 B27
Sex: Female
Age: Adult
Burial Type:
   Indeterminate. Evidence of cane along west side of
   body.
Comments:
   The grave was badly disturbed prior to excavation
   by late architectural construction. No grave goods
   were encountered.

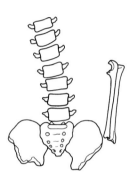

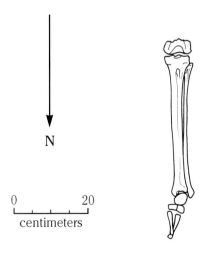

N

0   20
centimeters

Burial 51

Original Field Number: H45CM1 B31
Sex: Male
Age: 25-30
Burial Type:
  Indeterminate. Cane remnants.
Contents:
  Two ceramic vessels (1, 2).
  One copper chunk in mouth, too fragmentary to measure.
  One folded copper object (2.8 x 2.5 x 0.2 cm, 6.0 g) in left hand (A).
  One copper object, multiple folded sheets (2.6 x 3 x 0.2 cm, 5.0 g), in the left hand.
  One copper needle (10 cm long x 0.2 cm dia., 1.9 g) (B).
  One bone *mallero* (1.1 x 2.1 x 9.3 cm), inside left femur near the finger (C).
  One unmodified sea mammal bone.
Comments:
  The copper needle was found in the area beneath the burial and may or may not have been associated with it.

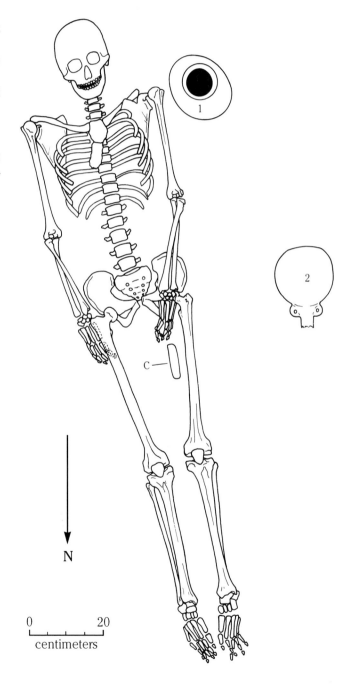

N

0 _____ 20
centimeters

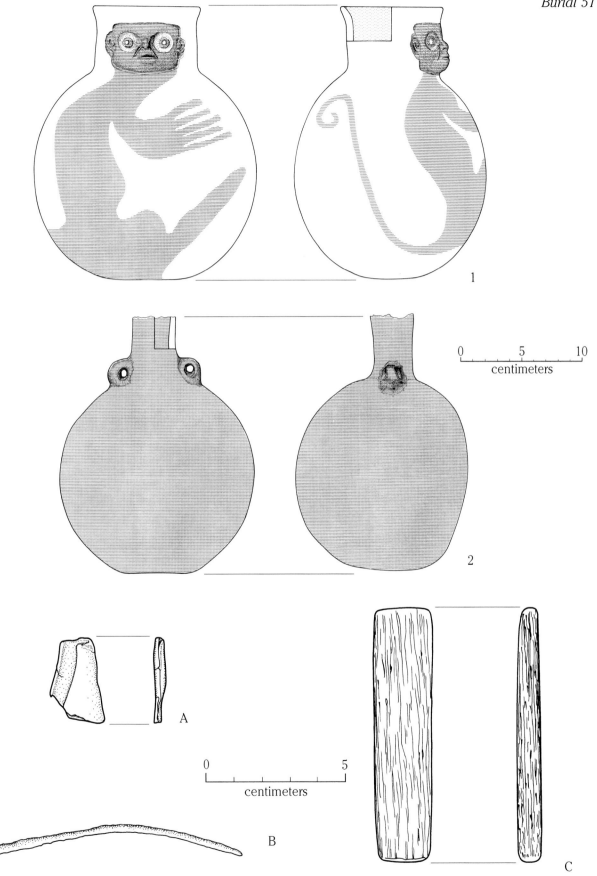

Burial 52

Original Field Number: H45CM1 B42
Sex: ?
Age: Approximately 1
Burial Type:
 Splint Reinforced.
Contents:
 One broken ceramic jar with white on red paint (1).
 Three small gourd bowls (G1-G3). Only one is illustrated. These were found in the area of the pelvis. One was upside down.
Comments:
 The burial was so badly disturbed prior to excavation it was not drawn. The body was extended north-south with head to the south.

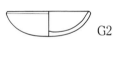

1

G2

0   5   10
       centimeters

Burial 53

Original Field Number: H45CM1 B41
Sex: Female
Age: 50+
Burial Type:
Cane Frame (?). Faint traces of cane beneath the body.
Contents:
Two ceramic vessels (1, 2).
> Ceramic 1 contained unidentifiable leaf fragments and a bast stopper.

Four gourds (G1-G4).
> G1, bowl (4.5 cm diameter x 10 cm high), positioned upright. It contained 1 *lucuma* (*Lucuma bifera*) seed.
> G2, upside down with the lid beneath the opening, contained 7 corncobs (*Zea mays*) wrapped with yarn, lime (?) cone (A), llama bone implement (awl? 11 cm long x 4 cm wide) (B), and a small shell (*Turbo niger*) with its top missing (bead?). One corncob (*Zea mays*) was wrapped in yarn.
> G3, bowl (12.5 cm diameter x 14 cm high), positioned upright inside G4. It contained 5.2 g of seaweed (*Gigartina chamissoi*) and insect pupae.
> G4, bowl (23 cm diameter), was badly decomposed.

Three copper objects in mouth, one-half of an ingot (14.2 g) (C), one folded sheet of copper (11.5 g) (D), and one-half of a convex pierced disk (13.7 g) (E).

Two textiles.
> Textile 1, outer shroud, wrapped over the face.
> Textile 2 wrapped over the face below textile 1.

Yarn, yellowish brown wool. At least 20 strands around upper part of skull.
Yarn, tan cotton, at least 9 strands near ear ornament.
Yarn, yellowish brown wool, at least 40 strands wrapped around a corncob in G2.
One stone spindle whorl (8.0 g) (F) above right wrist.
One stone spindle whorl (9.2 g) (G), on left side.
One wood ear ornament (H) originally inlaid at large end, beneath skull near left ear. Evidence of a dark brown adhesive in the recessed area at the large end. A dark discoloration encircles the middle of the rod.
One wood ornament (I) near the right ear, poorly preserved.
One pointed wood staff (4 cm diameter x 50 cm long).
One shell (*Spondylus*) labret (?) (J).

Comments:
> Spindle whorl F had been disturbed prior to excavation. The wood shaft was under the body, probably outside the cane frame and textile wrapping. The blunt end of wood shaft did not appear finished; therefore, originally it may have been longer. The shell (*Spondylus*) object (J) was found inside the skull. For further information on the textiles see Donnan and Donnan, this volume.

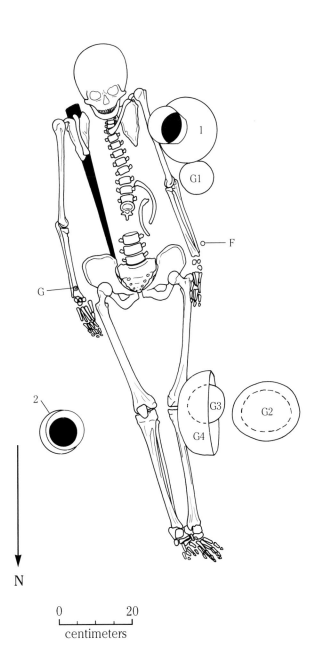

N

0 — 20
centimeters

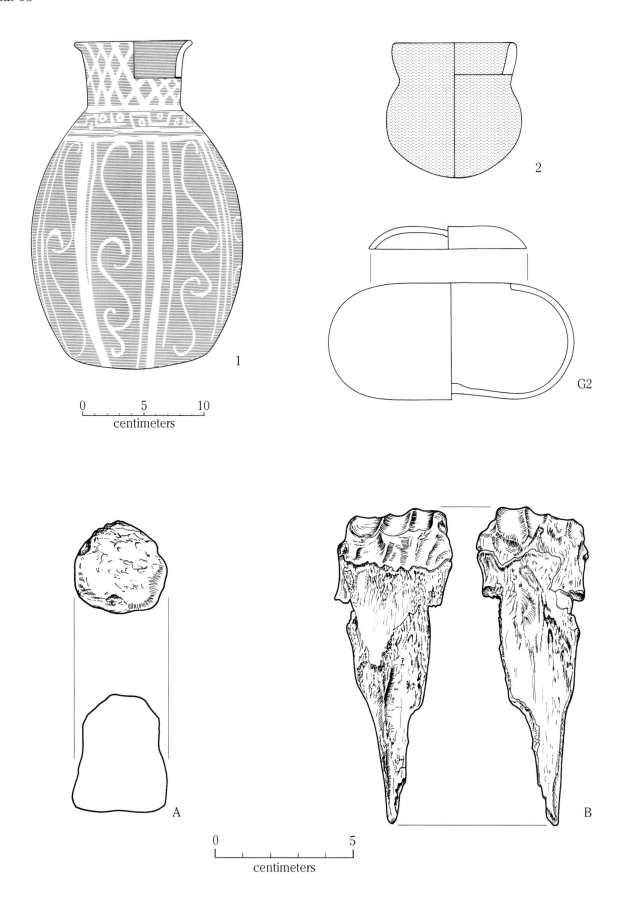

centimeters

centimeters

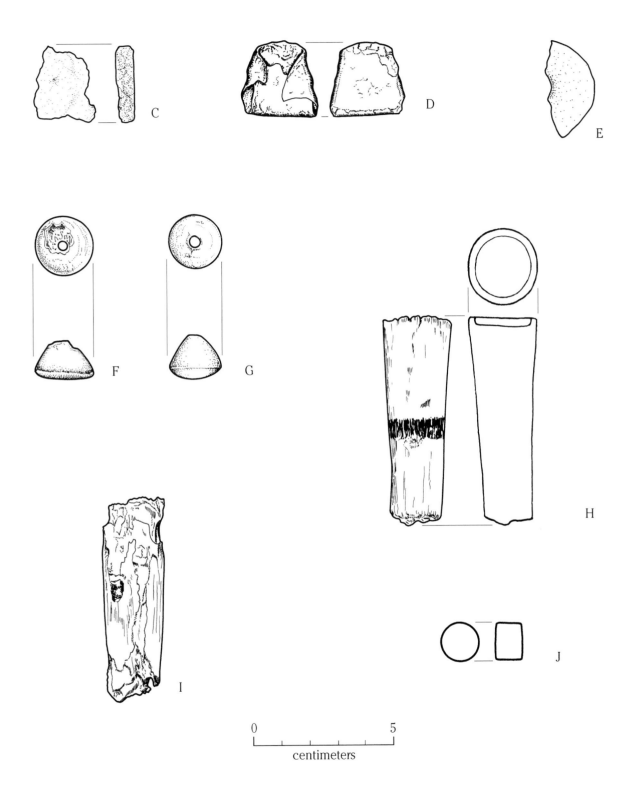

Burial 54

Original Field Number: H45CM1 B67
Sex: Male
Age: 30-40
Burial Type:
    Cane Frame.
Contents:
    One folded copper disk (5.4 x 3 x 1.1 cm, 17.7 g) in
        right hand.
    One bent sheet of copper (3 x 2.6 x 0.7 cm, 7.7 g) in
        left hand.
    One ingot fragment (2.6 x 1.7 x 0.7 cm, 10.8 g) on the
        chest.
    Copper sheeting (0.2 g) wrapped around a wood
        shaft, near left femur.
    Wood object, flat and tapered, above right shoulder.
    Wood object near right forearm, possibly from the
        same wood object above the right shoulder.
    One shell valve (*Mytilus* sp.) between the legs.
Comments:
    The burial was disturbed prior to excavation. The
    skull was missing.

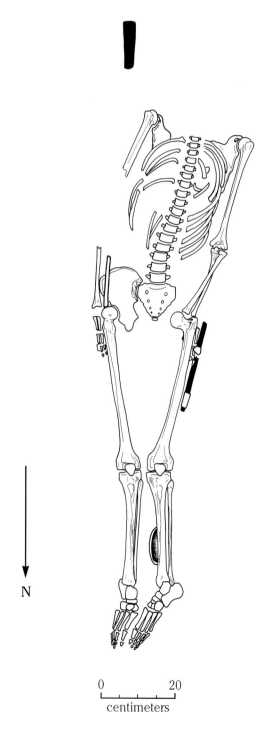

N

0   20
    centimeters

Burial 55

Original Field Number: H45CM1 B56
Sex: Male
Age: 30-35
Burial Type:
    Indeterminate. Only a few cane impressions under the body.
Contents:
    Green copper stains on bones of right hand.
    One copper chunk (1.8 x 1.3 x 0.9 cm, 5.7 g) in left hand.
Comments:
    The burial was badly disturbed prior to excavation. The skull was missing. The individual had severe compression fractures of the lumbar vertebrae. See Verano, this volume, for skeletal analysis.

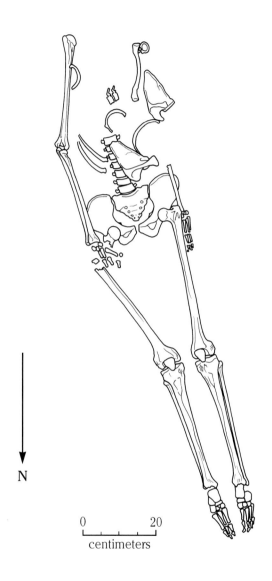

N

0   20
centimeters

Burial 56

Original Field Number: H45CM1 B60
Sex: ?
Age: Approximately 6 months
Burial Type:
   Splint Reinforced.
Contents:
   Two ceramic vessels (1, 2).
   One copper object (2 x 1.6 x 0.7 cm, 5.7 g) in mouth.
   One copper object (1.8 x 1.4 x 0.9 cm, 5.5 g) in right
        hand, wrapped with unspun cotton.
Comments:
   The body was positioned east-west with the head to
   the east, instead of the more usual position of north-
   south with the head to the south.

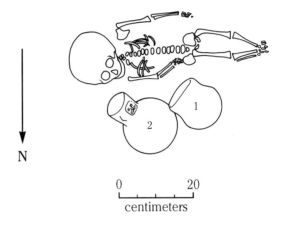

N

0   20
centimeters

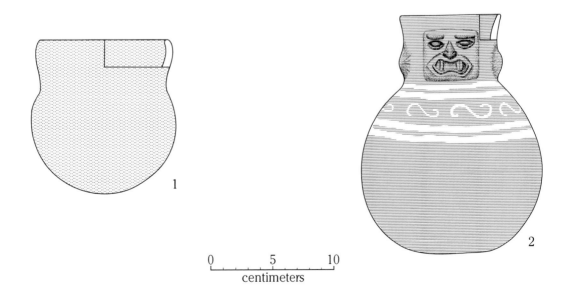

0   5   10
centimeters

Burial 57

Original Field Number: H45CM1 B61
Sex: Female
Age: 35-45
Burial Type:
    Indeterminate.
Contents:
    One copper chunk (2 x 1.6 x 0.6 cm, 6.6 g) in mouth

One copper chunk (1.5 x 1.2 x 0.5 cm, 4.0 g) in right hand.
One copper chunk (2.3 x 1 x 0.7 cm, 4.5 g) in left hand.
One stone spindle whorl (9.0 g) (A) with fragments of wood spindle.
One stone spindle whorl (6.5 g) (B).

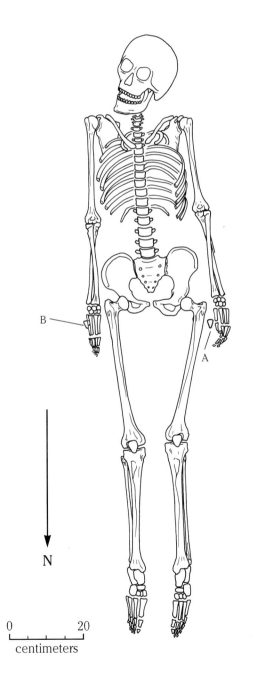

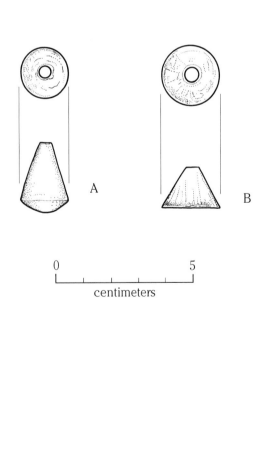

Burial 58

Original Field Number: H45CM1 B66a
Sex: Male
Age: 35-40
Burial Type:
    Indeterminate.
Contents:
    Two ceramic vessels (1-2).
        Ceramic 2, jar (19 cm diameter), was broken.
            Only the base remained.
Comments:
    Many bones of this burial were missing or out of
    position. An incomplete skeleton of a child (see
    Burial 59) was intermingled with this adult skeleton.

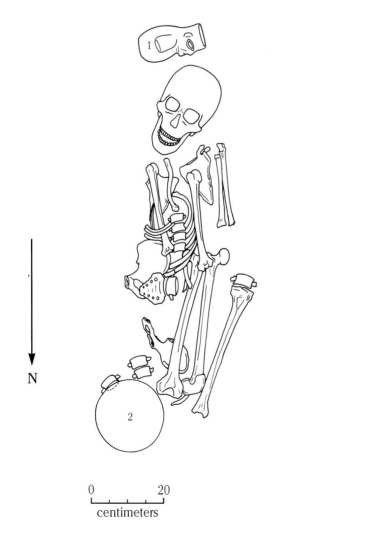

N

0   20
centimeters

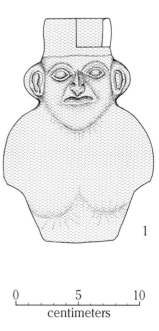

1

0   5   10
centimeters

Burial 59

Original Field Number: H45CM1 B66b
Sex: ?
Age: 2-2.5
Burial Type:
    Indeterminate.
Comments:
    The bones of this child were intermingled with the
    adult skeleton in Burial 58.

Burials 60-62

Original Field Numbers: H45CM1 B63-65
Sex: See individual descriptions.
Age: See individual descriptions.
Burial type: See individual descriptions
Contents: The burial goods at the north end of the tomb and the llama under the legs of the adults may be associated with any or all three of the burials.

> Four ceramic vessels (1-4).
>> Most of the jar neck of Ceramic 2 was missing prior to the burial.
> Ten gourds (G1-10).
>> G1 positioned upright, inside G2, over G3.
>> G2 positioned upright, under G1, over G3.
>> G3, bowl (10 cm diameter x 6 cm high), positioned upright under G1 and G2.
>> G4, oblate whole gourd (11 cm diameter), partially under Ceramic 2. It contained 22 bottle gourd seeds (*Lagenarira siceraria*).
>> G5, bowl (12 cm diameter x 2.5 cm high), partially under Ceramic 2.
>> G6, bowl (12.5 cm diameter x 2.5 cm high), lying on its side, under Ceramic 2.
>> G7, bowl (17 cm diameter x 2.5 cm high).
>> G8, bowl (20 cm diameter x 9 cm high), contained 8.5 g of seaweed (*Gigartina chamissoi*).
>> G10 on edge with opening down and to NE. It contained 7 g of seaweed (*Gigartina chamissoi*) and 2 leaf fragments.
> Llama under the three individuals. The head, upper neck, and pelvis were disturbed.
> Compacted llama dung (45 cm diameter x 20 cm thick) under the ceramics and gourds.

Comments:

> The three individuals appear to have been associated and contemporary with one another. The above listed contents were associated with Burials 60-62 at the north end of the burial pit. See individual descriptions of Burials 60-62 for contents associated with each individual.

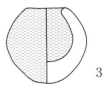

1

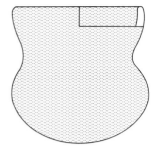

2

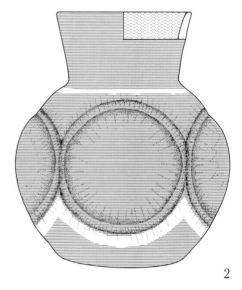

3

0   5   10
centimeters

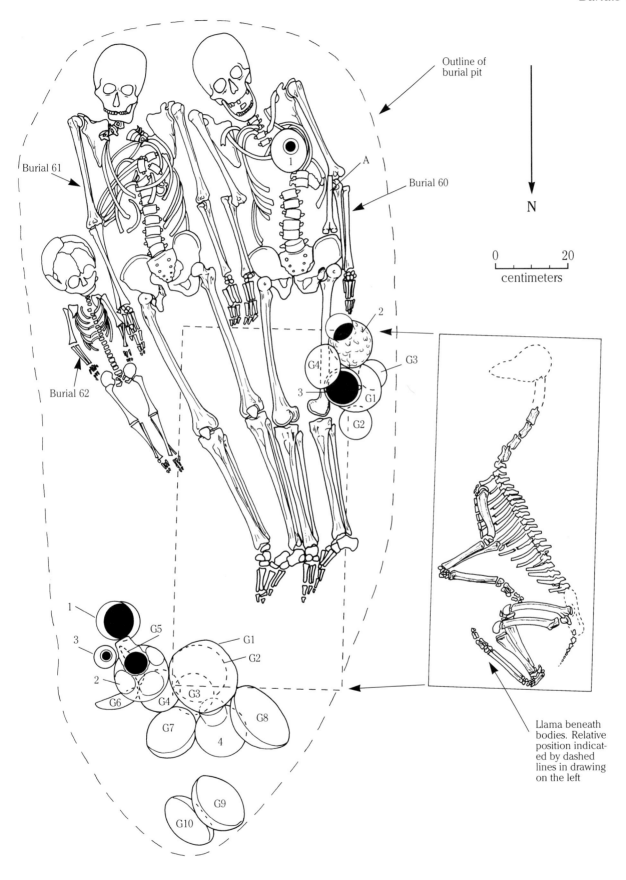

Outline of
burial pit

N

Burial 61

A

Burial 60

0   20
centimeters

Burial 62

2

G4   G3

3   G1

G2

1

G5

3   G1

2   G2

G6   G4   G3

G7   4   G8

G9

G10

Llama beneath
bodies. Relative
position indicat-
ed by dashed
lines in drawing
on the left

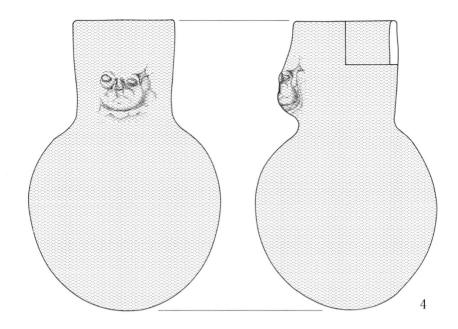

4

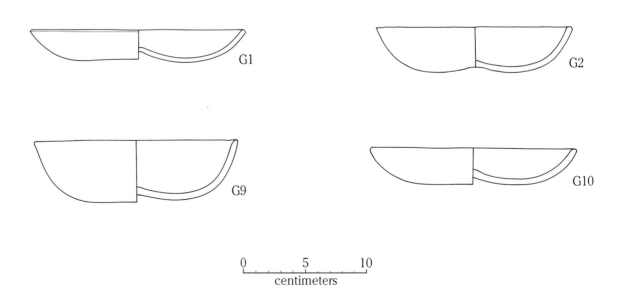

G1

G2

G9

G10

0   5   10
centimeters

Burial 60

Original Field Number: H45CM1 B63
Sex: Male
Age: 35-45
Burial Type:
    Indeterminate.
Contents: Associated with the male.
    Three ceramic vessels (1-3).
    Four gourds (G1-G4).
        G1, bowl (14 cm diameter x 3 cm high), posi-
            tioned upright, partially over G2 and G3,
            and under Ceramic 3. It contained 2 gm of
            seaweed (*Gigartina chamissoi*).
        G2, tall cup (9 cm diameter x 6 cm high), posi-
            tioned upright, partially under G1.
        G3, bottle-shaped (7 cm diameter x 9 cm high),
            partially under G1.
        G4, bowl (12 cm diameter x 5 cm high), upside
            down with the opening toward the north-
            west, over one corncob (*Zea mays*).
    One copper chunk (1.8 x 1.5 x 0.5 cm) in mouth.
    Two copper objects (2.6 x 1.6 x 0.1 cm and 3.8 x 3.2
        x 0.1 cm) in right hand.
    Copper fragments (approx. 2.6 x 2 x 0.1 cm) in left
        hand, similar to copper in right hand.
    One bone spatula made from llama cannon bone
        (A).
Comments:
    This individual's right humerus was substantially
    shorter than the left, indicating some disruption of
    growth during childhood or adolescence, but there
    was no apparent functional loss of the arm. See Ver-
    ano, this volume, for skeletal analysis. This was one
    of three individuals that appear to have been asso-
    ciated and contemporary with one another. See
    Burials 61 and 62.

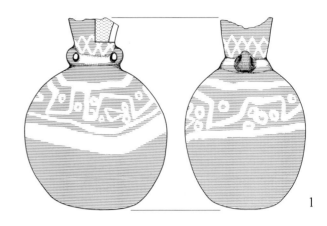

1

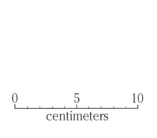

0   5   10
centimeters

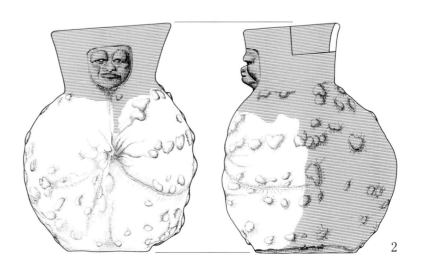

2

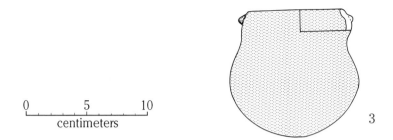

3

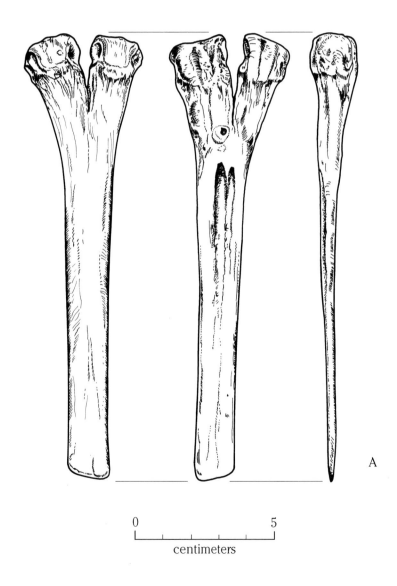

A

Burial 61

Original Field Number: H45CM1 B64

Sex: Female

Age: 30-40

Burial Type:

Indeterminate.

Contents:

Three copper objects (108.3 g) in mouth. Two were halves of ingots (4.4 x 3.3 x 1 cm and 4 x 3.2 x 0.8 cm), and the third was a chunk (3.2 x 2.1 x 1.2 cm).

One-half copper ingot in right hand (56.8 g). Other half in left hand.

One-half copper ingot in left hand (82.3 g). Other half in right hand.

One textile.

Textile 1 in area of right elbow.

One stone spindle whorl near right wrist (7.5 g) (A).

One stone spindle whorl near right hand (7.1 g) (B). The spindle was parallel to the body. A trace of the spindle extends 17 cm north of the spindle whorl.

Comments:

This was one of three individuals that appear to have been associated and contemporary with one another. See Burials 60 and 62. For further information on the textiles see Donnan and Donnan, this volume.

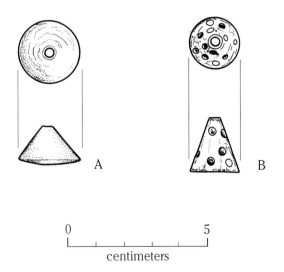

A

B

0   5

centimeters

Burial 62

Original Field Number: H45CM1 B65
Sex: ?
Age: Approximately 6 months
Burial Type:
  Splint Reinforced.
Contents:
  One copper chunk (2.2 x 2.1 x 0.7 cm, 9.7 g) in
    mouth.
  One-half of a copper ingot (2.6 x 2 x 0.4 cm, 6.2 g) in
    right hand.
  Two copper objects (9.3 g) (2.9 x 1.7 x 0.4 cm and
    3.3 x 1.9 x 0.4 cm) in left hand.
  Bead necklace. Representational beads are clus-
    tered under the chin with miniature war club in
    center.
    1 miniature war club (A).
    1 crab claw (B).
    2 carved shell miniature nose ornaments (C, D).
    1 carved shell disk (E).
    16 black-green beads.
    1 turquoise bead.
    1 white tubular bead.
    45 white beads.
Comments:
  This was one of three individuals that appear to have
  been associated and contemporary with one anoth-
  er. See Burials 60 and 61.

A

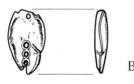

B

C

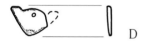

D

E

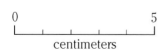

0   5
centimeters

Burial 63

Original Field Number: H45CM1 B40
Sex: ?
Age: 3-3.5
Burial Type:

Splint Reinforced. Canes appear to have been tied around the exterior of the shroud to keep the body rigid.

Contents:

Two ceramic vessels (1, 2).

Ceramic 1 contained unidentifiable plant remains.

Three gourds (G1-G3).

G1 positioned upright. It contained 2 corncobs (*Zea mays*).

G2, bowl (7 cm diameter x 4 cm high), upside down over Ceramic 2.

G3, bowl (16 cm diameter x 5.5 cm high), appears to have been placed over the head end of the burial wrapping.

One copper chunk (12.3 g) in mouth.

Five textiles.

Textile 1, an inner shroud wrapped around the body.

Textile 2, an outer shroud, wrapped around the entire body.

Textile 3 in the area of the head on top of the unspun cotton on the face.

Textile 4 near right shoulder of body.

Textile 5, cordage, used to tie the burial bundle together.

Unspun cotton on face.

Yarn, yellowish brown wool. Twenty strands around right wrist.

Yarn, tan cotton. At least 20 strands around right wrist.

Yarn, yellowish brown wool. At least 20 strands tied with a single strand of lighter colored wool. Near right wrist.

String, white cotton. Two groups of string, at least 20 strands in each group, tied in a single knot.

Bead necklace.

118 shell and stone beads.

1 long tubular shell bead.

4 short tubular shell beads.

3 shell pendants (one inlaid).

Twined mat, simple 1 over 1, apparently was placed over the coffin and grave contents after they were placed in the tomb.

Comments:

For further information on the textiles see Donnan and Donnan, this volume.

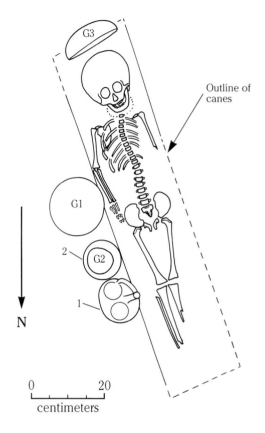

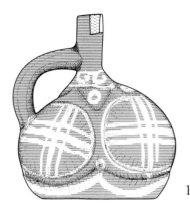

1

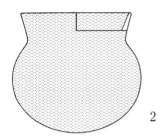

2

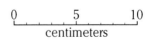

G1

Burial 64

Original Field Number: H45CM1 B50
Sex: Male
Age: 20-35
Burial Type:
   Indeterminate. Traces of cane under lower legs and feet.
Contents:
   One ceramic vessel (1).
   Three gourds (G1-G3).
      G1, bowl (15 cm diameter x 6 cm high), positioned upright.

G2, lid, horizontal.
G3, bowl (13 cm diameter x 3.5 cm high), positioned upright.
   One textile.
      Textile 1 near upper body.
   Yarn around right ankle.
   Yarn around left ankle.
Comments:
   The burial was badly disturbed prior to excavation probably as a result of digging the grave pit for the child (Burial 63) who was buried directly above.

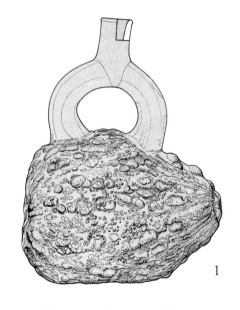

1

0   5   10
centimeters

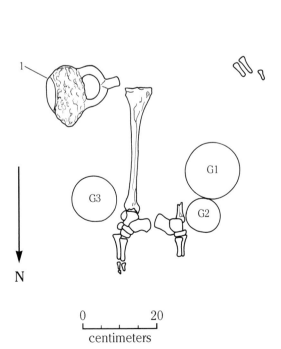

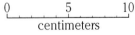

N

0   20
centimeters

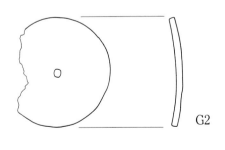

G2

0   5   10
centimeters

Burial 65

Original Field Number: H45CM1 B58
Sex: Female
Age: 30-40
Burial Type:
Indeterminate. Traces of cane under the body and along the sides.
Contents:
Three ceramic vessels (1-3).
Two ceramic spindle whorls (A, B).
Five gourds (G1-G5).
G1, bowl (11 cm diameter x 5 cm high), positioned upright.
G2, upside down over G3.
G3, bowl (16 cm diameter x 7 cm high), positioned upright under G2. It contained corncobs (*Zea mays*).

G4, bowl (12 cm diameter x 5.5 cm high).
G5, bowl (14 cm diameter x 5 cm high), upside down.
Green copper stains in mouth area.
One copper chunk (3.1 x 2.6 x 1 cm, 33.4 g) in right hand wrapped with unspun cotton.
One copper chunk (3.5 x 2.9 x 1 cm, 28.4 g) in left hand.
Comments:
The burial was disturbed prior to excavation. The skull was missing.

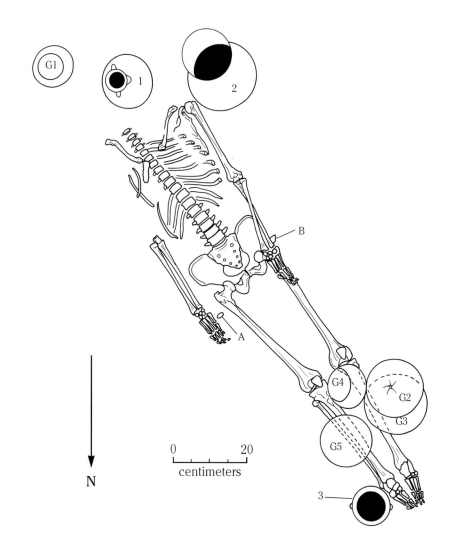

N

0   20
centimeters

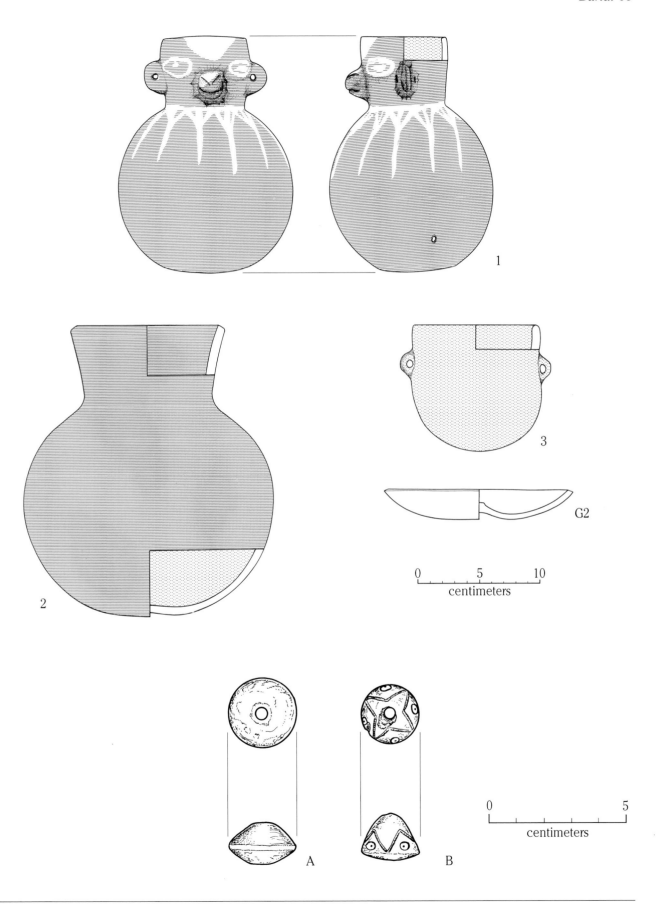

Burial 66

Original Field Number: H45CM1 B59
Sex: Female
Age: 30-40
Burial Type:
Indeterminate. Cane impressions were beneath the body and some cane was on top of the body.
Contents:
Two ceramic vessels (1, 2).
Two textiles.
Textile 1 near the legs.
Textile 2 near the legs.
Yarn, brown wool, S-Z2, around left ankle.
Comments:
The body was badly disturbed prior to excavation. It was definitely interred before Burial 65. For further information on the textiles, see Donnan and Donnan, this volume.

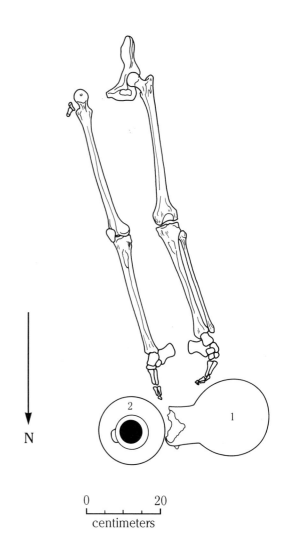

N

0   20
centimeters

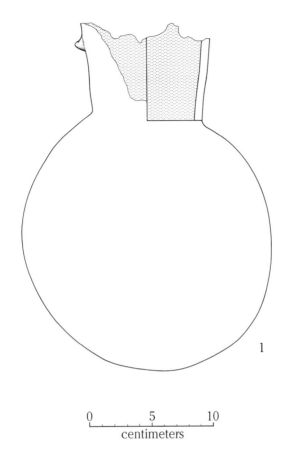

1

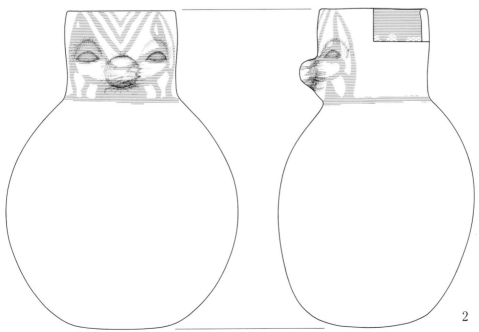

2

0   5   10
centimeters

Burial 67

Original Field Number: H45CM1 B51
Sex: Male
Age: 25-30
Burial Type:
    Indeterminate.
Contents:
    One ceramic vessel (1).
    One gourd (G1).
        G1, bowl (10 cm diameter x 5 cm high), positioned upright, impression only.

Llama skull near left shoulder.
Llama leg bone near right shoulder.
Comments:
    The skull was missing. It was not possible to determine whether this was because of disturbance, or if the skull was missing at the time of burial. The body was positioned east-west with the head to the east, instead of the more usual position of north-south with the head to the south.

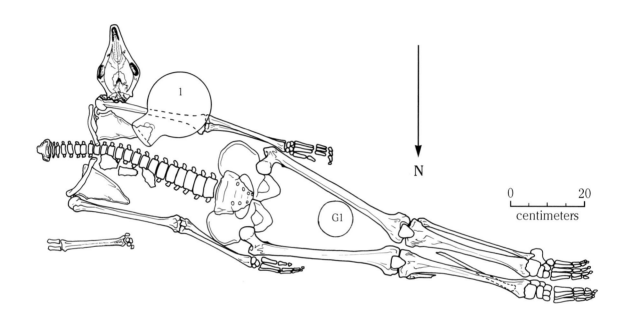

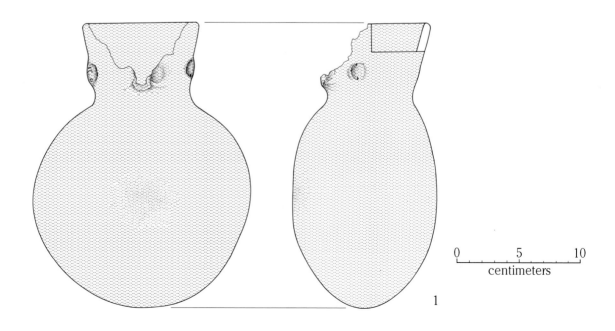

Burial 68

Original Field Number: H26CM1 B1
Sex: ?
Age: Approximately 9 months
Burial Type:
   Shroud Wrap (?).
Contents:
   One textile.
      Textile 1 under the body.
   Traces of brown yarn in area of right wrist.
   Traces of brown yarn in area of left wrist.
   Beads in area of left wrist.
      6 triangular nacre in three shapes: 2 (A), 2 (B),
         and 2 (C)
      19 tubular shell (4.8 mm - 11.5 mm diameter).
   Beads in area of right wrist.
      6 nacre under right wrist (D-I), one carved in
         the shape of a bird with a blue-green inlaid
         eye of faustite, a mineral similar to tur-
         quoise (I).
      24 tubular shell (*Spondylus*) (5 mm - 13.8 mm
         diameter). The elaborate beads were clus-
         tered together under the wrist, but the tubu-
         lar beads extended up to the elbow.
Comments:
   The burial pit was 24-27 cm below a hard compact
   "floor." The legs were tightly drawn back in a very
   unnatural way suggesting that they were originally
   extended, but that the bundle was folded back over
   itself, hyperextending the knees.

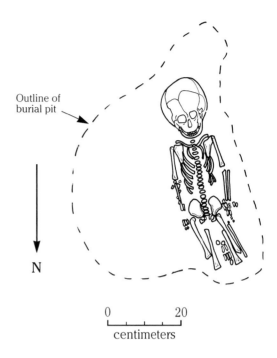

Outline of
burial pit

N

0   20
   centimeters

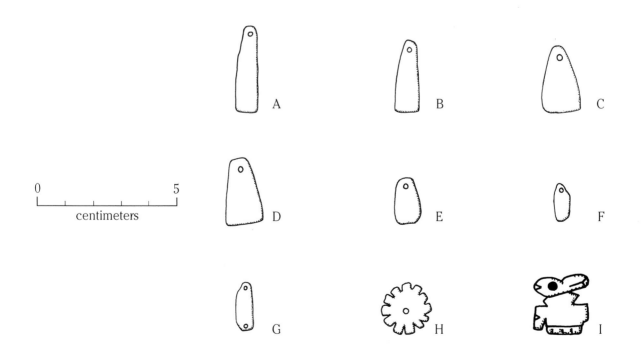

0   5
      centimeters

Burial 69

Original Field Number: H26CM1 B2
Sex: ?
Age: Approximately 1
Burial Type:
 Shroud Wrap.
Contents:
 One textile.
  Textile 1, a shroud (?) wrapped around the body.
 Traces of brown yarn around right wrist.
 Traces of brown yarn around left wrist.
 Beads in area of neck and head.
  4 whole shells (*Olivella*), perforated at the pointed end.
  54 shell (*Spondylus*), 33 disk, and 21 tubular (2.3 mm - 6.1 mm diameter).
  19 chrysocola (?) (2.3 mm - 3.1 mm diameter).
  56 gourd (1.7 mm - 6 mm diameter).
  10 carved nacre, 5 triangular pendants (A), 2 square (B), and 3 incomplete broken pendants.
 Beads in area of right wrist.
  10 small shell (*Spondylus*).
  2 small gourd.
  2 chrysocola (?).
 Beads in area of left wrist.
  4 small shell (*Spondylus*) in three sizes (2.2 mm - 11 mm diameter).
Comments:
 The burial was placed in an irregularly shaped pit which appeared to have been expanded to accommodate it. The pit cuts through a hardened floor and a refuse deposit. The fill around the body was very loose and darker than the surrounding matrix. The fill contained gray beach sand, silt, shell fragments, fish bone, charcoal, and sherds.

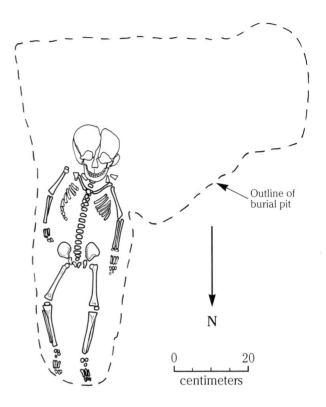

Outline of burial pit

N

0   20
centimeters

A

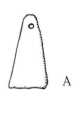

B

0   5
centimeters

Burial 70

Original Field Number: H26CM1 B3
Sex: ?
Age: 1-1.5
Burial Type:
    Shroud Wrap (?).
Contents:
    One textile.
        Textile 1 near the body
Comments:
    The burial was placed in slightly compacted sand
    containing cultural refuse.

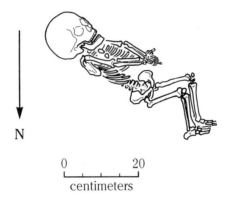

N

0   20
centimeters

Burial 71

Original Field Number: H28 B1
Sex: ?
Age: 4-5
Burial Type:
    Shroud Wrap.
Contents:
    Two ceramic vessels (1, 2).
    Ten gourds (G1-G10).
        G1, bowl (14 cm diameter x 3 cm high).
        G2, bowl (17 cm diameter x 4 cm high).
        G3, bowl (22 cm diameter x 6 cm high).
        G4, bowl (18 cm diameter x 4 cm high).
        G5, bowl (6 cm diameter x 4 cm high).

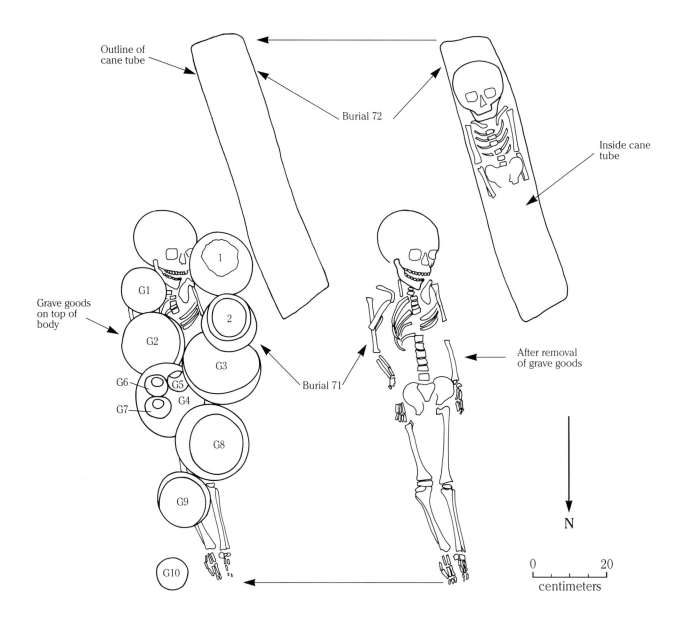

G6, bowl (6 cm diameter x 4 cm high).
G7, bowl (7 cm diameter x 4 cm high).
G8, bowl (20 cm diameter x 6 cm high).
G9, bowl (15 cm diameter x 13 cm high).
G10, bowl (8 cm diameter x 4 cm high).
One textile.
  Textile 1 in the gourd bowls and around the body.
Beads.
  2 perforated disk-shaped shell (*Spondylus*), near neck.
  1 perforated disk-shaped shell (*Spondylus*), at right wrist.
  1 perforated disk-shaped shell (*Spondylus*) bead, at left wrist.
Comments:
The burial pit was indistinguishable from the surrounding refuse deposit. It was near Burial 72, but not necessarily associated. The body appears to have been wrapped in a large textile. For further information on the textiles see Donnan and Donnan, this volume.

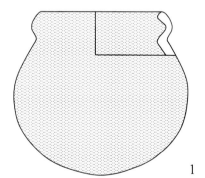

1

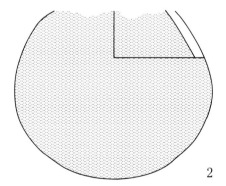

2

0   5   10
centimeters

Burial 72

Original Field Number: H28 B2
Sex: ?
Age: 1.5-2
Burial Type:
  Cane Tube.
Contents:
  Four textiles.
    Textile 1, an outer shroud, wrapped around the body. One side was folded over 1/2 inch and sewn closed. The extra material was gathered under the head.
    Textile 2, a middle shroud, wrapped around the body several times, and sewn closed.
    Textile 3, an inner shroud, wrapped around the body.
    Textile 4 in the area of the head.
  Unspun cotton in the area of the head.
Comments:
  The burial was placed in a shallow depression in *cascajo*, which was probably enlarged to fit. See Burial 71. The burial had been disturbed and the lower part of the body missing. It was near Burial 71, but it may have been buried sometime earlier. For further information on the textiles see Donnan and Donnan, this volume.

Burial 73

Original Field Number: H2 B1
Sex: Female
Age: 50+
Burial Type:
    Cane Frame.
Contents:
    [See next page]

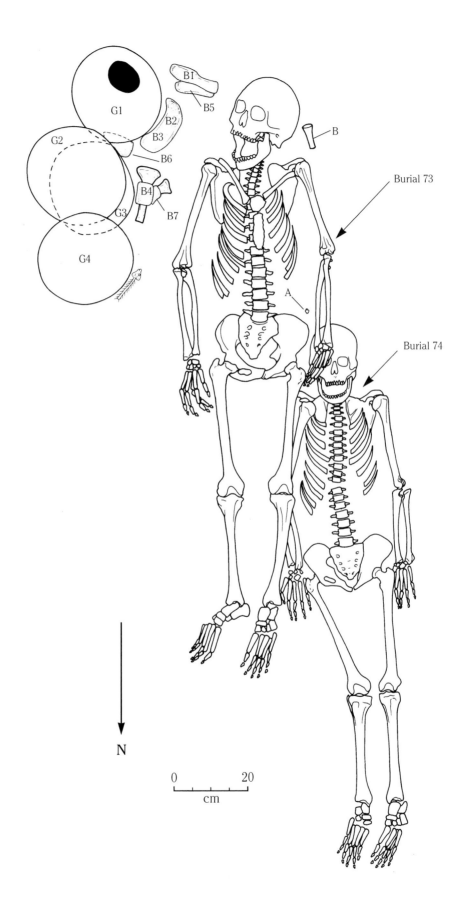

Burial 73

Contents:

One gray ceramic spindle whorl with unspun brown cotton at the base and remnants of a spindle inside (A).

Four gourds (G1-G4).

G1, incurved bowl (25 cm diameter), contained 11 corn kernels, 1 corncob with several fragments of corncobs (*Zea mays*), and fragments of a bag.

G2, bowl (26 cm diameter).

G3, bowl (23 cm diameter) contained a poorly preserved bag and 28 beans (27 *Phaseolus lunatus*, and 1 *Phaseolus vulgaris*).

G4, bowl (25 cm diameter).

Copper fragment in right hand.

Copper fragment in left hand.

Twelve textiles.

Textile 3 in the area of the torso.

Textile 4, a bag (B1), contained unidentifiable organic (food?) remains. The top was gathered and wrapped three times with cotton string.

Textile 5a, a bag (B2). The top was gathered and wrapped with cotton string.

Textile 5b, a bag (B3), contained one cotton (*Gossypium babadense*) seed and 35 corn (*Zea mays*) kernels.

Textile 6, a bag (B4), contained 59 corn (*Zea mays*) kernels, 4 corn (*Zea mays*) cupules, and 1 chile (*Capsicum sp.*) seed. The top was gathered and wrapped with cotton string. It was over a llama scapula, Textile 9, and another llama scapula.

Textile 7, a bag (B5), contained one chile (*Capsicum sp.*) seed and one coca (*Erythroxylum novogranatense*) endocarp.

Textile 8, a bag (B6), contained 2 kernels of corn (*Zea mays*). It was sewn with cotton string.

Textile 9, a bag (B7), contained 24 kernels of corn (*Zea mays*). It was under Textile 6 and one llama scapula, and over another llama scapula to which it was tied. It was sewn with cotton string.

Textile 12, a bag (B8), in G3, sewn together with cotton string.

Textile 13, a bag (B9), in G1.

Textile 14, an inner shroud, wrapped around the torso (the arms were outside).

Textile 15, an outer shroud, wrapped around the body and cane frame.

Yarn, gold wool (?), around the fingers on right hand.

One wood ear ornament (B), on left side of head. The front is inlaid with a chrysocola mosaic, and the rod is carved. (See Comments).

One shell pendant, triangularly shaped with two perforations, near the neck.

Plant remains in gourds and bags.

Fish bones near G4.

Llama bones.

Comments:

The burial pit was cut into *cascajo*. The tomb had been slightly disturbed prior to excavation. There was a large quantity of organic material (*totora*?) scattered across the north end of the burial pit, immediately above the lower legs and feet of Burial 73, and the lower body of Burial 74. Its original form and function could not be determined. An ear ornament, similar to the one on left side of head, was encountered in a disturbed area above the burial. This individual had a broken left leg that was well healed. See Verano, this volume, for skeletal analysis. For further information on the textiles see Donnan and Donnan, this volume. For further information on plant remains, see Gumerman, this volume.

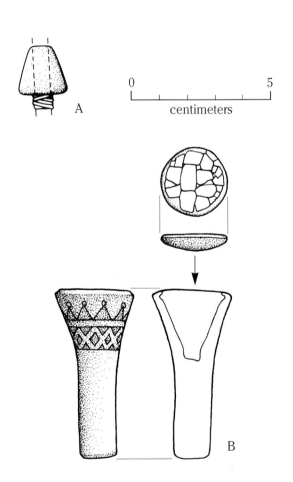

Burial 74

Original Field Number: H2 B2
Sex: Male
Age: 40-50
Burial Type:
    Indeterminate.
Contents:
    Seven textiles.
        Textile 1 adhering to the face and head
        Textiles 3, 4, 5, 8, 9, 10 in the general area of the
            body.
    Unspun cotton covering eyes.
    Yarn around fingers on right hand.
Comments:
    The burial pit was cut into *cascajo*. The *cascajo* was undercut and the body positioned under the resulting shelf of *cascajo*. See Burial 73. For further information on the textiles see Donnan and Donnan, this volume.

Burial 75

Original Field Number: H2 B3
Sex: Male
Age: 25-30

Burial Type:

Cane Frame. The frame was approximately 165 cm long and 20 cm wide. It was constructed with 11 long canes and 4 cane cross braces. Numerous reeds, laterally attached to a single cane, covered portions of the burial pit and the shrouded body. Reeds were placed along the sides of the legs, parallel to them, and covered the feet.

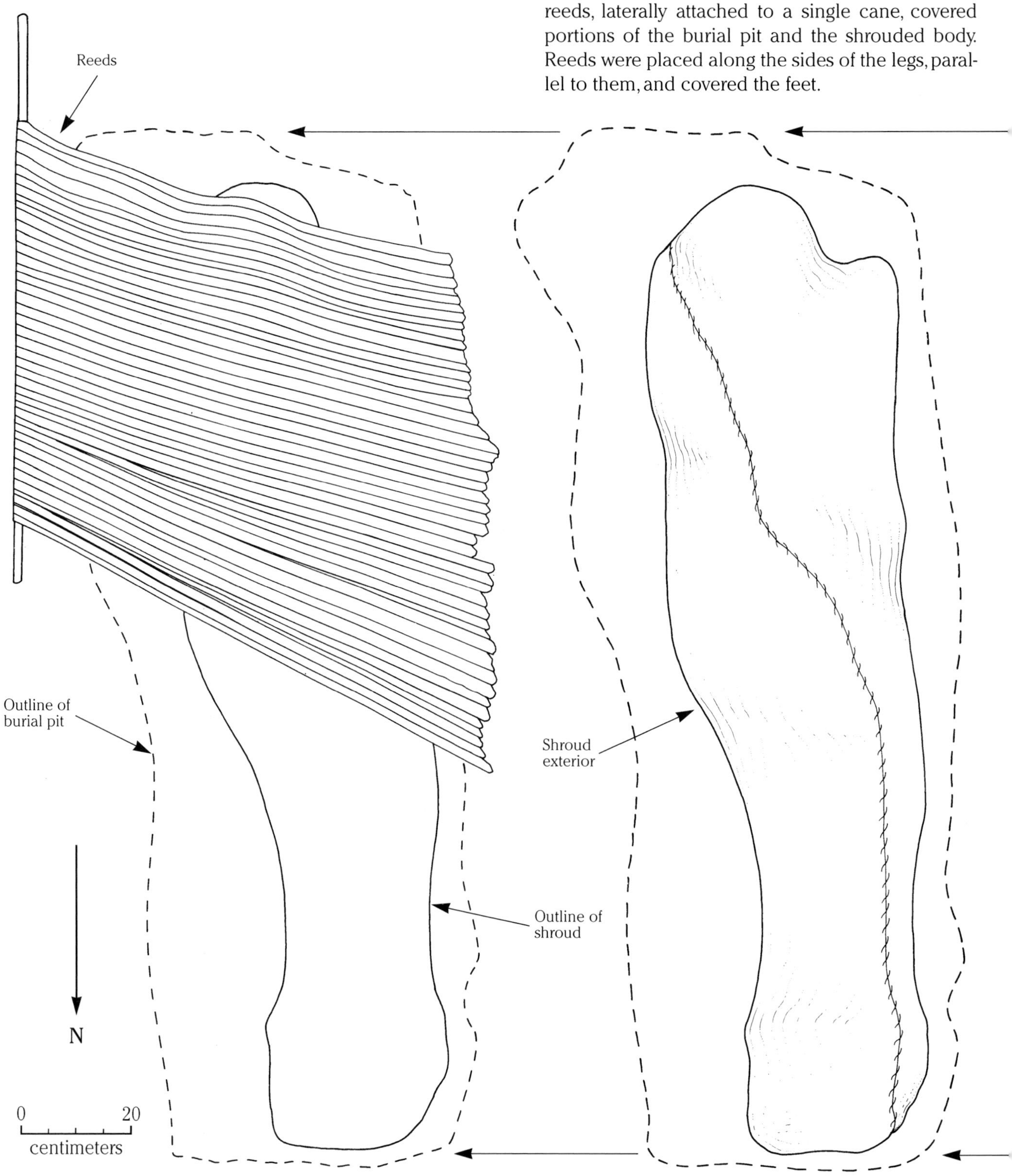

Reeds

Outline of
burial pit

N

0   20
centimeters

Shroud
exterior

Outline of
shroud

Contents:

One gourd (G1).

> G1 positioned upright. It was under the outer shroud, adjacent to the north side of the brick under the head. It contained beans, 6 *Phaseolus lunatus* and 25 *Phaseolus vulgaris*.

Thin sheets of folded copper in mouth (1.7 x 1.5 x 0.4 cm, 1.1 g).

Small piece of copper sheet in right hand (1.2 x 0.6 x 0.2 cm, 0.2 g).

Small piece of copper sheet in left hand (1.1 x 0.7 x 0.2 cm, 0.3 g).

[See next page]

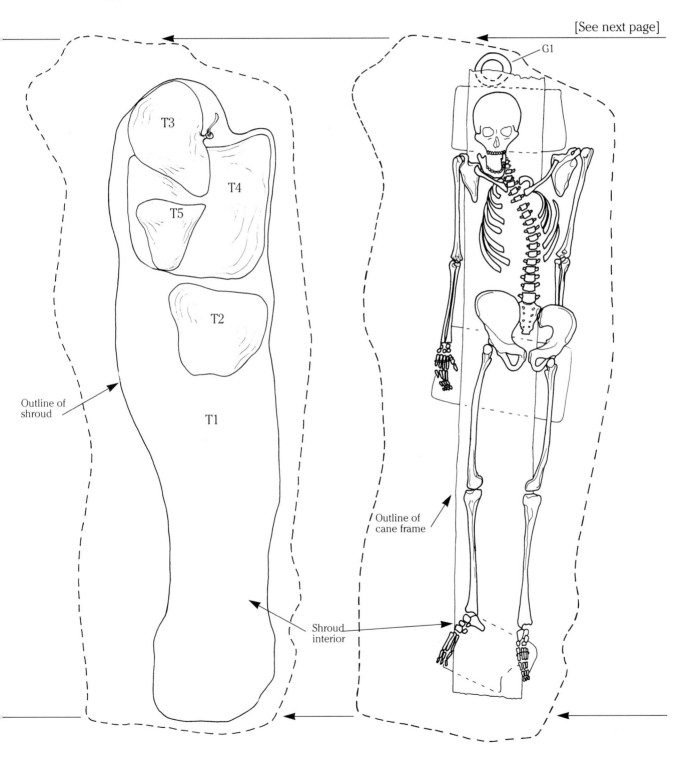

Outline of shroud

Shroud interior

Outline of cane frame

Nine textiles.

Textile 1, an outer shroud wrapped around the body and cane frame. Wrapping began beneath the right side of the body, passing under and over the body, then passing under the body again and ending with a selvage edge diagonally across the top central part of the body.

Textile 2, a loincloth, worn by the individual. It was gathered between the legs, brought up above the pelvis, and tied near the left hip.

Textile 3, a head cloth, wrapped around the head, covering the mouth and upper part of the face, leaving the chin exposed. It appears to have been tied on the left side of the head.

Textile 4, a shirt in the area of the upper body, covering the shoulders.

Textile 5, a bag, in the area of the chest. Contained a *mallero,* two wood objects, 135 coca leaf fragments, 3 coca endocarps (*Erythroxylum novogranatense*), 2 cotton (*Gossypium barbadense*) seeds, and 1 unidentifiable plant fragment.

Textile 6 covered the cane frame. The shrouded body was on top of this textile.

Textile 7 around Textile 5, with its corners tied together.

Textile 9 attached to *mallero* (A) inside Textile 5.

Textile 10, an inner shroud, wrapped around the body.

Yarn around right hand.

Yarn around left hand.

Yarn around right foot.

Yarn around left foot.

One stone *mallero* (A) inside the bag.

Two long wood objects (B, C) inside the bag (Textile 5).

Comments:

The burial pit was cut 20-25 cm into *cascajo.* An adobe was placed under the head, pelvis, and feet. For further information on the textiles see Donnan and Donnan, this volume.

[See previous page]

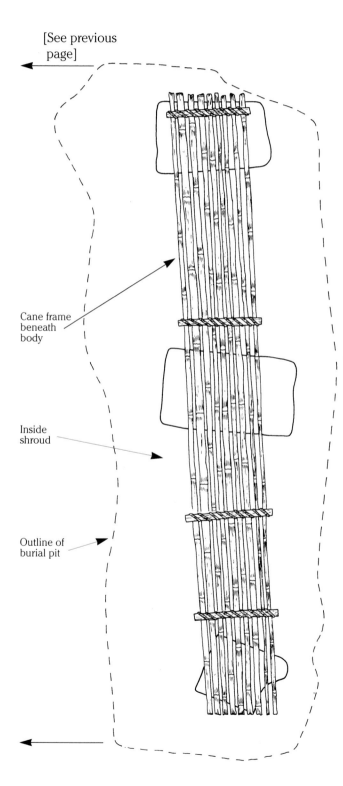

Cane frame beneath body

Inside shroud

Outline of burial pit

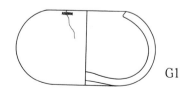

G1

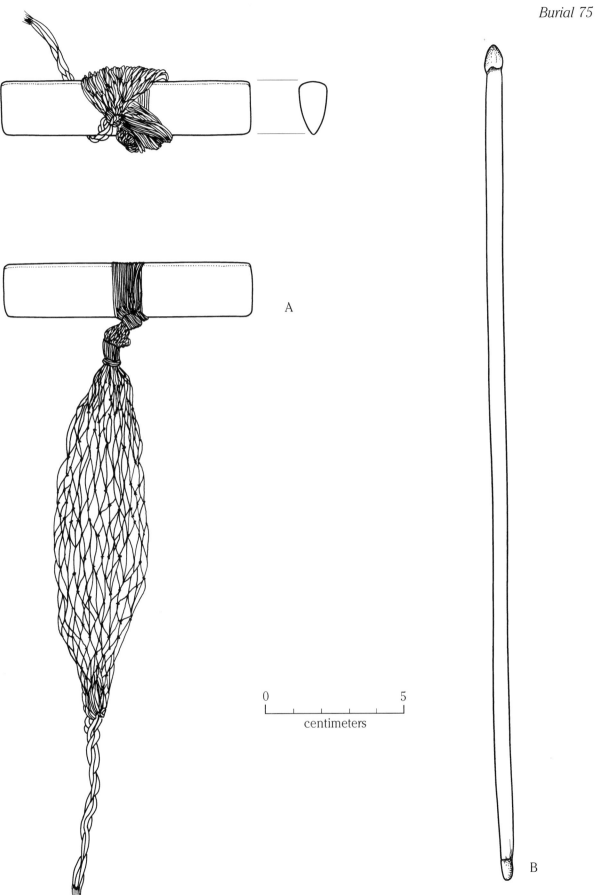

A

B

0 _____ 5
centimeters

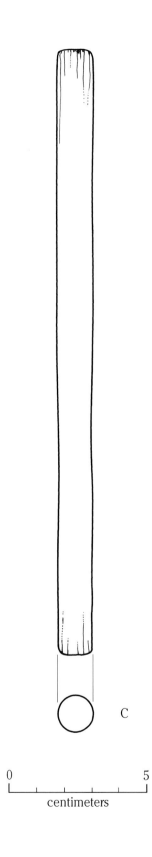

C

0   5
|__|__|__|__|__|
   centimeters

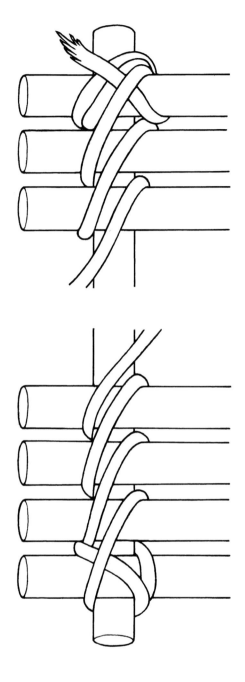

Details of cane lashing

Burial 76

Original Field Number: H1R5 B1a
Sex: Female
Age: 19-22
Burial Type:
    Shroud Wrap.

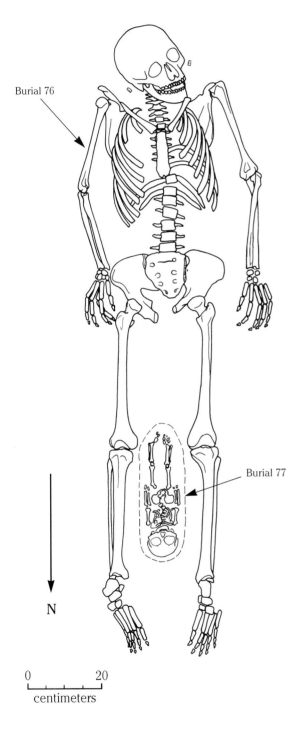

Burial 76

Burial 77

N

```
0          20
└─┴─┴─┴─┴─┘
  centimeters
```

Contents:
One copper spindle whorl near right wrist (A).
Fragments of sheet copper near mouth.
Silver sheet near mouth.
One textile.
    Textile 1, a shroud, wrapped around the body.
Beads around the right wrist.
    34 uniconically drilled shell (*Spondylus*?).
Beads around the left wrist.
    103 uniconically drilled lapis lazuli. They appear to have been on a single strand, double looped.
Beads around the neck.
    24 small shell.
    6 chrysocola (?).
Two small bone ear ornaments, one near each ear, each ornament inlaid with a single disk of chrysocola. Each disk incised with a small ring slightly off center (B, C).

Comments:
This is a double burial of a young adult female, Burial 76, with an infant, Burial 77, between her knees. The dashed line around the infant indicates the perimeter of a decomposed textile wrapping. The bodies lay in a shallow depression cut into a floor which lies directly on *cascajo*. A layer of reddish silty sand, which appears to be *cascajo* dug from under the floor, caps the burial. No outline of a grave pit could be defined. The body of the adult appears to have been wrapped in a large textile with the infant inside the shroud. There is no evidence of cane. See Burial 77.

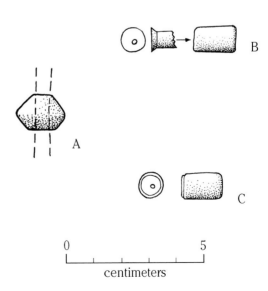

```
0                    5
└─┴─┴─┴─┴─┘
     centimeters
```

Burial 77

Original Field Number: H1R5 B1b
Sex: ?
Age: Less than 6 months
Burial Type:
   Shroud Wrap.
Contents:
   One textile.
      Textile 1, a shroud, wrapped around the body.
Comments:
   See Burial 76.

Burial 78

Original Field Number: H1R5 B2
Sex: ?
Age: 11-13
Burial Type:
    Cane Frame.
Contents:
    One textile.
        Textile 1, a shroud wrapped around the body.
Comments:
    The burial was in refuse, approximately 40 cm above *cascajo*. Faint evidence of textile and a cane frame beneath the body, with three cross braces: one under the head, the hips, and the feet.

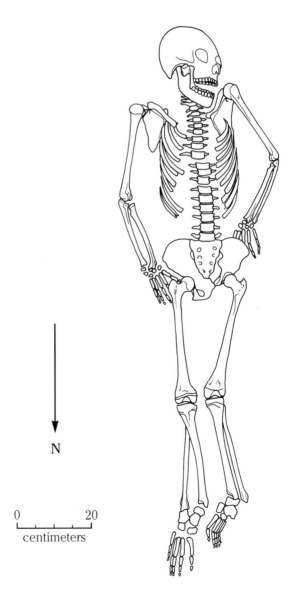

N

0   20
centimeters

Burial 79

Original Field Number: H20 B1
Sex: Female
Age: 25-30
Burial Type:
    Cane Frame.
Contents:
    Two ceramic vessels (1, 2).
    One ceramic spindle whorl (A).

Seven gourd impressions (G1-G7).
    G1 (10 cm diameter).
    G2 (18 cm diameter).
    G3 (25 cm diameter), contained dark, beach sand.
    G4 (8 cm diameter).
    G5 (8 cm diameter), contained squash (*Cucurbita* sp.) seeds.
    G6 (13 cm diameter).
    G7 (17 cm diameter), contained squash (*Cucurbita* sp.) seeds.

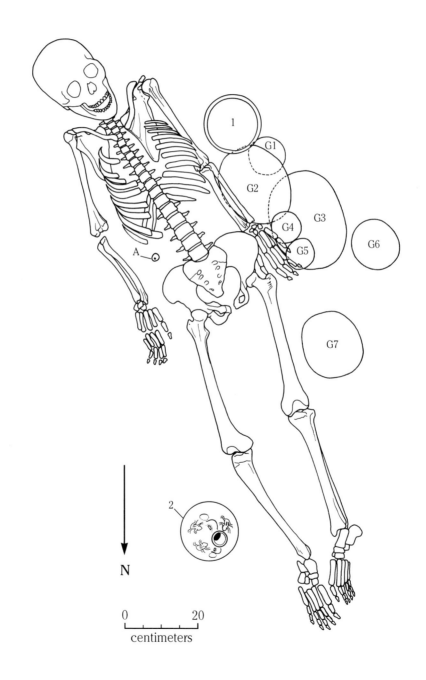

N

0   20
centimeters

Copper in mouth.

Copper in right hand.

Copper in left hand.

One textile.

    Textile 1, a shroud, wrapped around the body and cane frame.

Organic staining on left side of body in area of gourds.

Fish remains in area of gourds.

Comments:

    The burial pit was cut into *cascajo*. Llama toes, 5-10 cm above and to right of burial, possibly associated with burial. Remnants of the cane frame indicated it was 13 canes wide, and supported with four cross braces: one at the top and one at the bottom of the frame, one under the hips, and one under the knees. For further information on the textiles see Donnan and Donnan, this volume.

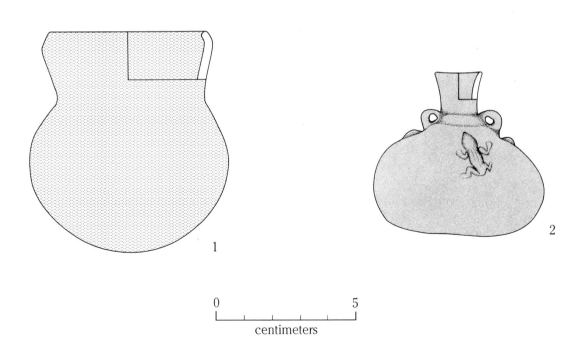

1

2

0   5

centimeters

Burial 80

Original Field Number: H31 B11

Sex: Male
Age: 30-40

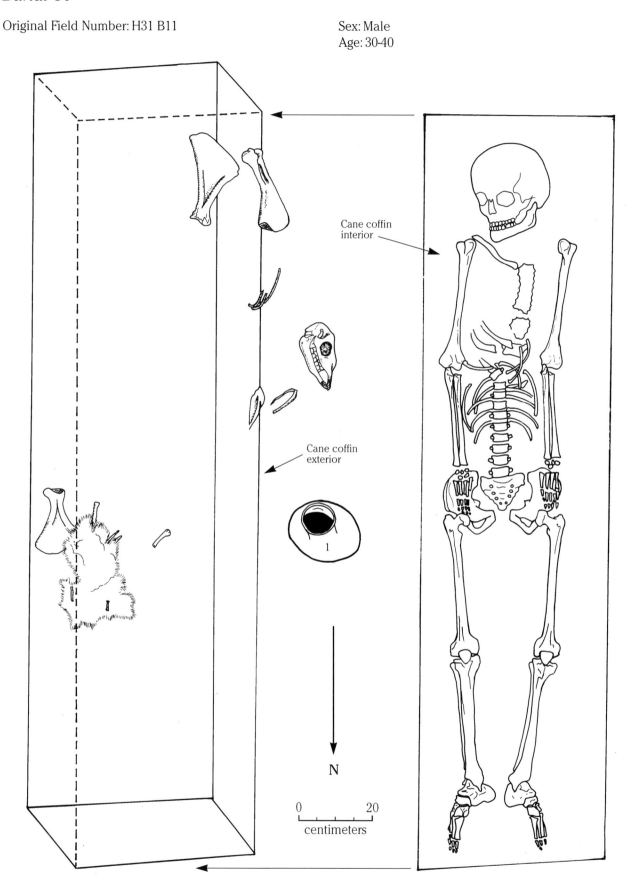

Cane coffin interior

Cane coffin exterior

1

N

0   20
centimeters

Burial Type:

Cane Coffin. The southern one-fourth of the coffin appears to have been wrapped with sedge rope.

Contents:

One ceramic vessel (1).

Ceramic 1, owl facing southwest.

Two gourds (G1, G2), containing llama rib bones beneath left hip, inside the coffin.

Copper fragment in mouth.

Sixteen textiles.

Textile 1, a loincloth, tied around hips.

Textile 3, an outer shroud, wrapped around body.

Textile 6a, a bag, above the chest on top of the coffin. (See Donnan and Donnan Fig. 13 this volume.)

Textile 7 under left side of head.

Textile 9 near head.

Textile 12 under head.

Textile 14 bundled under head.

Textile 17, a middle shroud, wrapped around body.

Textile 22, an inner shroud (?), wrapped around body.

Textile 24 under head.

Textile 29 near head.

Textile 16, a loincloth tie (?).*

Textile 19, a loincloth.*

Textile 13 over the cotton covering the face in area of the eyes.

Textile 28.*

Textile 30.*

Unspun cotton covering the face in area of the eyes, underneath Textile 13.

Red yarn wrapped around fingers of right hand, at mid-fingers.

Red yarn wrapped around fingers of left hand.

Yellow feather plume headdress ornament near right side of head (Fig. 17).

Llama bones on top of left side of cane coffin.

Llama rib bones in stacked gourds (G1, G2).

Llama bones and fur over right knee and lower leg, on top of coffin.

Immature llama cranium and forefeet on left side of body near the humerus, outside of coffin.

Guinea pig bones and fur over right knee and lower leg.

Fish remains under left side of head, inside of coffin.

Beans (*Phaseolus sp.*) under right side of head, inside of coffin.

Comments:

The burial was 1.5 meters below the base bricks of the east face of H31 near southeast corner. The pit was cut into *cascajo*. Five layers of plant material were placed above the burial, a single layer of adobes capped the plant material, and the adobes were sealed with clay 167 cm above the tomb. The hair on the individual was 21 cm long. For further information on the textiles see Donnan and Donnan, this volume. Cane from the coffin in this burial produced a radiocarbon date of 1350 ± 80 B.P. (A.D. 600), Beta-89546.

---

* This textile was discovered in the laboratory, when objects from the textiles were being analyzed. Its original location in the burial could not be determined.

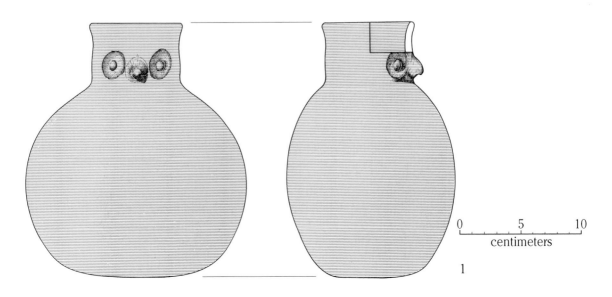

0   5   10
centimeters

1

Burial 81

Original Field Number: RG79 B1
Sex: ?
Age: Approximately 6 months
Burial Type:
  Shroud Wrap.
Contents:
  Two textiles.
      Textile 1, a shroud, wrapped around the body.
      Textile 2 wrapped around the head.
  Woven mat adhered to the skull.
Comments:
  The burial pit (52 cm long x 16 cm wide x 7 cm deep) was cut into the floor near a wall of a room. Numerous Moche sherds were in the surrounding refuse. The burial was partially disturbed, the lower legs were missing, and textile preservation was very poor.

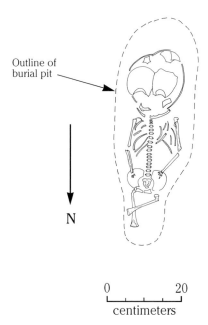

Outline of burial pit

N

0   20
  centimeters

Burial 82

Original Field Number: RG79 B2
Sex: Male
Age: 20-25
Burial Type:
Indeterminate.
Contents:
One textile.
Textile 1 over the pelvis.
Comments:
The burial was in loose fill of brown soil, sand, ash, and abundant shells and sherds. It had been disturbed prior to excavation. The skull, the top three vertebrae, the upper right arm, and some foot bones were missing. Some of the bones displayed considerable weathering on their upper surfaces suggesting that the skeleton had been partially exposed for some time. The burial is 1.5 meters south of Burial 83, but there is no evidence of association. For further information on the textiles see Donnan and Donnan, this volume.

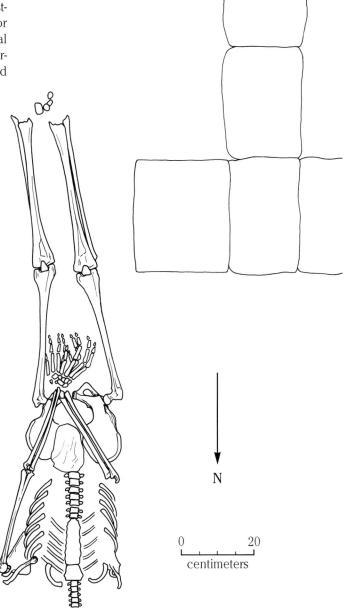

N

0   20
centimeters

Burial 83

Original Field Number: RG79 B3
Sex: Female
Age: 30-35
Burial Type:
    Shroud Wrap.
Contents:
    Three textiles.
        Textile 1, over the right shoulder, was attached to
            Textile 2.
        Textile 2 wrapped around the head attached to
            Textile 1.
        Textile 3, a shroud, wrapped around the body.
            The wrapping started from the left side of
            the body, encircled it, then ended with the
            selvage also along the left side. It was gath-
            ered between the legs.
Comments:
    The burial was in loose fill of brown soil, sand, shells
    and sherds. It was 1.5 m north of Burial 82, but there
    is no evidence of association. The lower right arm,
    some foot bones, and some left hand bones were
    missing. For further information on the textiles see
    Donnan and Donnan, this volume.

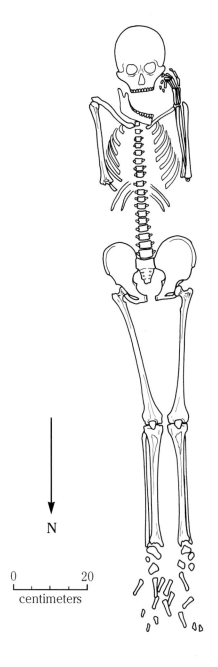

N

0   20
centimeters

Burial 84

Original Field Number: RG79 B4
Sex: Male
Age: 20-25
Burial Type:
    Shroud Wrap.
Contents:
    One textile.
        Textile 1, a shroud, wrapped around the body
        from left to right with the selvage ending
        along left side of body. The shroud was
        sewn along the selvage, gathering excess
        material under the seam.

Comments:
    The burial pit was indistinguishable from the sur-
    rounding loose fill. A stone was under the head, and
    adobes were under the pelvis and knees. For further
    information on the textiles see Donnan and Don-
    nan, this volume.

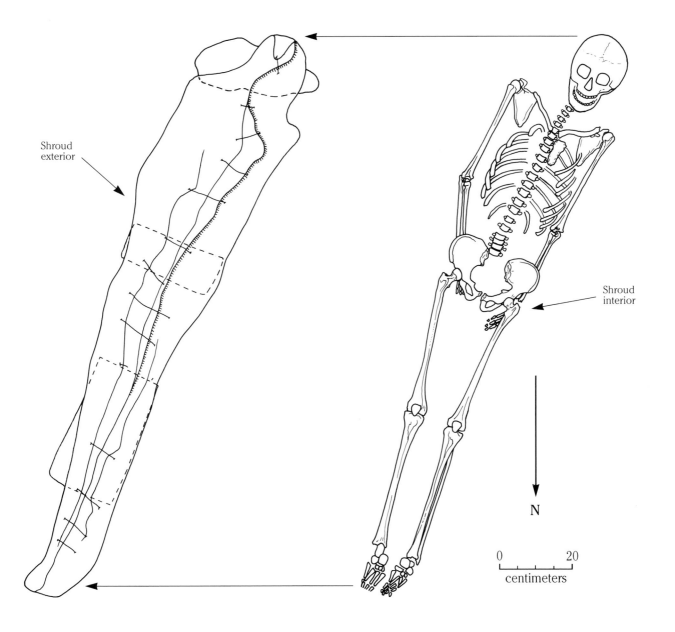

Shroud
exterior

Shroud
interior

N

0   20
    centimeters

RESUMEN:
Tumbas Moche en Pacatnamú

Entre 1984 y 1987 se excavaron ochenta y cuatro tumbas Moche (Tabla 1); del 1 a 67 provienen del cementerio H45CM1 (ver mapa y Figs. 1-2); tres (68-70), de un área que podría haber estado reservada para el entierro de niños; las restantes (71-84), de otras ocho áreas del sitio. 28 son adultos de sexo masculino, 27 del femenino, 2 adultos cuyo sexo no se pudo identificar, y 27 niños.

Preparación del Cuerpo

Todos los cuerpos estuvieron en posición extendida. La mayoría de las tumbas mejor conservadas carecían de restos de vestido; algunas conservaron una camisa (tumbas 4, 17), taparrabos (tumba 80) o ambos (tumba 75). Ninguna presentó calzado. La mujer en la tumba 2 tenía el pelo trenzado (Verano, Fig. 4, este volumen). En muchas, se usó lana para envolver la cabeza, manos, muñecas, tobillos, pies o piernas.

En las tumbas mejor preservadas hubo algodón sobre los ojos o cara, puesto antes que el cuerpo fuese envuelto en tejidos. Varios individuos presentaron algodón bajo la cabeza o debajo de todo el cuerpo. En algunos casos, la cabeza descansaba sobre tejidos, estaban debajo del cuerpo, sobre la cara, o envolvían la cabeza.

Envoltura del Cuerpo

Hubo cinco tipos que muestran la complejidad de las prácticas funerarias y reflejan el incremento de materia prima y uso de mano de obra.

Envoltura con Mortaja

El más simple consistió en envolver el cuerpo con una mortaja de algodón llano, cosiéndolo a lo largo de la parte superior (Fig. 4). En algunos casos se usaron dos o tres mortajas, siendo las interiores de tejido mas fino, no estando cosidas.

Refuerzo con Tablillas

El cuerpo fue envuelto con la mortaja y se usaron varillas de madera a lo largo del envoltorio, con la finalidad de mantener el cuerpo rígido (Fig. 5).

Bastidor o Camilla de Cañas

El cuerpo envuelto con la mortaja fue puesto sobre una camilla rígida de cañas; el fardo y la camilla fueron luego envueltos con otro tejido y cosidos (Fig. 6).

Tubo de Caña

El cuerpo era envuelto con una mortaja y luego con una estera que formaba un tubo, la cual era amarrada con sogas. En los extemos del tubo, algunas veces, se colocaban platos hechos de calabazas, poco profundos.

Ataúd de Cañas

El cuerpo envuelto en la mortaja era depositado dentro de una caja hecha con un bastidor de caña de grandes dimensiones, el cual había sido doblado en cuatro puntos, formando los lados del ataúd (Fig. 8). Los dos extremos fueron hechos de pequeños bastidores de cañas, que fueron colocados luego que el cadaver estuvo dentro del bastidor mas grande (Fig. 9). Algunos ataúdes fueron envueltos con sogas, formando complejos diseños.

El envoltorio de los cuerpos en una mortaja parece haber sido práctica universal de los Moche. Los cinco tipos de entierros parecen reflejar posición social y edad. Los niños eran enterrados envueltos en mortajas o en mortajas reforzadas con tablillas. Los adultos enterrados solo con una mortaja, tenían muy pocas ofrendas funerarias o carecían de ellas. Los sepultados en Camilla o Bastidor, Tubo, o Ataúdes de Cañas, eran adultos de sexo masculino o femenino, de más de 15 años de edad, y poseían un número mayor de ofrendas funerarias que los otros tipos de envoltorios funerarios.

Cámaras Funerarias

Las 84 tumbas eran pozos simples, de forma rectangular u ovalada, con pisos planos o ligeramente cóncavos y con una profundidad de 40 a 100 cms. La mayoría estaban orientados en un eje norte-sur, con la cabeza ubicada en el lado sur. Sólo una (Tumba 82) contuvo un individuo con la cabeza ubicada en el lado norte, mientras 4 (3, 16, 56 y 67) fueron depositados con la cabeza en el lado este.

Objetos Asociados

La mayoría contuvo piezas de cerámica (Figs. 10-13), aunque nunca más de seis. Las tumbas de adultos de ambos sexos contuvieron cantidades similares, mientras las de los niños menos; no hay evidencias de diferencias en la forma o tipo de cerámica entre hombres y mujeres, o adultos y niños, así como correlación entre sexo y edad e iconografía.

En prácticamente todas las tumbas con buena conservación, se recuperaron mates de calabaza (Fig. 14); se hallaron en mayor cantidad y número de tumbas que cerámica, llegando a recuperarse 21 piezas en una tumba (44).

Otras plantas fueron escasas (ver Gumerman, este volumen) y, normalmente, estuvieron dentro de los mates y la cerámica; además, dentro de ellos, se reportó restos de larvas e insectos, lo que denota que contuvieron comida preparada. La tumba 21 fué la única que presentó una cuchara, hecha de tutuma (Crescentia Cujete).

Restos de animales, completos o parciales, fueron frecuentes en sepulturas de adultos, pero raros en las de niños. 13 contuvieron restos de llamas, pero una sola (Tumba 60-62) contuvo un ejemplar completo. La ofrenda más común consistió en las cuatro patas y la cabeza, depositadas a un lado del cuerpo; se asocian, con mayor frecuencia, a tumbas con Bastidores o Camillas, Tubo, o Ataúdes de Caña. La tumba 80 presentó restos de Cuy y escamas de pescado, mientras las tumbas 9, 21, 73 y 79 presentaron huesos de pescado y la tumba 2, escamas de peces.

El cobre estuvo presente sin distinción de sexo o edad, pero sólo la tumba 76 presentó una delgada lámina de plata en la boca. El peso del cobre, por tumba, varió entre alrededor de 2 a 247 gramos; sin embargo, la mayoría contuvo entre 10 y 50 gramos. 47 tumbas presentaron cobre en la boca del individuo; 27 en la mano derecha y 31 en la izquierda. 18 presentaron cobre en la boca y en ambas manos; 4 en las manos, pero no en la boca. De 25 tumbas con cobre en la boca y en una o en ambas manos, sólo en dos casos el cobre de una de las manos pesó más que el de la boca, aunque con frecuencia el peso del metal en ambas manos es mayor que el de la boca. 13 lo tuvieron en un lugar diferente a la boca o las manos, pero fué de menor peso. El metal ubicado en la boca o en las manos estuvo, generalmente, envuelto en algodón o con hilo de este material, aunque hubo algunos que pudieron haberlo estado en fragmentos de tejido. La forma fué normalmente amorfa, aunque hubieron pedazos de láminas delgadas que habían sido dobladas varias veces (ver Lechtman, este volumen). Dos tumbas (17 y 31) presentaron fragmentos de cerámica en las manos, envueltas en algodón, como si fuesen ofrendas de cobre.

Entre los adornos de uso personal se recuperaron orejeras, en tumbas de mujeres adultas (2, 53, 73, 76), confeccionadas en madera o hueso y con incrustaciones de piedra (Fig. 16); collares, en 12 tumbas, hechos con conchas, piedras, cobre o pedazos de mates; brazaletes de diferentes materiales; y un penacho de plumas (Fig. 17) de un tipo presente en la iconografía Moche (Fig. 18).

Los varones presentaron mayor cantidad de textiles que las mujeres; los niños tuvieron menos que los adultos, pero esto puede deberse a la forma más simple de los envoltorios funerarios. En algunas tumbas se recuperaron piezas de vestido y accesorios, incluyendo camisas, mantos, taparrabos, tocados de cabeza y bolsas (ver Donnan y Donnan, este volumen); algunos lo tenían puesto, pero la mayoría había sido depositado al lado del cadáver.

Los husos se hallaron sólo en tumbas de mujeres: 20 de las 27 los tuvieron. Trece tenían uno, mientras siete poseyeron dos. La mayoría era de piedra o de cerámica, excepto por dos de cobre (Tumbas 34 y 76) y uno de coronta de maíz (31). Los malleros fueron exclusivos de los varones y se hallaron en tres tumbas (9, 15 y 75).

Entierros Múltiples

Hay por lo menos cuatro casos de entierros múltiples (Tumbas 44-45; 58-59; 60-62; y 76-77) Existe la posibilidad que algunos sean entierros secundarios, sobre todo en los casos de los niños. No hay evidencia de sacrificios humanos incluidos en la muestra.

Cronología

La muestra es difícil de adscribir cronológicamente. La mayoría no contenía cerámica que pudiese compararse con la secuencia de Larco. Las Tumbas 20 y 64 tenían piezas que pueden ser de la fase III (o fase tardía II). Las comparaciones con las tumbas excavadas por Ubbelohde-Doering permiten afirmar que practicamente todas las tumbas pertenecen a la fase III, con la única excepción de la Tumba 48 que contiene una pieza de cerámica de características Virú (Gallinazo). Las Tumbas 35 y 37 presentaron cerámica de ese estilo al lado de piezas Moche.

23 tumbas, en H45CM1, no contuvieron cerámica, pero estratigráficamente estuvieron mezcladas con las tumbas de la fase III. Fuera de este cementerio, no es posible fechar las tumbas sin cerámica, ya que carecen de asociaciones.

Tres fechados radiocarbónicos, provenientes de H45CM1, dan una apariencia tardía:

Tumba 20   1260 ± 80 A.P   750 N.E (Calibrada)
Tumba 25   1480 ± 80 A.P   510 N.E (Calibrada)
Tumba 80   1350 ± 80 A.P   600 N.E (Calibrada)

El fechado de 750 N.E. es sorprendente, pues corresponde a la fase V, ya que se espera un fechado de 400 N.E. para la fase III. Un fechado reciente, proveniente del cercano sitio Moche de Dos Cabezas, sugiere que la fase I no empezó hasta el 350 N.E. (Donnan, ms.). Por ello, al tratar la cronología absoluta Moche, es necesario revisar los fechados existentes, así como aumentar su número mediante fechados de las porciones de la secuencia para las que se tiene poca información.

Physical Characteristics and Skeletal Biology of the Moche Population at Pacatnamu

John W. Verano

Until recently, the physical characteristics of the Moche were known primarily from their depictions of themselves in ceramics. Despite the fact that Moche sites have been excavated by archaeologists since the early part of this century, only a handful of descriptions of Moche skeletal remains are available (Kroeber 1926, 1930; Stewart 1943; Verano 1987, 1991, 1994). Because Pacatnamu had an extensive Moche occupation and has provided abundant skeletal remains for study, it is a particularly important site for the study of the physical characteristics and skeletal biology of the Moche.

This report presents the results of analysis of Moche skeletal remains recovered from excavations and surface collections at Pacatnamu during the 1983-1987 field seasons. The sample is composed of the remains of 67 individuals from the H45CM1 cemetery, 17 individuals from excavation units in other areas of the site, and surface collections (approximately 590 specimens) made from three looted cemeteries (S2, S20, and S24, Fig. 1).

Surface Survey and Collection

Surface surveys conducted in 1983 and 1984 identified over 25 looted Moche cemeteries located within the architectural complex of Pacatnamu and scattered across the pampa within a radius of approximately two kilometers of the outer wall of the site (Fig. 1). Skeletal material on the surface of most of these cemeteries was sparse and poorly preserved, but cemeteries S2, S20, and S24 showed abundant and relatively well preserved skeletal remains. These cemeteries were selected for intensive surface collection and for limited test excavations to identify the form and stratigraphic context of the tombs (Fig. 2).

Skeletal Preservation

Bone preservation is generally very good at Pacatnamu, although Moche skeletons often show damage from salt crystal growth on their external surfaces and within hollow cavities of bones (Fig. 3). At Pacatnamu, salt crystal growth on bone is unique to the Moche burials. Late Period burials at the site have well preserved textiles and other organic material, and the bodies found in these tombs generally have well preserved skin and hair, with no evidence of salt crystal growth. The relatively poor preservation of organic material and the presence of salt crystals on Moche skeletons suggest that the soil surrounding them was wet at some time in the past. There is a growing body of archaeological evidence that heavy rains fell on the North Coast of Peru around A.D. 1100, during a major El Niño event (Nials et al. 1979a, b; Donnan 1986a:22, 1990; Shimada 1990).

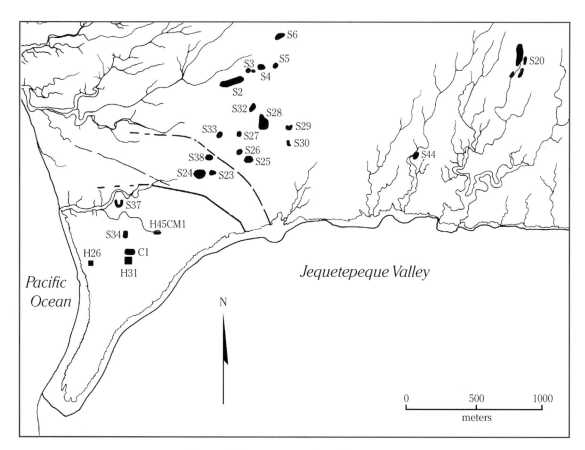

Figure 1. Moche cemeteries at Pacatnamu.

Figure 2. A looted Moche tomb in Cemetery S24.

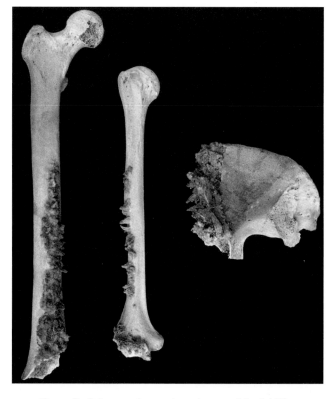

Figure 3. Salt crystal growth on bones of Burial 79.

Figure 4. Braided hair, Burial 2.

The preservational differences seen between Moche and Late Period burials at Pacatnamu provide further evidence of this event.

While all of the Moche burials we excavated were fully skeletonized, remains of hair (Fig. 4) occasionally were found. A Moche shaft tomb excavated by Ubbelohde-Doering at Pacatnamu in the late 1930s showed excellent organic preservation, including mummified human remains (Ubbelohde-Doering 1959, 1967). One of the individuals in this tomb, a female estimated to be 18 years of age, had tattooed designs on her forearms (*ibid*. 1967:30). The preservation of this burial was very unusual; all other Moche burials excavated by Ubbelohde-Doering were fully skeletonized.

Demographic Composition of Moche Cemeteries

One objective of surface collecting the Moche cemeteries was to establish a preliminary demographic profile of cemetery populations at the site. Examination of the skeletal material collected from the surface of cemeteries S2, S20, and S24 revealed that each contained skeletal remains representing all age groups, from infants to old adults. Based on a count of left innominates (Table 1, page 204), males and females were present in approximately equal numbers. Remains of infants and young children were relatively rare, however. This probably reflects the greater susceptibility of subadult remains to damage from looting and subsequent exposure on the surface,

although it is possible that not all infants and children were buried in cemetery areas (see H45CM1, below).

The H45CM1 Cemetery

The H45CM1 cemetery is important because it is the only cemetery at Pacatnamu that was found intact, and it has been excavated fully. The remains of 67 individuals were recovered from the cemetery. The age and sex distribution (Table 2, page 204) is similar to that of the surface-collected cemeteries, but provides greater precision. The greatest number of individuals fall into either the 0-4 year or adult age categories, while relatively few fall into the child and adolescent age range (ages 5-19). The age distribution for H45CM1 (Fig. 5) is consistent with a U-shaped mortality curve commonly observed in living human populations, where probability of death is highest during the first year of life, declines during early childhood and adolescence, and climbs sharply again in the adult years (Acsádi and Nemeskéri 1970; De Jong 1972). Among adolescents and adults for which sex could be determined on skeletal criteria, 23 were classified as male and 23 female. Based on its overall age and sex distribution, H45CM1 can be considered a representative mortuary population, although one might expect a larger number of individuals in the 0-0.9 year group.

It is possible that some infants were buried in locations other than the cemetery area. Isolated burials of infants and young children have been

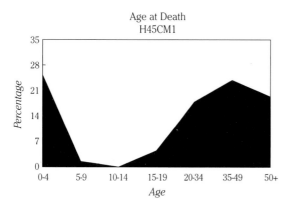

Figure 5. Mortality curve of H45CM1.

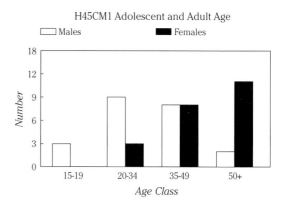

Figure 6. Adolescent and adult mortality profile of H45CM1.

found in various locations at Pacatnamu. During the 1987 field season, a group of three Moche child burials was discovered in a small ravine southeast of Huaca 26 (see Site Map, pages 18-19). No adult remains were found in this ravine, suggesting that the location may have been reserved for the burial of children. Although infants may be underrepresented in H45CM1, the burial of a fetus (Burial 27) was found in the cemetery, accompanied by grave goods (Donnan and McClelland, this volume). The maximum width of the distal end of the humerus of Burial 27 measured approximately 7.0 millimeters, which, according to age standards developed by Fazekas and Kósa (1978), corresponds to a fetal age of 4.5 to 5.0 lunar months.

Mortality and Sex

The adolescent and adult mortality profile for H45CM1 is presented in Figure 6. Males and females show notable differences in mortality patterns. A substantially larger proportion of males in H45CM1 died as adolescents (15-19 years) and young adults (20-34 years), while the majority of females were old adults (50+ years). If these observed frequencies accurately reflect the mortality experience of the population sample from which H45CM1 was drawn—rather than factors such as sampling error or differential burial practices by sex—the data indicate that Moche females outlived males by an average of 19 years, based on mean age at death. Mortality differences such as these might reflect either engagement in more hazardous activities by men, greater resistance to infectious disease in females, or some combination of factors. Unfortunately, specific cause of death rarely can be determined from the skeleton. The only individual in the H45CM1 cemetery for whom probable cause of death can be

inferred is Burial 14, a young adult male who suffered multiple fractures, apparently as a result of a fall.

Physical Characteristics of the Moche

Ancient Peruvian coastal populations traditionally have been described as broad headed (brachycephalic) peoples of relatively short stature (Hrdlička 1911, 1914, 1938; Newman 1943, 1947; Stewart 1943). This is a fair generalization for the Moche at Pacatnamu, who can be classified as broad headed, with wide faces and relatively narrow noses (Table 3, page 205). It should be noted, however, that approximately half of the Moche crania—both males and females—show artificial cranial deformation (Table 4, page 205), which takes the form of a mild to pronounced flattening of the occipital region (Fig. 7). The flattening is sometimes symmetrical relative to the coronal plane, but more often it is more pronounced on the left or right side (Table 4). Mild occipital flattening probably would not be perceptible in the living person, although pronounced cases might be. Examination of the skulls, however, reveals both visible and measurable broadening of the cranial vault in those that show occipital flattening (Verano 1987:109-120).

The form of cranial deformation seen at Pacatnamu is common in cranial collections from coastal Peru. It has been given various names, including "tabular erecta" (Imbelloni 1933), "fronto-occipital" (Stewart 1943), and "deformación por cuna" (Weiss 1972). Because of its minimal effect on the shape of the skull and its variability in expression, it is generally considered to be an unintentional result of infant cradleboarding rather than a conscious attempt to alter the shape of the head (Stewart 1943; Weiss, 1972).

Interestingly, no depictions of infants in cradleboards are known from Moche art, nor have physi-

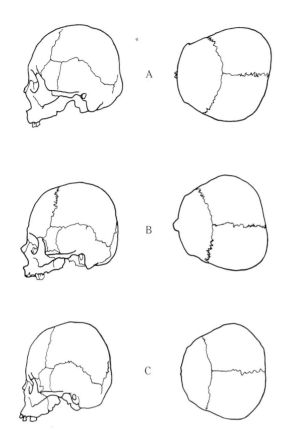

Figure 7. Examples of cranial deformation at Pacatnamu. Illustrations A and B show asymmetrical occipital flattening; Illustration C shows symmetrical flattening.

cal remains of cradleboards been found in a Moche context. However, well preserved cradles and objects which may have been associated with cradleboarding have been recovered from Late Intermediate Period contexts at several sites, including Pacatnamu (Stewart, 1943; Weiss 1972; Verano and Cordy-Collins 1986; Verano 1994). Late Intermediate Period skulls at Pacatnamu show the same type of deformation as do Moche skulls, suggesting that a similar mechanism produced the deformation (Verano 1987). The lack of recovery of cradleboard paraphernalia from Moche contexts simply may reflect the relatively poor preservation of organic material from this time period.

Living Stature

Estimates of adult stature for the Moche population at Pacatnamu are presented in Table 5, page 206. Stature estimates calculated for Moche burials at Complejo El Brujo, located at the mouth of the Chicama Valley (Verano and Anderson n.d.), and for a larger mixed time period surface collection from

the Chicama Valley (Hrdlička 1938), as well as summary data from two modern samples from the Lambayeque Valley (Lasker 1962) are presented for comparison. For the skeletal samples, living stature was estimated from maximum femoral length using stature formulae developed by Genovés (1967). For burials excavated at Pacatnamu, sex was determined on the basis of pelvic morphology. Surface-collected femora from Pacatnamu were sexed by maximum femoral head diameter, based on distributions developed from pelvically-sexed individuals.[1] Hrdlička sexed his disassociated femora on the basis of general size and robusticity. The modern Lambayeque Valley sample is derived from measurements of living volunteers in the towns of Monsefú and San José by Gabriel Lasker (Lasker 1960, 1962).

Based on the Genovés formulae, Moche males at Pacatnamu averaged 157.6 centimeters (5'2") in height, with a range of 148.2 to 168.7 centimeters. Moche females averaged 146.8 centimeters (4'10"), with a range of 139.4 to 156.0 centimeters. Moche male stature at El Brujo averaged 159.9 centimeters, slightly higher than the Pacatnamu mean, while the small female sample from El Brujo averaged 146.6 centimeters. Hrdlička's Chicama Valley sample falls very close to the Pacatnamu and El Brujo values.

Results indicate that the prehistoric stature estimates are quite similar to living stature recorded for modern inhabitants of two traditional north coast communities. The similarity between the prehistoric and modern data indicates that adult stature in native North Coast populations has not changed substantially over the past 1,500 years.

Physical Variation between Cemetery Populations

One of the principal research questions that emerged from the surface survey of cemeteries at Pacatnamu was why the Moche buried their dead in more than 25 discrete cemeteries rather than in a single or small number of larger communal mortuary areas. One approach was to examine how much physical variation existed between different cemetery populations at the site, to determine whether or not cemetery samples appeared to represent genetically distinct groups. Since samples of crania were available for H45CM1 and the three

1. Maximum femoral head diameter was measured for a sample of 36 pelvically-sexed males and 28 pelvically-sexed females from Pacatnamu. Males showed a mean maximum femoral head diameter of 45.47 ± 2.25 mm, females 39.89 ± 1.57 mm. Based on these distributions, isolated femora with a femoral head diameter of less than 41.0 mm were classified as female, while those with a diameter greater than 43.0 mm were classified as male. Femora falling within the range of overlap (41.0 mm $< x < 43.0$ mm) were excluded from stature estimates.

surface-collected cemeteries, a study of cranial variation was conducted.

We used a set of craniofacial measurements, selected for their usefulness in identifying between-population differences (Howells 1973; Jantz 1973) and for their freedom from the effects of fronto-occipital deformation (Verano 1987: 109-120). Samples of adult crania from cemeteries S2, S20, S24, and H45CM1 were compared, using multivariate tests of distance and discrimination (canonical discriminant function analysis, Norusis 1985:93-98). Results of the analyses indicated that sufficient between-cemetery variation was found in craniofacial morphology to effectively distinguish the cemetery samples from one another (Fig. 8) and to assign isolated crania to their respective cemetery with a high degree of accuracy (Table 6, pages 207-208). For male crania, statistically significant generalized distances (Mahalanobis D^2) were found for the majority of between-cemetery comparisons, also indicating substantial differences between the different samples. Male and female crania were analyzed separately to avoid confounding size differences and unequal sample sizes with morphological differences between samples. Interestingly, females showed slightly less between-cemetery differences. This is indicated by values for Mahalanobis D^2 and by location of group means on canonical discriminant functions 1 and 2, which encompass the majority of between-group variation among samples (Fig. 8).

Since differences in craniofacial morphology between cemetery samples can be assumed to reflect genetic differences between groups, these results suggest that cemetery membership at Pacatnamu was based on lineage group. The greater between-cemetery differences found between males may indicate that females married out of their natal group, while males did not.

The Spanish Chronicler, Cieza de León, who traveled through the Jequetepeque Valley in 1547, noted that the Indians in the valley buried their dead by kinship group in the hills and bluffs above the valley floor:

> "En muchos valles de estos llanos, en saliendo del valle por las sierras de rocas y de arena ay hechas grandes paredes y apartamientos, adonde cada linage tiene su lugar establecido para enterrar sus difuntos..." Cieza de León 1984 [1553]:197.

Multivariate comparisons of Moche crania from different cemeteries at Pacatnamu suggest that burial by kinship group had considerable antiquity in the Jequetepeque Valley.

Diet and Nutrition

Data on Moche diet as reconstructed from the analysis of refuse deposits are presented by Gumerman in this volume. Additional information on diet can be derived from the analysis of stable istotopes in bone. In particular, a number of studies have demonstrated that

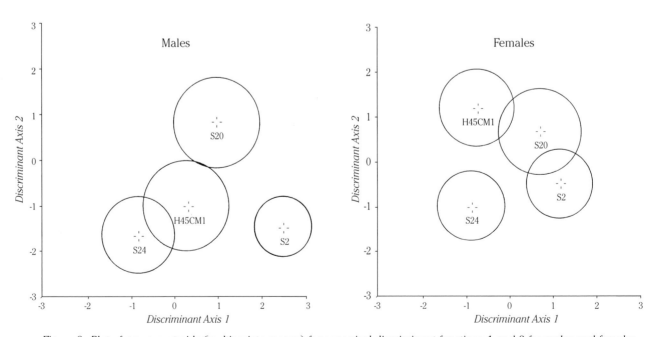

Figure 8. Plot of group centroids (multivariate means) for canonical discriminant functions 1 and 2 for males and females from cemeteries S2, S20, S24, and H45CM1.

$^{13}C/^{12}C$ and $^{15}N/^{14}N$ isotopic ratios of bone collagen can be used to estimate the relative proportions of marine versus terrestrial food sources in the diet (Schwarcz and Schoeninger 1991; Ambrose 1993). Such analyses can provide an independent test of results derived from the study of plant and faunal remains in refuse deposits.

Based on analyses of bone collagen from a sample of animals representing diverse environments and feeding strategies, Schoeninger and DeNiro (1984; also DeNiro 1987) developed an expected set of carbon and nitrogen isotopic ratios for animals following different dietary regimes. These expected values are diagrammed in Figure 9, where $^{13}C/^{12}C$ ratios are shown on the horizontal axis, and $^{15}N/^{14}N$ ratios on the vertical axis. The empty circle at the center of each box represents the mean isotopic ratio for the sample; the outer limits of each box represent two standard deviations from the mean (95 percent confidence interval). It can be seen that nitrogen isotopic ratios in bone collagen effectively distinguish marine from terrestrial feeders. Carbon ratios also can distinguish marine from terrestrial feeders, provided that C_4 plants, like maize, do not constitute a substantial portion of the terrestrial animal's diet. Note that the

terrestrial herbivore box in Figure 9 reflects a sample of exclusively C_3 plant eaters. Substantial consumption of C_4 plants (as might be expected in a maize-consuming population) would shift the ^{13}C value further to the right, towards less negative values.

Paleodietary reconstruction at Pacatnamu provides some information on the relative proportion of marine and terrestrial protein sources in the diet, as well as indirect data on the types of plant foods consumed by the Moche and Late Intermediate Period populations (Verano and DeNiro 1993). For the study, samples of femoral cortical bone were collected from nine Moche and ten Late Period burials. Collagen extracted from the ground bone samples was combusted, CO_2 and N_2 extracted, and isotopic composition of the carbon and nitrogen determined by mass spectrometer using procedures described in DeNiro and Epstein (1981) and Schoeninger and DeNiro (1984). Results are listed in Table 7, page 209, and plotted in Figure 9. The Pacatnamu Moche and Late Period human samples show substantial overlap with the isotopic signature of marine invertebrate and vertebrate eaters, indicating that marine protein was a major component of the diet. The mean values for $^{13}C/^{12}C$ ratios of –13.0 and –13.5 also suggest substantial consumption of C_4 plants such as maize. These results are consistent with the Moche diet reconstructed from refuse deposits at Pacatnamu: a mixed diet of C_3 and C_4 plants, with substantial consumption of marine protein.

Health and Disease

All skeletal material excavated and surface collected at Pacatnamu was examined for evidence of pathology. The descriptions below are limited to the most commonly observed pathologies and focus on those for which relative frequencies by age and sex can be calculated.

Degenerative Joint Disease (Osteoarthritis)

Degenerative changes in the joints of skeletons reflect the types of activities and stresses placed on particular joints during life. Examination of the frequency and distribution of degenerative joint disease, therefore, provides information on the activity patterns of ancient populations (Ortner 1968; Jurmain 1977). Data were collected on the frequency of degenerative joint changes by age, sex, and location in the skeleton for the H45CM1 cemetery sample. Degenerative changes were moderate, with no advanced patterns such as eburnation (articular cartilage destruction to the point of bone-to-bone contact) or severe distortion of the articular surfaces. The frequency of degenerative changes showed a strong correlation with age, as would

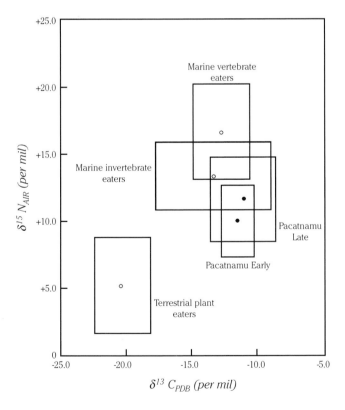

Figure 9. Stable carbon and nitrogen isotope values for Pacatnamu Moche and Late Intermediate Period bone collagen samples plotted against values derived from animals of known diets (after DeNiro 1987 and Verano and DeNiro 1993).

be expected. Degenerative changes in joints of the articular skeleton were found in all older adults, and in several younger adults as well. The hips, knees, shoulders, and elbows were most frequently affected. Arthritic changes in the temporomandibular joints also were common in old adults.

Degenerative changes at the hip and knee can be assumed to reflect weight-bearing stresses borne by these joints (Steinbock 1976:279), while changes at the shoulder and elbow joints reflect wear and tear from activities involving the upper limbs. Knee joints of both Moche and Late Intermediate Period skeletons at Pacatnamu often show a distinctive pattern of arthritis, characterized by an area of pitting and sclerosis on the posterior aspect of the lateral condyle of the femur (Fig. 10). The location of the lesion corresponds to the surface of the femoral condyle that would support upper body weight when a person is in a squatting position with the knees strongly flexed, and therefore appears to reflect habitual postural behavior during work or rest. Extension of normal joint surfaces and development of distinctive facets have been associated with habitual squatting or kneeling in other skeletal samples (Trinkaus 1975; Ubelaker 1979), but to my knowledge the only other finding of porous lesions of this kind is in a sample of isolated Peruvian femora from the Hrdlička Paleopathology Collection (Tyson and Alcauskas 1980).

The small number of young adult females and old adult males in the H45CM1 sample makes it difficult to compare the incidence of degenerative joint disease by sex. However, from the limited data available, there are no obvious sex differences in incidence or location. Within the context of degenerative joint disease, some changes were noted in non-synovial joints. Five adults in H45CM1 (three females and two males) showed intervertebral disc herniations or *Schmorl's nodes* (Ortner and Putschar 1981:430), which generally are believed to result from trauma to the intervertebral discs associated with lifting or carrying heavy objects. The Moche population at Pacatnamu, while not tall, was robust and strongly built, with prominent muscle markings observed in both men and women, reflecting a physically active lifestyle.

Comparative data on degenerative joint disease in ancient Peruvian populations are few and are difficult to compare with the present sample, because they are derived primarily from surface collected specimens with poor archaeological context. In Table 8, page 210, the incidence of joint involvement for H45CM1 adults is compared with data from Chicama Valley surface collections published by Hrdlička (1914). Hrdlička's figures record surprisingly low frequencies of degenerative joint disease compared with that of the H45CM1 cemetery. I suspect that Hrdlička classified only the most pronounced cases as arthritic, or perhaps his sample included a larger proportion of young individuals.

Rheumatoid Arthritis

Rheumatoid arthritis is a disease of connective tissue whose specific causes are still incompletely known. Although well-documented clinically, it is difficult to identify with certainty in archaeological remains, and

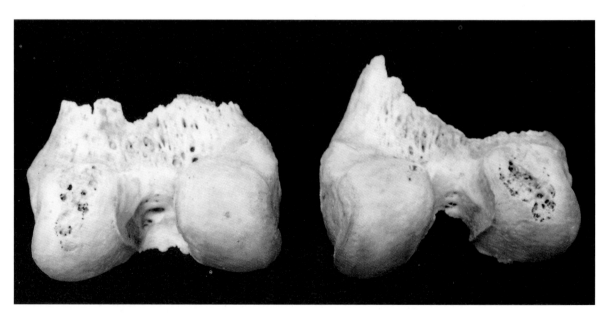

Figure 10. Arthritic changes (pitting and sclerosis) on the posterior aspect of the lateral femoral condyles.

debate continues about its antiquity in human populations (Ortner and Putschar 1981; Rogers, et al. 1987). However, rheumatoid arthritis shows some features, such as bilateral involvement of specific joints and a tendency to result in joint fusion, that help distinguish it from osteoarthritis.

Several examples of vertebral fusion and one example of sacroiliac joint fusion were found in surface material from Cemeteries S2 and S20. A single case of vertebral fusion was found in a burial from H45CM1. Most of these cases could represent either rheumatoid arthritis or a much rarer condition known as ankylosing spondylitis (Steinbock 1976; Ortner and Putschar 1981).

One specimen collected from the surface of Cemetery S2, consisting of the first four thoracic vertebrae, shows fusion of the intervertebral diarthrodial joints and fusion at the vertebral bodies. Costal pits on the vertebral bodies are pitted and lipped, and also suggest rib fusions, although no ribs were recovered. Another specimen from S2 consists of five thoracic vertebrae (T6-T9, T11), one lumbar vertebra (L1), and the left and right ninth ribs. Vertebrae T6-T9 are fused together at their diarthrodial joints. The left and right ninth ribs are also fused to the costal pits of T8/T9. There is no fusion of the vertebral bodies, as was seen in previous examples.

Another specimen from S2 is the left innominate and sacrum of a young adult female. The sacrum is fused to the left ilium. The right innominate was not found, but the right auricular surface of the sacrum looks normal, indicating that the fusion was not bilateral.

Burial 31, a female over 50 years of age, shows fusion of the second and third cervical vertebrae at both the intervertebral synovial joints and at the bodies.

Dental Pathology

Following degenerative joint disease, the most common pathological condition observed in the Moche skeletal collections is dental disease. Table 9, page 211, presents a tabulation of data in the H45CM1 sample, including the incidence of caries, antemortem tooth loss, abscesses, and periodontal disease. Caries were identified by visual inspection, as recommended by Rudney, et al. (1983). A tooth was scored absent antemortem if its alveolar socket(s) showed remodeling. Periodontal disease was scored present if there was pronounced alveolar resorption around tooth roots. Data are limited to adults, as only one juvenile showed dental caries.

Data in Table 9 indicate that caries and tooth loss were significant problems for H45CM1 adults. While the small sample of young adults (age 20-34) shows few dental pathologies, middle adults (age 35-49) show an average of 4.9 teeth (16.4 percent) lost antemortem, and caries present on an average of 4.1 (19.3 percent) of the remaining teeth. Old adults (age 50+) show an average of 17.2 teeth (53.6 percent) lost antemortem, with caries present on an average of 3.6 (39.9 percent) of those remaining. Tooth wear in this sample is moderate, so it can be assumed that most antemortem tooth loss was a result of caries, periodontal disease, or both.

Burial 53, an old adult female, illustrates the types of oral pathologies common in H45CM1 adults (Fig. 11). Present are multiple periapical abscesses of the upper teeth, pronounced alveolar resorption around the lower tooth roots, antemortem loss of seven teeth and interproximal caries on six.

The types of dental pathologies seen in H45CM1 adults, especially the frequency of caries, antemortem tooth loss, and periodontal disease, suggest that dental problems were a source of considerable suffering for the Moche population at Pacatnamu. In comparison to other skeletal samples from the site, H45CM1 does not appear to be unusual in this regard. It is difficult to quantify dental pathologies in surface-collected material because most skulls and mandibles are disassociated, and frequently much of the anterior dentition has fallen out. However, general observations of surface-collected skulls indicate a frequency of caries and antemortem tooth loss in the posterior dentition that is similar to the H45CM1 cemetery sample. Dental problems such as these were not only a source of pain and suffering, but a significant health concern as well, due to the risk of the spread of infection from abscessed teeth. Loss of appetite and difficulty of chewing were probably also common problems for adults with dental pathologies.

The high incidence of dental pathologies among the Moche at Pacatnamu is consistent with a growing body of data on dental disease among prehistoric agricultural populations in various parts of the world (Turner 1979; Cohen and Armelagos 1984; Powell 1985). These studies indicate a high incidence of caries and related dental pathologies in agriculturally-based populations with diets rich in carbohydrates and soft foods. The Moche diet, adequate as it may have been in terms of nutritional content (see below), nevertheless, was responsible for significant dental problems in adults.

Nutritional Stress Indicators

Indicators of nutritional stress during the childhood growth period, such as cribra orbitalia, porotic hyperostosis, and non-specific periostitis (Goodman et al. 1984), were relatively rare in the Moche skeletal collections from Pacatnamu,[2] in contrast to some of the

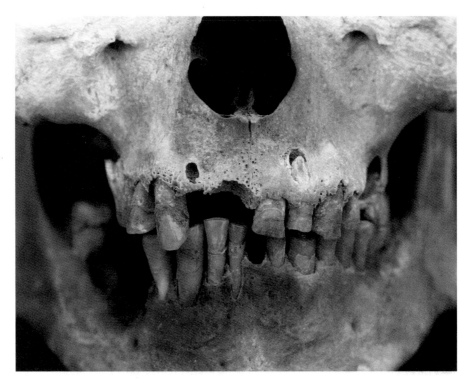

Figure 11. Anterior view of the dentition of Burial 53.

Late Period cemetery samples from the site (Verano 1992). Table 10, page 212, gives frequencies of porotic hyperostosis and cribra orbitalia for Moche and Late Period surface collections. Porotic hyperostosis and cribra orbitalia, porous lesions found on the skull vault and orbital roofs, are considered to represent a physiological response to iron deficiency anemia, which can be caused and exacerbated by dietary deficiencies, intestinal parasites, infectious disease, and their synergistic effects (Goodman et al. 1984; Stuart-Macadam 1985, 1987a, 1987b; Kent 1986; Walker 1986).

Only one individual from the H45CM1 cemetery, Burial 3, showed porotic hyperostosis and cribra orbitalia. He also had active periostitis on both femoral shafts, suggesting that he was suffering from some infectious process at the time of death (Goodman et al. 1984). Periosteal reactions were occasionally seen on infants' and children's bone surfaces collected from cemeteries S2, S20, and S24, but they were uncommon. Observed frequencies for Cemetery S2 are presented in Table 11, page 212. No cases were seen in the infant and child burials from Cemetery H45CM1; Burial 3, as noted above, was the only individual to show periostitis.

The low frequency of skeletal stress indicators suggests that the Moche population at Pacatnamu had an adequate diet and that factors such as crowding, contaminated drinking water, and intestinal parasite load were not significant problems.[3]

Trauma

Fractures, dislocations, and other evidence of trauma were uncommon in Moche skeletal remains from Pacatnamu. Two examples of healed fractures were found during surface collections of cemeteries S2 and S4. Healed fractures were found in one skeleton from Huaca 2 and in another from the H45CM1 cemetery (see Site Map, pages 18-19). A case of unhealed multiple fractures was found in a skeleton from the H45CM1 cemetery.

An isolated left humerus of an adult (probably male) collected from the surface of S2 shows a probable healed fracture of the distal metaphysis (Fig. 12). The distal end is deviated medially, and shows osteoarthritic lipping of the trochlea and capitulum and new bone deposited in the olecranon and coronoid fossae.

A partial skeleton of a 25-30 year old female from S2 shows healed compression (lateral wedge) fractures of

---

2. Enamel hypoplasias, also commonly used as stress indicators, were difficult to record systematically, because of the heavy postmortem loss of single rooted teeth in surface-collected crania and other factors such as tooth wear and antemortem loss.

3. The frequencies of porotic hyperostosis and cribra orbitalia are substantially higher in some Late Intermediate Period cemeteries at Pacatnamu, such as S1 and S8. Increased social stratification and changes in settlement pattern and density may be factors (Verano 1992).

the eleventh and twelfth thoracic vertebrae (Fig. 13). The vertebral column above the level of the fracture deviates at a nearly 90 degree angle to the right side, due to collapse and wedging of the bodies of T11 and T12. The intervertebral diarthrodial joints of vertebrae T11, T12, and L1 are fused, and a shelf of bone has grown out to support the fracture area. The neural arches of vertebrae T11-L1 are noticeably flattened, suggesting that the trunk habitually rested on these surfaces. Most ribs are relatively normal in shape, although all vertebral and sternal articular surfaces show osteoarthritic lipping and pitting. The body of the sternum shows pronounced anterior bowing, suggesting that the thoracic cage was deformed as a result of postural changes following the vertebral injuries. Interestingly, the hip and knee joints appear normal, except for some minor arthritic changes, suggesting that the woman was able to walk following stabilization of the spinal injury. Her humeri show pronounced deltoid tuberosities, which would be expected if she used her arms extensively to help support her weight. The cause of the spinal fractures is unknown, but this type of

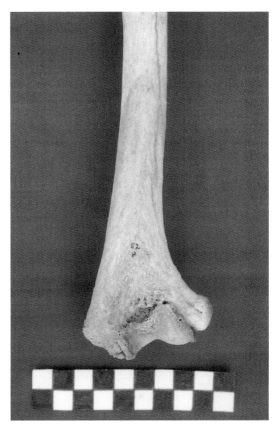

Figure 12. Distal portion of the left humerus showing a probable healed fracture, with medial displacement and arthritic changes (S2-055P).

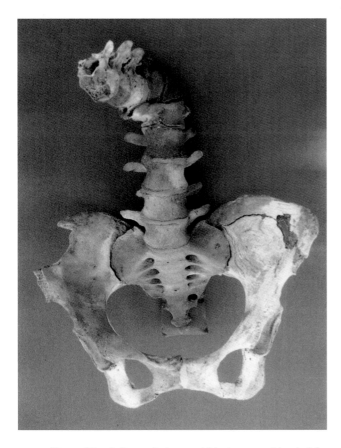

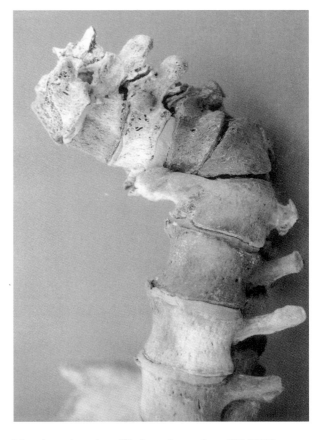

Figure 13. a) General view and b) close-up of healed fractures of the eleventh and twelfth thoracic vertebrae (S4-112P).

injury in an adolescent or young adult suggests a fall from some height. The ultimate cause of death could not be determined from the skeletal remains.

Burial 73, the skeleton of an old adult female, showed a well-healed midshaft fracture of the left fibula. The left tibia showed no evidence of fracture or other abnormality. Burial 55 showed healed compression fractures of the third and fourth lumbar vertebrae. There is extensive bony reaction and fusion of the anterior surfaces of the bodies. The neural arch of the fifth lumbar vertebra was fractured as well, (Spondylolysis, Merbs 1989) and remained ununited.

Burial 14 showed multiple bone fractures that appear to have occurred at or around the time of death. Most apparent was a midshaft fracture of the right femur, which showed overriding of the fractured ends and lateral rotation of the leg distal to the fracture (Fig. 14a). This is typical of the presentation of femoral shaft fractures in clinical settings due to contraction of thigh muscles following injury (see Burial 14 drawing, Donnan and McClelland, this volume). Examination of the skeleton following excavation revealed numerous additional fractures, including the neck of the right femur, ten right ribs and five left ribs (Fig. 14b), the left transverse processes of

vertebrae T3-10, the spinous processes of T3-5 (Fig. 14c), and the centrum of vertebra L4. Small fractures and damaged areas also were noted on the proximal ends of both tibiae and fibulae and on the greater tuberosity of the right humerus. A complete fracture also was present through the acromion process of the right scapula.

The overall pattern of fractures is suggestive of rapid deceleration injury. The most likely scenario in this case is a fall from a substantial height, such as from the bluff top above the Jequetepeque River Valley. None of the fractures shows evidence of healing, so it is likely that internal injuries suffered during the fall were the cause of death.

Trauma or Infection

Burial 5 had a healed injury that may be the result of trauma, infection, or both. The left orbit is abnormal in its shape and surface features (Fig. 15). Its surfaces show extensive deposits of new bone that overlie the normal cortex. The supraorbital margin is irregular, and also covered with a deposit of new bone, which extends onto the frontal bone over the left eye. Infection or serious injury to the eye is the most likely diagnosis, and it is likely that this individual lost the use of it.

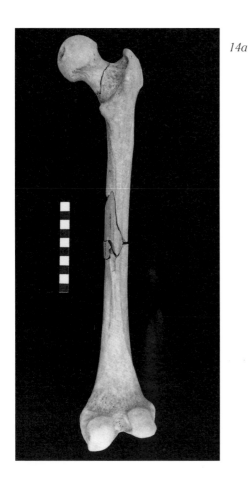

14a

14b

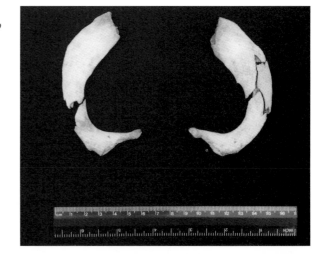

14c

Figure 14. a) Right femur, b) first ribs, and c) thoracic vertebrae T2-9 of Burial 14.

Tumors of Bone and Cartilage

Two examples of benign bony or cartilaginous tumors were found in the Moche skeletal sample from Pacatnamu. The first example, from Cemetery S2, is a nearly complete left femur (missing the distal epiphysis) of an adult male (Fig. 16a). It shows a large bony growth on the postero-medial aspect of the distal metaphysis (Fig. 16b). Although damaged, its external dimensions are estimated to have been approximately 41 millimeters x 47 millimeters. The growth appears to be bilobular and consists of a thin layer of cortical bone underlain by variable coarse and fine trabeculae. The femur is otherwise normal in appearance. A likely diagnosis is a slow-growing, benign tumor.

The second example is Burial 12, a young adult male. The metacarpal of the left thumb shows evidence of a soft tissue growth within the shaft of the bone (Fig. 17). The growth produced a ragged-edged defect in the shaft of the bone and enlargement and distortion of the distal joint surface. Its location and characteristics suggest that it may be a benign cartilaginous tumor known as a chondroma (Ortner and Putschar 1981:370).

Developmental Anomalies

Several examples of developmental anomalies were found. The head of the left radius of Burial 24, an adult female, is unusual in form (Fig. 18). Its articular surface is convex rather than concave, as it should be. The area with which it articulates with the humerus (the capitulum) has compensated by becoming a concave surface, also the reverse of the normal condition. The compensatory growth of the humerus and the lack of any signs of osteoarthritis suggest that this is a rare congenital or developmental malformation in the ossification of the radial epiphysis.

The right humerus of Burial 60, an adult male, shows a flattened head with an irregular joint surface. The right humerus is substantially shorter than the left (272 millimeters maximum length, vs. 350 millimeters for the left humerus), indicating that there was some disruption of growth at the proximal epiphysis during childhood or adolescence. The distal joint surfaces are normal in appearance, and the right radius and ulna are normal in size and robusticity, indicating that there was no apparent functional loss of the arm due to its short length or unusual morphology.

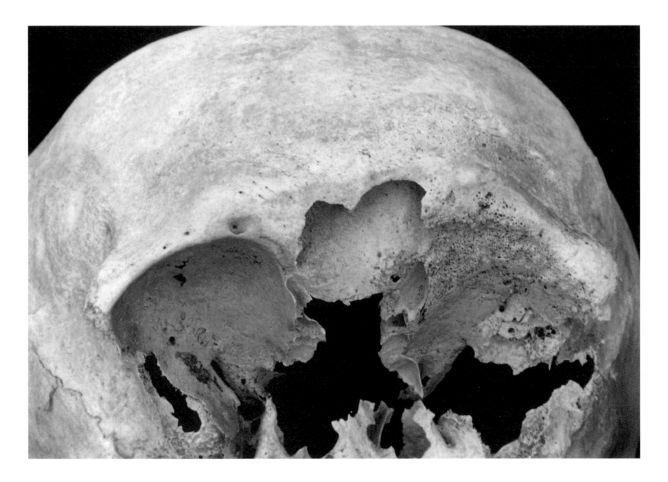

Figure 15. Frontal view of the calvaria of Burial 5, showing abnormal appearance of the left orbit.

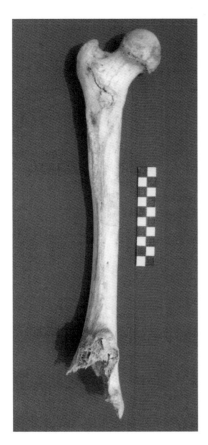

16a

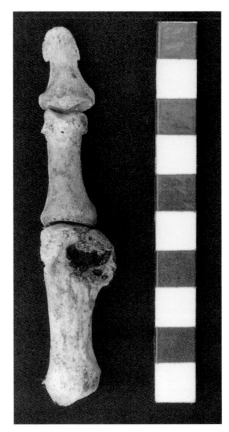

Figure 17. First metacarpal and phalanges of the left thumb of Burial 12, showing an expansive lesion at the distal end of the metacarpal.

16b

Figure 16. a) General and b) close-up views of a left femur, showing a bony tumor at the distal metaphysis (S2-074P).

One partial vertebral column of an adult female, collected from Cemetery S2, showed a developmental anomaly known as a sagittal cleft or "butterfly" vertebra, caused by persistence of the fetal notochord (Schmorl and Junghanns 1971; Mann and Verano 1990). The ninth thoracic vertebra has an elliptical defect in the right posterior half of the body, adjacent to the midline. The defect is partially cleft at its posterior margin, extends through both end-plates, and measures 9 millimeters x 12 millimeters. The margins of the defect are smooth and gently sloping, and the body is mildly asymmetrical. The eighth thoracic vertebra exhibits mild compensatory bulging of its inferior end-plate to accommodate the convex superior endplate of T9. The tenth and eleventh thoracic vertebrae show mild anterior wedging, but no other anomalies were noted. This is one of four cases of sagittal cleft vertebra I have identified from surface-collected and excavated Moche skeletal material at Pacatnamu. The other three examples came from Late Intermediate Period contexts.[4] Sagittal cleft vertebrae

---

4. A description of one of the Late Period cases has been published (Mann and Verano 1990).

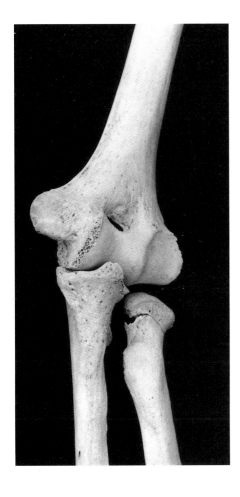

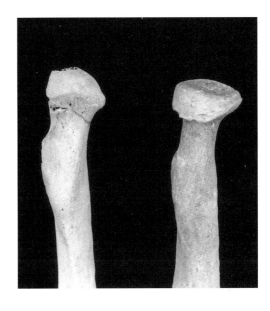

Figure 18. (Left) Bones of the left arm of Burial 24; (above) comparison of the proximal ends of the left (abnormal) and right (normal) radii.

rarely are reported in the paleopathological literature, and the specific cause of these developmental defects is unknown, but the number of cases found at Pacatnamu appears to be unusual.

Summary

The Moche skeletal collections recovered by the Pacatnamu Project constitute the first large and well documented sample of Moche skeletal remains to be reported. The sample consists of 84 burials and approximately 590 isolated skeletal elements surface collected from looted cemeteries. Analysis of these remains provides information on the demographic composition of cemeteries at Pacatnamu, as well as data on the physical characteristics and skeletal pathology of the Moche people.

Patterns of microvariation in facial morphology between different Moche cemetery samples at Pacatnamu support a hypothesis of burial by kinship group. This pattern of mortuary behavior, which was noted by Cieza de Leon among the indigenous population of the Jequetepeque Valley during the Early Colonial Period, appears to have considerable antiquity on the north coast.

Living stature for the Moche at Pacatnamu averaged 158 centimeters (5'2") for males and 147 centimeters (4'10") for females, values similar to those reported for present day inhabitants of traditional communities on the north coast. Although not tall, the Moche show little evidence of nutritional stress in the skeleton and dentition, suggesting that they enjoyed a nutritionally adequate and reliable diet.

Patterns of degenerative joint disease, as well as several examples of intervertebral disk herniations, suggest an active lifestyle, involving substantial wear and tear on the upper body and limbs. Evidence suggesting elevated mortality in adolescent and young adult males, in comparison to adult females, in the H45CM1 cemetery may indicate differential activity patterns in males which put them at greater health risk than females.

Recent years have seen a substantial increase in the number of Moche skeletal remains available for study. Ongoing archaeological projects at various north coast Moche sites are producing not only larger, but also better documented collections than were available previously. The coming years should witness further advances in our understanding of the physical characteristics, paleodemography, and health of the ancient Moche.

Table 1

Sex Composition of Surface Collected Cemeteries
Based on a Count of Left Innominates

Cemetery	Males		Females	
	N	%	N	%
S2	39	57.4	29	42.6
S20	17	58.6	12	41.4
S24	13	43.3	17	56.7

Table 2

Age and Sex Distribution of H45CM1

Age	N	%	Males	Females	Sex Unknown
Fetal	1	1.5	–	–	1
< 1 year	7	10.4	–	–	7
1-4 years	10	14.9	–	–	10
5-9 years	1	1.5	–	–	1
10-14 years	–	0.0	–	–	–
15-19 years	3	4.5	3	–	–
20-34 years	12	17.9	9	3	–
35-49 years	16	23.9	8	8	–
>50 years	13	19.4	2	11	–
Adult (age Indeterminate)	4	6.0	1	1	2
Totals	67	100.0	23	23	21

Table 3

Craniofacial Indices of Moche Crania at Pacatnamu

Index	Value		Classification
Males	Undeformed (N=19)	Deformed (N=17)	
Upper Facial Index	49.0	47.4	Wide or Broad Face (Euryeny)
Nasal Index	47.2	46.6	Narrow Nasal Aperture (Leptorrhiny)
Orbital Index	87.8	88.4	Average or Medium Orbits (Mesoconchy)
Females	Undeformed (N=14)	Deformed (N=20)	
Upper Facial Index	49.1	48.9	Wide or Broad Face (Euryeny)
Nasal Index	48.7	50.5	Average or Medium (Mesorrhiny)
Orbital Index	91.1	91.2	Narrow Orbits (Hypsiconchy)

Definition of Indices

Upper Facial Index: upper facial height x 100 / bizygomatic breadth

Nasal Index: nasal breadth x 100 / nasal height

Orbital Index: orbit height x 100 / orbit breadth

(Bass 1971:68-69). Classifications follow Bass.

Table 4

Frequency of Cranial Deformation by Cemetery (Males and Females Combined)

Cemetery	N	Undeformed N	Undeformed %	Deformed N	Deformed %
S2	34	16	47.1	18	52.9
S20	25	5	20.0	20	80.0
S24	18	12	66.7	6	33.3
H45CM1	14	3	21.4	11	78.6
Misc. Burials	5	2	40.0	3	60.0
Total	96	38	40.0	58	60.0

Table 5

Adult Stature Estimates for Pacatnamu Compared with El Brujo, Hrdlička's Chicama Valley Mixed Temporal Sample, and Two Modern North Coast Communities

Males

Sample	Period	N	Mean Stature (cm)	Range (cm)
S2	Moche	19	156.7	150.4-168.7
S24	Moche	17	158.3	153.1-165.8
H45CM1	Moche	17	157.8	148.2-164.6
El Brujo	Moche	9	159.9	152.7-166.3
Chicama	Mixed	1,000	157.2	(not given)
San José	Modern	46	156.6	(not given)
Monsefú	Modern	67	158.6	(not given)

Females

Sample	Period	N	Mean Stature (cm)	Range (cm)
S2	Moche	18	147.4	139.4-156.0
S24	Moche	21	146.2	140.4-153.4
H45CM1	Moche	13	146.9	139.5-153.7
El Brujo	Moche	4	146.6	141.4-154.4
Chicama	Mixed	350	144.7	(not given)
San José	Modern	49	145.1	(not given)
Monsefú	Modern	97	145.8	(not given)

Sources: Hrdlička 1938; Lasker 1962; Verano 1987, Verano and Anderson n.d.

Table 6

Canonical Discriminant Function Analysis, Crania from Cemeteries S2, S20, S24, and H45CM1

I. Males

Canonical Discriminant Functions

Function	Eigenvalue	Percent of Variance	Wilk's Lambda	Significance
1	1.95	66.35	0.160	.0016
2	0.87	29.45	0.475	.1265
3	0.12	4.21	0.889	.7866

Classification of Grouped Cases by Discriminant Functions
Predicted Group Membership

Actual Group	N	S2	S20	H45CM1	S24
S2	14	12 (85.7%)	1 (7.1%)	1 (7.1%)	0 (0%)
S20	6	1 (16.7%)	4 (66.7%)	1 (16.7%)	0 (0.0%)
H45CM1	6	0 (0%)	1 (16.7%)	3 (50%)	2 (33.3%)
S24	8	0 (0%)	0 (0%)	1 (12.5%)	7 (87.5%)

Overall percentage of cases correctly classified: 76.5%
Prior Probability for each group: 0.25

Mahalanobis Generalized Distances Between Cemetery Samples
($*p < .05$ $**p < .01$)

	S2	S20	H45CM1
S20	5.26**		
H45CM1	3.69*	1.65	
S24	9.22**	7.18**	0.41

[Table 6, cont.]

II. *Females*

Canonical Discriminant Functions

Function	Eigenvalue	Percent of Variance	Wilk's Lambda	Significance
1	0.95	42.60	0.193	.0151
2	0.82	36.55	0.376	.0424
3	0.46	20.85	0.682	.1614

Classification of Grouped Cases by Discriminant Functions

Predicted Group Membership

Actual Group	N	S2	S20	H45CM1	S24
S2	10	7 (70.0%)	1 (10.0%)	0 (0.0%)	2 (20.0%)
S20	7	1 (14.3%)	4 (57.1%)	1 (14.3%)	1 (14.3%)
H45CM1	8	0 (0.0%)	1 (12.5%)	6 (75%)	1 (12.5%)
S24	10	1 (10.0%)	1 (10.0%)	0 (0.0%)	8 (80.0%)

Overall percentage of cases correctly classified: 71.4%
Prior Probability for each group: 0.25

Mahalanobis Generalized Distances between cemetery samples
(*p < .05   **p < .01)

	S2	S20	H45CM1
S20	1.89		
H45CM1	4.21*	2.67	
S24	3.33	3.92	3.21

(Source: Verano 1987)

Table 7

Isotopic Ratios, Carbon/Nitrogen Ratios, and Percent Collagen by Weight for Individual Bone Samples.

<u>Moche Samples</u>

Specimen	% Collagen by Weight	C/N Ratio	$\delta^{13}C$	$\delta^{15}N$
S2-4	11.3	3.2	-11.7	+10.6
S2-2	15.1	3.2	-12.6	+9.2
S2-3	15.2	3.1	-11.4	+11.0
S2-1	10.4	3.2	-11.8	+11.7
S2-5	8.4	3.2	-11.2	+7.3
S2-6*	0.7	4.4	-14.4	+13.0
Burial 73	19.4	3.3	-11.0	+10.8
Burial 79	21.7	3.2	-13.0	+10.7
Burial 80	22.6	3.3	-12.4	+11.0

* % Collagen by weight and carbon/nitrogen ratio values indicate postmortem alteration. This specimen was removed from the analysis (see Verano and DeNiro 1993).

<u>Late Intermediate Period Samples</u>

Specimen	% Collagen by Weight	C/N Ratio	$\delta^{13}C$	$\delta^{15}N$
S8-1	10.7	3.1	-10.5	+14.2
S8-2	19.4	3.2	-13.5	+11.6
S8-3	22.5	3.2	-11.5	+10.7
S1-1	8.8	3.2	-10.5	+12.1
S1-2	15.0	3.1	-9.3	+12.1
S1-3	18.2	3.1	-9.7	+14.2
H31 B1	27.8	3.3	-12.4	+11.0
H31 B12	24.3	3.3	-10.4	+11.7
C1 B1	23.3	3.2	-13.0	+11.5
H1M1 B2	24.6	3.3	-11.0	+8.2

<u>Summary Statistics</u>

Sample	Mean $\delta^{13}C$	S.D.	Min	Max	Mean $\delta^{15}N$	S.D.	Min	Max
Moche	-11.9	0.7	-13.0	-11.0	+10.2	1.3	+7.3	+11.7
Late Period	-13.0	2.9	-15.6	-9.1	+7.3	1.8	+4.5	+9.1

Table 8

Frequency of Degenerative Joint Changes in Pacatnamu (H45CM1) Adults, Compared with Hrdlička's Chicama Valley Series (Hrdlička 1914:62-69).

Joint	Observable N	Arthritic	% Incidence
Pacatnamu (H45CM1)			
Shoulder	61	9	14.8
Elbow	63	13	20.6
Wrist	61	0	0.0
Hand	61	2	3.3
Hip	61	15	24.5
Knee	59	16	27.1
Ankle	61	0	0.0
Foot	58	2	3.4
Chicama Valley			
Shoulder	593	1	0.2
Elbow[1]	1149	34	3.0
Wrist	556	1	0.2
Hand	—	—	—
Hip	1210	16	1.3
Knee[2]	1991	14	0.7
Ankle[3]	1047	2	0.2
Foot	—	—	—

1. Frequencies for distal humerus, proximal radius and proximal ulna averaged.

2. Frequencies for distal femur and proximal tibia averaged.

3. Frequencies for distal tibia and fibula averaged.

Table 9

Dental Pathology in H45CM1 Adults

Burial	Age/Sex	Caries/ Observable Teeth	%	Antemortem Tooth Loss/ Observable* Teeth	%	Abscesses	Periodontal Disease
20	YAM	0/16	0.0	0/16***	0.0		
47	YAM	1/32	3.1	0/32	0.0		
14	YAM	0/32	0.0	0/32	0.0		
21	MAM	1/2	50.0	14/16***	87.5		
42	MAF	7/32	21.9	0/32	0.0	1	++
34	MAM	6/27	22.2	5/32	15.6		+
44	MAF	1/28	3.6	4/32	12.5		
51	MAM	2/32	6.3	0/32	0.0		
11	MAF	4/22	18.2	10/32	3.1	3	
4	MAM	0/27	0.0	5/32	15.6	1	
24	MAF	0/28	0.0	3/28**	10.7		
2	MAF	3/27	11.1	5/32	15.6		
57	MAF	9/27	33.3	5/32	15.6		
60	MAM	16/24	66.7	8/32	25.0	4	
61	MAF	6/23	26.1	9/32	28.1		
58	MAM	0/32	0.0	0/32	0.0	2	
30	OAF	1/1	100.0	27/32	84.4		
28	OAF	4/7	57.1	23/32	71.9		
22	OAF	4/10	40.0	10/32	31.3		
31	OAF	5/5	100.0	27/32	84.4		++
29	OAF	3/19	15.8	13/32	40.6		
18	OAF	12/13	92.3	19/32	59.4		
38	OAF	2/11	18.2	11/32	34.4		
13	OAF	1/12	8.3	20/32	62.5		
10	OAF	1/13	7.7	19/32	59.4		
53	OAF	6/22	27.3	10/32	31.3	3	
5	OAM	1/19	5.3	13/32	40.6		
19	OAF	2/7	28.6	25/32	78.1		
9	OAM	5/26	19.2	6/32	18.8		+

Key to Abbreviations

YAM = Young Adult Male   MAM = Middle Adult Male   OAM = Old Adult Male

YAF = Young Adult Female   MAF = Middle Adult Female   OAF = Old Adult Female

* Assumes adult originally had a full complement of 32 teeth (none congenitally absent)

** Third molars congenitally absent

*** Mandible only, no maxilla present.

+ Present

++ Pronounced

Table 10

Cribra Orbitalia and Porotic Hyperostosis in Pacatnamu Cemeteries

Cemetery	Cribra Orbitalia		Porotic Hyperostosis	
	Frequency	%	Frequency	%
Moche Occupation				
S2	1/29	3.4	3/31	9.7
S20	1/34	2.9	1/32	3.1
H45CM1	1/62	1.6	1/62	1.6
Late Intermediate Period Occupation				
S1	15/38	39.5	15/44	34.1
S8	15/55	27.3	8/50	16.0
S9	1/20	5.0	0/20	0.0

Table 11

Frequency of Periostitis on Subadult Skeletal Elements Surface Collected from Cemetery S2

Bone	Present/ Observable	Comments
Femur	0/10	
Tibia	2/6	#1: Estimated age: 6 months to 1 yr.; #2: Estimated age: 1-1.5 yrs.
Fibula	0/5	
Humerus	1/5	Estimated age: 6 months to 1.5 yrs.
Ulna	0/1	
Radius	0/1	

Age estimates are based on long bone length, using data from Ubelaker 1989, Table 14.

RESUMEN:
Características Físicas y Biología del Esqueleto de la Población Moche en Pacatnamú

Hasta hace poco las características físicas de los Moche eran conocidas por las representaciones de ellos mismos en cerámica. Aquí se presentan los resultados del análisis de las osamentas recuperadas en Pacatnamú entre 1983 y 1987: 67 individuos provenientes de H45CM1, 17 de excavaciones en otras áreas del sitio, y la recolección de restos en superficie (aproximadamente 590 especímenes) hecha en tres cementerios depredados (S2, S20 y S24; Fig. 1).

Exploraciones de Superficie y Recolección

Entre 1983 y 1984 se identificaron más de 25 cementerios Moche disturbados, pero sólo tres (S2, S20 y S24) mostraron material abundante y bien preservado, por lo que fueron escogidos para recolección de superficie y excavaciones de prueba, para identificar la forma y el contexto estratigráfico de las tumbas (Fig. 2).

Preservación de los Esqueletos

La preservación de los huesos es generalmente buena en Pacatnamú, aunque los esqueletos Moche muestran, con frecuencia, adherencias de cristales de sal en la superficie y en las cavidades (Fig. 3); ello sugiere que el suelo que los rodea estuvo húmedo en algún momento del pasado, lo que se asocia con evidencias de un periodo de lluvias (Niño de grandes proporciones) alrededor del 1100 N.E. en la Costa Norte del Perú. Las diferencias en preservación entre el material Moche y el de los periodos tardíos confirma este hecho.

Composición Demográfica de los Cementerios Moche

El examen del material en superficie reveló que todos los grupos de edad estuvieron representados y que tanto hombres como mujeres estuvieron presentes en aproximadamente números iguales (Tabla 1). Sin embargo, los restos de niños fueron relativamente más escasos, lo que sugiere que no todos ellos fueron enterrados en cementerios.

El Cementerio H45CM1

El único cementerio hallado intacto y excavado completamente. Se recuperaron 67 individuos; la distribución por sexo y edad (Tabla 2) es similar a la recolectada en superficie, pero permite un mayor grado de precisión. La mayoría de individuos está entre 0-4 años o en las edades adultas; pocos están en el rango de niñez o adolescencia (5-19 años). Esta distribución es consistente con la curva de mortalidad en U de las poblaciones humanas, donde la mayor incidencia de mortalidad se dá durante el primer año de vida, declina durante la niñez y adolescencia y asciende durante la edad adulta (Fig. 5). La baja frecuencia de infantes entre 0-0.9 años sugiere que ellos fueron enterrados en otas áreas.

Mortalidad y Sexo

Hombres y mujeres muestran diferencias en mortalidad (Fig. 6). Una proporción mayor de varones, en H45CM1, murieron como adolescentes (15-19 años) y jóvenes adultos (20-34 años), mientras la mayoría de mujeres murió como adultos viejos (50+ años). Si esto es correcto, las mujeres vivieron, basándonose en la edad promedio al momento de muerte, 19 años más que los hombres.

Características Físicas de los Moche

La población de la costa ha sido conocida como braquicefálica, que es una buena generalización para los Moche de Pacatnamú (Tabla 3). Casi la mitad de los cráneos muestran deformación artificial (Tabla 4), en la forma de un achatamiento de la región occipital (Fig. 7). Sin embargo, no hay evidencia de "cunas" para producir estas deformaciones, ni tampoco son representadas en el arte Moche (Donnan, comunicación personal).

Estatura

Los hombres Moche, en Pacatnamú, midieron, como promedio, 157.6 cms., con un rango entre 148.2 a 168.7 cms.; las mujeres promediaron 146.8 cms. y un rango de 139.4 a 156.0 cms. (Tabla 5). Los resultados muestran que se trata de estimados similares a los de poblaciones contemporáneas en la costa norte, lo que muestra que la estatura no ha variado, de manera significativa, en los últimos 1500 años.

Variaciones Físicas entre Poblaciones de Cementerios

Una de las interrogantes que surgió de los recorridos de superficie de los cementerios en Pacatnamú fué: ¿Porqué los Moche enterraron a sus difuntos en más de 25 cementerios discretos, en vez de en uno sólo o en un número menor de cementerios? Las mediciones cráneo faciales fueron usadas para determinar las diferencias entre la población, junto con pruebas multivariables y análisis canónico de funciones discriminantes. Se identificaron suficientes diferencias como para distinguir las muestras de un cementerio con respecto a los demás (Fig. 8). Así mismo, los cráneos femeninos mostraron menores diferencias que los de los varones. Desde que estas diferencias reflejan características genéticas, los resultados sugieren que los cementerios corresponden a grupos de parentesco o linajes y que las mujeres se casaban fuera de su grupo de parentesco, mientras los hombres no.

Dieta y Nutrición

El análisis del colágeno contenido en los huesos ha permitido estimar las proporciones de alimentos de origen marino y los de origen terrestre consumidos por la población. Esta información se cruza con la evidencia que proviene de las excavaciones arqueológicas, con la finalidad de verificar y precisar las conclusiones.

El análisis del colágeno de 9 individuos Moche y 10 pertenecientes al periodo Tardío del sitio (Tabla 7 y Fig. 9) muestra que las proteinas provenientes de vertebrados e invertebrados marinos fueron un componente muy importante de la dieta, así como la ingesta de plantas como el maíz.

Salud y Enfermedad

Todo el material óseo fué examinado para determinar evidencias de patologías.

Enfermedad Degenerativa de las Articulaciones (Osteoartritis)

Los cambios degenerativos en las articulaciones reflejan el tipo de actividades durante la vida. Las articulaciones de la rodilla, en los Moche y en la población del periodo Tardío, muestran con frecuencia signos de artritis en una forma que sugiere largos periodos de una postura con las rodillas flexionadas; 5 adultos (tres mujeres y dos hombres), provenientes de H45CM1, mostraron hernia de los discos intervertebrales, lo cual es consecuencia de cargar excesivo peso.

Artritis Reumatoide

Varios ejemplos de fusión vertebral y uno del sacroiliaco fueron recuperados en los cementerios S2 y S20, mientras sólo se halló uno en H45CM1. Otros casos en el cementerio S2 incluyen fusión intervertebral de las cuatro primeras vértebras toráxicas, fusiones de costillas a las vértebras, y fusión del sacro al ilium.

Patología Dental

Despues de las enfermedades de las articulaciones, la patología dental fué la más común. Caries y pérdida de dientes fueron problemas significativos en H45CM1 (Tabla 9). Los adultos jóvenes (20-34) muestran pocos problemas, mientras los adultos medios (35-49) muestran un promedio de pérdida de 4.9 dientes (16.4%) y 4.1 (19.3%) de caries en los dientes que les quedan; los adultos mayores (50+) muestras un promedio de pérdida de 17.2 dientes (53.6%) y caries en 3.6 (39.9%) de los que les quedan. El desgaste de los dientes es moderado, por lo que las pérdidas parecen haber sido causadas por caries, enfermedades peridontales, o ambas. De las observaciones se deduce que los problemas dentales fueron

fuente de considerable sufrimiento entre la población Moche en Pacatnamú. Ello puede haberse debido a una dieta rica en carbohidratos y alimentos de textura suave.

Indicadores de Stress Nutricional

La baja frecuencia de indicadores de stress en las osamentas sugiere que la población Moche en Pacatnamú tuvo una dieta adecuada y que factores tales como hacinamiento, agua contaminada y parásitos intestinales no fueron problemas significativos.

Trauma

Fracturas, dislocaduras y otras evidencias de trauma son raros entre los Moche de Pacatnamú. Hay ejemplos de fracturas curadas provenientes de los cementerios S2, S4 y H45CM1; también los hay de aquellas que no se curaron, en H45CM1. La fractura de la columna vertebral (Fig. 13) en una mujer de 25-30 años de edad muestra la soldadura de la misma en un ángulo de 90°; el examen de los huesos permite afirmar que fué capaz de volver a caminar, pero ayudándose intensivamente con los brazos. La osamenta recuperada en la Tumba 14 (Donnan y McClelland, este volumen) muestra múltiples fracturas (Fig. 14a, b y c), como si hubiese caido por el barranco que rodea Pacatnamú; los huesos no muestran evidencias de curación, por lo que es posible que la persona haya fallecido debido a las lesiones internas que sufrió.

Trauma o Infección

La Tumba 5 muestra un individuo con una herida curada que puede ser consecuencia de trauma, infección o ambos. La órbita ocular izquiera (Fig. 15) muestra anormalidades en la forma y en la superficie. Es muy probable que el individuo perdiera la vista en ese ojo.

Tumores del Hueso y Cartílago

Dos ejemplos de tumores benignos al hueso o cartílago: uno, proveniente de S2, es un fémur (Fig. 16a y b) y afectó la cabeza del hueso. En otro (Tumba 12), un adulto joven del sexo masculino, el metacarpo del dedo gordo de la mano izquierda muestra evidencia de crecimiento de tejido blando (Fig. 17).

Anomalías del Desarrollo

Se registraron varios ejemplos de anomalías, como el radio izquierdo de la mujer de la Tumba 24, cuya superficie articular es convexa, en vez de cóncava (Fig. 18); o el húmero derecho del varón de la Tumba 60, con la cabeza del hueso achatada y la superficie de la articulación irregular; además, el hueso es de menor tamaño que el del lado izquierdo.

Moche Textiles from Pacatnamu

Christopher B. Donnan
Sharon G. Donnan

Pacatnamu is one of the few archaeological sites where Moche textiles have been excavated. A small but important sample of these was excavated by Heinrich Ubbelohde-Doering prior to 1973, including several of the most elaborate Moche textiles that are known (Ubbelohde-Doering 1952, 1960, 1967; Keatinge 1978; Conklin 1979; Hecker and Hecker 1977, 1982, 1995). Our excavations, conducted at Pacatnamu between 1983 and 1987, yielded an additional large sample of Moche textiles which, although less elaborate than some found by Ubbelohde-Doering, provides an excellent opportunity to reconstruct the essential features of Moche weaving at this site. Moreover, the sample includes the first significant collection of Moche garments and accessories found archaeologically. Because most of the garments and accessories are from burials of individuals whose sex and age are known, it is possible to identify some that were sex and/or age specific. Of particular interest is the correlation of garments and accessories in our sample with similar items worn by individuals depicted in Moche art.

The sample consists of 181 textiles,[1] all but two of which came from burials.[2] These have been compiled into Table 1, Moche Textile Sample, pages 233-240, in which each textile is assigned a number. In this report, textiles from burials are cited by their burial and textile numbers shown in Table 1. The two textiles not recovered from burials are referenced by their source locations and textile numbers at the end of Table 1.

Nearly all of the textiles are incomplete and in poor condition because of decomposition prior to excavation. Some particularly fragile textiles that could not be removed were analyzed in situ. Those that could be removed were carefully conserved and maintained in optimum storage conditions.

Fibers and Yarns

The predominant fiber was cotton, in various natural colors, including white, tan, and light brown. Usually, both warps and wefts of cotton textiles were the same color, although in a few instances they were different, creating a decorative appearance. Wool[3] was much less common than cotton. Bast fiber was not used in weaving textiles, but was commonly made into cordage and rope. Human hair was occasionally made into cordage.

---

1. This does not include traces of textiles that were recognized during excavation, but for which no information could be recovered.

2. Some additional textile fragments were recovered from our excavations of Moche architecture and refuse at Pacatnamu. Although they are not discussed in this report, they are very similar to the textiles in this sample.

3. Throughout this report, the term wool refers to camelid fibers.

Figure 1. Plain weave with supplemental weft (Burial 2 Textile 3).

Cotton was used to create the basic structure in all plain weave, twill, gauze, double cloth, and net fabrics, and was used for warp yarns in all tapestries. It also was used occasionally for supplemental wefts. Wool apparently was not used for warps,[4] but was used to create elaborate textiles: weft elements of tapestries, supplemental weft elements in a variety of weaves, and threads for embroideries and couching.

Cotton yarns usually were S-spun and single-ply. Less than 10% of the S-spun yarns were plied, and in all cases they were plied Z2. Z-spun cotton yarns are uncommon, and all examples are single-ply. The only regular use of plied cotton yarns was for making nets (see *Netting* below) and for string used in sewing. Net yarns usually had two elements S-spun and Z-plied, while sewing strings varied from two to eight elements, S-spun and Z-plied.

In contrast to cotton, nearly all wool yarns were plied. The majority were S-spun and plied Z2. There were only four textiles with unplied wool yarn, and only one of these (Burial 4 Textile 5) was Z-spun.

In two textiles (Burial 20 Textile 7, Burial 21 Textile 7), cotton and wool were plied together to form some weft yarns, while the others were only of wool.

Except for tapestries, where warps were cotton and wefts were wool, or where wool was used to create a weft stripe among otherwise cotton wefts, the textiles in the sample usually had warps and wefts of the same fiber, and the warp and weft yarns in a single textile tended to be similar in spin, ply, and thickness.

Cloth Panels

The Moche weavers' fundamental approach to cloth was to weave rectangular panels that were used individually or sewn together to create garments and accessories. No attempt was made to shape the cloth panels as they were woven, or to cut and tailor them into fitted garments and accessories.

The widths of the textiles never exceeded what could be woven easily on a backstrap loom. Widths range from 30 to 85 centimeters, but most are between 40 and 50 centimeters. The only exceptions are narrow bands that served as the ties for loincloths (See *Loincloths* below), and narrow bands of tapestry that were sewn along the edges of head cloths (See *Head Cloths* below) or sewn together to form elaborate shirts. These textiles were woven with a loom width of less than 5 centimeters. The lengths of the textiles in the sample range from 18 cm (Burial 80 Textile 6) to 210 centimeters (Burial 25 Textile 1).

Weaves

Plain Weave

Approximately 50 percent of the textiles in the sample are plain weave. The warps and wefts of the plain weaves are always balanced. About two-thirds of the plain weaves have single warps and wefts; the others

---

4. Two textiles with wool wefts had warps that could not be identified (Burial 36 Textile 1, Burial 46 Textile 1).

*Figure 2. Plain weave with supplemental weft
(Burial 20 Textile 3).*

have paired warps and wefts. Some with single warps and wefts are open plain weave, but there is no open weave with paired warps and wefts. This suggests that Moche weavers used single warps and wefts when they wanted an open, light-weight fabric, and paired warps and wefts when they wanted a more tightly woven, heavier fabric.

One open plain weave textile with fine cotton warps and wefts has supplemental wefts of various colors of thicker cotton yarn, creating light and dark bands (Fig. 1). Another plain weave textile decorated with supplemental wefts consists of two panels of cloth—each a light colored cotton plain weave with paired warps and wefts (Fig. 2). One panel is undecorated, and the other has a geometric design created with supplemental weft, utilizing dark paired cotton yarns. The dark yarns are two-ply and substantially thicker than the single-ply light cotton yarns in the basic fabric. One shirt in the sample (Burial 75 Textile 4) has sleeves of cotton plain weave, with supplemental wool wefts forming stripes. It was made of twill weave with supplemental wool wefts forming stripes (see *Shirts* below).

Two open plain weave textiles have elaborate supplemental weft decoration (Figs. 3, 4). Each was woven with fine, single-ply cotton yarns. The one in Figure 3 has a supplemental weft design depicting a head, shown frontally, with serpent-like appendages. The head has a fanged mouth, almond-shaped eyes, a necklace of large beads, and appears to be wearing a headdress. The design was created using six colors of supplemental weft elements—the white yarns are cotton and the other five are wool. The eyes and nose were outlined with embroidery of brown, two-ply cotton yarn. This textile fragment

was probably from the front part of a shirt (see *Shirts* below).

The textile in Figure 4 has a geometric design created with four colors of supplemental wool weft, alternating on a diagonal grid.

Twill Weave

Approximately 25 percent of the textiles in the sample are twills. More than 70 percent of the twills are 2/2 and all but one of the remainder are 2/2 with paired warps and wefts. The exception, a 2/1 twill with paired warps and wefts (Fig. 5), is the only twill with a complex design. Two twills (Burial 7 Textile 2, Burial 21 Textile 4) have warp stripes, created by sections of light colored cotton warps alternating with sections of dark colored cotton warps (Fig. 6). A few of the twills have slight variations in the color used for warp and weft yarns, which emphasize the structure of the twill (e.g., Burial 2 Textile 1). One twill (Burial 14 Textile 2) is decorated with stripes of supplemental cotton wefts, and another (Burial 75 Textile 4) is decorated with stripes of supplemental wool wefts.

Gauze Weave

The six gauze textiles in the sample appear to have been head cloths. One had an elaborate tapestry border sewn to it (see *Head Cloths* below); the others were without elaboration. All six were made of single-ply cotton yarn and were plain gauze weave (see Emery 1980: Fig. 282).

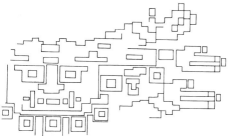

Figure 3. Left, elaborate shirt patch of open plain weave with supplemental weft (Huaca 45 Textile 1); below, detail of the design.

Tapestry Weave

The ten tapestries in the sample have single-ply cotton warps. All but three have two-ply wool wefts. Two exceptions (Burial 20 Textile 7 and Burial 21 Textile 7) have light-colored wefts of two-ply bichrome yarns consisting of white cotton and gold wool. Burial 21 Textile 7 also has dark brown wefts and gold wefts of single-ply wool. The other exception (Fig. 7) is the most elaborate tapestry in the sample. It is a sleeveless shirt, recovered from refuse in Room Group 79. It was made of twelve panels of cloth, sewn together vertically. The red and yellow wefts are two-ply Z-spun wool yarns, while the white and tan wefts are single-ply Z-spun cotton yarns.

Three tapestries were woven as narrow bands to be sewn onto the edges of plain weave or gauze textiles (see *Head Cloths* below). These are between 2.5 and 3.5 centimeters wide and were woven with one straight edge and one scalloped edge (Figs. 8-10). None of the three has a complete length, but the incomplete length of one (Figs. 8, 9, 10) is 86 centimeters.

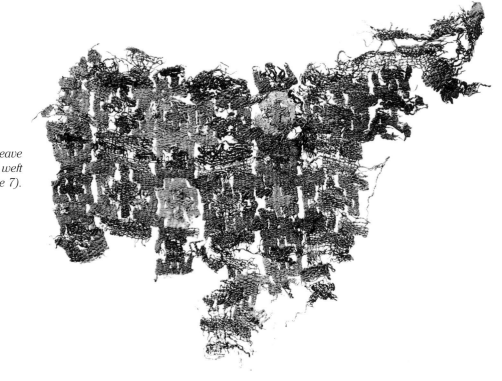

Figure 4. Open plain weave with supplemental weft (Burial 80 Textile 7).

Figure 5. Shirt of 2/1 twill, left, reconstruction of complete shirt; right, detail of weave and pattern (Burial 32 Textile 1).

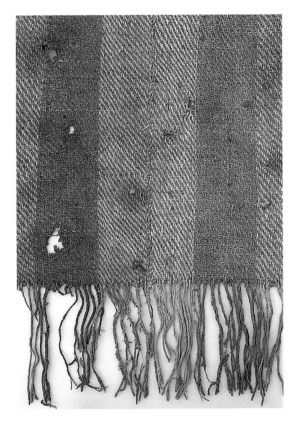

Figure 7. Above, tapestry weave shirt; below, detail of weave and pattern (RG 79 Textile 1).

Figure 6. Twill with warp stripes (Burial 21 Textile 4).

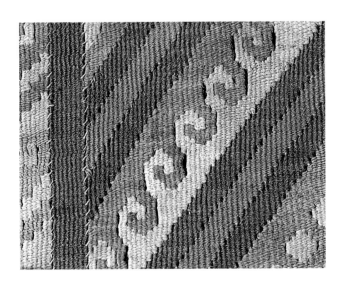

Two tapestries are part of five layers[5] sewn together, one on top of the other, to form a thick, quilt-like object (Fig. 11). Both are polychrome slit tapestry with wool wefts. The function of this object is unknown.

The other tapestries are fragments. None has complete length or width. One appears to have had a

5. Four layers of textile and one of unspun cotton.

Figure 8. Detail of a head cloth tapestry band (Burial 25 Textile 4).

Figure 9. Detail of a head cloth tapestry band (Burial 5 Textile 2).

Figure 11. Quilted fabric (Burial 20 Textile 8).

Figure 10. Tassel end of a head cloth tapestry band (Burial 5 Textile 2).

Figure 12. Tapestry (Burial 80 Textile 24).

Figure 13. Left, double-cloth flat bag; right, detail of weave and pattern (Burial 80 Textile 6).

Figure 14. Double-cloth from a cylindrical bag (Burial 75 Textile 5).

complex design, but it was too badly decomposed for the design to be reconstructed (Fig. 12). The others (Burial 20 Textiles 5, 7, 9; Burial 80 Textile 24) appear to have had large, geometric patterns in contrasting light and dark colors, but their poor condition made it impossible to reconstruct the original design.

Double-cloth

The sample includes three examples of double-cloth: a bag (Fig. 13), part of another bag (Fig. 14), and part of a head cloth (Fig. 15). Each consists of one layer of brown cotton plain weave and another of tan cotton plain weave. On one bag (Fig. 13) the brown layer has paired warps and wefts, while the tan layer has single warps and wefts. On the other bag (Fig. 14) both the brown and tan layers have paired warps and wefts, and on the head cloth (Fig. 15) both the brown and tan layers have single warps and wefts.

Wool elements, which were added to the design on each of the double cloths, resemble tapestry. Warp floats from the ground weave were interlaced with supplemental discontinuous wool wefts.[6]

Figure 15. Double-cloth from a head cloth (Burial 75 Textile 3).

---

6. This technique has been reported previously for Moche textiles (Donnan 1973; Conklin and Versteylen 1978; Conklin 1979; Prümers 1995).

Netting

The nine examples of netting all appear to be fishing nets. Five had been used as rope to tie objects into bundles. Another (Burial 75 Textile 9) is an unfinished net (Donnan and McClelland, this volume, Burial 75). It is still attached to, and wrapped around, a stone *mallero*, a spacer used to create a consistent mesh size in tying nets.

Garments and Accessories

Most of the textiles are so fragmentary that we could not reconstruct their original size and form or determine their original function. The more complete ones, however, can be identified as garments or accessories.

Shirts

Seven of the eight shirts in the sample are sleeveless. Three of these are small, and apparently were made for infants or children. Each consists of a single panel of cloth. The length was folded in half and sewn along the sides with a space left unsewn on each side to create an arm opening (Fig. 16a-c).

One single-panel sleeveless shirt of tan cotton plain weave (Fig. 16a) was in the grave of an eight-month-old infant. The sides were sewn with blue cotton threads. The neck slit appears to have been created during weaving by leaving several warps unwoven in the center of the textile. The unwoven warps subsequently were divided into two groups, one on either side of the neck open-

Figure 17. Warriors wearing decorative shirts.

ing, bound together, and secured to the adjacent fabric with an overcast stitch. Blue thread reinforced the ends of the slit, and white thread reinforced the sides.

The largest single-panel sleeveless shirt (Fig. 16b) was in the grave of a two-year-old child. It was made of tan cotton plain weave with paired warps and wefts, and had fringe along both the front and back hem created by Z-plying groups of two to eight warp yarns. The neck slit on this shirt was too decomposed for precise analysis; however, it appears to have been created in the same way as the previous example.

The third single-panel sleeveless shirt (Figs. 5, 16c) was in the grave of a three-month-old infant. It is the unusual 2/1 twill with patterned decoration discussed above (see *Twill Weave*). Its design sometimes is seen on clothing depicted in Moche art (Fig. 17). The neck opening was not created when the textile was being woven. Instead, it was formed by an irregular horizontal tear which was not subsequently reinforced with sewing.

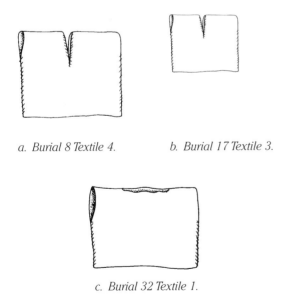

a. Burial 8 Textile 4.   *b. Burial 17 Textile 3.*

c. Burial 32 Textile 1.

Figure 16. Single-panel shirts.

In addition to the single-panel sleeveless shirts, there are three sleeveless shirts made of two panels. The widths of the panels were sewn together to form a central vertical seam, with a space left unsewn near the center of the seam to create a neck opening (Fig. 18). The lengths of the panels were then folded in half and sewn along the sides with a space left unsewn on each side to create an arm opening.

The largest of the two-panel sleeveless shirts (Fig. 18a) was made of tan cotton 2/2 twill with paired warps and wefts. It is undecorated and is 105 centimeters from shoulder to hem and 90 centimeters wide. The hem would have been below the knee on the average Moche adult. Thus it may have had the appearance of the long garment usually worn by females in Moche art (Fig. 19). It was found in the grave of an adult, whose sex could not be determined.

The other two-panel sleeveless shirts are wide but rather short. One (Fig. 18b) was made of tan cotton 2/2 twill with Z-spun yarns. The other (Fig. 18c) was made of brown cotton 2/2 twill with two white cotton warp stripes along the sides of each panel. Both were found in graves of adult males. They resemble the short shirts

Figure 19. Woman wearing a long shirt.

worn by some males depicted in Moche art (Fig. 20), who also usually wear either a short skirt (Fig. 20a) or a loincloth (Fig. 20b).

The final sleeveless shirt was made of multiple panels, and was the most elaborately woven Moche textile that we recovered from Pacatnamu (Fig. 7). It is so small (36 centimeters wide and 29 centimeters high) that it could only have been worn by a young infant. It was made of twelve panels of tapestry, sewn together

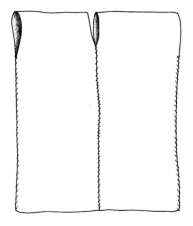

a. Burial 25 Textile 1.

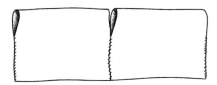

b. Burial 4 Textile 3.

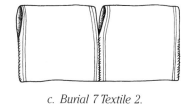

c. Burial 7 Textile 2.

Figure 18. Two-panel shirts.

20a   20b

Figure 20. Warriors.

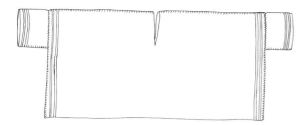

Figure 21. Sleeved shirt (Burial 75 Textile 4).

Figure 22. Detail of warp stripes on center panel of shirt in Figure 21 (Burial 75 Textile 4).

vertically (see *Tapestry Weave* above). The vertical neck slit and arm holes are similar to those on the two-panel sleeveless shirts discussed above.

In addition to sleeveless shirts, there is one shirt with sleeves (Fig. 21). It was made of three rectangular panels of cloth—two forming the front and back, and one forming both sleeves. The two panels forming the front and back are each 96 centimeters long and 46 centimeters wide, with all four selvages intact. Each was woven as 2/2 cotton twill, with supplemental weft stripes of wool near the upper and lower edges (Fig. 22). These panels were turned 90 degrees so that the weft stripes became vertical along the sides of the shirt (Fig. 21). A

neck slit was formed by cutting some of the warp yarns in each panel midway along their length, and finishing the edges of the cuts with closely spaced overcast stitches. The two panels were placed one on top of the other and sewn together, from the neck slit across to the upper corners and from the lower corners upward to the place where the sleeves would be attached. Assembling the shirt in this way resulted in stitches across the top of the shoulders, similar to those on the garment worn by the adult female in Figure 23.

The two sleeves appear to have been made from a single panel of cloth 26 centimeters long and 32 centimeters wide. In contrast to the 2/2 twill weave of the front and back panels, the sleeve panel was 1/1 cotton plain weave. Like the central panels, it was woven with wool weft stripes near its upper and lower edges. It was cut in half across the warps; each half was subsequently made into a sleeve by sewing the two short ends together with an overcast stitch. While the outer edge of each sleeve had an original selvage and was decorated with stripes (Fig. 24), the inner edge was cut cloth and undecorated. The inner edges were sewn to the central panel of the shirt to form sleeves.

Figure 23. Nursing female wearing a shirt with stitches on the shoulder.

Figure 24. Detail of warp stripes on the sleeve of the shirt in Figure 21 (Burial 75 Textile 4).

A final step in creating the shirt was to sew a braided tassel of red and white wool yarn to the front, just below the neck slit (Fig. 25). This tassel was created by folding in half several 15-centimeter lengths of white yarn and red yarn, separating them into four groups, and subsequently braiding the groups together. The unbraided end then was wrapped with white yarn. Individuals in Moche art (Fig. 26) sometimes wear tassels like this.

The sleeved shirt had greater width than height, and would have resembled the short two-panel sleeveless shirts (Fig. 18b, c). Like them, it was probably worn with either a short skirt (Fig. 20a) or a loincloth (Fig. 20b).

In addition to the eight relatively complete shirts discussed above, there was one identifiable fragment (Fig. 3) from the front of a shirt, in the area immediately beneath the neck slit. The shirt had been made of a single panel of open plain weave cotton cloth. The neck slit was created during the weaving process by using discontinuous weft elements, and was not subsequently reinforced with sewing. An elaborate design had been created with supplemental weft immediately beneath the neck slit. In Moche art individuals are shown wearing shirts with similarly located decorative elements (Fig. 27).

It should be noted that only one of the shirts in the sample had sleeves. In Moche art, both sleeveless (Fig. 20) and sleeved (Fig. 28) shirts are depicted; usually,

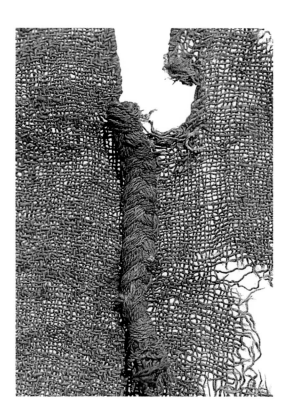

Figure 25. Tassel on the shirt in Figure 21 (Burial 75 Textile 4).

Figure 26. Individual wearing a shirt with a tassel in front.

Figure 27. Individual wearing a shirt with
a shirt patch in front.

Figure 28. Warriors wearing sleeved shirts.

however, it is not clear whether the shirt had sleeves (e.g., Fig. 29). This is not surprising when one considers their width. The two-panel adult shirts in our sample are between 86 and 100 centimeters wide, and thus would have extended at least 20 centimeters beyond each shoulder. This extension could have resembled a sleeve that covered approximately half of the upper arm.

Loincloths

Only one of the seven loincloths in the sample (Burial 21 Textile 5) is sufficiently complete that its original form can be reconstructed, but fragments of the others are so similar that they can be identified confidently as loincloths.

Six loincloths consist of a large rectangular cloth with a narrow band sewn along each weft selvage (Fig. 30). In all but one of these, the rectangular cloth was made of either one or two panels of 2/2 cotton twill. The exception (Burial 41 Textile 1) was made of a single panel of plain weave with paired warps and wefts. The ties were narrow bands of cotton plain weave, folded in half along their lengths, and then sewn to the rectangular cloth with an overcast stitch. The loincloths were worn by being brought up between the legs, the ties

Figure 29. Coca chewers with shirts and circular bags.

Figure 30. Loincloth (Burial 21 Textile 5).

wrapped around the waist from front to back and back to front, and then tied.

In addition to the six loincloths with ties, there was one that consisted only of a large rectangular panel, without ties. It would have been worn in the same fashion as the others, but simply tied at the corners.

The center panel of the one nearly complete loincloth (Burial 21 Textile 5) measured 98 by 80 centimeters. It would have fitted rather loosely—as corroborated by depictions of loincloths in Moche art (Fig. 20b).

All seven loincloths were found in graves of adult males. In Moche art they appear to be worn exclusively by males and usually are worn with a shirt covering the torso.

Head Cloths

Nine textiles can be identified as head cloths. All were found either wrapped around the head or in a fragmentary state near the head. One (Burial 16 Textile 4) was in a child's grave, and another (Burial 25 Textile 4) was in the grave of an adult whose sex could not be determined. The other seven were in adult male graves. Six of the nine were made of gauze. Since these include every gauze textile in the sample, it may be that gauze textiles were used exclusively as head cloths.

Eight head cloths are rectangular, consisting of a large cotton panel of gauze or open plain weave cloth. None is sufficiently intact to enable us to reconstruct its complete form or dimensions. The most elaborate has decorative bands of tapestry sewn along the edges. All the tapestry bands were woven with one straight and one scalloped edge (Figs. 8-10), and the straight edge was sewn to the large cloth panel. It is not known whether the elaborate tapestry bands were sewn only along one side of the large cloth panels, or to two or more sides. It is clear, however, that some of the bands were longer than the selvages of the large cloth panel to

Figure 31. Individual wearing a plain rectangular head cloth.

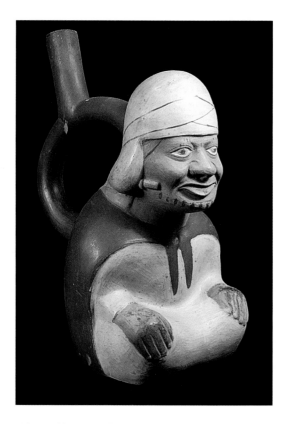

Figure 32. Individual wearing a plain rectangular head cloth and a long cape.

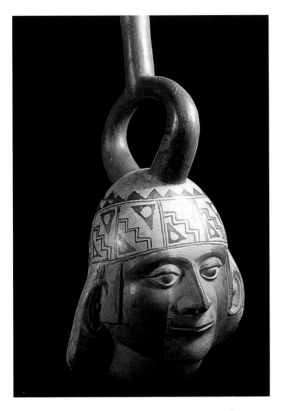

Figure 33. Individual wearing a rectangular head cloth with a scalloped tapestry band.

Figure 35. Individual wearing a rectangular head cloth with a tasseled band.

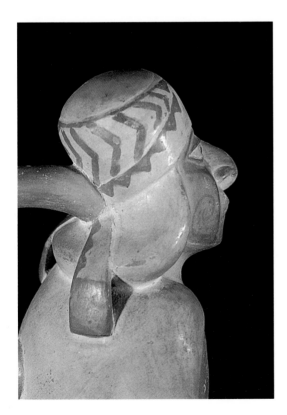

Figure 34. Individual wearing a rectangular head cloth with a scalloped tapestry band.

which they were sewn, and thus would have extended well beyond its corners. The decorative tapestry band on one head cloth terminated in tassels (Figs. 9, 10).

It is interesting to compare the rectangular head cloths in our sample with those worn by adult males in Moche art. In some depictions, males wear plain head cloths without decorative tapestry bands (Figs. 31, 32) like some in our sample. Others wear head cloths that clearly have decorative tapestry bands (Fig. 33). These almost invariably exhibit the distinctive scalloped edge that characterizes the tapestry bands in our sample. Some individuals wear elaborate tapestry bands that extend beyond the corners of the rectangular panel, hanging down as ties (Fig. 34). Others wear head cloths with tassels (Fig. 35).

It is noteworthy that an individual in a Moche weaving scene (Fig. 36) appears to be weaving elaborate tapestry bands with one scalloped edge and one straight edge. These bands probably were being woven for head cloths (see Donnan 1978:175).

In addition to the eight rectangular head cloths, there is a triangular one. It was made from three panels of cloth—one rectangular and one square panel of plain weave, and one square panel of double-cloth (Figs. 15, 37a). These were sewn together to form a large square panel measuring 52 by 52 centimeters (Fig. 37a). The panel was then folded diagonally to form a triangle, and the open sides of the triangle were sewn so that the triangular cloth became a large, closed pocket (Fig. 37b). The triangular cloth was subsequently folded (Fig. 37c), and tied around the head (Fig. 37d). In Moche art this type of head cloth is generally worn by fishermen (Fig. 38). It is interesting that the headcloth was found in the grave of an adult male (Burial 75) who was buried with an unfinished fishing net.

Long Capes

One final garment in our sample of Moche textiles is a large cloth panel that probably was worn as a long cape. In Moche art, individuals often are depicted wearing rectangular cloth panels that have two adjacent corners pulled up over the shoulders and tied across the chest (Fig. 32). The cloth panel covers the shoulders and hangs down the back. Many of the large plain cotton cloths in our sample probably were used for this purpose prior to serving as burial shrouds. Generally, they were made of two or three panels of cloth, sewn together along their warp selvages with an overcast stitch. Some were plain weave with either single or paired warps and wefts, while others were twill weave with either single or paired warps and wefts.

Bags

There are two bags in the sample, one flat and the other cylindrical. The flat bag (Figs. 13, 39) is remarkably similar to a Moche bag excavated at Huaca del Sol in the Moche Valley in 1972 (Conklin and Versteylen 1978: Figures 4,5; Conklin 1979: 169). Its basic weave was double-cloth with supplemental weft on warp floats (see *Double-cloth* above). The design includes a frontal warrior wearing a large crescent-shaped headdress ornament and holding weapons in his extended hands.

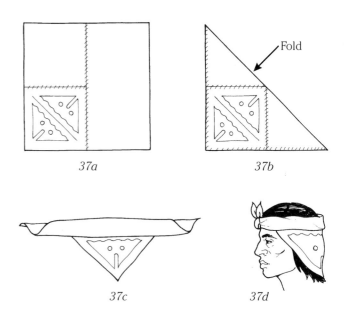

Figure 37. Construction of the triangular head cloth (Burial 75 Textile 3).

The bag was woven as a single rectangular panel, 18 centimeters long and 34 centimeters wide, with warp yarns extending approximately 4 centimeters beyond the woven area at the bottom (Figs. 13, 39a). The panel

Figure 36. Weaver, who appears to be weaving scalloped tapestry bands for head cloths (detail from a fineline painting of a weaving scene).

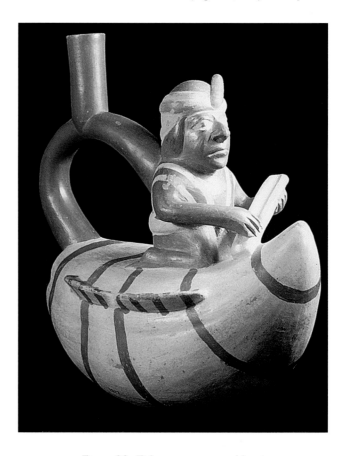

Figure 38. Fisherman on a reed boat.

then was folded in half and sewn along the bottom and open side (Fig. 39b). Cotton loops for a drawstring were sewn along the upper edge of the bag, and a cotton drawstring was inserted through the loops. A fringe along the lower edge of the bag was created by Z-plying groups of warp yarns (Figs. 13, 39c).

The cylindrical bag consisted of one panel of double cloth (Fig. 14) that formed the sides, and a smaller panel of plain weave with supplemental weft that formed the bottom (Fig. 40). Both panels appear to have been scraps of larger textiles that were worn and tattered prior to being assembled into a bag as shown in Figure 41.[7]

Realizing that the Moche had both flat and cylindrical bags, it is interesting to look at the way bags are depicted in Moche art. Presumably, flat bags have relatively straight bottom edges, which may or may not have fringe (Fig. 42), while cylindrical bags have rounded bottoms and no fringe (Figs. 29, 43).

The Moche Weaving Tradition

Our Pacatnamu textiles conform in most respects to what has been reported earlier about Moche weaving (O'Neale and Kroeber 1930; O'Neale 1946; Strong and Evans 1952; Bennett and Bird 1964; Ubbelohde-Doering 1967; Donnan 1973; Conklin 1979; Prümers 1995). All reported examples of Moche textiles exhibit remarkable consistency in the use, spin, and ply of cotton and wool fibers. Only tapestries utilized much wool, but even they were woven with cotton warps, and usually used cotton rather than wool for areas of white weft. This implies that wool was more scarce and therefore more valuable than cotton in Moche society. Moreover, it indicates that Moche weavers appreciated the strong colors of dyed wool, and valued it as a means of elaborating their textiles.

Plain weaves and twill weaves woven with either single or paired warps and wefts were the most common textile structures. Some were elaborated with supplemental weft.

Double-cloth was used to produce textiles with figurative and geometric designs. Moche double-cloth often was elaborated by weaving supplemental wool wefts on cotton warps that were allowed to float at specific places in the design.

The most colorful textiles were tapestry. Because of the amount of wool used in the weft, and the time and skill required in weaving tapestry, the Moche probably saw these as their most valuable textiles. It should be noted that none of the tapestries in our sample had

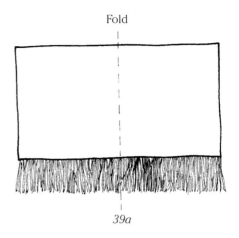

Fold

39a

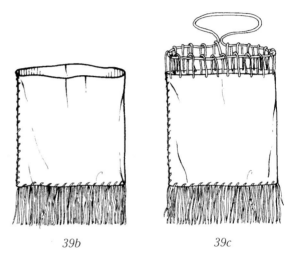

39b   *39c*

Figure 39. *Construction of the flat bag (Burial 80 Textile 6).*

interlaced weft outlining, a characteristic of many, though not all, of the previously reported Moche tapestries (Conklin 1979:173-180). Nor did we find tapestries with eccentric wefts (*ibid.*: 176); all had designs formed on a square matrix.

The identifiable garments and accessories in our sample are particularly valuable because they closely correspond to garments and accessories worn by individuals in Moche art. Moreover, our examination of actual examples has given us valuable insights into their depictions in Moche art—the various types of shirts, headcloths elaborated by tapestry bands with scalloped edges, triangular headcloths worn by fishermen, long capes, and flat and rectangular bags.

We found very few highly decorated textiles in our sample, suggesting that common people in Moche society normally did not have access to elaborate textiles, particularly those with complex iconography. Occasionally, however, they were able to acquire worn fragments of elaborate textiles that perhaps had been discarded by the elite. Two of these were sewn together to create the cylindrical bag (Figs. 14, 41) and another was reused as

---

7. A similar bag from Pacatnamu was found by Ubbelohde-Doering at Huaca 31 (Prümers 1995: Abb. 56). It was 35 centimeters high, and appears to have had a rectangular (23.5 x 22 centimeters) rather than circular bottom.

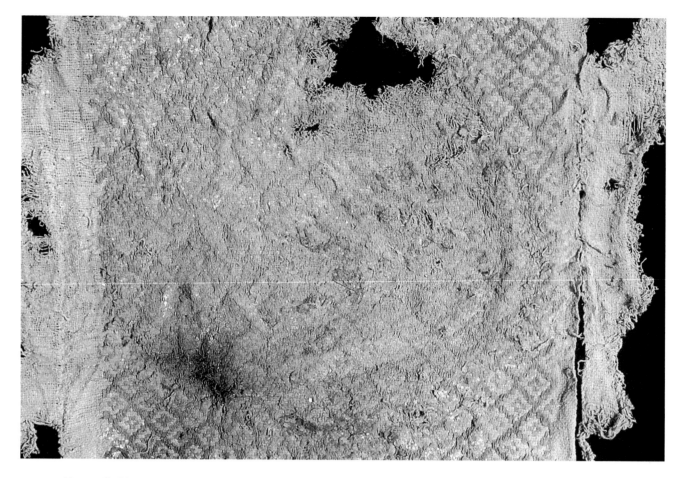

Figure 40. Plain weave with supplemental weft, used for the bottom of the cylindrical bag (Burial 75 Textile 5).

part of a head cloth (Fig. 37). Similarly, one of the most elaborate shirts in the sample (Fig. 5) appears to have been constructed of a decorative twill weave textile that originally was woven for another purpose.

Finally, our sample contains many old and heavily worn fabrics. These were often frayed at the edges, sometimes with portions of the selvages completely worn away. Holes in the fabrics were common—often sewn closed or patched with fragments of other textiles. The prevalence of heavily worn fabrics and the degree of wear tended to be greater in the burials of older adults than in those of young adults or children. This suggests that individuals may have had garments made for them when they were young adults; as they grew older their garments became worn and tattered, but were seldom replaced by new ones. Presumably, the investment of time and materials to make new garments was sufficiently taxing that clothes were kept and used even when they were quite tattered. It would seem that among the common people in Moche society, textiles were not easily acquired, and even when they were worn and tattered they still had value.

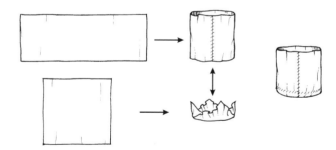

Figure 41. Construction of the Cylindrical bag (Burial 75 Textile 5).

Figure 42. Individual with a flat bag.

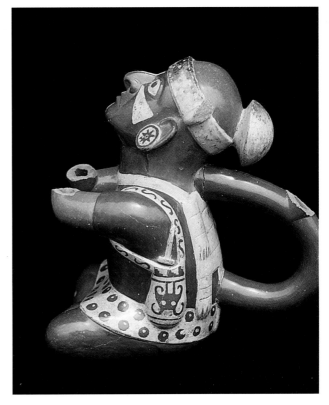

Figure 43. Individual with a cylindrical bag.

KEY TO TABLE 1

The textile numbers in Table 1 are the original field numbers. All cotton and wool products, including string, yarn, and unspun cotton were given textile numbers; however, string, yarn, and unspun cotton, as well as textiles that were too fragmentary to be analyzed, are not included in Table 1. Thus, some textiles numbers are missing (e.g., Textile 1 in Burial 73 which was unspun cotton).

DIMENSIONS:
All dimensions are in centimeters. Bold numbers stand for complete dimensions.
Length (L) and width (W) are indicated when they are complete and can be determined.
Many of the textiles were degraded into multiple fragments. Only the dimensions of the largest fragment are listed.

WEAVE CODE:	FIBER CODE:	S/P CODE:	COLOR CODE:		
ww=warps and wefts	C=cotton	o=overspun	B=brown	N=black	T=tan
	W=wool		W=white	Y=yellow	L=blue
			O=orange	G=gold	R=red

For further information on the textiles, see the individual burial descriptions in Donnan and McClelland, this volume.

Table 1. Moche Textile Sample

BURIAL	TEXTILE	PANELS	OBJECT	WEAVE	DIMENSIONS		WARP Fib	s/p	End/cm	Color	WEFT Fib	s/p	End/cm	Color	HEADINGS	NOTES
Burial 1	Textile 1	2	Shroud		20	x 17										1
			Panel A	Open Plain	10	x 2	C	Z1	8	B	C	Z1	8	B		
			Panel B	Open Plain	19	x 15	C	Z1	8	B	C	Z1	8	B		
	Textile 2	2	Loincloth		22	x 17										1
			Central Panel	2/2 Twill	22	x 14	C	S1	12	B	C	S1	4	B		
			Tie	Plain, Paired w w	9	x 5W	C	S1	12	B	C	Z1	8	B		
Burial 2	Textile 1	2	Outer Shroud		92	x 67									Pattern in colors?	1
			Panel A	2/2 Twill	92	x 38	C	S1	11	B	C	S1	13	B		
			Panel B	2/2 Twill	83	x 42	C	S1	11	B	C	S1	13	B		
	Textile 2	2	Inner Shroud		124	x 90										1, 2
			Panel A	2/2 Twill	116	x 40	C	S1	12	B	C	S1	15	B		
			Panel B	Plain	30	x 56	C	S1	10	B	C	S1	10	B		
Fig. 1	Textile 3	3			37L	x 50										1
			Panel A	Plain			C	S1o	20	B	C	S1o	20	B		
				Supp. Weft							C	S1	10	B		
				Supp. Weft							C	S1	4	W		
			Panel B	Plain			C	S1o	20	B	C	S1o	20	B		
				Supp. Weft							C	S1	10	B		
				Supp. Weft							C	S1	4	W		
			Panel C	Plain			C	S1o	20	B	C	S1o	20	B		
	Textile 4	2			50	x 41										1
			Panel A	2/2 Twill	47	x 30	C	S1	11	B	C	S1	11	B		
			Panel B	Plain	32	x 21	C	S1	12	B	C	S1	12	B		
Burial 3	Textile 1	1		Open Plain	31	x 8	C	S1	12	B	C	S1	18	B		
Burial 4	Textile 1	4	Outer Shroud		168	x 44										1
			Panel A	2/2 Twill	23	x 16	C	S1	9	B	C	S1	9	B		
			Panel B	2/2 Twill	68	x 12	C	S1	9	B	C	S1	9	B		
			Panel C	2/2 Twill	98	x 46	C	S1	9	B	C	S1	9	B		
			Panel D	2/2 Twill	27	x 16	C	S1	9	B	C	S1	9	B		
	Textile 2	2			130L	x 82W										1
			Panel A	2/2 Twill	130L	x 41W	C	S1	13	B	C	S1	11	B	1 Row, 2 Wefts	
			Panel B	2/2 Twill	106L	x 41W	C	S1	13	B	C	S1	11	B		
Fig. 18b	Textile 3	2	Shirt		37H	x 100W										
			Bodice Panel A	2/2 Twill	74L	x 50W	C	Z1	12	T	C	Z1	12	T	1 Row, 1 Cord SZ2	
			Bodice Panel B	2/2 Twill	39	x 40	C	Z1	12	T	C	Z1	11	T		
	Textile 4	2			85	x 60										1
			Panel A	Open Plain	85	x 45W	C	S1o	14	B	C	Z1o	16	B		
			Panel B	Open Plain	85	x 15	C	S1o	14	B	C	Z1o	16	B		
	Textile 5	2	Head Cloth		44	x 32										1, 3
			Central Panel	Open Plain	44	x 29	C	S1	7	B	C	S1	8	B		
			Band	Slit Tapestry	44	x 3W	C	SZ2	10	T	W	Z1	42	B		
											C	S1	23	W		
											W	SZ2	26	G		
	Textile 6	1	Head Cloth	Gauze	80	x 46	C	S1o	6	T	C	S1o	3	T		
Burial 5	Textile 1	1	Outer Shroud	Open Plain	52	x 40W	C	S1o	6	B	C	S1o	4	B		
Figs. 9, 10	Textile 2	2	Head Cloth													1
			Central Panel	Open Plain	22	x 21	C	SZ2	8	B	C	SZ2	6	B		
			Band	Slit Tapestry	71	x 3.5W	C	SZ2	11	W	W	SZ2	32	B		3
											C		SZ2	32	W	
				Tassels on Band												4
	Textile 3	1	Head Cloth	Gauze	13	x 17	C	S1	6	T	C	S1	2	T		
	Textile 4	1		2/2 Twill	28	x 17	C	S1	8	B	C	S1	6	B		
Burial 6	Textile 1	1	Shroud	2/2 Twill, Paired w w	21	x 9	C	S1	20	B	C	S1	18	B		
	Textile 2	1	Llama Wrapping?	Net												5, 6
Burial 7	Textile 1	2	Shroud		108	x 108W										1
			Panel A	2/2 Twill, Paired w w	108	x 58W	C	S1	18	B	C	S1	12	B	1 Row, 4 Wefts	
			Panel B	2/2 Twill, Paired w w	68	x 50W	C	S1	18	B	C	S1	12	B		
Fig. 18c	Textile 2	2	Shirt		40H	x 86W										7
			Bodice Panel A	2/2 Twill	80L	x 43W	C	S1	8	B	C	S1	8	B		
							C	S1	4	W						
			Bodice Panel B	2/2 Twill	80L	x 43W	C	S1	8	B	C	S1	8	B		
							C	S1	4	W						
	Textile 3	3			41	x 48										1, 8
			Panel A	Plain	30	x 20	C	S1	10	B	C	S1	10	B		
			Panel B	Plain	41	x 30	C	S1	10	B	C	S1	10	B		
			Panel C	Plain	14	x 30	C	S1	19	B	C	S1	18	B	Plain, 0.5 wide	
	Textile 4	1	Head Cloth	Gauze	160	x 32	C	S1o	6	B	C	S1o	3	B		
Burial 8	Textile 1	1	Outer Shroud	2/2 Twill, Paired w w	77	x 48W	C	S1	22	T	C	S1	20	T		
	Textile 2	1	Middle Shroud	Plain, Paired w w	134L	x 84	C	S1	12	B	C	S1	14	B	1 Row, 4 Wefts	
	Textile 3	2	Inner Shroud		80	x 120										1
			Panel A	Plain, Paired w w	79	x 70	C	S1	12	B .	C	S1	10	B		
			Panel B	Plain, Paired w w	80	x 60W	C	S1	12	B	C	S1	10	B		
Fig. 16b	Textile 4	1	Shirt		30	x 36W										9
			Bodice Panel	Plain	60	x 36W	C	S1	13	T	C	S1	11	T	1 Row, 2 Wefts	

Table 1. Moche Textile Sample (cont.)

BURIAL	TEXTILE	PANELS	OBJECT	WEAVE	DIMENSIONS	WARP				WEFT				HEADINGS	NOTES
						Fib	s/p	End/cm	Color	Fib	s/p	End/cm	Color		
Burial 9	Textile 1	1 ?		2/2 Twill	2 x 1	C	S1	10	T	C	S1	8	T		
Burial 10	Textile 1	1 ?		2/2 Twill			S1			C					5
Burial 11	Textile 1	1	Outer Shroud	2/2 Twill, Pair w w	23 x 14	C	S1	14	B	C	S1	14	B		
	Textile 2	2			25 x 22										1
			Panel A	Open Plain	9 x 4	C	S1	12	T	C	S1	8	T		
			Panel B	Open Plain	25 x 18										
	Textile 3	1		2/2 Twill	14 x 9	C	S1	12	B	C	S1	9	B		
Burial 12	Textile 1	1 ?													5
	Textile 2	1	Shroud	Plain, Paired w w	11 x 11	C	S1	14	T	C	S1	12	T		
	Textile 3	1		2/2 Twill	23 x 20	C	S1	15	T	C	S1	13	T		
Burial 14	Textile 1	1		Plain	3 x 3	C	S1	10	B	C	S1	12	B		
	Textile 2	1		2/2 Twill, Paired w w	8 x 4	C	S1	10	B	C	S1	14	B		10
				Supp. Weft						C	S1	12	Y		
Burial 15	Textile 1	1	Inner Shroud	Plain	16 x 10	C	S1	14	T	C	S1	9	T		
	Textile 2	1	Outer Shroud	2/2 Twill		C	S1		B	C			B		5
	Textile 3	1		Plain, Paired w w		C			B	C			B		5
	Textile 4	1		Plain, Paired w w	4 x 5	C	S1	22	T	C	S1	18	T		
	Textile 5	1		2/2 Twill	1.5 x 1	C	S1	8	B	C	S1	10	B		
Burial 16	Textile 1	2	Outer Shroud		95 x 98W										1
			Panel A	Plain	95 x 49W	C	Z1	14	T	C	Z1	11	T	1 Row, 2 Wefts	
			Panel B	Plain	95 x 49W	C	Z1	14	T	C	Z1	11	T		
	Textile 2	2	Inner Shroud		54 x 98W										1
			Panel A	Plain	54 x 49W	C	Z1	14	T	C	Z1	14	T		
			Panel B	Plain	54 x 49W	C	Z1	10	T	C	Z1	12	T		
	Textile 3	1	Cordage	Net	40L										11
	Textile 4	1	Head Cloth	Gauze	55 x 45	C	S1	6	T	C	S1	4	T		
Burial 17	Textile 1	2	Shroud		104 x 104W										1
			Panel A	Plain, Paired w w	100 x 52W	C	S1	16	T	C	S1	12	T		
			Panel B	Plain, Paired w w	104 x 52W	C	S1	16	T	C	S1	12	T		
	Textile 2	1	Cordage	Net	14L										12
Fig. 16a	Textile 3	1	Shirt		52L x 60W										13
			Bodice Panel	Plain, Paired w w	104L x 60W	C	S1	16	T	C	S1	12	T	2 Rows, 4 Wefts	
	Textile 4	1		Plain, Paired w w	4 x 2	C	S1	10	T	C	S1	8	T		
Burial 18	Textile 1	1	Shroud	Open Plain	6 x 8	C	S1	9	T	C	S1	7	T		5
	Textile 2	1		Plain, Paired w w	4 x 2	C	S1	14	T	C	S1	10	T		
Burial 20	Textile 1	2	Outer Shroud		80 x 150W										1
			Panel A	Plain, Paired w w	80 x 75W	C	S1	20	T	C	S1	16	T	1 Row, 4 Wefts	
			Panel B	Plain, Paired w w	80 x 75W	C	S1	20	T	C	S1	16	T	1 Row, 4 Wefts	
	Textile 2	3	Inner Shroud		67 x 97										1, 14
			Panel A	2/2 Twill	67 x 52W	C	S1	20	T	C	S1	20	T	1 Row, 4 Wefts	
			Panel B	2/2 Twill	29 x 15	C	S1	20	T	C	S1	20	T		
			Panel C	2/2 Twill	21 x 20	C	S1	20	T	C	S1	20	T	1 Row, 4 Wefts	
Fig. 2	Textile 3	2			24 x 21										
			Panel A	Plain, Paired w w	24 x 9	C	S1	14	T	C	S1	14	T		
			Panel B	Plain, Paired w w	24 x 12	C	S1	14	T	C	S1	14	T		
				Supp. Weft						C	SZ2	6	B		
	Textile 4	2			18 x 47										1, 15
			Panel A	Plain	18 x 47	C	SZ2	7	T	W	ZS2	26	R		
			Panel B	Open Plain	18 x 34	C	S1	7	B	C	S1	7	B		
	Textile 5	2			9 x 8										16
			Panel A	Slit Tapestry		C		5		W	SZ2	20	B		
										W	SZ2	20	Y		
										W	SZ2	20	G		
			Panel B	Open Plain	2 x 3	C	S1	8	T	C	S1	10	T		
	Textile 7	1			14 x 7										17
				Slit Tapestry		C	S1	6	T	C	S1	26	W		
										W	SZ2	32	YG		
										W	SZ2	24	N		
Fig. 11	Textile 8	4			16 x 15										18
			Panels A and B	Slit Tapestry	16 x 15	C	SZ2	7	T	W	SZ2	36	Y		
										W	SZ2	36	R		
										W	SZ2	36	B		
										W	SZ2	36	N		
			Panels C and D	Plain	12 x 9	C	S1	8	T	C	S1	8	T		
	Textile 9	4			19 x 15										19
			Panel A	Tapestry	5 x 12	C	SZ2	8	T	W	SZ2	22	B		
			Panel B	Plain	17 x 17	C	S1	12	T	C	S1	12	T		
			Panel C	Open Plain	12 x 17	C	S1	20	T	C	S1	20	T		
			Panel D	Plain, Paired w w	23 x 12	C	S1	12	T	C	S1	10	T		
	Textile 10	1		Net	21 x 7										20
	Textile 11	1		Plain, Paired w w	6 x 5	C	S1	20	T	C	S1	20	T		

Table 1. Moche Textile Sample (cont.)

BURIAL	TEXTILE	PANELS	OBJECT	WEAVE	DIMENSIONS			WARP Fib	s/p	End/cm	Color	WEFT Fib	s/p	End/cm	Color	HEADINGS	NOTES
Burial 21	Textile 1b			Net	13	x	16										21
	Textile 1c	1		2/2 Twill	18	x	12	C			T	C			T		5
	Textile 2	2	Outer Shroud		112	x	149W	C	S1	16	T	C	S1	9	T		1
			Panel A	2/2 Twill	97	x	75W										
			Panel B	2/2 Twill	113	x	74W										
	Textile 3	2	Inner Shroud	Plain	134	x	146W										1
			Panel A		112	x	70W	C	S1	9	T	C	S1	9	T	1 Row, 2 Wefts	
			Panel B		92	x	46	C	S1	9	T	C	S1	9	T		
Fig. 6	Textile 4	3			75	x	119										1, 22
			Panel A	2/2 Twill, Paired w w	31	x	48	C	S1	10	T	C	S1	10	B	1 Row, 4 Wefts	
								C	S1	10	B						
			Panel B	2/2 Twill, Paired w w	75	x	47W	C	S1	10	T	C	S1	10	B	1 Row, 4 Wefts	
								C	S1	10	B						
			Panel C	2/2 Twill, Paired w w	56	x	24	C	S1	10	T	C	S1	10	B	1 Row, 4 Wefts	
												C	S1	10	T		
Fig. 30	Textile 5	3	Loincloth														1
			Central Panel	2/2 Twill	140L	x	80W	C	S1	20	T	C	S1	20	T	1 Row, 4 Wefts	
			Tie	Plain	138L	x	4W	C	S1	13	T	C	S1	5	T		
			Tie	Plain	138L	x	4W	C	S1	13	T	C	S1	5	T		
	Textile 6	1	Cordage	Net	20	x	15										23
	Textile 7	1		Slit Tapestry	25	x	21	C	SZ2	7	W	C	SZ2	32	W		17
												W	S1	36	G		
												W	S1	28	B		
Burial 22	Textile 1	1		Plain	23	x	16	C	S1o	17	T	C	S1o	8	T	1 Row, 3 Wefts	
	Textile 2	1	Shroud	Plain, Paired w w	11	x	6	C	S1	16	T	C	S1	14	T		
Burial 24	Textile 1	1 ?	Shroud	Plain, Paired w w													5
Burial 25	Textile 1	2	Shirt		105L	x	90W										1
Fig. 18a			Bodice Panel	2/2 Twill, Paired w w	210L	x	45W	C	S1	18	T	C	S1	12	T	1 Row, 4 Wefts	
			Bodice Panel	2/2 Twill, Paired w w	204L	x	45W	C	S1	18	T	C	S1	12	T		
	Textile 2	3			209L	x	182										1
			Panel A	2/2 Twill, Paired w w	209L	x	59	C	S1	24	T	C	S1	16	T		
			Panel B	2/2 Twill, Paired w w	209L	x	66	C	S1	24	T	C	S1	16	T		
			Panel C	2/2 Twill, Paired w w	209L	x	57	C	S1	24	T	C	S1	16	T		
	Textile 3	1		Open Plain	19	x	8	C	S1	11	B	C	S1	11	B	1 Row, 2 Wefts	
Fig. 8	Textile 4	2	Head Cloth														1
			Central Panel	Gauze	27	x	11	C	S1	12	T	C	S1	5	T		
			Band	Slit Tapestry	86	x	2.5	C	SZ2	7	T	W	ZS2	24	B		
												W	ZS2	10	W		
	Textile 5	1															1, 24
			Panel A	Plain	34	x	23	C	S1o	10	T	C	S1	8	T		
			Panel B	Plain	46	x	24	C	S1o	10	T	C	S1	8	T		
	Textile 6	1		Plain	51	x	27	C	S1	13	T	C	S1	9	T	1 Row, 2 Wefts	
	Textile 7	2			72	x	82W										1
			Panel A	Plain	72	x	45W	C	S1o	10	T	C	S1o	10	T		
			Panel B	Plain	72	x	37W	C	S1o	10	T	C	S1o	10	T		
	Textile 8	1		Slit Tapestry	27	x	18	C	S1o	8	W	C	S1	24	W		
												W	S1	44	Y		
												W			R		
Burial 26	Textile 1	2	Shroud		27	x	60										1
			Panel A	Plain	27	x	41W	C	S1	12	T	C	S1	9	T	1 Row, 2 Wefts	
			Panel B	Plain	23	x	20	C	S1	12	T	C	S1	9	T		
Burial 27	Textile 1	1	Shroud	2/2 Twill	2	x	1	C	S1		T	C	S1		T		5
Burial 29	Textile 1	1	Outer Shroud	Plain	5	x	3	C	S1	9	B	C	S1	5	B		
	Textile 2	1	Middle Shroud	2/2 Twill	4	x	4	C	S1	12	T	C	S1	10	T		
	Textile 3	1	Inner Shroud	Plain, Paired w w	11	x	5	C	S1	20	T	C	S1	16	T		
Burial 31	Textile 1	3	Outer Shroud		132L	x	136W										
			Panel A	Plain, Paired w w	132L	x	45W	C	S1	14	T	C	S1	10	T	1 Row, 4 Wefts	
			Panel B	Plain, Paired w w	128	x	43W	C	S1	14	T	C	S1	10	T		
			Panel C	Plain, Paired w w	130	x	48W	C	S1	14	T	C	S1	10	T		
	Textile 2	2			77	x	61										1
			Panel A	2/2 Twill	77	x	30	C	S1	21	T	C	S1	14	T		
			Panel B	2/2 Twill	77	x	31	C	S1	21	T	C	S1	14	T		
	Textile 3	1	Inner Shroud	Plain, Paired w w	110	x	91	C	S1	18	B	C	S1	12	B		25
	Textile 4	1		Plain, Paired w w	28	x	30	C	S1	24	T	C	S1	14	T		
Burial 32	Textile 1	1	Shirt		28L	x	37W										
Figs. 5, 16c			Bodice Panel	2/1 Twill, Paired w w	56L	x	37W	C	Z1	22	W	C	Z1	26	B	1 Row, 4 Wefts	
	Textile 2	1	Head Cloth ?	Gauze	25	x	18	C	S1o	10	T	C	S1o	5	T		
Burial 33	Textile 1	1	Shroud														5
Burial 34	Textile 1	1 ?		Plain, Paired w w													5

Table 1. Moche Textile Sample (cont.)

BURIAL	TEXTILE	PANELS	OBJECT	WEAVE	DIMENSIONS	WARP				WEFT				HEADINGS	NOTES
						Fib	s/p	End/cm	Color	Fib	s/p	End/cm	Color		
Burial 36	Textile 1	1 ?		Weft Face						W	SZ2				5
Burial 40	Textile 1	1		Plain, Paired w w	4 x 5.5	C	S1	10	T	C	S1	12	T		
Burial 41	Textile 1	2	Loincloth		18 x 20										1, 26
			Central Panel	Plain, Paired w w	16 x 18	C	S1	14	T	C	S1	14	T	1 Row, 4 Wefts	
			Tie	Plain	15 x 9	C	S1	10	T	C	S1	7	T		
	Textile 2	1 ?	Shroud	Plain, Paired w w											5
Burial 43	Textile 1	1		Plain, Paired w w	3 x 1	C	S1	16	B	C	S1	8	B		
	Textile 2	1 ?		Plain	2L x 1	C	S1		B						5
Burial 44	Textile 1	1		Plain	5 x 3	C	S1	9	T	C	S1	9	T		
	Textile 2	1		Plain, Paired w w	3 x 5	C	S1	18	T	C	S1	6	T		
Burial 45	Textile 1	1 ?	Shroud?												5
Burial 46	Textile 1	1		Weft Face	6 x 2					W	SZ2	18	B		5
Burial 48	Textile 1	1 ?	Shroud?												5
Burial 53	Textile 1	1		2/2 Twill	6 x 1.5	C	S1	14	B	C	S1	7	B		
	Textile 2	1		2/2 Twill	7 x 6	C	S1	13	B	C	S1	13	B		
Burial 61	Textile 1	1		2/2 Twill, Paired w w		C	S1	22	B	C	S1	22	B		
Burial 63	Textile 1	1	Inner Shroud	2/2 Twill	42 x 30	C	S1	13	T	C	S1	13	T		
	Textile 2	1	Outer Shroud	Plain	44 x 21	C	S1	12	T	C	S1	9	T		
	Textile 3	2			42 x 48										1
			Panel A	Open Weave	14 x 7	C	Z1	12	T	C	Z1	10	T		
			Panel B	Open Weave	42 x 41W	C	Z1	12	T	C	Z1	10	T		
	Textile 4	1 ?													5
	Textile 5	1	Cordage	Net	13										27
Burial 64	Textile 1	1 ?													5
Burial 66	Textile 1	1		Plain, Paired w w	3 x 2	C	S1	18	B	C	S1	12	B		
	Textile 2	1		Open Plain	2 x 2	C	S1	10	B	C	S1	8	B		
Burial 68	Textile 1	1 ?													5
Burial 69	Textile 1	1 ?	Shroud?												5
Burial 70	Textile 1	1 ?													5
Burial 71	Textile 1	1		Plain, Paired w w	10 x 5	C	S1	20	B	C	S1	16	B		
Burial 72	Textile 1	2	Outer Shroud		48 x 106										1
			Panel A	Plain	48 x 53W	C	S1	10	B	C	S1	10	B		
			Panel B	Plain	47 x 53W	C	S1	10	B	C	S1	10	B		
	Textile 2	1 ?	Middle Shroud	Plain	100 x 38	C	Z1	10	B	C	Z1	14	B	1 Row, 2 Wefts	
	Textile 3	1 ?	Inner Shroud	Plain	41 x 85W	C	S1os	18	B	C	S1os	18	B	2 Rows, 2 Wefts	
	Textile 4	1 ?		Open Plain	32 x 10	C	S1	9	BL	C	S1	9	B		
Burial 73	Textile 3	1		Open Plain	20 x 18	C	S1	10	T	C	S1	7	T		
	Textile 4	1	Bag	2/2 Twill	26 x 23	C	S1	18	B	C	S1	18	B		28
	Textile 5a	1	Bag	Open Plain	32 x 34	C	Z1	15	T	C	Z1	10	T		28, 29
	Textile 5b	1	Bag	Open Plain	36 x 38	C	S1	14	B	C	S1	12	B	1 Row, 2 Wefts / 1 Row, 4 Wefts	28, 29
	Textile 6	1	Bag	Plain, Paired w w	27 x 18	C	S1	16	B	C	S1	10	B		28
	Textile 7	1	Bag	Plain, paired w w	9 x 7	C	S1	14	T	C	S1	14	T		28
	Textile 8	1	Bag	Plain, Paired w w	21 x 23	C	S1	20	T	C	Z1	14	T		28
	Textile 9	1	Bag	Plain, Paired w w	28 x 17	C	S1	14	T	C	S1	14	T		28
	Textile 12	1	Bag	Plain, Paired w w	25 x 29	C	S1	18	T	C	Z1	12	T		28
	Textile 13	1	Bag	Plain	42 x 10	C	S1	10	T	C	S1	12	T		
	Textile 14	3	Inner Shroud		133 x 70										1
			Panel A	Open Plain	72 x 48W	C	Z1	11	B	C	Z1	11	B		
			Panel B	Open Plain	66 x 48W	C	Z1	11	B	C	Z1	11	B		
			Panel C	Open Plain	70 x 33										
	Textile 15	2	Outer Shroud												
			Panel A	Plain, Paired w w	58 x 33	C	S1	14	B	C	S1	10	B		
			Panel B	Plain, Paired w w	106 x 67	C	S1	14	B	C	S1	10	B		1
Burial 74	Textile 1	3	Panel A	Open Plain	9 x 10	C	S1o	14	B	C	S1o	14	B		1
				Supp. Weft						C	SZ2	7	B		
			Panel B	Open Plain	5 x 4	C	S1o	10	B	C	S1o	10	B		
			Panel C	Plain	2 x 5	C	S1	9	B	C	S1	12	B		
	Textile 3	1		Plain, Paired w w	4 x 4	C	S1	18	B	C	S1	14	B		
	Textile 4	1		Open Plain	12 x 5	C	S1	10	B	C	S1	12	B		
	Textile 5	1		Open Plain	12 x 11	C	S1o	10	T	C	S1o	9	T	1 Row, 2 Wefts	30
	Textile 8	1		Plain, Paired w w	8 x 1	C	S1	12	B	C	S1	8	B		
	Textile 9	1		Plain, Paired w w	42 x 61	C	S1	16	T	C	S1	16	T		
	Textile 10	1		Open Plain	25 x 18	C	S1	10	B	C	S1	10	B		
Burial 75	Textile 1	2	Outer Shroud		150 x 75										1
			Panel A	2/2 Twill, Paired w w	150 x 59	C	S1	18	T	C	S1	18	T		
			Panel B	2/2 Twill, Paired w w	112 x 56	C	S1	18	T	C	S1	18	T		
	Textile 2	2	Loincloth	2/2 Twill	40L x 53	C	S1	13	T	C	S1	16	T		1, 31
					40 x 53	C	S1	13	T	C	S1	16	T		

Table 1. Moche Textile Sample (cont.)

BURIAL	TEXTILE	PANELS	OBJECT	WEAVE		DIMENSIONS		WARP Fib	s/p	End/cm	Color	WEFT Fib	s/p	End/cm	Color	HEADINGS	NOTES
Burial 75	Textile 3	3	Head Cloth		56	x	56										1, 32
Figs. 15, 37			Panel A	Open Plain	28	x	28	C	S1	8	T	C	S1	8	T		
			Panel B	Open Plain	56	x	28	C	S1	8	T	C	S1	8	T		
			Panel C	Double Cloth	28	x	28	C	S1	16	T	C	S1	17	T		
				Plain				C	S1	16	T	C	S1	17	T		
				Plain				C	S1	10	B	W	ZS2	10	B		
				Supp. Weft								W	ZS2	10	G		
Figs. 21-24	Textile 4	3	Shirt														1, 33
			Bodice Front	2/2 Twill	96L	x	46W	C	S1	15	T	C	S1				
			Stripes	Supp. Weft								W	SZ2-ZS2		BR		
			Bodice Back	2/2 Twill	96L	x	46W	C	S1	15	T	C	S1				
			Stripes	Supp. Weft								W	SZ2-ZS2		BR		
			Sleeves	Plain	32L	x	26W	C	S1	13	T	C	S1	13	T	Double Warp	
			Stripes	Supp. Weft								W	SZ2-ZS2	15	BR		
Figs. 14, 41	Textile 5	2	Bag		21H	x	20D										5, 34
			Side Panel	Double Cloth	29	x	58										
				Plain, Paired w w				C	Z1	24	T	C	Z1	24	T		
				Plain, Paired w w				C	S1	16	B	C	S1	16	B		
				Supp. Weft								W	ZS2	12	Y		
Figs. 14, 42			Bottom Panel	Plain, Paired w w	53	x	27	C	S1	9	T	C	S1	9	T		
				Supp. Weft , Paired								C	S1	8	B		
	Textile 6	1		Open Plain	60L	x	37	C	S1	13	T	C	S1	13	T	2 Wefts	35
	Textile 7	2			47	x	50										1, 36
				Plain	34	x	49	C	S1	12	T	C	S1	12	T		
				Plain	13	x	32	C	S1	12	T	C	S1	12	T		
	Textile 9	1	Net		14	x	14										37
	Textile 10	1	Inner Shroud	Plain, Paired w w	76	x	49	C	S1	12,18	TW	C	S1	12	T	4 Wefts	38
Burial 76	Textile 1	1	Shroud	Plain				C				C					5
Burial 77	Textile 1	1 ?	Shroud														5
Burial 78	Textile1	1 ?															5
Burial 79	Textile 1	1 ?	Shroud	Plain, Paired w w													5
Burial 80	Textile 1	2	Loincloth														1
			Central Panel	2/2 Twill	71	x	40	C	S1o	13	T	C	S1o	16	T	1 Row, 2 Wefts	
			Tie	Plain, Paired w w	56	x	5	C	S1o	20	B	C	S1o	9	T	1 Row, 2 Wefts	
	Textile 3	2	Outer Shroud		112	x	61W										1
			Panel A	2/2 Twill	112	x	30W	C	S1o	13	B	C	S1o	11	B	1 Row, 2 Wefts	
			Panel B	2/2 Twill	106	x	31W	C	S1o	13	B	C	S1o	11	B	1 Row, 2 Wefts	
Figs. 3, 39	Textile 6	1	Bag		18L	x	17W										39
				Double Cloth	18L	x	34W										
				Plain, Paired w w				C	S1o	10	T	C	S1o	10	T	1 Row, 2 Wefts	
				Plain				C	S1o	8	B	C	S1o	10	B		
				Supp. Weft								W	SZ2		G		
Fig. 4	Textile 7	1		Open Plain	11	x	26	C	S1o	6	B	C	S1o	11	B		40
				Supp. Weft								W	ZS2	42	R		
				Supp. Weft								W	ZS2	42	Y		
				Supp. Weft								W	S1	26	B		
				Supp. Weft								W	ZS2	32	B		
	Textile 9	1		Open Plain	14	x	4	C	S1o	11	B	C	S1o	11	B		
	Textile 12	1		Open Plain	19	x	12	C	S1o	8	B	C	S1o	6	B		
				Supp. Weft								W	SZ2	20	G		
	Textile 13	1		Open Plain	24	x	12	C	Z1	13	B	C	Z1	13	B		
	Textile 14	2		Open Plain	20	x	13										1, 41
			Panel A	Open Plain	20	x	5	C	S1o	6	B	C	S1o	6	B		
			Panel B	Open Plain, Embroidered	16	x	8	C	S1o	6	B	C	S1o	6	B		
	Textile 16	1	Loincloth tie?	Plain, Paired w w	22	x	5W	C	S1	16	B	C	S1	12	B		42
												C	Z1	12	B		
	Textile 17	1	Middle Shroud	Open Plain	40	x	33	C	S1	17	B	C	S1	14	B		
	Textile 19	3	Loin Cloth														1
			Panel A	2/2 Twill	27	x	18	C	S1	13	B	C	S1	11	B	1 Row, 2 Wefts	
			Panel B	2/2 Twill	21	x	11	C	S1	11	B	C	S1	12	B		
			Tie	Plain, Paired w w	29	x	5	C	S1	14	B	C	S1	11	B		
	Textile 22	2	Inner Shroud ?		70	x	82										1
			Panel A	Open Plain	40	x	12	C	S1o	11	T	C	S1o	11	T		
			Panel B	Open Plain	70	x	68W	C	S1o	11	T	C	S1o	11	T		
Fig. 12	Textile 24	1		Open Plain-Slit Tapestry	17	x	18	C	S1o	13	B	C	S1o	18	B		40, 43
								C	S1o	12	B	W	SZ2	30	G		
												W	SZ2	30	R		
												W	SZ2	30	Y		
	Textile 28	1		Plain	13	x	18	C	S1o	10	B	C	S1o	13	B		
	Textile 29	1		Plain	7	x	3	C	S1o	9	T	C	S1o	11	T		
	Textile 30	1		Plain	10	x	7	C	S1o	10	B	C	S1o	13	B	1 Row, 2 Wefts	

Table 1. Moche Textile Sample (cont.)

BURIAL	TEXTILE	PANELS	OBJECT	WEAVE	DIMENSIONS			WARP				WEFT				HEADINGS	NOTES
								Fib	s/p	End/cm	Color	Fib	s/p	End/cm	Color		
Burial 81	Textile 1	1 ?	Shroud														5
	Textile 2	1 ?															5
Burial 82	Textile 1	1		Plain Pair w Single w				C	S1	11	T?	C	S1	10 pairs	T?		5, 44
Burial 83	Textile 1	1		Net	113	x	21										45
	Textile 2	1		Plain	56	x	30	C	S1	17	T	C	S1	17	T		46
												W	SZ2	18	Y		
	Textile 3	8	Shroud		85	x	72										1, 47
			Panel A	Plain	17	x	4	C	S1	14	T	C	S1	14	T		
			Panel B	2/2 Twill, Pair w w	22	x	43	C	S1	20	T	C	S1	10 pairs	T		
			Panel C	2/2 Twill, Pair w w	24	x	61	C	S1	20	T	C	S1	10 pairs	T		
			Panel D	Plain, Paired w w	80	x	48	C	S1	22	T	C	S1	11 pairs	T		
			Panel E	Plain, Paired w w	72	x	41	C	S1	22	T	C	S1	11 pairs	T		
			Panel F	2/2 Twill	5	x	26	C	S1	17	T	C	S1	17	T		
			Panel G	2/2 Twill, Pair w w	60	x	40	C	S1	22	T	C	S1	11 pairs	T		
			Panel H	Plain	21	x	70	C	S1	15	B	C	S1	15	B		
Burial 84	Textile 1	2	Shroud		172	x	103										1
			Panel A	Plain, Paired w w	35	x	39	C	S1	16	W	C	S1	8 pairs	W		
			Panel B	Plain, Paired w w	172	x	70	C	S1	16	W	C	S1	8 pairs	W		
H45 Fig. 3	Textile 1	1	Shirt	Open Plain				C	S1	6	W	C	S1	11	W		
				Supp. weft								W					
				Supp. weft								W					
				Supp. weft								W					
				Supp. weft								W					
				Supp. weft								W					
				Supp. weft								W					
RG 79 Figs. 7, 18d	Textile 1	12	Shirt	Tapestry	36	x	29	C				W					

NOTES TO TABLE 1

1. These panels were sewn together.

2. This textile is composed of at least two heavily worn and frayed panels that are sewn, one on top of the other, as though for mutual reinforcement. In addition, there are many patches on both panels including twill patches on the plain weave panel and plain weave patches on the twill panel.

3. Scallops are produced by adding another warp yarn which is held in place with weft on each side of the scallop.

4. Brown yarns inserted through slits at the ends, folded in half, and bound with yellow wool, SZ2, and resin.

5. Very badly deteriorated; little or no analysis could be made.

6. Net: cotton, SZ2, mesh size 2 cm x 2 cm.

7. White warp yarns were used to create the narrow white stripes on the two panels.

8. Panels A and B are seamed together on one side at their selvages. Panel C is sewn to Panel A, perpendicular to the seam joining Panels A and B.

9. The sides of the shirt are sewn with blue cotton thread. The neck slit is finished with overcast white thread.

10. Brown background with yellow supplemental warp.

11. Net: cotton, SZ2, mesh size 1 cm x 1 cm, used as cordage.

12. Net: cotton, SZ2, mesh size 1 cm x 1 cm, used as cordage.

13. Warp fringe on the bottom of the shirt, both front and back.

14. Three panels sewn together along their side selvages.

15. The textile consisted of two panels of cloth lying one on top of the other and joined by couching threads. The upper (Panel A) is weft faced with red wool wefts. On the surface a geometric design was created in white wool yarns (SZ2S2), which were tacked in place with cotton threads (ZS2) that passed through the two layers of textile from the bottom (Panel B) side. These threads were allowed to float on the bottom side, while the upper side was left with a clean line pattern.

16. Textile was wrapped around two pieces of cane and tied with two tan wool yarns, SZ2.

17. Some weft yarns were plied cotton and wool.

18. Rectangular object, five layers: upper two tapestry, lower two plain weave, with unspun cotton between. SZ2 tan wool couching in a braid-like stitch (Fig. 11).

19. Four layers of textiles sewn together along one side. These four textiles are sewn one on top of the other—almost certainly as patches and/or repairs of tattered cloth. Panel D is folded.

20. Ball of net: cotton, SZ2, mesh size 1.5 cm x 1.5 cm.

21. Net: white cotton ZS2, mesh size 2.2 cm x 2.2 cm.

22. Warp stripes were created by using alternating tan and brown yarns. Fringe was created by twisting together groups of warp yarns.

23. Net: brown cotton, S1, mesh size could not be determined, used as cordage.

24. The two panels may have been from a single textile or from two textiles sewn together. They are not joined now.

25. This textile was patched with pieces of a similar textile.

26. This may have been a loincloth used as an outer shroud. The tie is made from a 9 cm wide band of plain weave that was apparently torn from another textile (it has only one selvage). It was folded approximately 4 cm from the selvage; then the torn edge was turned under about 1 cm and sewn to the selvage. This formed a band approximately 4 cm wide. The fold, opposite the sewn selvage and torn edge, was sewn to the selvage of the central panel forming the loincloth.

27. Net: cotton, SZ2, mesh size could not be determined, used as cordage.

28. The edges of a single panel of cloth were gathered together and then tied to form the bag.

29. Bags 5a and 5b were collected in the field as one textile. In the laboratory they were determined to be two.

30. This is one panel of cloth (the corner of a panel) that was tied into a knot.

31. The heading consisted of 36 rows of regular weave, then 11 pairs of paired wefts, presumably sewn in. Only the position of the textile relative to the corpse suggests that it is a loincloth; there is nothing about the construction to indicate one.

32. Embroidery yarn is orange-brown wool, ZS2.

33. Shirt composed of three panels: one for the front, one for the back, and one was cut in half to make the sleeves.

34. The spin of the yarns, Z1 and ZS2 in the side panel, is unusual.

35. Gauze over cane frame, under shrouded body.

36. Some corners of this textile were tied together.

37. Net: white cotton SZ2, mesh size 2.3 cm x 2.3 cm.

38. The warp stripes were created by clusters of thin white warps alternating with clusters of thicker tan warps.

39. Drawstring cord on bag, tan cotton, SZ3S2.

40. The open plain weave and slit tapestry are woven on the same warp yarns.

41. Embroidery using three wool yarns: red and yellow, SZ2; tan ZS2.

42. Each pair of weft yarns has one Z-spun yarn and one S-spun yarn.

43. The open plain weave has single warps and wefts. Warps are paired in the slit tapestry.

44. It could not be determined if the wefts were paired and the warps were single or vice versa.

45. Net: white cotton, SZ2, mesh size 2 cm x 2 cm.

46. Wool weft stripe heading consists of 0.8 cm of cotton plain weave and 1.5 cm of wool plain weave.

47. This textile was worn and patched many times utilizing fragments of at least seven different textiles.

RESUMEN:
Tejidos Moche de Pacatnamú

Pacatnamú es uno de los pocos sitios donde se han excavado, arqueológicamente, tejidos Moche, siendo Heinrich Ubbelohdde-Doering el primero, en 1937-38. Entre 1983 y 1987 se estudió una muestra de 181 tejidos, de los cuales todos, menos dos, provienen de tumbas (Tabla 1). 145 provinieron de H45CM1; 25 de la Huaca 2; 9 al sur de esa estructura; 18 del lado este de la Huaca 31; 7 del sureste de la Huaca 28; y 7 del conjunto que denominamos grupo 79. Casi todos fueron hallados incompletos o muy deteriorados.

Fibras e Hilos

Predominó el algodón, en colores naturales, mientras la lana fué menos frecuente. Para sogas y cuerdas se usaron otras fibras vegetales, así como cabello humano, en algunos casos. El algodón se usó para crear la estructura básica en la mayoría de los tejidos. En los tapices, principalmente, se combinaron hilos de algodón y de lana, en la trama y urdimbre.

Paneles de Tela

Los Moche tejían paneles rectangulares que luego usarían, individualmente o cosidos a otros, para crear vestido y accesorios. El ancho varía entre 30 y 85 cms., con la mayoría entre 40 y 50 cms. Las únicas excepciones son tiras usadas para amarrar los taparrabos y grecas en tapicería que se cosían en el borde de los turbantes o tocados de cabeza y como paneles centrales en camisas. El largo, en la muestra, varía entre 18 cms. (Tumba 80, tejido 6) y 210 cms. (Tumba 25, tejido 1).

Tejidos

Tejidos Llanos

Fueron aproximadamente 50% de la muestra. Los Moche usaron tramas y urdimbres simples, cuando quisieron producir tejidos ligeros, y en pares, cuando buscaron un tejido más apretado y pesado. El empleo de tramas suplementarias y el uso de algodón mas grueso y de otro color, les permitió crear diseños con bandas claras y obscuras (Fig. 1); también combinaron, para decoración, tramas suplementarias con tramas y urdimbres en pares (Fig. 2). La trama suplementaria les permitió plasmar elaborada iconografía (Figs. 3 y 4), añadiendo, además, hasta seis colores, donde el blanco es algodón y los otros cinco fibra de lana.

Tejido Diagonal

Forma 25% de la muestra. Más de 70% son 2/2 y todos los demás, menos uno, son 2/2 con trama y urdimbre en pares. La excepción, un 2/1 con trama y urdimbre en pares, es el único con un diseño complejo (Fig. 5).

Gasas

Los seis ejemplos parecen haber sido tocados de cabeza o turbantes. Uno tiene un borde de tapiz, mientras los otros son simples.

Tapices

Los diez en la muestra tienen urdimbres de hilo simple. Dos excepciones (Tumba 20, tejido 7 y Tumba 21, tejido 7) tienen tramas de color claro con hilo doble hecho de algodón blanco y lana color dorado. La otra excepción (Fig. 7) es el tapiz más elaborado (Fig. 7): una camisa sin mangas hallada en la basura del grupo 79, hecha de 12 paneles de tela, cosidos y unidos verticalmente. Las tramas rojas y amarillas son hilos de lana dobles torcidos en Z, mientras las tramas blancas y marrón claro fueron hechas de hilos simples de algodón torcidos en Z. Otros tapices son bandas (Figs. 8, 9 y 10) que miden entre 2.5 y 3.5 cms de ancho y hasta 86 cms. de largo.

Tejido Doble

Hay tres ejemplos: una bolsa (Fig. 13), parte de otra (Fig. 14), y parte de un tocado de cabeza (Fig. 15). Cada uno consiste de una capa de tejido simple marrón y otra de marrón claro. Se usaron tramas y urdimbres en pares, así como lana, en los diseños para darles aspecto de tapiz.

Redes

Los nueve ejemplares parecen haber sido hechos para pescar. Cinco fueron usadas como sogas para amarrar envoltorios, y una red (Tumba 75, tejido 9) estaba en proceso de confección, enrollada al mallero.

Ropa y Accesorios

La mayoría de los textiles estuvieron tan fragmentados, que no fué posible recontruir su tamaño original y forma o determinar su función original. Los más completos, sin embargo, pueden ser identificados como vestido y accesorios.

Camisas

Siete de las ocho en la muestra, carecen de mangas. Tres de ellas son pequeñas, para infantes (Fig. 16) y fueron hechas usando un solo panel. Tres de las de adultos, sin mangas, están hechas de dos paneles cosidos verticalmente, dejando un espacio abierto para el cuello y para los brazos (Fig. 18). La última de las camisas sin mangas fué el tejido Moche más elaborado, recuperado en Pacatnamú (Fig. 7), hecha para un infante, consta de doce paneles (ver tapices, arriba).

Hay una con mangas, hecha de tres paneles, dos para el cuerpo y una para las mangas (Fig. 21), tejida en diagonal, 2/2 (Fig. 22), las mangas estuvieron decoradas con bandas (Fig. 24).

Taparrabos

Sólo uno de los siete recuperados (Tumba 21, tejido 5) estuvo lo suficientemente completo como para ser reconstruido. Consisten de una tela rectangular con una cinta cosida a lo largo de la orilla de la trama (Fig. 30). Predomina el tejido diagonal 2/2, usando uno o dos paneles. Fueron recuperados en tumbas de varones adultos.

Tocados de Cabeza o Turbantes

Se identificaron 9 textiles y todos se hallaron alrededor de la cabeza o cerca de ella. Parecen haber estado en tumbas de varones, incluyendo un niño y un adulto cuyo sexo no pudo ser determinado. Seis de los nueve fueron hechos en gasa, constituyendo la totalidad de la muestra de este tipo de textil. Ocho son rectangulares y los más elaborados tienen una banda de tapiz en los bordes. Ellos, en diversas formas, aparecen en la iconografía Moche (Figs. 31-34). Hubo uno de forma triangular, hecho de tres paneles que fueron cosidos y luego doblados en diagonal para formar el tocado (Figs. 37a, b y c). Este tipo, en la iconografía, es usado por pescadores, y fué tecuperado en la tumba de un varón adulto (Tumba 75) que fué enterrado con una red en proceso de manufactura.

Capas Largas

Se trata de una pieza grande confeccionada usando dos o tres paneles de tejido, cosidos a lo largo del borde de la urdimbre. Algunas eran de tejido llano y otras en tejido en diagonal; ambos tipos podían tener trama y urdimbre simple o en pares. La capa cubría los hombros y la espalda, siendo amarradas, por las dos esquinas superiores, sobre el pecho (Fig. 32).

Bolsas

Hay dos en la muestra, una plana y la otra cilíndrica (Figs. 13 y 39). Hechas en tejido doble con trama suplementaria y urdimbre flotante, su construcción está ilustrada en las Figs. 39 y 41. En la iconografía Moche, las bolsas planas se representan con el borde inferior recto (Fig. 42), mientras las cilíndricas con el borde redondeado (Figs. 29 y 43).

La Tradición Textil Moche

La muestra exhibe consistencia, tanto entre los textiles que la conforman, como con aquellos conocidos y analizados por otros investigadores. El uso de lana es más frecuente en los tapices, pero aún allí la urdimbre es de algodón; probablemente las cualidades de la lana para ser teñida, así como el probable acceso restringido a ella, le adscribieron un valor más alto en la sociedad. Los tejidos más comunes son los llanos y los en diagonal, mientras el tejido doble fué muy usado para plasmar iconografía. Las piezas del vestido recuperadas en las excavaciones corresponden con aquellas representadas en la iconografía. Los tejidos muy elaborados fueron raros, lo que demuestra que la gente del común normalmente no tuvo acceso a ellos. Hubo un porcentaje significativo de ropa muy deteriorada por el uso, remendada y parchada con pedazos de otras telas, lo que fué más evidente entre los adultos mayores que entre los jóvenes y los niños. Esto sugiere que usaron su ropa desde que eran jóvenes, deteriorándose confome se hacían viejos y que raramente la reemplazaban. Esto indicaría que, entre la gente del común, el acceso a los tejidos no fué fácil, por lo que aún aquellos muy usados y remendados poseían un relativo alto valor.

Botanical Offerings in Moche Burials at Pacatnamu

George Gumerman IV

Remarkably well-preserved botanical offerings[1] were interred with many Moche burials at Pacatnamu (Fig. 1). This report analyzes the variety and frequency of botanical offerings found in these burials, and compares the food plants in burials to the full range of foods in the diet of the Moche people at Pacatnamu.

Botanical offerings were recovered from 30 of the 84 Moche burials excavated at Pacatnamu between 1983 and 1987 (Table 1, pages 247-248).[2] Nearly all burials with good organic preservation contained botanical offerings. Most burials without botanical offerings were either disturbed or poorly preserved. The counts of botanical items discussed below are based on the 30 well-preserved burials.

Most of the botanical offerings were in gourd bowls and plates (Fig. 2). Occasionally they were wrapped in textiles. They rarely were found in ceramic vessels, although many ceramic vessels contained insect pupae, suggesting they may have contained food or beverages at the time of burial. Several gourds and ceramic vessels contained organic residue, possibly from cooked, ground, or partially decomposed food, but the residue could not be identified under low-power (40X) magnification.

Botanical offerings found in the burials were relatively homogeneous, both in number of plant species buried with each individual and overall variety of species. The number of species in each burial was generally low; a few burials contained three plant species, but most burials contained only one or two.

We identified 17 plant species in the Moche burials. Of these, only three occurred with regular frequency: corn (*Zea mays*), bottle gourd seeds (*Lagenaria siceraria*), and seaweed (*Gigartina chamissoi*). Corn was the most common, occurring in 19 of the 30 burials. Offerings were typically cobs, many with their kernels still preserved (Fig. 3). Of the 117 cobs recovered, 73 could be measured in detail. They displayed great variation in cob morphology. The cobs had from 8 to 16 rows, and cob lengths and thicknesses varied widely (Gumerman 1994).

Corn found in Moche refuse at Pacatnamu is substantially different from corn recovered from Moche burials. More than 90 percent of cobs from Moche midden had 8 to 10 rows of kernels.[3] In contrast, more than 50

---

1. Throughout this report, the term botanical offerings does not include plant materials used in encasing the corpse (cane, rope, unspun cotton, etc.), gourds, or cotton textiles.

2. Some plant remains noted during excavations could not be analyzed because of their poor preservation. These are listed in Table 1, but were not used in the numerical summaries. Their presence, however, reinforces the observed patterns.

3. This pattern of low row numbers also was observed in corn from refuse and occupation levels at other Moche sites (Grobman et al. 1961; Pozorski 1976; Bird and Bird 1980; Grobman 1982; Sevilla 1994).

Figure 1. Gourd bowls filled with peanuts in Burial 9 *Figure 2. Gourd bowls filled with corn in Burial 17*

percent of the cobs in the burials had 14 to 16 rows of kernels (Fig. 4). This suggests that corn with high row numbers was intentionally chosen for burials (Gumerman, 1994).

Corn in burials was distributed across age and gender groups, as well as burial types (Table 1), although Cane Frame and Cane Coffin burials tended to have more corn than Shroud Wrap, Splint Reinforced, and Cane Tube burials (see Donnan and McClelland, this volume).

Although probably not used as food (Towle 1961), bottle gourd seeds were the second most frequent botanical offering in the Moche burials. They were found in 10 of the 30 well-preserved burials, and 425 bottle gourd seeds were recovered. They were associated with burials of different age, gender, and burial types (Table 1).

Seaweed was the third most common botanical offering (Fig. 5). It was recovered in 8 of the 30 burials (Table 1).[4] Seaweed may have been widely used prehistorically as a food, but because most of the plant is con-

sumed, it rarely appears in the archaeological record except when preserved as a burial offering.[5] All eight of the burials with seaweed were from cemetery H45CM1. Five were males and three were females. The total weight of seaweed and its frequency are similar in male and female graves.

Nearly 80 percent of the seaweed (by weight) was recovered from five Cane Frame burials (Table 1). Seaweed tended to occur most frequently with this burial type. In contrast, only two Cane Coffin burials and one burial of indeterminate type contained seaweed. It should be noted that two Cane Frame burials (2, 12) contained more than two-thirds of all the seaweed by weight. The sample size is quite small, however, and the correlation between Cane Frame burials and seaweed may be spurious.

In addition to corn, bottle gourd seeds, and seaweed, which were found in many burials, nine plant

---

4. This examination of the contextual association of seaweed excludes the group burial (60-62) where seaweed was not associated with a particular individual.

5. Today, *Gigartina chamissoi* is the most abundantly consumed Peruvian seaweed (Acleto 1986) and is available in Peruvian seafood restaurants, often served with ceviche.

Figure 3. Corn cobs from the Moche Burials (scale in cm)

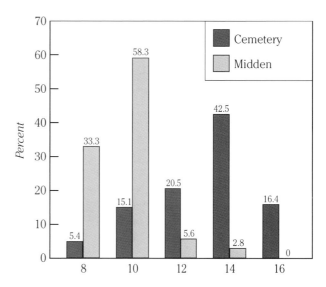

Figure 4. Corn (Zea mays) — Number of Rows

species were recovered less frequently (Table 1): common bean (*Phaseolus vulgaris*), lima bean (*P. lunatus*), coca (*Erythroxylum novogranatense*), peanut (*Arachis hypogaea*), squash (*Cucurbita maxima*), cotton (*Gossypium barbadense*), *pacae* (*Inga Feuillei*), *lucuma* (*Lucuma* sp.), and *espingo* (*Nectandra* sp.). Five individuals (Burials 22, 26, 42, 73, 75) were buried with common beans and one individual (Burial 15) with three fragments of seeds from the Fabaceae family.[6] Two burials (73, 75) contained lima beans. Coca leaves were found in Burial 73, and both coca seeds (endocarps) and coca leaves were found in Burial 75.[7] Two burials (73, 75) contained lima beans. Peanuts were found in only one (9), which contained 119 whole peanuts and several peanut shell fragments (Fig. 1). Squash also was recovered from only one burial (10). Cotton seeds were found in two (73, 75). *Pacae* pods were found in one (37). One seed of *lucuma* was found in Burial 53. Perhaps a whole fruit was placed in the grave, and had decomposed or was consumed by insects, leaving only the seed. One pierced cotyledon of *espingo* was recovered from Burial 43. *Espingo* cotyledons, often pierced and strung together, were not used as food, but as rattles in curing ceremonies (Towle 1961; Arriaga 1968; Donnan 1978).

The seeds of chile (*Capsium* sp.), *faique* (*Acacia* sp.), and *algarrobo* (*Prosopis* sp.) were found associated with a few burials, but appear not to have been deliberately placed there as offerings. Each of these species is wide-

Figure 5. Gourd bowl filled with seaweed in Burial 11

---

6. These are probably common beans, but fragmentation prevented identification of genus or species.

7. The scarcity of coca offerings in the Moche burials at Pacatnamu is interesting because coca was important ethnohistorically as a burial offering (Doyle 1988), and its use in Late Intermediate Period and Inca burials is well documented (e.g., Ravines and Stothert 1976; Dendy 1991).

spread in the refuse and fill at Pacatnamu, and their context in burials is unclear.

Most Moche burials at Pacatnamu did not contain botanical offerings. Poor preservation probably accounts for this, since the majority of burials without plant offerings were disturbed or poorly preserved. Interestingly, the generally well-preserved Moche burials from RG 79 (81-84) did not contain plant offerings, nor other offerings such as copper in the mouth or hands. The reason for this lack has not been determined.

Data from the Moche burials at Pacatnamu suggest that botanical offerings were not specifically related to sex, age, or burial type (except for the possible correlation between seaweed and Cane Frame burials). Moche burials excavated by Ubbelohde-Doering (1967, 1983) at Pacatnamu support these observations. Of particular interest is the large shaft tomb (E 1, found at Huaca 31) which contained 12 individuals, 9 of whom were in cane coffins. These were among the most elaborate burials recovered from Pacatnamu. They had numerous offerings, including abundant copper objects, elaborate textiles, ceramics, and gourd bowls. Some of the gourd bowls contained fish bones and one contained cotton fiber. Another was filled with peanuts, and what appears to be seaweed (Ubbelohde-Doering 1967: Figure 65).

Mortuary Botanical Offerings versus Diet of the Living

Analyses of Moche midden deposits at Pacatnamu suggest that Moche diet relied heavily on marine resources: shellfish and fish (Fig. 6). Agriculture appears to have been secondary to the marine subsistence base. In contrast, food offerings from Moche burials were mainly agricultural products. The high frequency of seaweed is the only significant exception to the predominance of agricultural food offerings. Minimal amounts of marine fauna were recovered from the burials: fish bones and scales from eight burials, unmodified shell from six burials, and one sea mammal bone.[8] Overall, marine fauna was surprisingly uncommon in the Moche burials, in contrast to its frequency in the Moche diet.

There are several alternative explanations for these differences between the diet of the living and the offerings for the dead. It is possible that the unidentified organic residue recovered in some of the gourd bowls and ceramic vessels is meat from terrestrial or maritime resources. If so, this would increase both the frequency of faunal resources and diversity of offerings. However, it is equally possible that the residue is agricultural, and

was so altered by cooking or poor preservation that it cannot be identified.

Differential preservation between burial offerings and food recovered from refuse could account for the observed differences; however, preservation was relatively good in both cases. Certain items may have been preserved better than others, causing a bias in their relative representation, but, since faunal bones are preserved better than vegetal remains, it is unlikely that differential preservation effected the observed patterns.

Finally, the selection of food offered to the burials may reflect the resources that were available at the time of burial. Seasonal availability and storability of certain resources may have affected the types of offerings. Although a combination of factors may explain the differences between burial offerings and the diet of the living, the most significant factor must have been cultural. A very limited inventory of food resources was utilized as offerings, while a different, more varied mix was used for subsistence needs.

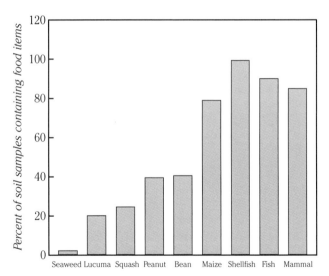

Figure 6. Relative frequency of food types from Moche refuse (n=48 samples)

---

8. Some of these appear to be intrusive (e.g., the few fish scales in Burial 9) and may not have been offerings.

Table 1. Botanical offerings and contextual associations from the Moche burials at Pacatnamu

	G3	G5	G7	G9	G10	G1	G2	G3	G1	G3	G4	G5	G6	G7	G10	G11	G12	G1	G4	G5	G6	G11	G13	G15	G17	G19
Burial Identification Number	2					4			5									6	7		9					
Sex	F					M*			M									M	M		M					
Age	35-45					30-35			50+									35-45	30-35		50+					
Burial Type	Cane Frame					Cane Frame			Cane Coffin									Cane Coffin	Cane Frame		Cane Coffin					
Number of Ceramic Vessels	1					1			2									2	1		2					
Number of Gourds	10					4			19									3	5		19					
Gourd Identification Number	G3	G5	G7	G9	G10	G1	G2	G3	G1	G3	G4	G5	G6	G7	G10	G11	G12	G1	G4	G5	G6	G11	G13	G15	G17	G19
Ceramic Identification Number																										
Textile Identification Number																										
Peanut *Arachis hypogaea* whole																					14	29	27			49
fragments																					6		3			6
Seaweed *Gigartina chamissoi* (gm)		0.5	43.2	26.7	1.3		6.3	#	6.1		8.6						5.0	1.5								
Bottle gourd seeds *Lagenaria siceraria*	10									5			11													
Corn *Zea mays* cobs					4	4/1*	3		5		2				4	3	5		3					3+	2	1

	G2	G1	G2	G1	G2	G5	G7	G2		G1	G3	G4	G5			G6	G8	G5	G6	G9	G14		G4
Burial Identification Number	10	11		12				14	15	17						20		21				25	26
Sex	F	F		M				M	?	?						M		M				?	?
Age	50+	30-40		25-35				20-25	6 mo	2						25-35		35-45				Adult	1-2
Burial Type	Cane Frame	Cane Frame		Cane Frame				Cane Coffin	?	Cane Frame/Cane Tube						Cane Coffin		Cane Coffin				Cane Coffin	Splint Reinforced
Number of Ceramic Vessels	1	1		0				3	0	1						3		3				0	0
Number of Gourds	2	3		8				3	2	6						8		16				2	5
Gourd Identification Number	G2	G1	G2	G1	G2	G5	G7	G2		G1	G3	G4	G5			G6	G8	G5	G6	G9	G14		G4
Ceramic Identification Number														2	3								
Textile Identification Number																							
Squash seeds *Cucurbita sp.*	43																						
Seaweed *Gigartina chamissoi* (gm)		11.5	1.0	5.6	14.4	15.5	24.3																
Bottle gourd seeds *Lagenaria siceraria*																		26	19	1	97+		
Common bean *Phaseolus vulgaris*																					4		29
Corn *Zea mays* cobs	2					7	3				#*	4	10			7	9					4	
Unidentifiable Fragments									3					#	#								
Leaf Fragments								#															

	G1		G1	G2		G2	G4			G2	G6	G9		G3	G7		G2	G4	G6	G7		G2	
Burial Identification Number	27	28	29					31	33				37			41					42		43
Sex	?	F	F					F	?				?			M					F		M
Age	Fetus	50+	50+					50+	ca. 18 mo.				4-5			25-30					30-40		25-45
Burial Type	Splint Reinforced	?	Cane Tube					Shroud Wrap	Splint Reinforced				Indeterminate			Cane Tube					Indeter.		Cane Frame
Number of Ceramic Vessels	0	3	1					0	1				2			6					5		1
Number of Gourds	1	2	6					1	9				15			7					10		0
Gourd Identification Number	G1		G1	G2		G2	G4			G2	G6	G9		G3	G7		G2	G4	G6	G7		G2	
Ceramic Identification Number		1			1				1				1			6					1		1
Textile Identification Number								T1															
Cotton seeds *Gossypium barbadense*		2											2										
Pacae *Inga Feuillei*													2										
Bottle gourd seeds *Lagenaria siceraria*	41**	3	5						1+				2	2	3							1+	
Espingo *Nectandra sp.*																							1
Common bean *Phaseolus vulgaris*																						1	
Corn *Zea mays* cobs				14				2		3	#							#*	#*	#*		1,#*	
kernels						*	*																
Unidentifiable Fragments											1+	s				#s					#s		

Table 1. Botanical offerings and contextual associations from the Moche burials at Pacatnamu (cont.)

Burial Identification Number	44				46	53				60-62(1)			60(2)	
Sex	F				M	F				M	F	?	M	
Age	25-35				Adult	50+				35-45	30-40	3-3.5	35-45	
Burial Type	Cane Tube ?				Indeter.	Cane Frame ?				?			Indeter.	
Number of Ceramic Vessels	2				1	2				4			3	
Number of Gourds	19				1	4				10			4	
Gourd Identification Number	G2	G8	G10	G15	G1		G1	G2	G3	G4	G8	G10	G1	G4
Ceramic Identification Number						1								
Textile Identification Number														
Seaweed *Gigartina chamissoi* (gm)									5.2		8.5	7.0	2	
Bottle gourd seeds *Lagenaria siceraria*		31	1	104	10					22				
Lucuma *Lucuma bifera*							1							
Corn *Zea mays*														
cobs	8		#					7						1
Unidentifiable Fragments														
Leaf Fragments	s		s			#						2		

Burial Identification Number	63	73							75	79		80
Sex	?	F							M	F		M
Age	3-3.5	50+							27-30	25-35		30-40
Burial Type	Splint Reinforced	Cane Frame							Cane Frame	Cane Frame		Cane Coffin
Number of Ceramic Vessels	2	0							0	2		1
Number of Gourds	3	4							1	7		2
Gourd Identification Number	G1	G1	G3						G1	G5	G7	
Ceramic Identification Number												
Textile Identification Number		T13		T5b	T6	T7	T8	T9	T5			
Squash seeds *Cucurbita sp.*										s*	s*	
Coca *Erthroxylum novoqranatense*												
leaf fragments									135			
endocarps						1			3			
Cotton seeds *Gossypium barbadense*				1					2			
Bean *Phaseolus sp.*												*
Lima bean *Phaseolus lunatus*		27							6			
Common bean *Phaseolus vulgaris*		1							25			
Corn *Zea mays*												
cobs	2	1+										
kernels		11			35	59	2	24				
cupules						4						
Leaf Fragments									1			

Key:
  # Several fragments
  + Plus several fragments
  * Noted during excavation, but not analyzed because of poor preservation
  s Seeds
  ** From whole gourd
  (1) These burials were in a single tomb, and appear to have shared the botanical remains listed below.
  (2) The botanical remains listed below appear to have been associated with this burial.

RESUMEN:
Ofrendas Botánicas en las
Tumbas Moche en Pacatnamú

Se recuperaron en 30 de las 84 Tumbas Moche excavadas en Pacatnamú (Fig. 1; Tabla 1). Estas pueden ser comparadas con las plantas usadas en el sitio, como parte de la dieta.

La mayoría de las ofrendas estaban dentro de platos y recipientes de calabazas (mates; Fig. 2), algunas veces envueltos en tejidos y raramenente dentro de cerámica. La mayoría de las tumbas contuvo una o dos especies, y raramente tres. Se identificaron 17 especies, pero sólo tres aparecen con frecuencia regular: maíz (Zea mays), semillas de calabazas (Lagenaria siceraria) y algas (Gigantina chamissoi). El maíz aparece en 19 de las 30 tumbas (Fig. 3); es diferente al que se usó en la alimentación, ya que mientras el usado para este fin, en el 90% de los casos, tenía de 8 a 10 ringleras, el que predomina en las tumbas tiene entre 14 y 16 (Fig. 4).

Las semillas de Calabazas fueron recuperadas en 10 de las 30 tumbas, mientras las algas lo fueron en 8 de 30 casos (Fig. 5) y, como característica, de manera exclusiva en H45CM1. Frijoles, pallares, coca, maní, zapallo, algodón, pacae, lúcuma e ishpingo, son los otros productos vegetales encontrados con más frecuencia en las tumbas. Semillas de ají, algarrobo y faique, aunque aparecieron asociadas con algunas tumbas, no parecen haber sido depositadas intencionalmente.

Los problemas de preservación parecen haber afectado al resto de las tumbas, en las cuales se presume que también hubieron ofrendas botánicas, pero éstas no se han conservado.

Ofrendas Botánicas y Dieta de la Población

El análisis de los basurales Moche sugiere que la población dependió, principalmente, de los recursos marinos, siendo los productos agrícolas secundarios en importancia. Sin embargo, en las tumbas, se recuperaron pocos ejemplares de huesos de pescado y conchas marinas. La explicación en esta diferencia parece haber sido cultural, ya que sólo un número limitado de plantas fué utilizado como ofrendas, mientras se usó una variedad mucho mayor para satisfacer las necesidades de alimentación.

Copper Artifacts from Moche Burials at Pacatnamu

Heather Lechtman

Twelve burials from Cemetery H45CM1 at Pacatnamu yielded 15 heavily corroded copper or copper alloy artifacts (one artifact from each of Burials 4, 5, 10, 17, 18, 28, 38, 48, 53, and 60; two artifacts from Burial 34; and three artifacts from Burial 40). Fourteen artifacts are small, solid, irregularly-shaped chunks or fragments of metal. They range in size from approximately 1.7 x 1.3 x 0.5 centimeters to 3.5 x 2.7 x 0.5 centimeters. The remaining artifact, from Burial 5, is made of one or more pieces of thin metal sheet, folded over along three sides to form a roughly rectangular packet, measuring approximately 4.2 x 2.8 centimeters. The thin sheet is heavily corroded and entirely mineralized in some areas. It was not sampled for chemical or metallographic analysis.

Most of the artifacts appear to be lumps of metal that solidified from a melt, but were not cast into a mold. They may be bits of cast cakes or ingots. Others show evidence of having been shaped by working, but even these objects (e.g., Burial 10 Cu3 and Burial 28 Cu1) appear to be fragments of larger items.

Three representative artifacts were sampled for chemical analysis and microstructural interpretation: two cast chunks and one slightly worked piece. Table 1, page 253, shows that all three are made of impure copper. The range and concentration of impurities indicate that the copper was smelted from ore. The slightly worked piece (Burial 38 Cu2/MIT 3813) has considerably more arsenic than either of the two cast chunks, but the arsenic impurity level is too low to consider the material an arsenic bronze. It is a low arsenic copper-arsenic alloy.[1]

Metallographic examination of cross sections cut from each of the cast chunks reveals virtually identical microstructures. Figure 1 illustrates a typical area just beneath the corroded surface of one sample (Burial 34 Cu1/MIT 3812). While molten, the copper dissolved a considerable amount of oxygen. Upon solidification, some of the oxygen combined with copper to precipitate the second phase, Cu_2O (the tiny, dark dots in Fig. 1). The Cu_2O inclusions form a fine Cu-Cu_2O eutectic microconsituent (gray in the photomicrograph) surrounding the undistorted, primary copper dendrites (white, branching structures in Fig. 1). Another sample (Burial 4 Cu2/MIT 3814) exhibits a similar cast microstructure.

The microstructure of the worked piece, shown in Figure 2 (Burial 38 Cu2/MIT 3813), is quite different. Here too, the photomicrograph shows a zone of metal just beneath the corroded surface. As a result of hammering and low temperature annealing, the Cu_2O inclusions have become larger and are randomly distributed throughout the section. It may be that the presence of

---

1. Definitions of arsenical copper, low arsenic, copper-arsenic alloy, and arsenic bronze are given in Hosler, Lechtman, and Holm 1990: fn 2.

Figure 1. Photomicrograph of cross section of copper chunk (Burial 34 Cu1/MIT 3812). This is a polished section, showing undistorted, large copper dendrites surrounded by a very fine copper oxide eutectic microconstituent. Larger Cu$_2$O inclusions outline the primary dendrite arms. Magnification: 50

Figure 2. Photomicrograph of cross section of worked copper (Burial 38 Cu2/MIT 3813) Large, roughly spherical Cu$_2$O inclusions are distributed randomly throughout the section. The metal is fully recrystallized, with smaller, equiaxed grains and annealing twins near the surface and larger grains toward the interior of the piece. Magnification: 100. Etchant: Potassium dichromate

arsenic in the alloy helped to deoxidize the melt so that less Cu$_2$O formed during solidification. Dendrites are no longer present. Instead, equiaxed grains containing annealing twins have recrystallized, and the piece has been left in the annealed condition. The grains near the corroded surface are somewhat smaller than those deeper within the body of the piece, indicating that the surface metal was worked (hammered) more than the interior. Overall, the object was lightly worked.

Table 1

Analytical Results

Artifact No.	MIT No.	Description	Composition (Weight %)							
			Ag	As	Au	Bi	Ni	Pb	Sb	Sn
Burial 34 Cu1	3812	Cast chunk	0.097	0.017	0.016	0.0025	0.007	0.0098	0.003	<0.001
Burial 38 Cu2	3813	Cast chunk, slightly worked and annealed	0.234	0.288	0.023	0.0319	0.008	0.4647	0.030	0.001
Burial 4 Cu2	3814	Cast chunk	0.117	0.004	<0.001	0.0025	0.004	0.0166	0.002	0.001

Key: Ag, As, Au, Sb were determined by neutron activation analysis (INAA)
Bi, Ni, Pb, Sn were determined by inductively coupled plasma mass spectrometry (ICP-MS)

RESUMEN:
Artefactos de Cobre de las
Tumbas Moche en Pacatnamú

Doce tumbas del Cementerio H45CM1 arrojaron 15 artefactos de cobre o de aleaciones de cobre, los cuales estaban muy oxidados. La mayoría de los arterfactos son pedazos de metal fundido, aunque algunos de ellos muestran evidencia de haber sido trabajados, pero en ningún caso se trata de piezas completas.

El análisis de tres de los artefactos muestra que fueron manufacturados usando cobre impuro, fundido de menas nativas. El análisis metalográfico revela practicamente idénticas microestructuras en las piezas de metal fundido y algunas diferencias en el que fué trabajado, como consecuencia del martillado a que fué sometido.

A Moche Cane Coffin from Pacatnamu

Christopher B. Donnan
Daisy Barreto C.

A few Moche cane coffins have been excavated archaeologically, and they also have been noted in Moche artistic representations. None, however, has been described in sufficient detail to fully understand their form, their manufacture, or exactly how they would have functioned. One of the Moche burials we excavated at Pacatnamu in 1985 had an unusually well-preserved cane coffin, which provided an excellent opportunity to conduct a detailed study of its construction. The understanding we gained enabled us to build a full-scale replica of the coffin. This report discusses the excavated cane coffin, the insights gained from building the replica, and how this cane coffin compares to others that have been reported previously.

Our excavations of Moche burials at Pacatnamu uncovered ten examples of cane coffins (see Donnan and McClelland, this volume). Most of these were in poor condition, and few details of their construction could be recovered, but the coffin of Burial 20 (Fig. 1) was remarkably well preserved and provided an excellent opportunity to conduct a detailed analysis of its dimensions, materials, and construction. By building a full-scale replica as the original coffin was being excavated, we were able to determine the quantity of materials used, and to estimate the time and labor needed for construction. Moreover, we were able to reconstruct the precise sequence in which the ropes were tied at each stage of construction. This provided key insights regarding when and how the body was placed in the coffin, and substantially enhanced our understanding of Moche cane coffin burials.

The original coffin of Burial 20 was a rectangular container, 168 centimeters long, 50 centimeters wide, and 27 centimeters high (Fig. 1). At its north end the top had decomposed, but all other parts were preserved. Weight of the soil above the coffin had caused it to compress slightly at the south end, but the rope and cane elements in that area were not broken.

Construction

The coffin was constructed exclusively of rope and cane. The rope was made from *enea* (*Typha angustifolia*) and the cane was *caña brava* (*Gynerium saggittatum*). Both materials are readily available along the margins of the Jequetepeque River, and are abundant in the marshy delta area near Pacatnamu. They can be obtained throughout the year,[1] and would have been easily transported by hand from their source to Pacatnamu.

---

1. There is a belief among the local people that it is best to obtain *caña brava* and *enea* during the *luna menguante* (waning moon), because it insures that these materials will last longer than those harvested at other times.

Figure 1. The cane coffin of Burial 20 with the replica under construction on the right

Enea normally grows only in standing water. Our workers, who were adept at making the type of *enea* rope used in the original coffin, said they prefer stalks that are mature and have a soft texture. They refer to this type as "*enea hembra*" (female *enea*). The *enea* rope was two ply. Each ply consisted of single stalks of *enea*, joined to one another at their ends, and tightly S-twisted along their lengths. Joining one stalk to another was accomplished by having approximately 7 centimeters of the narrow end of one of the stalks folded inside the wide end of the adjacent stalk (Fig. 2). The overlapping section was then S-twisted in the same fashion as the rest of the stalk. Twisting was accomplished by tightly winding the *enea* around a short piece of cane, as shown in Figure 3.

Figure 2. Folding the small end of a stalk of enea *inside the large end of the adjacent stalk*

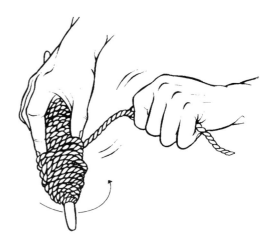

Figure 3. Twisting one strand of enea *around a short piece of cane*

Figure 4 (left and above). Plying two strands of twisted enea *by tying one of the single strands to a post and tightly wrapping another single strand around it*

After long segments of the single S-twisted elements were produced, two of them were Z-plied to create the finished rope. Plying was achieved by tying two of the single elements to a post, and tightly wrapping one around the other in a counter-clockwise direction (Fig. 4).

The canes used in constructing the coffin were straight, mature stalks. The sides, top, and bottom of the coffin were made in a single operation from 70 lengths of cane. Sixty-seven of these, which will be called *length canes*, would ultimately extend along the length of the

coffin. They were 168 centimeters long and had an average diameter of 2.7 centimeters. The remaining three canes were *cross braces*. They were 154 centimeters long and had an average diameter of 2.8 centimeters.

Before the 67 length canes were lashed to the three cross braces, each cross brace was crimped using a stone hammer at three places to facilitate subsequent bending (Fig. 5). Once crimped, the canes were carefully bent to right angles (Fig. 6) and subsequently relaxed to their original straight form.

The length canes then were ready to be lashed to the cross braces. We found that this could be accomplished most easily with three individuals, one at each cross brace, simultaneously lashing the individual length canes as they were added. Each length cane was usually secured with a single loop around the cross brace (Figs. 7, 8). At the three places where the cross braces had been crimped, however, the lashing cord made an extra loop around the cross brace, thus creating extra

Figure 5. Crimping a cross brace in preparation for bending

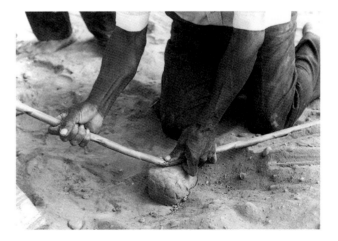

Figure 6. Bending a crimped cross brace

Figure 7. Lashing a length cane to a cross brace

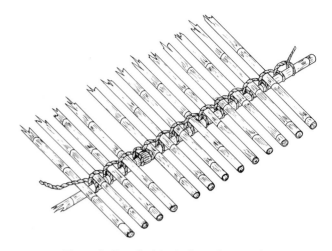

*Figure 8. Detail of the lashing that attaches
the cross braces to the length canes*

space between the adjacent length canes (Fig. 8). The double loop prevented binding when the cross braces were subsequently bent 90 degrees to form the sides, top, and bottom of the coffin.

The two ends of the coffin were constructed individually. Each end piece consisted of 13 horizontal canes and two vertical cross braces. The horizontal canes were 45 centimeters long and averaged 1.8 centimeters in diameter, while the cross braces were 23 centimeters long and averaged 1.5 centimeters in diameter. The horizontal canes were lashed to the cross braces using the same technique employed in lashing the length canes to their cross braces.

The two end pieces were then ready to be attached to the large cane frame that would form the sides, top, and bottom of the coffin. Before the end pieces were attached, the corpse and grave goods that were to be inside the coffin would have been placed on the bottom panel of the coffin (Fig. 9). Then the top panel, would have been folded up and over the corpse and grave contents (Fig. 10). With one side of the coffin still open, the end pieces were put in position and securely tied to the side, top, and bottom panels (Fig. 10). Leaving one side of the coffin open during this process facilitated tying the end pieces in place.

Once the end pieces were securely tied in place, the second side panel was bent up to close the coffin, and secured by doubling one long length of rope over each of the three cross brace ends (Fig. 11). These double ropes were then pulled tight across the top of the coffin, and wrapped around the coffin many times (Fig. 12). At the foot of the coffin, the double rope was wrapped around the coffin 21 times, forming a set of 42 cords. At the center the double rope was wrapped around the coffin 28 times, forming a group of 56 cords, and at the head the double rope was wrapped around the coffin six times, forming a group of 12 cords.

Additional ropes, running parallel to the length of the coffin, were then woven in among the groups of cords (Fig. 13).

Material and Time for Construction

The coffin was built from 100 pieces of cane—70 for the sides, bottom, and top, and 15 for each of the two end pieces. The 100 pieces totaled 130 meters in length.

A total of 268 meters of rope was used in constructing the coffin and wrapping the exterior. Of this, 34 meters were used to build the two end pieces and the piece that formed the sides, bottom, and top of the coffin. The end pieces were tied to the top, bottom, and sides by 11 meters of rope (5.5 meters at each end). The exterior was wrapped with 224 meters of rope. Thus, the wrapping required nearly *five times* as much rope as that used in all other parts of the coffin construction.

The amount of time required to prepare the raw materials, make the rope, and construct the coffin is difficult to assess. In part, this is because parts of the process were new to us and had to be developed as the work proceeded. Also, we cut the canes with steel machetes. Presumably, cutting and trimming raw materials would have been more time consuming with the tools employed by the Moche.

Once the rope material was cut and transported to the production locale, one individual can produce 1 meter of finished rope every 10 minutes. Thus, 268 meters could have been produced in approximately 45 man-hours.

Once the cane was harvested and transported to the location where the casket was to be built, it could be cut to the required lengths by one individual in approximately 6 hours. Three individuals could then assemble the coffin in approximately 5 hours—a total of about 15 man-hours. The time needed to make the 45 meters of

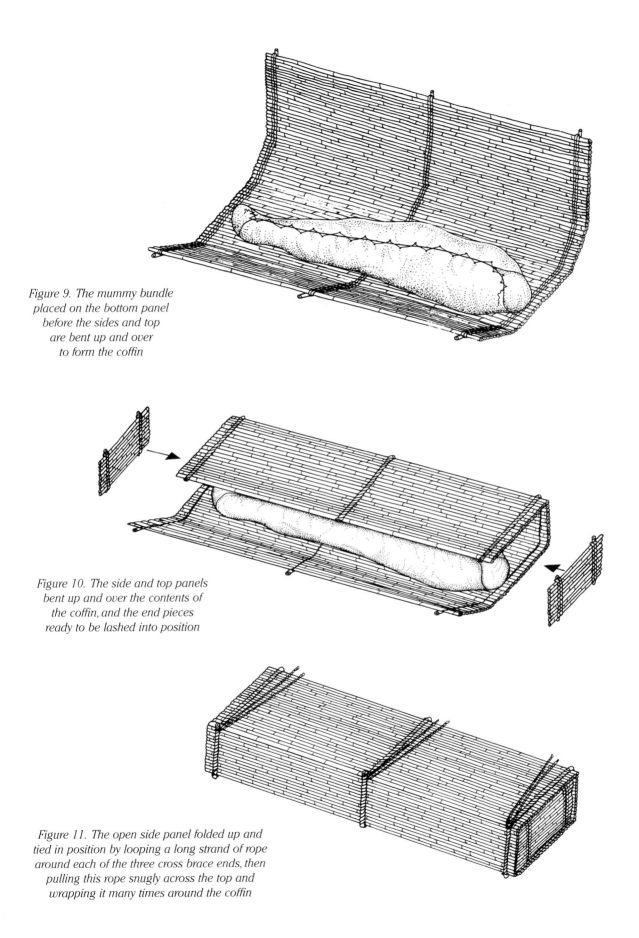

Figure 9. The mummy bundle placed on the bottom panel before the sides and top are bent up and over to form the coffin

Figure 10. The side and top panels bent up and over the contents of the coffin, and the end pieces ready to be lashed into position

Figure 11. The open side panel folded up and tied in position by looping a long strand of rope around each of the three cross brace ends, then pulling this rope snugly across the top and wrapping it many times around the coffin

Figure 12. Wrapping the coffin

rope used to construct the coffin is approximately 8 hours. Therefore, to make the rope, cut the canes, and assemble the coffin would have required approximately 29 man-hours.

Wrapping the coffin required a greater labor investment. The 224 meters of rope used in the wrapping would have required 37 man-hours to produce. The wrapping itself was facilitated by having two individuals work together. It required approximately 2 hours—a total of 4 man-hours. Thus, while it would have required 29 man-hours to construct the coffin, 41 man-hours were required to wrap it with rope.

Why was so much material and labor invested in elaborate wrapping? It would have slightly strengthened the coffin, but the increase in strength was not really necessary for the cane coffin to function adequately, and certainly would not warrant the extensive investment of time and materials. It is interesting that the wrapping is concentrated at the head, center, and foot of the coffin. These areas would correspond to areas of head, hands, and feet of the individual inside the coffin—places where the greatest quantity and quality of grave goods usually were placed in Moche burials. Perhaps

the location of the wrapping on the exterior of the coffin was related to the importance of these areas of the corpse inside.

The complexity of the wrapping, and the care with which it was executed, suggest that it was meant to enhance the appearance of the coffin. It may well be that the coffin was to be seen by many people, and the wrapping was meant to impress. Perhaps it was a form of offering.

The finished coffin was extremely rigid, and would have supported easily the weight of an adult body—even when carried only by the two ends. In Moche art (Fig. 14), rectangular coffins are lowered into deep graves with ropes (Donnan and McClelland 1979). Given their strength and rigidity, cane coffins could have been lowered in this way without difficulty.

It should be noted that although this coffin appears similar to coffins of the western tradition, with a box-like lower section and lid, it clearly was not conceptualized by the Moche as a box, and it was not built as a box-like structure with lid. Rather, it was a means of *wrapping* the body with cane, analogous to the Cane Tube burials discussed by Donnan and McClelland (this volume). The large cane frame essentially was wrapped *around* the body, and then the end pieces were tied into position.

Comparison with Other Moche Cane Coffins

Heinrich Ubbelohde-Doering published the first descriptions of Moche cane coffins, which he had excavated in 1938 at Pacatnamu in tombs on the north side of Huaca 31 (see Site Map, pages 18-19). Most of these coffins were in poor condition, and almost no details of their size or form could be reconstructed. In one deep shaft tomb, however, nine well-preserved cane coffins were found. No detailed description of these has been published, but scale drawings and photographs of them *in situ* provide considerable information regarding their size and construction (Ubbelohde-Doering 1964: Photos 62, 64, and 65; 1983: 54-57).

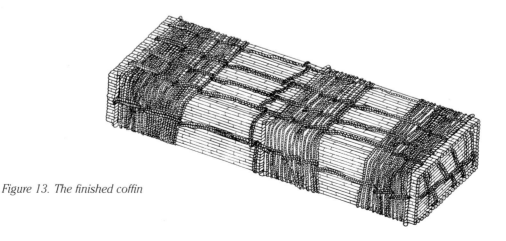

Figure 13. The finished coffin

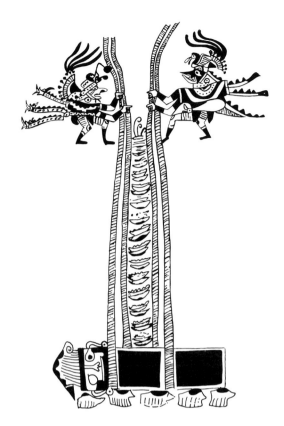

Figure 14. Moche fineline painting showing a rectangular coffin being lowered with ropes into a deep grave

The nine coffins varied considerably in size (see Table 1, page 263). Those visible in the photographs appear to be similar to the one that we replicated, utilizing the same type of cane and two-ply S-spun *enea* rope. It is not possible to determine how the canes were tied, nor how the end pieces were assembled and tied to the main frame, but several of the coffins had

ropes wrapped around them many times. Ubbelohde-Doering (1983: 22) stated that two of the coffins had pairs of ropes running lengthwise at regular intervals, as part of the elaborate wrapping.

In 1946 a Moche cane coffin burial was excavated by Duncan Strong and Clifford Evans at Huaca de la Cruz in the Viru Valley (Strong 1947; Strong and Evans 1953). The coffin was described as a well built rectangular box, constructed of canes reinforced with cross braces at each end and in the middle. The cross braces were securely tied with two-ply sedge rope, and similar ropes were tied around the entire cane coffin about one-third of the distance from each end. In addition, a coarse, cotton twilled cloth had been sewn over the entire exterior of the coffin (Strong and Evans 1953: 153).

Although the cane coffin from Huaca de la Cruz was similar in most respects to the one we replicated at Pacatnamu, there appears to have been one significant difference. The top of the coffin is said to have been hinged as a lid that opened along the side (*ibid.*). If so, the construction of the coffin, as well as how and when its contents were placed inside, differed dramatically from the one we replicated at Pacatnamu. The coffin would have been conceptualized as a box, and would have been loaded from the top *after* construction, rather than a frame that was wrapped around the contents *during* construction.

More recently, a cane coffin burial was excavated at Huaca de la Luna in the Moche Valley (Uceda *et al.* 1994: 280-296). It contained an adult male, and was inside the mud brick matrix of the pyramid. An isometric drawing of the coffin indicates that ropes had been wrapped around the coffin many times near the foot, center, and presumably also the head (Uceda *et al.* 1994: Fig. 8.19).

Cane coffin burials also have been reported from Sipán in the Reque Valley (Alva and Donnan 1993). They

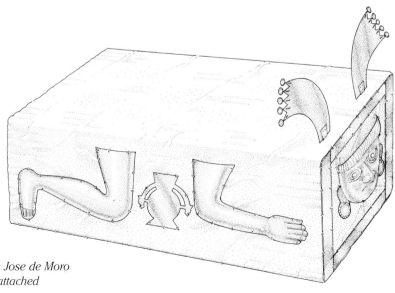

Figure 15. A cane coffin from San Jose de Moro with sheet metal elements attached

were in royal tombs and contained bodies of men, women, and children who were buried with the principal individual. They also were found in graves of adult males who were buried individually. Unfortunately, none was sufficiently well preserved that construction details could be observed. Nevertheless, all evidence suggests they were similar in form, material, and construction to the Moche cane coffins reported elsewhere.

Finally, cane coffins have been excavated at the site of San Jose de Moro in the Jequetepeque Valley (Donnan and Castillo 1992, 1994; Castillo and Donnan 1994a). They were found in large, room-size chamber tombs and contained the body of the principal individual. None of these was sufficiently well preserved so that details of construction could be observed. It was clear, however, that two of the coffins containing adult females had been covered with cloth and had sheet metal arms, legs, and masks sewn on the exterior of the cloth (Fig. 15).

The cane coffins that have been reported have a considerable range of dimensions (see Table 1). The one from Huaca de la Cruz in the Viru Valley was unusually large. Its length and depth were greater than any other cane coffin reported, and its width was greater than most. It had more than three times the volume of the smallest cane coffin (Ubbelohde-Doering's Burial E I g from Pacatnamu). However, it is also the only cane coffin that contained two bodies—a young child above an adult. There was an unusually large number of associated objects, many of which were *inside* the coffin. It is likely that this cane coffin was deliberately made large in order to contain the volume of material that was to be placed within it.

Clearly, the tradition of cane coffin burials was widespread both temporally and geographically. Although their earliest known occurrence is at Sipán, dating approximately to A.D. 300, they may have been used by the Moche before that time.[2] They continued to be made until near the end of the Moche style, approximately A.D. 750—the date for the cane coffins at San Jose de Moro (Donnan and Castillo 1992, 1994; Castillo and Donnan 1994a).

Geographically, they have been reported from many of the river valleys in both the northern and southern part of the Moche kingdom (Donnan and Castillo 1994). It is likely that as more Moche graves are excavated archaeologically in the other valleys, additional cane coffin burials will be uncovered. As the sample of Moche cane coffins continues to expand with future archaeological excavation, it is hoped that researchers will record all observable details of their size and construction, and thus continue to refine our understanding of this aspect of Moche culture.

---

2. Larco (1945: 26) states that cane coffins are commonly found in Viru (Gallinazo) burials, but he does not describe or illustrate them. Bennett (1950) makes no mention of cane coffins in his description of a large sample of Viru (Gallinazo) burials.

Table 1

Dimensions of Cane Coffins

		Length cm	Width cm	Height cm	Volume cc	Individual(s)
Jequetepeque Valley, Pacatnamu						
Grave E I	a	200	70	20	280,000	adult
	b	180	40	25	180,000	18 yr. old female
	c	195	60	25	292,500	adult
	d a	190	40	23	174,800	adult
	d b	190	35	23	152,950	adult
	e	192	45	25	216,000	adult
	f	175	55	25	240,625	adult
	g	185	40	20	148,000	adult
	h	187	50	21	196,350	adult
Burial 20		168	50	27	226,800	adult male
Viru Valley, Huaca de la Cruz		235	57	35	468,825	adult male and child
Moche Valley, Huaca de la Luna		205	50	25	256,250	adult male

RESUMEN:
Un Ataúd de Caña de Pacatnamú

Aunque algunos ataúdes de caña se han excavado arqueológicamente y hay representaciones de ellos en la iconografía Moche, ninguno ha sido descrito con suficiente detalle. En Pacatnamú, en 1985, se excavaron diez de ellos (ver Donnan y McClelland, este volumen), pero el de la Tumba 20 estuvo especialmente bien preservado (Fig. 1).

El análisis se realizó mediante la construcción de una réplica, con el fín de determinar la cantidad de material usado, tiempo y técnicas empleadas. El original medía 1.68 mts. de largo, 50 cms. de ancho y 27 cms. de alto (Fig. 1).

Construcción

Se usó soga hecha de enea (Typha angustifolia) y caña brava (Gynerium saggittatum), materiales que crecen en las proximidades al río Jequetepeque. La soga fué confeccionada usando tallos simples de enea, ligeramente torcidos en S (Fig. 3), y unidos para formar largos segmentos (Fig. 2), los cuales fueron torcidos en Z, a continuación, y amarrados a un poste, para trenzarlos uno alrededor del otro, en sentido anti-horario (Fig. 4), creando el producto final.

Para construirlo se usaron 70 cañas; 67 de 1.68 mts. de largo y un diámetro promedio de 2.7 cms., dispuestas a lo largo, y 3 a lo ancho, de 1.54 mts. y 2.8 cms. de diámetro. Las transversales fueron golpeadas con una piedra en tres puntos diferentes (Fig. 5), para permitir doblarlas posteriormente (Fig. 6) y poder formar el cajón.

Para unir las cañas a las tres transversales, se hizo con tres individuos, los que amarraban cada caña con un nudo simple (Figs. 7-8) al transversal que cada uno de ellos manejaba. En cada punto donde los transversales fueron golpeados, se usó un nudo doble, con el fín de crear espacio entre las cañas adyacentes (Fig. 8), con el fin de poder doblar el tejido para crear los cuatro lados del ataúd.

Los dos extremos se hicieron individualmente, usando 13 cañas horizontales de 45 cms. de largo y 1.8 cms. de diámetro, y dos transversales de 23 cms. de largo y 1.5 cms de diámetro.

Antes de poner los extremos, el cuerpo y las ofrendas debía de depositarse sobre la parte correspondiente al fondo de la estructura de cañas (Fig. 9); luego, se dobla para formar un lado y la parte superior (Fig. 10). Con un lado todavía abierto, se ponían los extremos, asegurándolos con soga, para luego cerrar el ataúd, atando el lado abierto a los transversales (Fig. 11). Para ello, se usaron sogas dobles que, además, se enrollaron varias veces alrededor del ataúd (Fig. 12). A los pies, dió 21 vueltas, formando un grupo de 42 cuerdas; en el medio, 28 veces y 56 cuerdas; y a la cabecera, 6 veces y un grupo de 12 cuerdas. Luego, se pusieron algunas sogas a lo largo del ataúd, las que pasaron por entre los grupos de cuerdas, para darle solidez a la estructura (Fig. 13).

Material y tiempo empleado en la Construcción

Se usaron 100 piezas de caña, con un largo total de 130 mts.; además, 268 mts. de soga, de los cuales 224 fueron usadas para el amarre del exterior, mientras sólo se usaron 44 mts. en la construcción de la estructura misma.

Cada metro de soga se hizo en alrededor de 10 minutos, por lo que toda la soga se pudo producir en 45 horas-hombre. El corte y preparación de la caña tomó alrededor de 6 horas; 3 personas armaron la estructura en 5 horas, o 15 horas-hombre. Si sumamos el corte, armado y la soga (44 mts., 8 horas de confección), tenemos que el ataúd mismo tomó 29 horas; sin embargo, el atado exterior requirió 224 mts. de soga (37 horas de confección) y 4 horas-hombre de trabajo en el amarrado, totalizando 41 horas de trabajo.

El refuerzo del ataúd no justifica esta cantidad de trabajo, ya que podría haberse logrado por medios más económicos; indudablemente, el esfuerzo se justifica sólo por el efecto decorativo que tuvo o porque fué considerado como otro tipo de ofrenda funeraria.

Aunque el ataúd parece ser similar a los de la tradición occidental, éste no fué conceptualizado por los Moche como una caja con una tapa, sino como un envoltorio de cañas alrededor del cadáver, con los extremos de forma rectangular, por lo que la forma total adopta esa configuración.

Comparación con Otros Ataúdes de Cañas

Heinrich Ubbelohde-Doering publicó las primeras descripciones de los ataúdes que excavó, en 1938, en el lado norte de la Huaca 31, en Pacatnamú. Los nueve ataúdes (ver Tabla 1) eran de diferentes dimensiones, y parecen haber sido construidos siguiendo la misma técnica.

En 1946, Duncan Strong y Clifford Evans excavaron, en la Huaca de la Cruz, Valle de Virú, un ataúd de características similares, pero de mayor tamaño (Tabla 1) y envuelto en un tejido de algodón. Otra diferencia es que se abría por la parte superior, lo que lo haría similar en concepto al ataúd occidental.

Recientemente, otro ataúd fué excavado en la Huaca de la Luna. Contenía un varón adulto y las características parecen ser similares al descrito.

En Sipán han sido recuperados tantro en tumbas reales como en entierros individuales, pero ninguno estuvo lo suficientemente bien preservado como para observar los detalles de construcción.

En San José de Moro, en el Valle del Jequetepeque, fueron hallados en tumbas de cámara y aunque no estuvieron muy bien preservados, es claro que fueron recubiertos con tejidos que tenían cosidos brazos, piernas y máscaras confeccionados con láminas de metal (Fig. 15). Además, se trataba de entierros de mujeres de alto rango.

La tradición de Ataúdes de Caña cubrió una extensa área geográfica, tanto en la parte sur como norte del territorio Moche, y un largo periodo de tiempo: desde el 300 N.E., en Sipán, hasta cerca del final del periodo Moche, alrededor del 750 N.E., en San José de Moro.

Moche Fineline Ceramics at Pacatnamu

Donna McClelland

Although there are thousands of examples of Moche slip painted ceramics with fineline drawings in museums and private collections throughout the world, nearly all were looted from burials by grave robbers, and have no reliable provenience as to the site or even the valley from which they came. This makes it extremely difficult to reconstruct the regional differences that must have existed in fineline painting, as well as the distribution of fineline ceramics from one site or region to another. If the Moche fineline tradition is ever to be adequately understood, it is imperative that archaeologists systematically publish all examples that can be documented from specific sites.

During his 1938-39 field season at Pacatnamu, Heinrich Ubbelohde-Doering excavated three ceramic bottles with fineline drawings from two shaft tombs (1983:Abb. 49, 55.3, 56.3). These provided the first archaeologically documented examples from Pacatnamu. Between 1983 and 1987, our project found no additional examples of complete ceramic vessels with fineline drawings, but 65 sherds with fineline drawings were recovered. When combined with the three complete examples excavated by Ubbelohde-Doering, these sherds provide valuable insights into the distribution, iconography, chronology, and source of fineline ceramics at Pacatnamu.

Distribution

The Moche ceramics that were excavated at Pacatnamu between 1983 and 1987 were used to determine the area of Moche occupation (Fig. 1). Sherds with fineline drawings, which represent an extremely small percentage of the excavated Moche ceramics, were found within a limited area of the Moche occupation (Fig. 1). Although the three bottles with fineline drawings excavated by Ubbelohde-Doering were associated with burials, none of the 84 Moche burials described in this volume contained any fineline bottles or sherds. Some of the fineline sherds may have been from vessels that were associated with burials that had been looted, but others clearly were found in Moche refuse, which indicates that these ceramics were not created solely as burial offerings.

The Moche Archive

The Moche Archive at UCLA contains photographs of approximately 20,000 objects of Moche art from museums and private collections all over the world. Of these objects, over 2,000 are ceramics with fineline drawings. Because fineline drawings contain a wealth of information, we have made a considerable effort to photograph as many of these ceramics as possible, and have

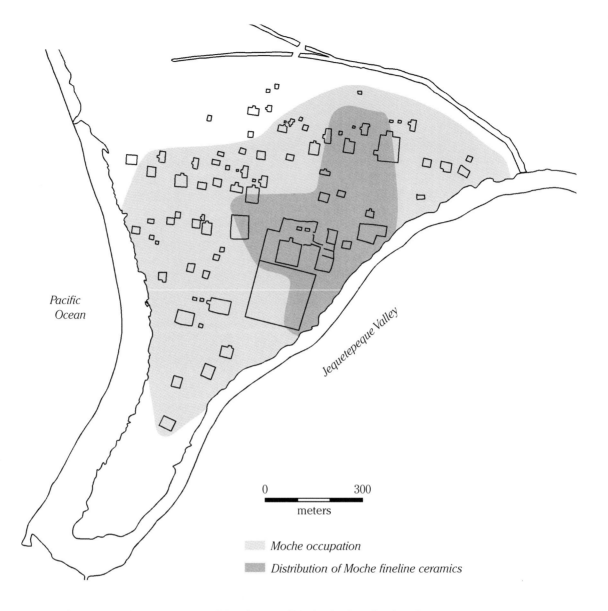

Figure 1. Moche occupation and distribution of Moche fineline sherds at Pacatnamu.

produced over 500 rollout drawings from these photographs. In addition, we systematically catalogue rollout drawings published by other scholars. Therefore, the Moche Archive contains an extremely large data base of Moche fineline drawings.

There is a great deal of repetition in subject matter, layout, and designs among these drawings. Although details of drawing style vary from artist to artist, specific scenes are remarkably consistent. Even though a sherd is small and displays only a fragment of a drawing, this consistency often enables us to identify and describe the complete drawing of which it was a part. When a fragmentary drawing on a sherd can be matched to a drawing on a whole bottle, it sometimes is possible to infer the phase of the sherd.

The Pacatnamu Sample

Of the 65 sherds with fineline drawings that were recovered from Pacatnamu between 1983 and 1987, 18 could be matched with very similar drawings in the Moche Archive.

Bands of Geometric Designs

Eleven sherds have fragments of geometric designs in bands. Seven of these have a stepped design (Fig. 2)[1] similar to those in Figure 3. The sherd in Figure 4

---

1. All sherd illustrations are 1:1, unless otherwise noted.

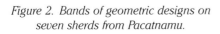

Figure 2. Bands of geometric designs on seven sherds from Pacatnamu.

Figure 3. Stirrup spout bottle with geometric designs in bands. Rautenstrauch-Joest Museum, Köln.

Figure 4 Disk design on a sherd from Pacatnamu.

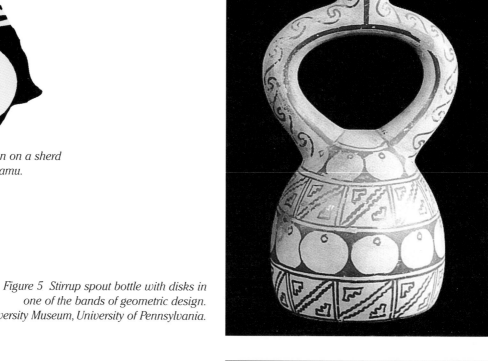

Figure 5 Stirrup spout bottle with disks in one of the bands of geometric design. University Museum, University of Pennsylvania.

Figure 6. Triangular elements on a sherd from Pacatnamu.

Figure 7. Stirrup spout bottle with triangular elements in one of the bands of geometric design. The British Museum, London.

Figure 8. Interlocking wave design on a sherd from Pacatnamu.

Figure 9. Right-angled spiral on a sherd from Pacatnamu.

Figure 10. Stirrup spout bottle with a right-angled spiral. Fowler Museum of Cultural History, University of California, Los Angeles.

11a

11b

11c

11d

11e

Figure 11. Rollout drawing of the tule boats on a stirrup spout bottle (Fig. 12).
Highlighted areas correspond to parts of a ray and sections
of the boat on sherds (11a-e) from Pacatnamu.

Figure 12. Stirrup spout bottle chamber with rays and tule boats.
Private collection, Lima.

displays a circular disk, similar to the one that alternates with stepped designs in bands in Figure 5. A triangular element on one sherd (Fig. 6) appears in one of the bands of geometric design in Figure 7. Interlocking waves on one sherd (Fig. 8) appear in a band on the broken stirrup spout bottle (Fig. 2). Finally, the right-angled spiral on the sherd in Figure 9 is similar to the snakes in a band in Figure 10, and the design on top of this sherd resembles the design on top of the chamber in Figure 10.

Tule Boats

Six fineline sherds have fragments of complex tule boat scenes. Five of these (Figs. 11a-11e) are comparable to the tule boats on the bottle in Figures 11 and 12. Two (Figs. 11a, b) display parts of the rays between the two boats, two (Figs. 11c, d) contain sections of the boat. Figure 11e also represents a section of the boat with a portion of its anthropomorphized leg. The sixth sherd (Fig. 13a) is from a tule boat in the form of a rayed crescent (Figs. 13, 14).

Strombus Monster

Four fineline sherds (Figs. 15a-d) have fragments of Strombus Monster scenes (Figs. 16, 17). Two of these (Figs. 15a, b) are part of the monster's head; one (Fig. 15c) displays a section of the outer lip of its shell and parts of its legs and tail; and the fourth (Fig. 15d) is part of the monster's mouth. A fifth sherd (Fig. 18) appears to have the markings of the Strombus Monster's body.

Triangular Head

One sherd (Fig. 19) shows part of a triangular head. It matches an abstract animal on the bottle in Figure 20.

Running Figures

The sherd in Figure 21, a fragment of a running scene, depicts a hand holding a bag similar to those in Figure 22.

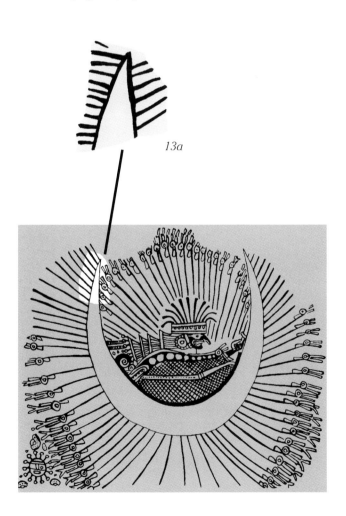

Figure 13 Rollout drawing of rayed crescent tule boat (Fig. 14) with a sherd (13a) from Pacatnamu.

Figure 14 Stirrup spout bottle with a crescent tule boat. Private collection, Lima.

15a

15b

15c

15d

Figures 15. Sections of a Strombus Monster on sherds from Pacatnamu.

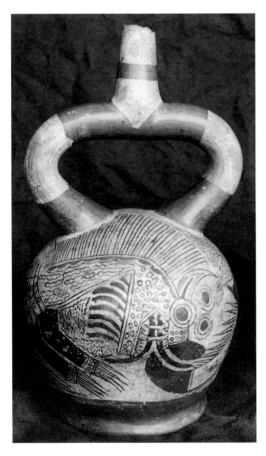

Figure 17. Rollout drawing of the Strombus Monster on the stirrup spout bottle in Figure 16.

Figure 16 Stirrup spout bottle with the Strombus Monster. Private collection, Lima.

Figure 18. A sherd from Pacatnamu with markings similar to those of the Strombus Monster.

Figure 19 Triangular head on a sherd from Pacatnamu.

Figure 20. Stirrup spout bottle with a triangular headed animal.
Peabody Museum, Harvard University, Cambridge.

Figure 21. Detail of runners on a sherd from Pacatnamu.

Figure 22. Anthropomorphized bird runners. Detail from a rollout drawing from a flaring bowl.

Figure 23. A foot and leg on a sherd from Pacatnamu.

Figure 24. Flower element on a sherd from Pacatnamu.

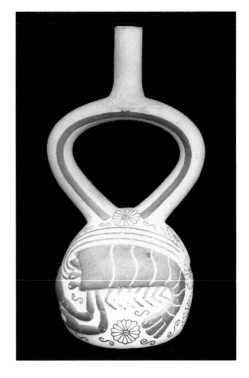

Figure 25. Stirrup spout bottle with
crayfish and flower elements.
Field Museum of Natural History, Chicago.

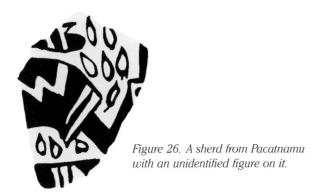

Figure 26. A sherd from Pacatnamu
with an unidentified figure on it.

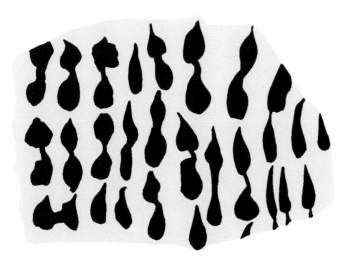

Figure 27. Pelage markings on a sherd from Pacatnamu.

Figure 28. Stirrup spout bottle with a feline.
Private collection, Buenos Aires.

Figures 29. Feathers on two sherds from Pacatnamu.

The feathers in front of the hand suggest that the runner is behind an anthropomorphized bird runner. Although it is not possible to identify the type of runner holding the bag, it is probably another anthropomorphized animal, because the Moche rarely mixed human and anthropomorphized animal runners in the same scene.

Nonspecific Design Elements

Although the fineline sherds discussed above could be matched to specific, identifiable scenes, ten sherds have design elements that are not unique to any one scene, and could have appeared in a number of different scenes. The lower leg in Figure 23 could be attached to almost anyone. The flower-like element in Figure 24 appears in the background of many ocean or estuary scenes (Fig. 25). These elements also occur in bands alternating with bands of other geometric designs.

The sherd in Figure 26 appears to be another runner holding a bag. The arm and leg positions are consistent with those of runners; however, the figure is wearing a shirt, which runners rarely do. Alternatively, this may have been a fighting warrior, since they have similar arm and leg positions and wear shirts like this. If it is a warrior, the hand might be holding a club.

The sherd in Figure 27 is covered with feline pelage markings like those in Figure 28. Although the markings can be identified, there is no way to determine what the original drawing looked like. The sherd is highly convex and might be from a modeled feline ceramic that was painted with pelage markings.

Two sherds (Fig. 29) display only feathers. Moche plumage markings are not unique to any one species, so it is not possible to identify the birds being depicted. Moreover, birds appear in so many different scenes that even if we could identify the birds on the sherds from their feathers, we could not identify the original drawing in which they appeared.

Two fox-headed snakes were depicted on another sherd (Fig. 30). These represent the fox-headed belt endings worn by supernatural figures in many different activities (e.g., Figs. 31, 32).

Part of a head can be seen in Figure 33. However, the fragment is so incomplete that we cannot identify the figure, nor the scene in which he occurs.

The sherd in Figure 34 has the jaw and hand of a creature with teeth, whiskers, and a protruding tongue that are similar to those of an anthropomorphized fish (Fig. 35). The hand holds an object shaped like a tumi (ceremonial knife), similar to the one held by the fish. The fish can hold the blade either up or down, so the position of the blade is not significant. Not so easily explained are the rectangular objects suspended from the creature's tumi, tongue, and lip.[2]

Two fineline sherds (Figs. 36, 37) seem to contain parts of complex scenes, but there is not enough information to identify them. Although the Moche character Iguana can be identified by the serrated tail in Figure 36, Iguana appears in many complex scenes. There are several jars below him, suggesting a ritual activity. The waves and circular netting in Figure 37 suggest a maritime setting. Perhaps it will be possible to identify the activities that were portrayed on these two sherds as more fineline ceramics are recorded and more iconographic studies are completed.

Unidentifiable Sherds

The remaining 30 fineline sherds in the sample (Figs. 38, 39) are so fragmentary that it is not possible to match them with any known fineline scene at this time. Nevertheless, they are illustrated here with the expectation that some of them will be matched or identified as additional complete fineline drawings become available.

Chronology

The style and complexity of Moche fineline drawings changed through time, and so did the activities and characters that were depicted. Therefore, it is often possible to use the drawings on fineline sherds to identify the Moche phase in which they were produced.

---

2. This sherd is from a Moche plate, an exceedingly rare ceramic form for fineline drawing.

Figure 30. Fox-headed snakes on a sherd from Pacatnamu.

Figure 31. Stirrup spout bottle illustrating
fox-headed snake belts.
The Art Institute of Chicago.

Figure 32. Detail of a rollout drawing from a stirrup spout
bottle (Fig. 31) showing fox-headed snake belts
on Wrinkle Face (left seated figure).

Figure 33. Supernatural head on a sherd from Pacatnamu.

*Figure 34. Part of a mythical animal head
on a sherd from Pacatnamu.*

*Figures 36 Unidentified complex scene
on a sherd from Pacatnamu.*

*Figure 37. Unidentified complex scene
on a sherd from Pacatnamu.*

*Figure 35. Stirrup spout bottle with a fish
demon holding a tumi.
Museo Arqueológico de la Universidad de Trujillo.*

Nearly all the fineline sherds in our sample can be identified as Moche V. This includes all with the bands of geometric design (Fig. 2), the tule boats (Figs. 11a-e, 13a), and the Strombus Monster (Figs. 15a-d). The majority of the unidentified sherds (Figs. 38, 39) are probably also Phase V, based on the style of painting.

Geometric designs decorate ceramics in every phase, but in Phase V they are painted in bands. A bottle with bands of geometric designs was excavated by Ubbelohde-Doering (1983: Abb. 56.3) at Pacatnamu. Twenty-two bottles in the Moche Archive with bands of geometric designs all date to Moche V. They are widespread geographically in Phase V and have been documented by Christopher Donnan in the Santa Valley (1973: Plate 7E), by Garth Bawden in the Moche Valley (1977: Figs. 92-94), and by Izumi Shimada in the Lambayeque Valley (1976: 188, 194, 225).[3]

Phase V tule boats are distinctive, and the crescent boat was produced only in Phase V.

---

3. This style of geometric designs in tiers also was being produced by the Panzaleo culture in Ecuador on a goblet during the same time period (Salvat y Crespo 1977:191).

Although it is possible that the sherd with Runners (Fig. 21) belongs to Phase IV, the execution of the line is more similar to the painting style of Phase V.

One sherd in our sample may have been produced in Moche II or III. The triangular head on the sherd in Figure 19 is only found on ceramics of Phase II or III in the Moche Archive, and the broad painted line is characteristic of fineline drawing prior to Phase IV.

San José de Moro

The Phase V fineline ceramics that have been found at Pacatnamu are remarkably similar to those from the site of San José de Moro, located less than twenty-five kilometers away. The Moche Archive includes 89 fineline painted bottles from San José de Moro.[4] The close match between tule boats from Pacatnamu and those on a bottle from San José de Moro suggests they even may have come from the same production center. It is likely that this center was San José de Moro.

Summary

When the 65 Moche fineline sherds from Pacatnamu were compared with photographs of whole bottles in the Moche Archive, some complex scenes could be identified, and in some cases the phase in which they were produced could be determined. Comparison with the fineline drawings from San José de Moro suggests that the Pacatnamu fineline ceramics were produced at San José de Moro. Only the high status burials at Pacatnamu (Ubbelohde-Doering 1983) contained fineline ceramics. Their limited distribution within the area of Moche occupation at Pacatnamu also suggests they were regarded as elite ware. In contrast to the majority of Moche ceramics, which are from looted tombs and have little or no provenience, field-collected sherds offer an important resource to study the distribution, chronology, iconography, and production of fineline ceramics. The publication of sherds with fineline drawings as well as whole ceramics will expand this valuable corpus of data.

---

4. Nine were excavated in 1991 and 1992 from very high status burials in deep shaft tombs at San José de Moro (Donnan and Castillo 1992, n.d.).

Figure 38. Unidentified elements on sherds from Pacatnamu.

Figure 39. Unidentified elements on sherds from Pacatnamu.

RESUMEN:
Dibujos en Línea Fina Moche en Pacatnamú

Aunque hay miles de ejemplos de cerámios Moche con línea fina, casi todos han sido saqueados, por lo que carecen de proveniencia, tanto del sitio o valle de donde proceden. Ubbelohde-Doering excavó en Pacatnamú, en 1938-39, tres piezas decoradas con línea fina; entre 1983 y 1987 no ubicamos otras piezas de este tipo, pero recuperamos 65 fragmentos de cerámica decorados con esta técnica.

Distribución

La cerámica recuperada ha servido para determinar el área de ocupación Moche en el sitio (Fig. 1). Las decoradas con línea fina, que representan un porcentaje menor en la muestra, se hallan todas dentro del área de ocupación Moche (Fig. 1). Aunque algunas pueden provenir de tumbas saqueadas, la gran mayoría de los fragmentos proviene de los basurales Moche.

El Archivo Moche

El Archivo Moche, en UCLA, contiene fotografías de aproximadamente 20,000 objetos Moche provenientes de Museos y colecciones privadas de todo el mundo. De ellos, mas que 2000 corresponden a cerámica decorada con línea fina, las que están sistemáticamente catalogadas. Aunque los detalles de los dibujos varían de artista a artista, hay mucha repetición en la temática, diseño y distribución de los elementos, por lo que las escenas y los temas son muy consistentes. Esto permite asociar un fragmento con un dibujo completo y, aún, identificar la fase cuando fue pintado.

La Muestra de Pacatnamú

18 de los 65 fragmentos pueden ser identificados usando la muestra del Archivo Moche.

Diseños Escalonados Geométricos

Once fragmentos tienen este diseño. Siete están pintados con un diseño escalonado (Fig. 2) similar al de la Fig. 3. Las variaciones de este motivo pueden verse en las Figs. 4-10.

"Caballitos" o Embarcaciones de Totora

Seis fragmentos muestran complejas escenas con embarcaciones de totora. Cinco (Figs. 11a-11e) son comparables a las embarcaciones de las Figs. 11 y 12. La sexta (Fig. 13a) es parte del tipo mostrado en las Figs. 13 y 14.

Monstruo Strombus

Cuatro (Figs. 15a-d) poseen diseños asociados con la escena del Monstruo Strombus (Figs. 16-17). Dos son parte de la cabeza (Fig. 15a-b); una (Fig. 15c) es el borde de la concha, piernas y cola; otra (Fig. 15d) es parte de la boca; y la última (Fig. 18), las marcas del cuerpo.

Cabeza Triangular

Un fragmento (Fig. 19) coincide con el animal abstracto de la Figura 20.

Individuos Corriendo

El tiesto de la Figura 21 muestra la mano sosteniendo una bolsa, similar a la de la Figura 22.

Elementos No-específicos de Diseño

Aunque los elementos descritos arriba son específicos de esas escenas, diez fragmentos tienen diseños que se presentan en más de una escena. Por ejemplo, la pierna de la Fig. 23 puede ser adscrita a casi cualquier individuo. La "flor" de la Fig. 24 aparece en escenas marinas o de estuarios (Fig. 25); el fragmento de Fig. 26 puede ser otro corredor; la Fig. 27 muestra pelambre de felino, como en Fig. 28; Fig. 29 muestra plumas, pero la escena concreta no puede identificarse por la diversidad de contextos en las que ellas se muestran; las serpientes con cabeza de zorro (Fig. 30) también aparecen en diferentes escenas (p. ej. Figs. 31 y 32); hay parte de una cabeza en Fig. 33, mientras Fig. 34 muestra la mandíbula y la mano de una criatura con dientes, bigotes, y larga lengua, como la del pez antropomorfizado (Fig. 35). Por último, dos fragmentos (Figs. 36 y 37) muestran partes de escenas complejas.

Fragmentos Inidentificables

Treinta (Figs. 38-39) están tan fragmentados, que no pueden identificarse, pero es posible que se pueda hacer en el futuro.

Cronología

El estilo y la complejidad del dibujo en línea fina cambió a través del tiempo, así como cambiaron las actividades y los caracteres que se representaron. Por ello, es posible fechar, de manera relativa, los fragmentos recuperados.

Casi todos ellos pueden adscribirse a la fase V, incluyendo las no identificadas, basándonos en el estilo y tipo de línea. Sin embargo, es posible que los corredores (Fig. 21) pertenezcan a la fase IV, aunque la línea sea más

*similar a la de la fase V. Por último, un fragmento puede
haber sido producido en la fase II o III (Fig. 19), ya que el
motivo aparece sólo en esas fases y el tipo de línea usado
es anterior a la fase IV.*

San José de Moro

*Los fragmentos pertenecientes a la fase V, recupera-
dos en Pacatnamú, son muy similares a los de San José
de Moro, ubicado a menos de 25 kms. de distancia. En el
Archivo Moche hay dibujos de 89 botellas pintadas provenientes de ese sitio y las similitudes entre las Embarcaciones de Totora de ambos sitios sugiere que las piezas
fueron hechas en el mismo taller, probablemente en Moro.*

The Offering Room Group

Alana Cordy-Collins

During the 1984 excavations at Pacatnamu an Offering Room Group was discovered which appears to be unique at the site. Analysis and interpretation of its contents afford new insights into Moche ceremonial practice in the Jequetepeque Valley.

The room group is part of a late Moche architectural complex immediately northwest of Huaca 1 (Fig. 1a). The walls of this complex were constructed using sundried mud brick set in mud mortar. The exterior of the complex was remodeled during the succeeding Lambayeque period, thus obscuring its original outward appearance. However, much of the original interior wall surface is unmodified and intact, and it is clear that it never was plastered. A north-south wall, also built during the Lambayeque period, subsequently divided the Moche architecture into an eastern and western section. The eastern section was the focus of investigation.

Substantial excavation of this section revealed a three-room structure measuring 5 meters east-west by 4 meters north-south (Fig. 1b). Room 1 and Room 2 have single doorways in their north walls, which open directly into Room 3. There is a step down from the bricked and plastered floors of Rooms 1 and 2 onto the bedrock floor of Room 3. Rooms 1 and 2 each had a single post hole, but were empty of cultural remains. Room 3, however, is remarkable because of its abundant contents. A set of wood posts once stood in the room, apparently to support a cane roof. At some point the room burned, reducing the posts to charcoal, baking the interior surfaces of the walls, and charring the cane roof. The room contents, which included ceramics, bone, metal, textile, shell, and organic residue, also were altered by the intense heat of the fire.

Ceramics

Approximately 400 small, unslipped, redware hand modeled pots, known locally as *ofrendas*, were found in six major and two minor clusters at the room's west and east ends (Fig. 2).[1] The majority of the pots are plain, but 50 are decorated and are classifiable into five stylistic types (Fig.3); the plainware can be considered a sixth type (see Appendix for a discussion of the types, and Figs. 10-16). Two clusters contained only plain *ofrendas*. The other four clusters contained *ofrendas* of various types. All *ofrendas* had raw cotton embedded in their necks which was burned to a delicate ash by the fire.

In addition to the *ofrendas*, five hand-modeled, shallow, unslipped redware pedestal bowls with crenelated rims (Fig. 4) were nested together in one cluster.

---

1. Three-hundred fifty-three are intact. An additional 47 to 50 broke as the room settled.

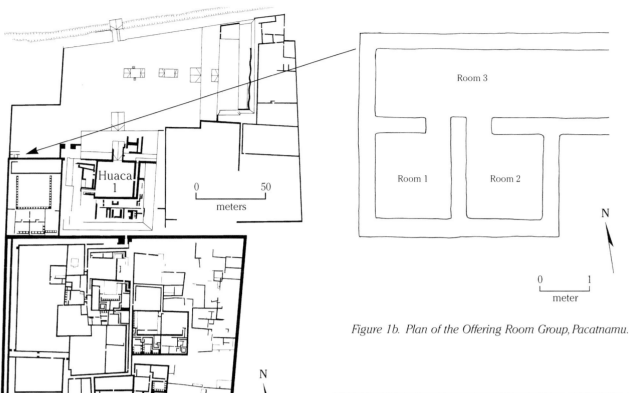

Figure 1a. Huaca 1 Complex showing location
of the Offering Room Group.

Figure 1b. Plan of the Offering Room Group, Pacatnamu.

These types of *ofrendas* and bowls appear to be unique
to Room 3; no other examples have been found at
Pacatnamu.[2]

Finally, four large mold-made ceramic vessels were
found apart from the ceramic clusters. Two are jars modeled in the form of a crayfish (Fig. 5). Another vessel is a
jar modeled in the form of a woman carrying a jar on her
back (Fig. 6). These three pieces have clear antecedents
in earlier Moche pottery. The fourth vessel also is a jar,
modeled in the shape of a bird (Fig. 7). Although the two
crayfish jars are painted with only red and cream slip, the
woman carrying a jar and the bird are painted with red,
cream, and black slip. The presence of black slip on
these latter vessels identifies them as Huari related.

---

2. A few of the decorated *ofrenda* types were excavated at the post-
Moche site of Chotuna in the Lambayeque Valley (Donnan n.d.a.),
and smaller versions of the plain *ofrendas* have been found elsewhere at Pacatnamu, at San Jose de Moro (another late Moche site
in the Jequetepeque Valley), and at Chotuna.

Figure 2. View of Room 3 from the east
before removal of contents.

Figure 3. Five decorated ofrenda *types on the left; plain example on the far right.*

Bone

Seven partial human skeletons were recovered from Room 3. The bones appear to have been dry when they burned because they are not warped as fresh bone is when exposed to extreme heat. Males and females were represented, and their ages ranged from approximately 10 to 50 years (John Verano, personal communication, 1984).

Incomplete remains of three animals were recovered: avian and canine bones were found mixed with camelid ribs bearing cut marks. All were intermingled with the bones of three adult humans. Also recovered was an isolated partial adult camelid skeleton, consisting of the cranium and long bones (Fig. 8). Two features of this camelid are noteworthy: its hind feet are four-toed rather than the normal two-toed, an occurrence related to inbreeding (Altamirano n.d.); and the bones are warped, indicating they were fresh at the time of the fire.

Metal

Four copper objects were found near the four-toed camelid remains: a large bent spatula (Fig. 9) and three flat, unidentifiable fragmentary objects that exhibit textile impressions.

Textile

Textile was found in two contexts: charred with some of the human bone, and impressed on the three flat copper pieces. That adhering to the bone was not analyzable, but scrutiny of fiber impressions on the copper revealed that the fabric was woven from S over-spun cotton, 3 to 6 millimeters thick (Susan Bruce, personal communication, 1984). Because so little textile survived, no conclusions could be drawn about the original appearance or number of pieces.

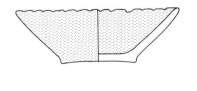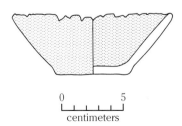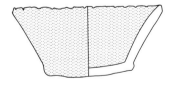

Figure 4 Three of the five crenelated bowls.

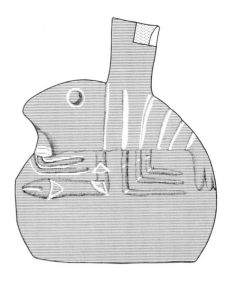

0 — 5
centimeters

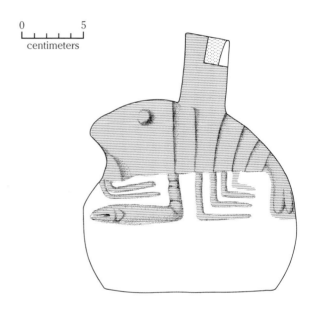

Figure 5. Pair of crayfish-shaped jars.

Shell

Seven disc and five tubular beads were found in the eastern part of the room. The disc beads are light pink; the shell type has not been identified. The tubular beads range from light purple to light orange, and probably are made from *Spondylus calcifer* and *Spondylus princeps* shell.

Organic Residue

The organic material seems to be residue from a liquid. Most pottery is likely to have contained the substance;

a few of the vessels broke during the fire and the liquid ran across the breaks and was baked onto them. Impressions of the clustered pots result from the sandy ash in which they were stacked having been drenched by the liquid and baked by the fire simultaneously. The raw cotton in the neck of the vessels was probably intended as stoppers.

The human bones, located apart from the *ofrendas*, also exhibit scorched residue. Because they were dry at the time they burned, the organic residue on them must be the remains of something poured over them about the time of the fire. Some bone actually may have been immersed in liquid, because a few samples show scorched organic material inside as well as outside.

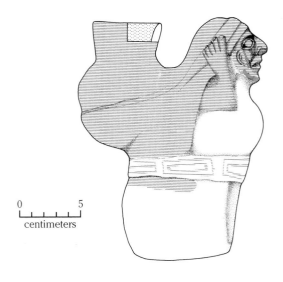

0 _____ 5
centimeters

Figure 6. Jar modeled in the form of a woman carrying a jar on her back.

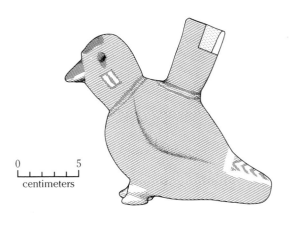

0 _____ 5
centimeters

Figure 7. Jar modeled in the form of a bird.

Finally, there are spots on the floor of the room, suggesting that liquid was poured directly onto it. A 10-centimeter-deep area of sand shows a stain throughout, and a hole which had been dug at a sharp angle (making it unlikely to have enclosed a post) exhibits traces of burned organic liquid.

Date

A late Moche temporal assignment for the room is indicated by both relative and absolute dates. Donald McClelland has identified the mud bricks as late Moche (McClelland 1986). Three of the larger ceramics are late Moche in style, while the fourth has affinities to the contemporary Huari style. In addition, one type of the small pots has a press-molded human face, which seems to be a variant of the "New King" image on ceramics found only in late Moche period deposits at Pacatnamu (Fig. 11). Finally, an uncalibrated radiocarbon date of A.D. 710,[3] obtained from the wood charcoal of the burned posts, places the find as late Moche, at the time when Huari influence (Middle Horizon 1B) was reflected in ceramic and textile styles of the North Coast.

---

3. (1240 ± 60 B.P.) #Beta-12285. Beta Analytic, Inc. (April, 1985).

Figure 8. Camelid mandible and forelegs in situ.

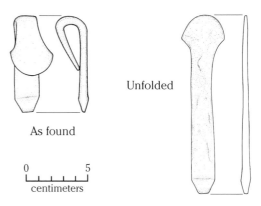

Figure 9. Copper spatula.

Interpretation

The Offering Room Group is a singular discovery at Pacatnamu, suggesting that it served an unusual purpose. Several lines of evidence argue for its ceremonial function. The placement, association, and treatment of objects deposited therein imply the enactment of a ritual. Many of the objects are unique, such as the four mold-made vessels (Fig. 5-7); no other examples of these types have been found at Pacatnamu, either isolated or in association with each other. However, other object types have been found as ritual grave goods elsewhere at Pacatnamu: the 400 ceramic *ofrendas* are larger, more elaborate versions of smaller *ofrendas* found with contemporaneous burials and slightly later as caches. Another frequent burial offering is a llama skull and forelegs grouped together. Copper, usually bent or broken, is a traditional accompaniment for the dead, usually placed in the mouth or hands. Textiles, too, have been found as burial offerings clearly distinct from the cloth in which the deceased was clothed or enshrouded. Shell jewelry occasionally is found in burial contexts, and the rare *Spondylus* shell always seems to have been an item worthy of offering status at Pacatnamu (Verano and Cordy-Collins 1986).

The only apparent nontraditional offering is the liquid. However, the absence of liquid in burials may be simply the result of desiccation or evaporation; most elaborate grave ceramics are empty, and often small *ofrendas* are found with cotton stoppers, suggesting that originally they may have contained liquid. If the Offering Room Group had not burned and thereby scorched the liquid, all traces of the substance likely would have disappeared.

The most curious of the room's contents, however, are the partial human remains. It is clear from the desiccated state of the bone that the individuals had been dead for some time prior to their deposition in Room 3. These remains may have been curated bodies. This also would account for copper and textile as funerary goods. The Moche conserved certain deceased individuals to be interred at some later time as special offerings (Alva and Donnan 1993: 125). Their incompleteness in this instance may result from disintegration either in the storage facility or in their transport from it to Room 3.[4]

Two items of evidence suggest that the Offering Room Group burned very soon after its contents were assembled there: the llama bone warped, indicating that it was fresh when burned; and liquid in the bottles had not evaporated or desiccated when the bottles baked. Although we cannot conclude whether the burning was intentional or accidental, there is evidence indicating it was intentional. A 20-centimeter layer of compacted ash under the north wall of Room 3 and beyond it for over a meter demonstrates that prior burning had taken place in the area, before the room was reduced in size by the Lambayeque construction of the north-south wall. Furthermore, destruction by fire is a known Andean means of transferring offerings from human supplicants to the gods. For example, the Inca of Cuzco burned fine textiles every morning as a way of presenting valued commodities to the supreme deity, *Inti* (Murra 1980). Another tradition still practiced in the highlands of Peru is the offering of food and drink. In fact, libations routinely are presented to the deified earth before beginning any important undertaking. Thus, the presence of liquid, not only in the vessels, but also on the floor of the room, would be appropriate in the context of offerings.

4. Curated interments were found at the contemporaneous site of San Jose de Moro, also in the Jequetepeque Valley. These are less complete than the earlier interments discussed by Alva and Donnan. It may be that during late Moche times the interment of curated bodies was somewhat more careless than in earlier times.

Sequence

Analysis of the relative position of the architectural and artifactual features of the Offering Room Group allows for a reconstruction of the general sequence of events that took place there:

1. The area of the Offering Room Group was allocated.

2. Rooms 1, 2, and 3 were constructed (Fig. 1b).
   a. Walls were erected.
   b. Floors of Rooms 1 and 2 were bricked and plastered.
   c. Bedrock floor of Room 3 was left covered with 20 centimeters of ash from at least one earlier burning event.
   d. Post holes were dug in the three rooms.
   e. A cane roof was installed.

3. The contents of Room 3 were prepared and placed on the floor.
   a. The *ofrendas* were filled with liquid and plugged with cotton.
   b. The *ofrendas* were stacked in clusters, probably in gourds or some other perishable containers.
   c. The crenelated dishes were included in one stack.
   d. The four elaborate ceramics were placed directly on the floor.
   e. The human bone along with its associated textiles, copper, and shell beads—and probably the fragmentary canine, avian, and camelid bone—were introduced.
   f. The diagonal hole in the floor was dug.
   g. A four-toed llama was sacrificed and its cranium and lower long bones were deposited.
   h. Liquid was poured over everything.
   i. The fire took place.

4. Time elapsed.

5. The Lambayeque north-south wall was erected.

This scenario is simple and straightforward; it attempts to account only for the general sequence of events as they can be reconstructed from the extant material. However, other related activities may have taken place, such as prayers, incantations, and ritual feasting and drinking. Because we do not know the exact nature of the ceremony, we can only postulate who the celebrants and officiants might have been. Nonetheless, based upon ethnographic and ethnohistoric comparisons, and on the nature of the offerings, we can suggest a more detailed, but hypothetical, reconstruction that includes a more human dimension:

Prior to the final burning, there had been at least one other burning in the Offering Room Group. This suggests that the area was dedicated to such a ceremony. We can imagine workmen constructing the rooms under the guidance of experienced practitioners of the sacred: bricks being formed, dried, and mortared into position; wood posts cut and fitted into their floor sockets; and a cane thatch roof woven and secured above the posts. We can further envision the selection of four fine pottery vessels—perhaps even commissioned for the offering ceremony. It would appear that less-skilled potters fashioned the *ofrendas*. (The six types may have reflected specific individuals or groups.) Subsequently, someone was responsible for preparing the liquid, possibly *chicha* (corn beer) and for decanting it into the *ofrendas*, over the bones, and onto the floor. The rare polydactyl camelid was slaughtered for this event, but because the entire animal was not included, we can imagine a feasting ceremony wherein the celebrants partook of the more succulent portions (the meatier ribs and quarters which are absent from the room). In addition, someone exhumed the human ancestral bones and re-deposited them here. Finally, the room was set afire as the culmination of the ceremony.

Addendum

As this article was going to press, we made an archaeological find which provides some time depth for the ceremony enacted in the Offering Room Group. During the 1995 field season at the early Moche site of Dos Cabezas, a Moche architectural complex located in the delta of the Jequetepeque Valley just south of Pacatnamu, our excavations uncovered an earlier example of the ceremony. Although considerably larger in scale, the Dos Cabezas find was essentially the same: a rectangular room wherein disarticulated human bone was mixed with articulated camelid bone and ceramic *ofrendas*. Over this layer, a fire of wood beams had been lit and covered with mud bricks. The differences between the two events are minor and may be attributable to the several centuries that separate them. While the second discovery brings us no closer to understanding the meaning of the fire ceremony, it does underscore its importance to the Moche society of the Jequetepeque Valley.

APPENDIX: *Ofrenda* Ceramic Typology

The *ofrendas* recovered from Room 3 are classified as six types based upon morphological characteristics. All have bulbous chambers and round bottoms, except for one pedestal-based example of Type 1, and they lack handles. They are hand modeled, oxidation-fired, and range in height between 7 and 12.5 centimeters.

Type 1:

A small modeled anthropomorphic or zoomorphic face is situated at the vessel shoulder, just below the short cylindrical spout (Fig. 10).

Type 2:

An anthropomorphic head (the "New King") is press molded onto the neck of the short cylindrical spout (Fig. 11). One example has a single modeled zoomorphic "arm" affixed to the vessel chamber below the face.

Type 3:

An anthropomorphic face is hand modeled into the area between the vessel shoulder and the short spout (Fig. 12). Several examples have pinched out ears and nose. The eyes and mouth are incised.

Type 4:

In most examples a somewhat bulbous anthropomorphic face serves as the spout. In other examples (Fig. 13) the anthropomorphic face is modeled directly into the chamber. In these cases a short spout surmounts the head. All examples have incised eyes and pinched out ears and nose. Mouths usually are incised, but can be appliquéd. Occasionally, hair is indicated by parallel incisions. The characteristic feature of this type is a pair of deeply incised "+" motifs, one on each cheek or arranged horizontally on the chamber.

Type 5:

There is more variation in this type than in the other four. All have faces, some modeled into the neckless chamber, others on the short neck (Fig. 14). Most faces are hand formed with pinched out ears and/or nose, but a few bottles have a press molded face. The distinctive feature of this type is an "arm," either the right or left, appended to the vessel chamber. The arm is zoomorphized.

Type 6:

Plain (Fig. 3, far right).

Miscellaneous:

Two pieces are unique. One has two hand-modeled zoomorphs, ventral side up, each with a line incised vertically down its middle (Fig. 15). The other has the spout bent at an angle onto which is modeled a zoomorphic face with incised features (Fig. 16).

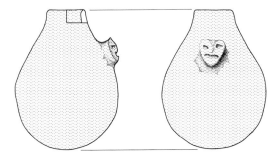

Figure 10. *Type 1* ofrenda.

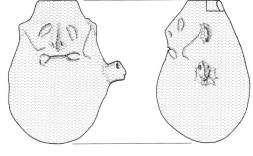

Figure 14. *Type 5* ofrenda.

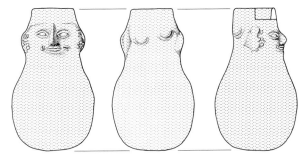

Figure 11. *Type 2* ofrenda.

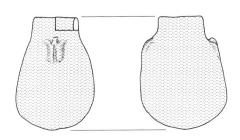

Figure 15. Ofrenda *with two animal appliqués.*

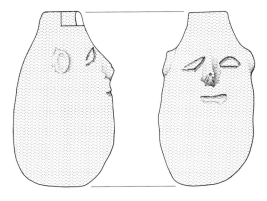

Figure 12. *Type 3* ofrenda.

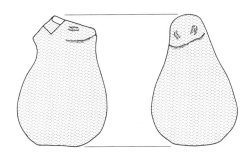

Figure 16. Ofrenda *with zoomorphic face on bent jar neck.*

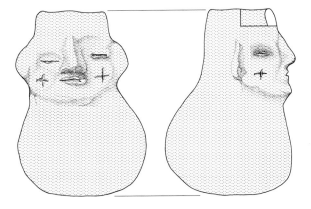

Figure 13. *Type 4* ofrenda.

0   5
centimeters

RESUMEN:
El Cuarto de las Ofrendas

Durante las excavaciones de 1984 se descubrió una habitación con características únicas en Pacatnamú; forma parte de un complejo arquitectónico Moche tardío ubicado al noroeste de la Huaca 1 (Fig. 1), construido con adobes y remodelado durante la subsecuente ocupación Lambayeque, lo que dificulta establecer sus características originales. La estructura medía 5 mts. este-oeste y 4 mts. norte-sur (Fig. 1b). Las dos habitaciones más pequeñas (1 y 2) tenían una puerta en la pared norte, la que daba al cuarto más grande (3), donde se hallaron las ofrendas. Este último tuvo postes para soportar un techo y sufrió un episodio de incendio que redujo casi todo el contenido orgánico a carbón y cenizas; el material recuperado en esta habitación incluye cerámica, huesos, metales, tejidos, conchas y residuos orgánicos.

Cerámica

Fueron halladas, aproximadamente, 400 pequeñas piezas de cerámica roja, modelada a mano, sin pintura, conocida en la zona como ofrendas. Estaban formando seis grupos grandes y dos pequeños (Fig. 2); 353 estaban intactas, pero entre 47 y 50 estaban rotas. Alrededor de 50 estaban decoradas y son clasificables en 5 tipos (Fig. 3); el sexto tipo estaría formado por aquellas sin decoración (ver Apéndice).

Cinco tazones con pedestal, hechos de cerámica roja sin pintar (Fig. 4), fueron depositados juntos en otro grupo, mientras cuatro piezas hechas con molde (Fig. 5), fueron depositadas en el piso, pero sin formar parte de los grupos. Dos tenían la forma de camarones, pintados crema y ocre (Figs. 6); otra representa una mujer cargando un recipiente de cerámica (Fig. 7); y la última tenía la forma de un pájaro (Fig. 8). Estas dos últimas piezas eran de color ocre, crema y negro. La presencia del color negro sugiere una influencia Huari.

Hueso

Las osamentas incompletas de siete personas, de ambos sexos y entre 10 y 50 años de edad, fueron consumidas por el fuego, el que ocurrió mucho después de su deceso, ya que los huesos no se torcieron con el calor.

Los esqueletos incompletos de por lo menos tres animales, pájaro, canino y camélido, estuvieron mezclados con los de por lo menos tres humanos. El camélido (Fig. 9) tenía tres dedos, en vez de los dos normales, y sus huesos estaban torcidos, lo que denota que estuvo recién muerto cuando fué sometido al fuego.

Metal

Se recuperaron cuatro objetos de metal, cerca del camélido: una espátula doblada (Fig. 10) y otros tres no identificables, con impresiones de tejido.

Tejidos

Se observó en dos contextos: calcinado con algunos de los huesos humanos, e impreso en las piezas de cobre. Este último estuvo hecho con hilo torcido en S.

Concha

En la porción este de la habitación se hallaron siete cuentas circulares y tres tubulares; las circulares eran ligeramente rosadas, mientras las tubulares variaban de púrpura claro a naranja claro, por lo que pueden haber sido hechas de Spondylus calcifer o Spondylus princeps.

Residuos Orgánicos

Se trata, aparentemente, de residuos de líquidos, ubicados en la mayoría de la cerámica; con el fuego y la rotura de algunas piezas, se esparció en el piso y se endureció, así como sobre algunos de los huesos humanos. Algunas de las manchas en el piso sugieren que también fué asperjado.

Fechado

La datación absoluta y la relativa indican un fechado Moche tardío; los adobes son Moche tardíos y tres de las piezas de cerámica son claramente del mismo periodo. Un fechado radiocarbónico, sin calibrar, arrojó 710 N.E., Horizonte Medio 1b, época de influencia Huari.

Interpretación

La ubicación, asociación y tratamiento de los objetos implica la realización de un ritual. Algunos de los objetos ofrendados son únicos (las 4 piezas de cerámica o el líquido), mientras otros, como las ofrendas, restos de llamas, textiles, cobre y conchas se han hallado en diversas partes del sitio. Las osamentas humanas parciales corresponden a un tipo de entierro secundario que se ha registrado en Sipán, quizá tambien dentro de un contexto de ofrenda.

El fuego parece haber sido intencional y se habría iniciado poco después de haberse depositado las ofrendas, como lo sugiere el líquido (que no estaba seco o evaporado) y los huesos de llama, que eran frescos. Probablemente se trató de la realización de un ritual que, como posteriormente, durante la época Inca, implicó la quema de las ofrendas.

Acleto O., César
1986   *Algas Marinas del Perú de Importancia Económica.*
        Departamento de Botánica Serie de Divulgación,
        No. 5. Museo de Historia Natural "Javier Prado,"
        Universidad Nacional Mayor de San Marcos. Lima.

Acsádi, Gyorgy., and J. Nemeskéri
1970   *History of Human Life Span and Mortality.*
        Akadémiai Kiadó. Budapest.

Altamirano, Alfredo
n.d.   *Sacrificios de Camélidos* en Pacatnamú. Ms. on
        file in the Archive of Moche Art. University of
        California, Los Angeles.

Alva, Walter
1988   Discovering the New World's Richest Unlooted
        Tomb. *National Geographic* 174(4):509-550.

Alva, Walter, and Christopher B. Donnan
1993   *Royal Tombs of Sipán.* Fowler Museum of Cultural
        History. University of California, Los Angeles.

Ambrose, Stanley H.
1993   Isotopic Analysis of Paleodiets: Methodological and
        Interpretive Considerations. In *Investigations of
        Ancient Human Tissue: Chemical Analysis in Anthro-
        pology.* Mary K. Sandford (ed.). Gordon and
        Breach. Amsterdam.

Arriaga, Pablo José de
1968   *The Extirpation of Idolatry in Peru.* L. Clark Keating
        (ed. and trans.). University of Texas Press. Lexington.

Bawden, Garth
1977   *Galindo and the Nature of the Middle Horizon in
        Northern Coastal Peru.* Ph.D. dissertation, Depart-
        ment of Anthropology. Harvard University.

Bennett, Wendell C.
1950   The Gallinazo Group, Virú Valley, Peru. *Yale University
        Publications in Anthropology* 43. Yale University
        Press, New Haven.

Bennett, Wendell C., and Junius B. Bird
1964   *Andean Culture History.* American Museum of
        Natural History. New York.

Bird, Robert McK., and Junius B. Bird
1980   Gallinazo Maize from the Chicama Valley, Peru.
        American Antiquity 45(2):325-332.

Calancha, Fray Antonio de la
1977-1981 [1638] *Crónica Moralizada.* Ignacio Prado Pastor
        (ed.). Universidad Nacional Mayor de San Marcos.
        Lima.

Castillo B., Luis Jaime, and Christopher B. Donnan
1994a   La Ocupación Moche de San José de Moro,
        Jequetepeque. In *Moche: Propuestas y Perspecti-
        vas.* Santiago Uceda and Elías Mujica (eds.).
        Universidad Nacional de La Libertad. Trujillo.
1994b   Los Mochicas del Norte y los Mochicas del Sur. In
        Vicus. Colección Arte y Tesoros del Perú. Banco
        de Lima. Lima.

Cieza de León, Pedro de
    1984 [1553] *La Crónica del Perú.* Vol. 1. Fondo Editorial
        Pontificia Universidad Católica del Perú-Academia
        Nacional de la Historia. Lima.

Conklin, William J
    1979 Moche Textile Structures. In *The Junius B. Bird
        Pre-Columbian Textile Conference, May 19th and
        20th, 1973.* Ann P. Rowe, Elizabeth P. Benson, and
        Anne-Louise Schaffer (eds.). The Textile Museum
        and Dumbarton Oaks. Washington, D.C.

Conklin, William J, and Eduardo Versteylen
    1978 Appendix 1: Textiles from a Pyramid of the Sun
        Burial. In *Ancient Burial Patterns of the Moche
        Valley, Peru.* Christopher B. Donnan and Carol J.
        Mackey. University of Texas Press. Austin.

Cordy-Collins, Alana
    1996 Lambayeque. In *Andean Art at Dumbarton Oaks.*
        Elizabeth H. Boone (ed.). Dumbarton Oaks.
        Washington, D.C.

De Jong, Gordon F.
    1972 Patterns of Human Fertility and Mortality. In
        The Structure of Human Populations. Geoffrey A.
        Harrison and Anthony J. Boyce (eds.). Clarendon
        Press. Oxford.

Dendy, John Holmes
    1991 *A Descriptive Catalog and Preliminary Analysis of
        Botanical Remains from Archaeological Excava-
        tions at Chiribaya Alta, Lower Osmore Drainage,
        Peru.* M.A. thesis, Department of Anthropology,
        Washington University. St. Louis.

DeNiro, Michael J.
    1987 Stable Isotopy and Archaeology. *American Scientist*
        75:182-191.

DeNiro, Michael J. and Samuel Epstein
    1981 Influence of Diet on the Distribution of Nitrogen
        Isotopes in Animals. *Geochimica et Cosmochimica
        Acta* 45:341-351.

Donnan, Christopher B.
    1973 *Moche Occupation of the Santa Valley, Peru.*
        University of California Press. Berkeley.
    1978 *Moche Art of Peru.* Museum of Cultural History.
        University of California, Los Angeles.
    1986a Introduction. In *The Pacatnamu Papers, Volume I.*
        Christopher B. Donnan and Guillermo A. Cock
        (eds.). Museum of Cultural History. University of
        California, Los Angeles.
    1986b The City Walls at Pacatnamu. In *The Pacatnamu
        Papers, Volume 1.* Christopher B. Donnan and
        Guillermo A. Cock (eds.). Museum of Cultural
        History. University of California, Los Angeles.
    1986c The Huaca 1 Complex. In *The Pacatnamu
        Papers, Volume 1.* Christopher B. Donnan, and
        Guillermo A. Cock (eds.). Museum of Cultural
        History. University of California, Los Angeles.

    1990 An Assessment of the Validity of the Naymlap
        Dynasty. In *The Northern Dynasties: Kingship and
        Statecraft in Chimor.* Michael E. Moseley and
        Alana Cordy-Collins (eds.). Dumbarton Oaks.
        Washington, D.C.
    1995 Moche Funerary Practice. In *Tombs for the Living:
        Andean Mortuary Practices.* Tom D. Dillehay (ed.).
        Dumbarton Oaks. Washington, D.C.
    n.d.a. *Excavations at Chotuna.* Ms. on file in the Archive
        of Moche Art. University of California, Los Angeles.
    n.d.b. *Excavations at Dos Cabezas.* Ms. on file in the
        Archive of Moche Art. University of California,
        Los Angeles.

Donnan, Christopher B., and Luis Jaime Castillo B.
    1992 Finding the Tomb of a Moche Priestess. *Archaeology*
        45(6):38-42.
    n.d. *Excavations at San José de Moro.* Ms. on file in
        the Archive of Moche Art. University of California,
        Los Angeles.

Donnan, Christopher B., and Guillermo A. Cock (eds.)
    1986 *The Pacatnamu Papers, Volume I.* Museum of
        Cultural History. University of California,
        Los Angeles.

Donnan, Christopher B., and Carol J. Mackey
    1978 *Ancient Burial Patterns of the Moche Valley, Peru.*
        University of Texas Press. Austin.

Donnan, Christopher B. and Donna McClelland
    1979 *The Burial Theme in Moche Iconography.* Studies
        in Pre-Columbian Art and Archaeology 21.
        Dumbarton Oaks. Washington D.C.

Doyle, Mary Eileen
    1988 *The Ancestor Cult and Burial Ritual in Seventeenth
        and Eighteenth Century Central Peru.*
        Ph.D. dissertation, Department of History.
        University of California, Los Angeles. University
        Microfilms. Ann Arbor.

Emery, Irene
    1966 *The Primary Structure of Fabrics.* The Textile
        Museum. Washington, D.C.

Fazekas, I. Gy, and F. Kósa
    1978 *Forensic Fetal Osteology.* Akadémiai Kiadó.
        Budapest.

Genovés, Santiago
    1967 Proportionality of the Long Bones and Their Rela-
        tion to Stature Among Mesoamericans. *American
        Journal of Physical Anthropology* 26:67-77.

Goodman, Alan H., Debra L. Martin, George J. Armelagos, and
  George Clark
    1984 "Indications of Stress From Bone and Teeth." In
        Paleopathology at the Origins of Agriculture. Mark
        Nathan Cohen and George J. Armelagos (eds.).
        Academic Press. New York.

Grobman, Alexander
    1982   Maiz (Zea mays). In *Precerámico Peruano. Los Gavilanes. Mar, Desierto y Oasis en la Historia del Hombre.* Duccio Bonavia (ed.). Corporación Financiera de Desarrollo S.A. COFIDE. Instituto Arqueológico Alemán. Lima.

Grobman, Alexander, Wilfredo Salhuana, and Ricardo Sevilla with Paul C. Mangelsdorf
    1961   *Races of Maize in Peru, Their Origins, Evolution and Classification.* Publication 915. National Academy of Science-National Research Council. Washington, D.C.

Gumerman IV, George
    1994   Corn for the Dead: The Significance of Zea mays in Moche Burial Offerings. In *Corn and Culture in the Prehistoric New World.* Sissel Johannessen and Christine A. Hastorf (eds.). Westview Press. Boulder.

Hecker, Giesela, and Wolfgang Hecker
    1982   *Pacatnamú, Vorspanische Stadt in Nordperu.* Materialien zur Allgemeinen und Vergleichenden Archäologie, Band 5. Verlag C.H. Beck. München.
    1985   *Pacatnamú y sus Construcciones, Centro Religioso Prehispánico en la Costa Norte Peruana.* Verlag Klaus Dieter Vervuert. Frankfurt.
    1990   Bestattete und Beigaben aus der Nordperuanischen Ruinenstadt Pacatnamú. *Baessler-Archiv.* Neue Folge, Band XXXVIII, 117-260. Berlin.
    1991   *Die Huaca 16 in Pacatnamú. Eine Ausgrabung an der Nordperuanischen Küste.* Berlin.
    1992   Huesos Humanos como Ofrendas Mortuorias y Uso Repetido de Vasijas. Detalles sobre la Tradición Funeraria Prehispánica de la Región Costeña Nordperuana. *Baessler-Archiv.* Neue Folge, Band XL, 117-195. Berlin.
    1995   *Die Grabungen von Heinrich Ubbelohde-Doering in Pacatnamu, Nordperú.* Dietrich Reimer Verlag. Berlin.

Hecker, Wolfgang, and Giesela Hecker
    1977   *Archäologische Untersuchungen in Pacatnamú, Nord-Peru.* Indiana, Beiheft 9. Berlin.
    1984   Erläuterungen von Beigaben und Zeitstellung Vorspanischer Gräber von Pacatnamú, Nordperú. *Baessler-Archive.* Neue Folge, Band XXXII, 159-212. Berlin.

Hosler, Dorothy, Heather Lechtman, and Olaf Holm
    1990   *Axe-Monies and Their Relatives.* Studies in Pre-Columbian Art and Archaeology 30. Dumbarton Oaks. Washington, D.C.

Howells, William W.
    1973   *Cranial Variation in Man: A Study by Multivariate Analysis of Patterns of Difference Among Recent Human Populations.* Papers of the Peabody Museum of American Archaeology and Ethnology 67. Harvard University.

Hrdlička, Aleš
    1911   Some Results of Recent Anthropological Exploration in Peru. *Smithsonian Miscellaneous Collection* 56(16). Washington, D.C.
    1914   Anthropological Work in Peru in 1913, with Notes on the Pathology of the Ancient Peruvians. *Smithsonian Miscellaneous Collection* 61(18). Washington D.C.
    1938   The Femur of the Old Peruvians. *American Journal of Physical Anthropology* 23(4):421-462.

Imbelloni, José
    1933   Los Pueblos Deformadores de los Andes. La Deformación Intencional de la Cabeza como Arte y como Elemento Diagnóstico de las Culturas. *Anales del Museo Argentino de Ciences Naturales* 37(75):209-253.

Jantz, Richard L.
    1973   Microevolutionary Change in Arikara Crania: A Multivariate Analysis. *American Journal of Physical Anthropology* 38(1):15-26.

Jurmain, Robert D.
    1977   Stress and the Etiology of Osteoarthritis. *American Journal of Physical Anthropology* 46:353-366.

Keatinge, Richard W.
    1978   The Pacatnamu Textiles. *Archaeology* 31:30-41.

Kent, Susan
    1986   The Influence of Sedentism and Aggregation on Porotic Hyperostosis and Anemia: A Case Study. *Man* 21(4):605-636.

Klein, Jeffrey, J.C. Lerman, P. E. Damon, and E.K. Ralph
    1982   Calibration of Radiocarbon Dates: Tables Based on the Consensus Data of the Workshop of Calibrating the Radiocarbon Time Scale. *Radiocarbon* 24(2):103-150.

Kroeber, Alfred L.
    1926   Archaeological Explorations in Peru. I. Ancient Pottery from Trujillo. *Anthropology Memoirs* 2(1). Field Museum of Natural History. Chicago.
    1930   Archaeological Explorations in Peru. II. The Northern Coast. *Anthropology Memoirs* 2(2). Field Museum of Natural History. Chicago.

Larco Hoyle, Rafael
    1945   *La Cultura Virú.* Sociedad Geográfica Americana. Buenos Aires.
    1948   *Cronología Arqueológica del Norte del Perú.* Sociedad Geográfica Americana. Buenos Aires.

Lasker, Gabriel W.
    1960   Variances of Bodily Measurements in the Offspring of Natives and Immigrants to Three Peruvian Towns. *American Journal of Physical Anthropology* 18:257-261.
    1962   Differences in Anthropometric Measurements Within and Between Three Communities in Peru. *Human Biology* 34:63-70.

Mann, Robert W., and John W. Verano
1990   Congenital Spinal Anomalies in a Prehistoric Adult Female from Peru. Case Reports on Paleopathology No. 13. *Paleopathology Newsletter* 72:5-6.

McClelland, Donald
1986   Brick Seriation at Pacatnamu. In *The Pacatnamu Paper, Volume 1.* Christopher B. Donnan, and Guillermo A. Cock (eds.). Museum of Cultural History. University of California, Los Angeles.

Merbs, Charles F.
1989   Spondylolysis: Its Nature and Anthropological Significance. *International Journal of Anthropology* 4(3):163-169.

Murra, John
1980   *The Incas.* Odyssey. WGBH, Boston.

Newman, Marshall T.
1943   A Metric Study of Undeformed Indian Crania from Peru. *American Journal of Physical Anthropology* 1:21-45.
1947   Indian Skeletal Material from the Central Coast of Peru. *Papers of the Peabody Museum of American Archaeology and Ethnology* 27(4). Harvard University.

Nials, Fred L., Eric E. Deeds, Michael E. Moseley, Sheila G. Pozorski, Thomas G. Pozorski, and Robert A. Feldman
1979a   El Niño: The Catastrophic Flooding of Coastal Peru. *Field Museum of Natural History Bulletin* 50 (7):4-14. Chicago.
1979b   El Niño: The Catastrophic Flooding of Coastal Peru, Part II. *Field Museum of Natural History Bulletin* 50 (8):4-10. Chicago.

O'Neal, Lila M.
1946   Mochica (Early Chimu) and Other Peruvian Twill Fabrics. *Southwestern Journal of Anthropology* 2(3):269-294.

O'Neal, Lila M., and Alfred L. Kroeber
1930   *Textile Periods in Ancient Peru.* University of California Publications in American Archaeology and Ethnology 28(2). University of California Press. Berkeley.

Norusis, Marija J.
1985   *SPSSx Advanced Statistics Guide.* McGraw-Hill. San Francisco.

Ortner, Donald J.
1968   Description and Classification of Degenerative Bone Changes in the Distal Joint Surfaces of the Humerus. *American Journal of Physical Anthropology* 28:139-156.

Ortner, Donald J., and Walter G.J. Putschar
1981   Identification of Pathological Conditions in Human Skeletal Remains. *Smithsonian Contributions to Anthropology* No. 28. Smithsonian Institution Press. Washington, D.C.

Powell, Mary L.
1985   The Analysis of Dental Wear and Caries in Dietary Reconstruction. In *The Analysis of Prehistoric Diets.* Robert I. Gilbert and James H. Mielke (eds.). Academic Press. New York.

Pozorski, Sheila Griffis
1976   *Prehistoric Subsistence Patterns and Site Economics in the Moche Valley, Peru.* Ph.D. dissertation, Department of Anthropology, University of Texas, Austin. Microfilms International. Ann Arbor.

Prümers, Heiko
1995   Ein ungewöhnliches Moche-Gewebe aus dem Grab des "Fürsten von Sipán." (Lambayeque - Tal, Nordperu). *Beiträge zur Allgemeinen und Vergleichenden Archäologie* Band 15. Verlag Philipp von Zabern. Mainz.

Ravines, Rogger, and Karen Stothert
1976   Un Entierro Común del Horizonte Tardío en la Costa Central del Perú. *Revista del Museo Nacional* 42:153-206. Lima.

Rogers, Juliet, Tony Waldron, Paul Dieppe, and Iain Watt.
1987   Arthropathies in Paleopathology: The Basis of Classification According to Most Probable Cause. *Journal of Archaeological Science* 14:179-193.

Rudney, Joel D., Ralph V. Katz, and John W. Brand
1983   Interobserver Reliability of Methods for Paleopathological Diagnosis of Dental Caries. *American Journal of Physical Anthropology* 62:243-248.

Salvat, Juan, y Eduardo Crespo
1977   *Arte Precolombino de Ecuador.* Salvat Editores, S.A. Barcelona.

Schmorl, Georg, and Herbert Junghanns
1971   *The Human Spine in Health and Disease.* Grune and Stratton. New York.

Schoeninger, Margaret J., and Michael J. DeNiro
1984   Nitrogen and Carbon Isotopic Composition of Bone Collagen from Marine and Terrestrial Animals. *Geochimica et Cosmochimica Acta* 48:625-639.

Schwarcz, Henry P., and Margaret J. Schoeninger
1991   Stable Isotope Analyses in Human Nutritional Ecology. *Yearbook of Physical Anthropology* 34:283-321.

Sevilla, Ricardo
1994   Variation in Modern Andean Maize and Its Implications for Prehistoric Patterns. In *Corn and Culture in the Prehistoric New World.* Sissel Johannessen and Christine A. Hastorf (eds.). Westview Press. Boulder.

Shimada, Izumi

1976   *Socioeconomic Organization at Moche V Pampa Grande, Peru: Prelude to a Major Transformation to Come.* Ph.D. dissertation, Department of Anthropology, University of Arizona, Tucson. Microfilms International. Ann Arbor.

1990   Cultural Continuities and Discontinuities on the Northern North Coast of Peru, Middle-Late Horizons. In *The Northern Dynasties: Kingship and Statecraft in Chimor.* Michael E. Moseley and Alana Cordy-Collins (eds.). Dumbarton Oaks. Washington, D.C.

Steinbock, R. Ted

1976   *Paleopathological Diagnosis and Interpretation.* Charles C. Thomas. Springfield, Illinois.

Stewart, T. Dale

1943   Skeletal Remains with Cultural Associations from the Chicama, Moche, and Viru Valleys, Peru. *Proceedings of the U.S. National Museum* 93. Washington, D.C.

Strong, William Duncan, and Clifford Evans, Jr.

1947   Finding the Tomb of a Warrior God. *The National Geographic Magazine* XCI(4):453-482. Washington, D.C.

1952   *Cultural Stratigraphy in the Virú Valley, Northern Peru: The Formative and Fluorescent Epochs.* Columbia Studies in Archaeology and Ethnology IV. Columbia University Press. New York.

Stuart-Macadam, Patty

1985   Porotic Hyperostosis: Representative of a Childhood Condition. *American Journal of Physical Anthropology* 66:391-398.

1987a   A Radiographic Study of Porotic Hyperostosis. *American Journal of Physical Anthropology* 74:511-520.

1987b   Porotic Hyperostosis: New Evidence to Support the Anemia Theory. *American Journal of Physical Anthropology* 74:521-526.

Towle, Margaret A.

1952   Appendix 2. Descriptions and Identifications of the Viru Plant Remains. In *Cultural Stratigraphy in the Virú Valley, Northern Peru: The Formative and Fluorescent Epochs.* Columbia Studies in Archaeology and Ethnology IV. Columbia University. New York.

1961   *The Ethnobotany of Pre-Columbian Peru.* Viking Fund Publications in Anthropology 30. Aldine Publishing Company. Chicago.

Trinkaus, Erik

1975   Squatting Among the Neandertals: A Problem in the Behavioral Interpretation of Skeletal Morphology. *Journal of Archaeological Science* 2:327-351.

Turner II, Christy G.

1979   Dental Anthropological Indications of Agriculture Among the Jomon Population of Japan. *American Journal of Physical Anthropology* 51:619-636.

Tyson, Rose A., and Elizabeth S. Dyer Alcauskas (eds.)

1980   *Catalogue of the Hrdlička Paleopathology Collection.* San Diego Museum of Man. San Diego.

Ubbelohde-Doering, Heinrich

1959a   Bericht über archäologische Feldarbeiten in Perú, (II). *Ethnos* 24 (1-2):1-32. Stockholm.

1959b   Bericht über archäologische Feldarbeiten in Perú, (III). *Ethnos* 25 (3-4):153-82. Stockholm.

1967   *On the Royal Highways of the Inca: Civilizations of Ancient Peru.* Praeger. New York.

1983   *Vorspanische Gräber von Pacatnamú, Nordperu.* Materialien zur Allgemeinen und Vergleichenden Arcäologie, Band 26. Verlag C. H. Beck. München.

Ubelaker, Douglas H.

1979   Skeletal Evidence for Kneeling in Prehistoric Ecuador. *American Journal of Physical Anthropology* 51(4):679-685.

1989   *Human Skeletal Remains: Excavation, Analysis, Interpretation.* Second edition. Taraxacum, Washington, D.C.

Uceda Castillo, Santiago, Ricardo Morales Gamarra, José Canziani Amico, and María Montoya Vera

1994   Investigaciones Sobre la Arquitectura y Relieves Polícromas en la Huaca de la Luna, Valle de Moche. In *Moche: Propuestas y Perspectivas.* Santiago Uceda and Elías Mujica (eds.). Universidad Nacional de la Libertad, Trujillo.

Verano, John W.

1987   *Cranial Microvariation at Pacatnamu: A Study of Cemetery Population Variability.* Ph.D. dissertation, Department of Anthropology. University of California, Los Angeles. Microfilms International. Ann Arbor.

1991   Moche: Perfil de un Antiguo Pueblo Peruano. *Revista del Museo de Arqueología* 2:104-113. Trujillo.

1992   Prehistoric Disease and Demography in the Andes. In *Disease and Demography in the Americas.* John W. Verano and Douglas H. Ubelaker (eds.). Smithsonian Institution Press. Washington, D.C.

1994   Características Físicas y Biología Osteológica de los Moche. In *Moche: Propuestas y Perspectivas.* Santiago Uceda and Elías Mujica (eds.). Universidad Nacional de La Libertad. Trujillo.

Verano, John W., and Laurel S. Anderson

n.d.   Análisis de Material Osteológico Humano del Proyecto Arqueológico Complejo "El Brujo." Informe Final de la Temporada 1995. Report submitted to the Complejo "El Brujo" Archaeological Project, November, 1995. Trujillo.

Verano, John W., and Alana Cordy-Collins

1986   H1M1: A Late Intermediate Period Mortuary
        Structure at Pacatnamu. In *The Pacatnamu Papers,
        Volume 1.* Christopher B. Donnan and Guillermo
        A. Cock (eds.). Museum of Cultural History.
        University of California. Los Angeles.

Verano, John W., and Michael J. DeNiro

1993   Locals or Foreigners? Morphological, Biometric and
        Isotopic Approaches to the Question of Group
        Affinity in Human Skeletal Remains Recovered
        From Unusual Archaeological Context. In *Inves-
        tigations of Ancient Human Tissue: Chemical
        Analysis in Anthropology.* Mary K. Sandford (ed.).
        Gordon and Breach. Amsterdam.

Walker, Phillip L.

1986   Porotic Hyperostosis in a Marine-dependent
        California Indian Population. *American Journal
        of Physical Anthropology* 69:435-354.

Weiss, Pedro

1972   Las Deformaciones Cefálicas Intencionales como
        Factores de la Arqueología. *Actas y Memorias del
        XXXIX Congreso Internacional de Americanistas*
        Vol. 1. Instituto de Estudios Peruanos. Lima.

Sources of Illustrations

Credits

Design and Layout   *Guillermo A. Cock*
                             Donald H. McClelland

Production Coordination   *Daniel R. Brauer*

Printing and Binding   *Golden Cup Printing Co., Ltd.*
                             Hong Kong